Bravura!

UNIVERSITY PRESS OF FLORIDA
Florida A&M University, Tallahassee
Florida Atlantic University, Boca Raton
Florida Gulf Coast University, Ft. Myers
Florida International University, Miami
Florida State University, Tallahassee
New College of Florida, Sarasota
University of Central Florida, Orlando
University of Florida, Gainesville
University of North Florida, Jacksonville
University of South Florida, Tampa
University of West Florida, Pensacola

UNIVERSITY PRESS OF FLORIDA

Gainesville · Tallahassee · Tampa · Boca Raton · Pensacola · Orlando · Miami · Jacksonville · Ft. Myers · Sarasota

Alex C. Ewing

Bravura!

Lucia Chase &
the American
Ballet Theatre

Library of Congress Cataloging-in-Publication Data
Ewing, Alex C.
Bravura!: Lucia Chase and the American Ballet
Theatre/Alex C. Ewing.
p. cm.
Includes index.
ISBN 978-0-8130-3376-1 (alk. paper)
1. Chase, Lucia, 1897–1986. 2. Dancers—United States—
Biography. 3. Choreographers—United States—Biography.
4. American Ballet Theatre. I. Title.
GV1785.C49E95 2009
792.80929–dc22
[B]   2009006565

The University Press of Florida is the scholarly publishing
agency for the State University System of Florida, comprising
Florida A&M University, Florida Atlantic University, Florida
Gulf Coast University, Florida International University, Florida
State University, New College of Florida, University of Central
Florida, University of Florida, University of North Florida,
University of South Florida, and University of West Florida

University Press of Florida
15 Northwest 15th Street
Gainesville, FL 32611–2079
http://www.upf.com

For Sheila

Contents

Acknowledgments   ix

PART 1   Prologue   1

1. Early Life   5

2. The Mordkin Ballet   25

3. Richard Pleasant   47

PART 2   4. Debut of Ballet Theatre   65

5. Life at Home   72

6. *Pillar of Fire*   84

7. Touring in Wartime   98

8. Jerome Robbins and *Fancy Free*   109

9. Covent Garden   124

10. Ballet Theatre Closes Down   141

PART 3 ⟶ 11. Troubles with the IRS 155

12. Revolution in Argentina 169

13. Adverse U.S. Tax Court
    Verdict 176

14. Alex Ewing at Ballet
    Theatre 182

15. Disastrous Cannes Fire 192

16. A Second Tragedy 204

PART 4 ⟶ 17. *Les Noces* 211

18. A Full-Length *Swan Lake* 218

19. Attempted Coup d'Etat 230

20. Balanchine and the New York
    City Ballet 238

21. Lucia Chase as Artistic
    Director 250

22. Sherwin Goldman 259

23. Troubles between Sherwin and
    Lucia 266

24. Makarova and
    Baryshnikov 276

25. Twyla Tharp's *Push Comes
    to Shove* 290

26. Baryshnikov Replaces
    Lucia 298

27. Last Years 311

28. Memorial Service 321

Index 325

Acknowledgments

Many people took an active interest in this book, but I would like to begin by expressing my gratitude and great debt to two informal editors without whose help this book probably would never have been published. Jill Greeson critiqued the first draft when it had little organization or literary style and when it could well have been dismissed out of hand. But she repeatedly encouraged me to move on to a second draft, and I was strongly fortified by the many illuminating comments she made along the way. Mina Samuels later made the same kind of painstaking review of the entire manuscript, never hesitating to point out weaknesses or excesses but always with great sensitivity, intelligence, and understanding, so that working with her was an extremely positive and pleasurable experience.

A considerable number of other people, many of them professionals in the dance or publishing worlds, also read various versions of what I had written, and I would particularly like to thank Chuck Adams, Mindy Aloff, Judith Bennahum, Claude Conyers, Jonathan Galassi, Robert Gottlieb, Don Lamm, Kate Medina, Zachary Morfogen, Penelope Niven, Suzanna Tamminem, and Lee and Miles Thompson.

Among the many interviews I had—many with former dancers or associates of Ballet Theatre and its Foundation—I was particularly assisted by Eleanor d'Antuono, Irina Baronova, Isabel Brown, Warren Conover, Eliot Feld, Cynthia Gregory, Sherwin Goldman, Ted Kivett, Ruth Ann Koesun, Robert Lindgren, Natalia Makarova, John Mehan, Terry Orr, Sono Osato, Florence Pettan, Donald Saddler, Karen Schwalb, Lupe Serrano, Frank Smith, Sallie Wilson, and Nancy Zeckendorf.

The administration and staff of Ballet Theatre were always kind and helpful, and my special thanks go to Myra Armstrong, Tina Escoda, Roseanne Forni, David Lansky, Kevin McKenzie, and Kelly Ryan.

I also am grateful to many friends and family members who read all or a portion of this book prior to publication and encouraged me with their kind comments. These include my children, Sandy, Eric, Cecilia, and Caroline, as well as Peggy and Jim Anderson, Jonathan and Jody Bush, Deirdre Carmody, J. Scott Cramer, Philip Dunnigan, Russell Flagg, Nancy Hart, Eric Larsen, David Lewittes, Harvey Loomis, Clifton Mathews, Carver Rudolph, Byam and Priscilla Stevens, and Francis and Seth Taft.

Special credit and thanks also go to several people who were principally involved in the preparation, promotion, and publication of this book: Mitchell Waters of Curtis Brown Ltd., who has served as its literary agent from the very beginning; the staff at the Dance Division of the New York Public Library at Lincoln Center for invaluable assistance in regard to photographs; Meredith Morris-Babb, director of the University Press of Florida, who has overseen all details of its publication; and Jacqueline Kinghorn Brown, project editor, Elaine Durham Otto, copy editor, and the Press staff, whose energetic and meticulous efforts distinguish it as one of the exemplary university presses in the country.

Over and beyond all those grand people just named, most important is my wife, Sheila, who has never doubted, whose interest and support have never wavered, and who is just about the sharpest and wisest reader any author could ever have. With deepest admiration, respect, and all my love, I dedicate this book to her.

Part 1

Prologue

O<small>N SUNDAY EVENING</small>, May 4, 1980, a mass of theater-goers, many in formal dress, hurry across the great plaza at Lincoln Center and crowd into the Metropolitan Opera House.

The American Ballet Theatre's spring season at the Met, one of the greatly anticipated events in New York's annual dance calendar, is not scheduled to begin until tomorrow. Tonight is a preview extravaganza celebrating the fortieth anniversary of America's national ballet company (originally called simply Ballet Theatre), which first burst onstage at the Center Theatre in New York City's Rockefeller Center on January 11, 1940, and in two hours established itself as one of the premier ballet companies of the world.

Scores of ABT's most illustrious alumni have streamed into town from all corners of the country and beyond in order to participate, or at least make an appearance, in tonight's gala. As reported in the Sunday edition of the *New York Times:*

> This 40th anniversary season is . . . a celebration of personal achievement.
>
> It is the last which will see Lucia Chase and Oliver Smith as company directors, posts they have occupied since 1945. The season also marks the 40 years that Miss Chase has served as the company's founding patron and long-term artistic director. . . . It is only fair to say that this season marks the end of an era.

Inside the Met, the houselights dim and the performance begins with a series of photographs projected on the curtain and a brief narration describing the company's historic debut at the old Center Theatre. A final image shows the four principal dancers—Karen Conrad, Nina Strogonova, Lucia Chase, and William Dollar—who performed that inaugural evening in the opening ballet, *Les Sylphides*.

Now, forty years later, the Met's great gold curtain rises to reveal dancers in the current American Ballet Theatre in the same opening tableau of *Sylphides*, this time with the lead danced by Kevin McKenzie (who in a few years will become artistic director of ABT). For the past four decades, *Les Sylphides* has been the company's signature piece, always meticulously rehearsed by Dimitri Romanoff, an original member of the company and its current regisseur, who tonight stands just offstage in the wings. Meanwhile, out in the audience, Lucia Chase, Agnes de Mille, Antony Tudor, Karen Conrad, Anton Dolin, Annabelle Lyon, Sono Osato, and Donald Saddler— also original members of Ballet Theatre—sit watching and remembering as the fortieth anniversary gala unfolds.

Next onstage are Alicia Alonso and Igor Youskevitch, who during the 1940s and 1950s were perhaps the leading pair of dancers in the world. Tonight they are back together again to dance the adagio from act 2 of *Giselle*. Following Alonso and Youskevitch is another celebrated ABT partnership, Erik Bruhn, the noble Dane, most classical of all male dancers, and Carla Fracci, star of Italy's La Scala. Only a few minutes have passed, and already it is clear that this evening is going to be an epochal event, the kind people will talk about for years.

Next to appear is Cynthia Gregory, who joined ABT in 1965 and two years later was raised to the rank of ballerina. Tonight she is performing the Rose Adagio from *The Sleeping Beauty*. Then a complete switch from Tchaikovsky and a palace ballroom scene to Leonard Bernstein and a Times Square bar, three sailors on shore leave, looking for girls and fun—the ballet *Fancy Free*, introduced thirty-six years ago by Jerome Robbins when he was a young soloist in Ballet Theatre. Tonight two of the three sailors in 1944's initial cast—Robbins and Harold Lang—appear in their original roles. The audience goes wild as the three sailors strut their stuff, each trying to outdo the others in order to impress the two girls they coaxed to accompany them into the bar.

The gala continues, featuring one longtime favorite after another, until a closing full-company curtain call brings all the ABT alumni out one by one to take their individual bows: Irina Baronova, one of the Ballet Russe's "baby ballerinas" in the early 1930s who led Ballet Theatre in its second year and who remains, nearly a half-century later, the favorite of many ballet devotees; Nora Kaye, ABT's first homegrown superstar and one of ballet's greatest dramatic dancers; Muriel Bentley, who danced fourteen years with the company; Alonso and Youskevitch, who come out onstage still in costume; Anton Dolin, who was the leading male dancer in Ballet Theatre for its first five years; then in quick succession, one after the other, almost faster than the dazzled audience can recognize and respond, out come Antony Tudor, Agnes de Mille, Melissa Hayden, Natalia Makarova, Jerome Robbins, Rudolf Nureyev, Hugh Laing, Ian Gibson, Miriam Golden, Ivan Nagy, Maria Karnilova, Donald Saddler, Ruth Ann Koesun, and Violette Verdy. The applause keeps growing as the audience greets each new face with fresh shouts and whistles and cheers from all over the house.

Nearing the end, the spotlight turns to focus on the company's directors, Lucia Chase and Oliver Smith, who have guided ABT's destiny for the past thirty-five years. Jerome Robbins steps forward to recall, back when he was a young dancer in the company and totally unknown as a choreographer, how Oliver Smith had believed in him and championed his first ballet, *Fancy Free*, which was an instant sensation and launched his career as the most dynamic choreographer/director in American theater.

Then it is Lucia Chase's turn. There is a surprise brief revue in which current ABT dancers reenact roles Lucia has danced in the course of her forty years with the company. Antony Tudor, ABT's choreographer laureate, walks out to present her with an overflowing bouquet of long-stemmed red roses. Agnes de Mille reads a congratulatory telegram from President Jimmy Carter before paying her own tribute: "It is thanks to Lucia's tenacity—Lucia, you know, is nine-tenths granite—that American Ballet Theatre has lasted longer than Diaghilev's Ballets Russes and stands today as a national treasure." Then de Mille, Robbins, Tudor, Smith, and all the others step back and push Lucia Chase out from their midst into center stage.

She stands alone, trim, auburn-haired, erect, and glowing, the diminutive, resolute figure who has been there all four decades from the very beginning of the company and who for the last thirty-five years has directed and safeguarded ABT through its trials and mishaps and grand successes leading up to this fabulous night. She bows several times, then turns and waves for everyone else to step forward and join her, but no one moves. They all hold back and leave her to stand out there by herself, alone in front of the entire company, past and present, facing the audience, which is now on its feet and cheering as cascades of rose petals are released from high above the stage and come fluttering down on the head of the laughing, teary, indomitable figure of my mother, Lucia Chase.

1. Early Life

She makes a great deal of noise for
such a small person.
—St. Margaret's School Yearbook, 1910

As a young girl, she was called "Lu" by her friends.
She was a dark-haired, green-eyed torrent of speeding laughter, dashing
down the two flights of stairs from her room on the top floor of Rose Hill,
the family homestead on Prospect Street in Waterbury, Connecticut. She
was always racing out the door to St. Margaret's School two blocks away, or
to tennis, or best of all, to rehearsal of whatever class play or musical show
she was currently in, invariably playing the leading role. Even back then,
she felt totally at home on the stage and was bursting to perform.

"Lucia is our actress," her fellow classmates wrote in the St. Margaret's
School yearbook. "We feel that if she follows the stage as a profession, she
will be unequaled. She also has a large sense of humor. Even in the midst
of study hours, it often overcomes her, and she makes a great deal of noise
for such a small person."

Lucia was younger than most of her classmates. Born in March 1897, she
had just turned fifteen in 1912. As her junior year was coming to an end,
she was more and more conscious of the exciting world out there. It was an
enormous stage, and she was standing in the wings, waiting for her cue to
go on.

The first quarter of the twentieth century marked the beginning of the peak era for the great watering places up and down the northeast coast—the Hamptons on Long Island, the Jersey and Connecticut shores, Newport and Watch Hill in Rhode Island, the long stretch of Cape Cod in Massachusetts, and Northeast and Bar Harbor up in Maine.

Families who could afford to take extended vacations adopted the habit of faithfully going back year after year to the same spot, even to the same great brown-shingled summer cottage, where everything and everyone was taken in—grandparents, parents, children, and nannies, along with steamer trunks and family pets, several generations armed with racquets, golf clubs, and beach umbrellas.

For the Irving Chases, summer meant Narragansett Pier in South County, Rhode Island, bordering on the Atlantic Ocean and facing Newport across the great expanse of Narragansett Bay. For the first ten years, they stayed in the Atlantic House, one of the stately hotels lining Ocean Road. But as the family grew larger, they acquired Miramar, a three-story, cedar-shingled residence on Ocean Drive originally built by Stanford White for Admiral Dewey.

Another important part of Chase family life in Narragansett was Sunset Farm. Situated on a narrow strip of land between Great Salt Pond and the Point Judith Country Club, a couple of miles short of the state beach at Scarborough, the farm was easily visible from all directions because of the imposing two-story East Indian bungalow looming close behind its stone-pillared entrance. The building was originally designed to serve as a club-house for a wealthy tycoon who had been turned down as a member of the Point Judith club across the road. After he had left Narragansett and the place was deserted for several years, Mrs. Irving Chase ("Mumsie") had acquired the farm, and it became a favored destination for her children and their friends to go. The bungalow was a tremendous space with long rows of high windows upstairs and a broad polished wood floor surrounding a great central staircase.

From childhood on, Lucia regarded Narragansett as the supremely right place to spend vacations. Now, in the summer of 1912, it was also the place to begin preparing for the rest of her life. According to letters written by her and from friends and family, there was no question in her mind regarding the immediate future, soon to be her last year as a senior at St. Margaret's School. But after graduation, then what? It seemed she had three options.

The first was to stay at home in Waterbury, where she could count on being an immensely popular debutante. Living at Rose Hill could be such fun, particularly since her two younger sisters, E.I. and Dee, were finally old enough to become great companions. Even as a teenager, she was virtually assured an active role in the Junior League, not only to do some "good works" but also to take part in their annual shows which were big events in Waterbury every year. And not to be overlooked, lately she had been receiving invitations, mostly from New Haven, for fall football games or all sorts of social events, highlighted by the famous Yale Senior Prom. And yet this sort of life didn't represent a real breaking-out, which soon she would be gloriously free to do.

More daring would be for her to recognize right now that the one thing she wanted in life was to pursue a career in the theater. For that, the place to go was certainly New York.

New York was less than two hours from Waterbury on the train, yet in some ways it might as well have been a foreign country. Unlike today, there wasn't a broad array of qualified places to study the arts. Children of prominent families in hometown America, particularly girls, were rarely given parental permission or even encouraged to contemplate making the attempt.

This sort of parental constraint was not a problem in Lucia's case. Despite his Connecticut Yankee cautionary habits, her father tended to let people go their own way as long as they left him to his. And perhaps her mother's strongest trait was the way she stood behind practically anything her five daughters wanted to do, unless the idea was absolutely insane.

"I was brought up to be responsible for myself," Lucia often explained. "My father and mother—if you wanted to do something very much and you could take care of yourself, you could talk them into it. We were not spoiled. We were just very well treated."

Yet however much she yearned for a career in the theater, the timing wasn't quite right. Although she was full of confidence, she was understandably hesitant, at fifteen, to strike out all by herself in New York.

The third possibility was to go to college. In the early 1900s, this was not yet a common recourse. College women were generally considered to be intellectuals, not widely considered to be one of the top feminine attributes. Nor was college the standard route for a professional career in the theater. Quite the opposite, there was something about college studies that represented the antithesis of all that was involved in trying to make it on the stage. A very ambitious, talented, determined woman might choose college or the performing arts, one or the other, but not both.

Waterbury, New York, or college? Lucia chose what amounted to a mini-step by spending the first few weeks of the fall at the Bryn Mawr Tutoring School in Philadelphia before returning to St. Margaret's to complete her senior year. The following fall, she set off for Philadelphia to begin life as a freshman at Bryn Mawr College, one of the most prestigious, proudly bluestocking women's educational institutions in the country.

College life was terrific: "Chemistry Lab is quite fun," she wrote her mother. "We do everything wrong, of course, and explode and burn up everything, but it's nice. The other morning, the poor little demonstrator blew up a gas tank or some gunpowder or something, and it went up in a cloud of smoke. No one's been killed yet though."

This was just Lucia's teenage way of talking: reports from the registrar's office reveal that she managed academic work very comfortably, with consistently good grades in English, mathematics, and particularly languages—German, Spanish, classic Greek—despite a full social schedule up and down the East Coast. Since Bryn Mawr was strictly an all-girls' school, Lucia was forever leaving campus to head for where the men were. Her favorite destination was Yale, a family tradition ever since an early maternal ancestor, Stephen Titus Hosmer, graduated from Yale in 1782. Both her father (class of 1880) and her mother were dedicated Yale supporters, and ultimately Lucia's husband, Tom (my father), my brother and I, and two of her three grandchildren all turned out to be Yalies. Lucia's enthusiasm for Yale was unbounded: in the next few years, she was invited to six senior proms at Yale, a daunting record that probably still stands.

Her popularity was legendary. The late De Witt Hanes, a lifelong friend, sitting on the sofa in her living room in Winston-Salem, N.C., reminisced about the time seventy years earlier when she went with my mother to one of the Yale proms. "Late in the evening, suddenly Lucia did a whole series of cartwheels across the dance floor and brought down the house. You never heard such stamping and whistling. My, she was fun."

Near the end of fall term in her junior year, Lucia was stricken with diphtheria and sent home. She spent most of the next two months in bed and only returned to Bryn Mawr in the spring of 1916. By then, though, she had missed four months, which was too much to make up: she would have to repeat junior year and not graduate until the spring of 1918.

Meanwhile, beyond the cloistered campus of Bryn Mawr, attention was shifting to the war raging in Europe. Lucia's interest in college began to wane as her original classmates were all lining up to graduate, while more and more of her principal male escorts were now in uniform, many of them overseas. Her old way of life was beginning to seem frivolous. What was the point of continuing with all that chemistry and Greek and math when so many of her friends were risking their lives? In the spring of 1917, Lucia packed up and went to New York.

She never completed her last year at Bryn Mawr. Once she left, she completely cut all her ties and no longer wanted to be associated in any way with her alma mater. Her overriding aim from this moment on was to pursue a career on the stage, and professional performers in the arts—particularly ballet dancers—at that time were simply not college graduates. The distinction of having gone to Bryn Mawr would have set her apart from all the other dancers when she was desperately trying to be one of them.

This almost complete about-face was steadfastly maintained for the rest of her life. Years later, when Bryn Mawr was anxious to pay tribute to Lucia Chase as one of its most prestigious alumnae, she as much as disavowed ever having gone to Bryn Mawr at all. Instead, she turned all her formidable energy and talent into forging a productive life for herself in New York, her new home which she immediately took to and where she would continue to live, a true inveterate New Yorker, for the next sixty-plus years.

Her first few months in New York were spent working with the Red Cross, serving as a driver to ferry soldiers and officials in and around Manhattan. But after the Armistice was signed and the war was over, her letters home were filled with accounts of classes and rehearsals, particularly those at the Vestoff-Serova School. Mr. Vestoff was a former premier danseur and ballet master in Moscow. His wife, Sonia Serova, was a former instructor of the Imperial Russian Ballet. Together they were known for training a good many dancers for the professional stage.

They want me to dance in a program at Wanamaker's Auditorium July 3rd. Also, they've asked the Vestoffs to put on a thing in the afternoon. I'd love to do it, and it's a pretty good chance.

Meanwhile, Lucia's social life continued at an astonishing pace. To quote Agnes de Mille, who had a very sharp eye when it came to assessing compatriots:

Until Brenda Frazer came along, Lucia Chase was the most popular girl of the nineteen twenties, no question. What Lucia had, what Lucia wore, what Lucia did made the social news. She was the stellar prom date, and when she tooted off to Yale or Princeton (I think not Harvard, or very, very rarely) in her smart little roadster, everyone talked. And she was always enthusiastic, always fun, always eager for adventure. And tireless? You could not wear her out!

Yet despite all the social gallivanting, preparing for a stage career began taking up more and more of Lucia's time, and for the next few years, Lucia continued to pursue all three major disciplines—singing, dancing, and acting—with encouraging results in each.

At the Vestoff-Serova School, dancers gave a recital each year in Carnegie Hall, and the 1925 spring performance marked Lucia Chase's first publicized appearance in New York. In a letter to her mother, Lucia wrote, "I was surprised to see the recital poster had on it 'The Mazurka' by V. Vestoff and Miss L. Chase. It will be fun—first time he's danced in 10 or 15 years! Alice and I are doing a tap number, an innovation in a Vestoff recital. My solo is "Pierette s'amuse" (!!)—in a white ballet skirt (!!), white wig and black velvet—like Pavlova!—and 4 Harlequins come in and fight over me."

That fall she had the principal part in the popular Junior League Frolic at the Strand Theatre in Waterbury, then back in New York she continued to take singing lessons from Mme. Gaudenzi in Carnegie Hall and studying at the Theatre Guild.

Near the end of June 1926, once the last Theatre Guild plays were over and the New York theater world dramatically slowed down, Lucia left town and headed for Narragansett, her heart and mind set on the beach and grand family get-togethers in Miramar.

As soon as she arrived, she began planning for a mid-August party out at Sunset Farm. A host of dinners were arranged to take place beforehand; then everyone would converge on the Farm, where the towering bungalow would be glowing with magic lanterns, fancy decorations, Eddie Wittstein's music, candles everywhere . . . the works.

It was as though Lucia sensed that this party would be a final fling to wind up what had been a wild, dizzy, happy decade.

The big weekend started with an officially sanctioned polo game on the field across the road from the entrance to the Point Judith Country Club. One of the two contestants that afternoon was the Freebooters, not one of the top-scoring teams on the Eastern Circuit but an adventure-loving outfit attracted by the prospect of a strenuous contest. For the man playing Number One on the Freebooters, Tom Ewing, good sport rather than victory was the principal thing. As the second-in-command and heir-apparent of the Alex Smith & Sons Carpet Company in Yonkers, a huge Ewing/Cochran family enterprise employing thousands of workers, Tom Ewing had challenges and pressures enough all week to fill every waking hour of the day, and because of work, he couldn't indulge in polo on a regular basis. However, every now and then there was an opening, like the one in Narragansett. According to Alex Carver, another Freebooter and Tom's oldest friend since childhood in Yonkers, there was also going to be a postgame clambake and party at the Scarborough Beach Club. Alex, who seemed to know almost everyone and everything that was going on, thought this was just the ticket to kick off the last part of the summer. I never heard who won the polo game that afternoon, but what happened next has been meticulously described by John William Andrews, a family acquaintance, who was commissioned by my grandfather to write "Portrait of a Young American" (completed in the late 1930s but never published) about the Cochran/Ewing family.

The big postgame affair at Scarborough was a costume party, which Tom Ewing as a rule cordially disliked. He didn't mind dressing up, but he much preferred his own evening clothes. Yet there was no getting out of it this time. The only recourse was for him and Alex Carver to have a couple of drinks to fortify themselves before getting dressed—Alex in a Pierrot costume and Tom in a sailor outfit, little gob hat, and wide flaring trousers that flapped as he walked. Then off they roared to the Scarborough Beach Club.

Alex had been right: it was a great crowd, with lots of people dancing when they got there. They stood together, two companionable out-of-town-ers content to relax on the sidelines and survey the couples out on the dance floor. After a few minutes, Tom noticed a dark-haired girl, dressed as a gypsy in a bright red skirt, whirling around the outside edge. She whipped past him and disappeared into the mass of moving bodies.

A moment later, he caught sight of her again on the far side. This time he followed her swirling path in and out among the other dancers. Tom seized Alex's arm.

"There," he said decisively, nodding after her as she passed by a third time.

"What?" Alex hadn't been paying particular attention, but Tom's unexpected fierce grip was hurting his arm.

"That girl."

"What about her?"

"Who is she?" Tom demanded brusquely.

"In the red skirt? Why, that's Lucia Chase."

"That's the girl I'm going to marry."

"What are you talking about? Are you crazy?" Alex knew how Tom liked to drink, but he was one person who could really hold his liquor and never lost his head.

"Introduce me," Tom said, pushing his friend out onto the floor. Alex went to cut in and had only taken a few steps when Tom was out tapping him on the shoulder.

"Lucia, this is Tom Ewing," Alex told her, and then stood still out in the middle of the floor, watching as they danced away together.

They had lunch the next day. Lucia was used to being in a crowd, particularly in Narragansett on a big polo weekend. But now she found herself seated a short distance away from the others, alone with a very serious man with dark brown eyes and an intense voice whom she had only just met the night before. He seemed to want to talk, but not aimlessly. Each time she brought up a subject, he would pause to consider it, taking a moment before making a slow, careful response, never relaxing into easy back-and-forth chatter, but focusing on the topic at hand. It was disconcerting and a little overpowering, especially on such a nice day at the beach with so much socializing going on.

Before they separated, almost to ease the embarrassment of abruptly getting up and leaving him sitting there, Lucia asked if he would like to attend a big party she and her family were giving the following Saturday at her mother's Sunset Farm. Tom gravely promised to come.

Returning to Narragansett the next weekend, this time without Alex Carver, Tom drove Lucia's sister, Elizabeth Irving (E.I.) out to the party at Sunset Farm. There was already a crowd of people, and more kept pouring in. Lucia was busy greeting guests yet also constantly out on the dance floor. Tom kept his eye on her and did little else. Around eleven o'clock, he cut in and asked her to step outside with him down into the little garden by the south door.

It was cool and rather damp, with a cold wind blowing in from Great Salt Pond on the southern edge of the farm. They sat on two little iron chairs out on the grass in quite dreary surroundings, the music sounding faintly from upstairs behind them. Lucia listened in amazement as Tom talked to her in a low but steady and intense voice.

He said he was twenty-nine (same age as she was) and came from a wonderful family, with parents he dearly loved. He was working very hard. Everything in his life was fine. All he wanted now, and it was the most important thing above all other considerations for him, was that she should be his wife. But she needn't worry. She could go right on doing exactly as she wanted. Nothing in her world had to change. All he wanted was just for them to be together forever.

Lucia was dumbfounded. Her party at that moment was at its height, with a couple of hours still to go. Next weekend was Labor Day, with a big crowd coming to stay at Miramar. After that, she was going back to New York and taking up again at the Theatre Guild, studying with its director, Reuben Mamoulian himself. Both in Narragansett and New York, she had plenty of admirers to squire her around. But nothing like this. She said that she appreciated all he had told her, but she didn't know how to respond.

Tom assured her that he understood. She should just think about it. Take all the time she wanted. He could wait. And with that he took her back inside to the dance.

They had lunch again the next day. Afterwards, before he drove off for Yonkers, Lucia asked if he'd like to come back for Labor Day weekend. Tom said he would.

The next night he wrote her from Yonkers:

Dearest Lucia: Played golf today. I'm a terrible golfer anyhow, but my game wasn't improved any by the fact that, instead of thinking about keeping the right elbow in and the right knee straight, etc., I was all the time thinking of Miss Lucia Chase and how lovely she is. It's very distracting. Alex [Carver] came to supper, and that brings us up to the present moment, ten o'clock on the most gorgeous evening, with all the crickets singing, and the most glorious moon, a regular "God what a night," only no good at all, absolutely none, because you're not here to see the moon with me. That was a much more lovely evening, years ago now, when we sat in the garden at Narragansett in the cold breeze, with no moon, and all the crickets' teeth chattering. There was my idea of an evening. I suppose it's because I'm happier than ever before that I remember.

After that, new letters started to arrive, one after another, each one fervent, not at all the kind of friendly banter Lucia was used to receiving from male friends. Although the words were slightly crazed, they didn't bother her. She even sort of liked them: they were exciting to read. After three arrived in as many days, she wrote one letter back:

Tom, my dear: How strange to think this is the first time I have ever written you, in fact have known you only a little more than a week!

She went on with little bits about Narragansett, then toward the end lowered her guard slightly:

I'm acquiring quite an interest in the mail, and if it keeps on treating me as well as it has since you went away, I'm afraid it will get worse! I've a funny singing in my soul too, and I don't know just what it is, but I think I know who put it there. Bye-bye, my Tom. Strange man. Who are you?

The next day Tom left for a family gathering in Sorrento, the Cochran/Ewing homestead in Maine where Tom had always felt most at ease.

It's very quiet and simple here, but I've loved this place all my life: there's something about it that lays hold of one. This has been a wonderful day, with an off-shore breeze blowing half a gale. I spent the morning sailing and it was glorious, though I expected to lose the mast overboard any minute. . . . Friday is getting nearer, but oh what a long two weeks!

There are no letters to give an account of that Labor Day weekend, but after they had both returned—Lucia to her new little Manhattan lair on West 58th Street and Tom to Yonkers—flowers arrived for "Miss Lucia Chase," Tom's way of signaling he was not letting up.

Although they were nearly thirty, neither one was accustomed to going out on any regular basis with the same person. Lucia was extremely social and thoroughly enjoyed men's company, but at the same time she fiercely defended her independence and warded off any personal commitment that might interfere with her theater ambitions, whereas Tom was too involved in his business and sports to pay much attention to cultivating any lady friends. The fact that they had both been living on their own for the past ten years without ever forming any close romantic attachments was unusual in the fast-moving social circle that they inhabited.

That fall, they managed to see each other at least every other night, usually with a letter from Tom for the ones in-between. The pattern might have continued like that for some time, but then two issues required sudden attention: the Theatre Guild, where Lucia was taking acting classes every day, gave notice that it was closing over the Christmas holiday and that all students would have two weeks off before having to report back; and "Popsie," Lucia's father, announced he was leaving for a trip to Europe before the end of the month, now only three weeks away.

Ever since that enchanted night at Sunset Farm when Tom had proposed marriage on the lawn beside the bungalow, he had kept his promise that he would never interfere in Lucia's relentless drive toward a professional career in the theater. Yet suddenly here at year's end was a perfect opportunity when the two of them might break away. Knowing how close Lucia was to her parents, Tom reneged on his promise to allow her all the time in the world and urged her to confide in her father.

Lucia did, at which point Tom wrote that if they were really going to take advantage of the Christmas holiday, she had to decide right now whether or not to marry him. What was her answer?

Lucia responded that she just couldn't simply say yes. Tom continued to press, and finally that weekend, she promised to give him an answer in a few days—perhaps by Thursday, which happened to be three months to the day since his first proposal out in the windy little garden. Still according to John Andrews's unpublished account: when the appointed hour came around on Thursday, Tom was at Lucia's apartment on the dot, ringing the bell insistently, impatient for the door to open.

Lucia appeared, dressed and ready to go out on the town.

"Well, how about it?" The question was out of Tom's mouth before his coat was off or the flowers presented.

"How about what?" Lucia asked.

"Will you marry me?"

Lucia's answer (never to be forgotten): "Why, really, I haven't thought about it." (Haven't thought about it?!!) Then the next moment, hesitatingly, she looked up into his face and said softly, "I guess so, Tom."

Their first home together was Lucia's little apartment on West 58th Street. The space was classic New York pied-a-terre, two rooms, a bathroom that gave out on an inner airshaft, and one extra closet. Tom simply packed the few belongings he had in his parents' townhouse and moved in with no fuss, not even listing his name by the front door or in the phone book.

Otherwise each one continued to follow exactly the same routine as before. Tom would get up early and drive to Yonkers, where he would work at the mills until late in the day, then often exercise with indoor polo at the Riding Club or outdoors at Whippany when the weather was right. Lucia began her day uptown at Serova's dance studio, went to Mme. Gaudenzi's brownstone house on the West Side for singing lessons, then spent afternoons at the Theatre Guild.

Although caught up now in an even broader circle of their combined friends, they wanted nothing more than to be together. With or without other people, it didn't really matter. The essential was simply the other one—Tom for Lucia, Lucia for Tom—each ecstatic and rather dazed at having found, in the midst of a busy workaday world, the perfect soul mate. By all accounts of those who knew them well, theirs was an absolutely idyllic match.

In the United States, the late 1920s were for many the best of times. The nation's economy was booming, and the stock market appeared to be permanently headed upwards. In Yonkers, the old Alex Smith & Sons carpet mills roared along at full speed. Huge auctions were held every spring and fall in downtown New York, often with a million yards of carpet dispersed in a single session.

Some of the younger, more thoughtful Alex Smith employees worried about how the increasingly headlong production had been achieved with almost no attempts at modernization. A great many, if not most, of the old machines were still powered by steam and were located in cavernous quarters, with little coordination between departments in the increasingly widespread factory complex. It was a similar story for the factory personnel: the day-to-day operations were directed by experienced and competent department heads, but the majority were aged and doggedly set in their thinking, almost to a man dedicated to maintaining the time-honored product line and methods of doing things.

Tom had little trouble falling in with this old-fashioned loyalty. He was by nature a traditionalist who liked things to stay as they were, just as they had been handed down by elders whom he loved and respected. Towering above them all was his uncle, Alex Smith Cochran, yachtsman, philanthropist, former president and still dominating influence at Alex Smith & Sons, a titan in his time who in Tom's opinion had the keenest mind, the highest standards, and the most generous spirit of any man he had ever encountered.

In the spring of 1928 Lucia was pregnant, a secret which well into the summer she shared only with her husband and her mother. The baby was due in January or early February, so there was plenty of time for others to find out later, particularly her theater and dance associates, with whom she wanted to continue working as long as she could. She kept on taking her dance classes through November, and afterwards she helped rehearse a show for the Junior League right up to the time predicted for her delivery.

All her life, Lucia had cherished the idea of having several children, just as her parents had done. Now this goal was intensified because Tom was starting to feel the same way. He had never paid much attention to children and had remained slightly aloof to all his Ewing nieces and nephews. However, this still-unborn infant would be his, a miracle which soon became the most important event on his horizon.

The baby was born February 11, 1929. It was a boy. Very healthy. And Lucia was fine, everything right. Tremendously all right. The boy would be named Thomas, the fifth Thomas Ewing in succession and the seventh in a direct line to have lived and breathed in America.

"Hip hip hooray," Lucia wrote her sister Eleanor ten days later:

Isn't it grand. I'm feeling like a million again, and if you could see our precious Tommy, he is the cutest little thing you ever saw, and not so little either! He has the most wonderful color, a lovely skin, and looks the picture of health—in fact he's quite perfect. And as for Tom, you've never seen anyone so excited over anything. He's sure Tommy is the most beautiful baby that ever was born.

If life could ever be perfect, it surely was now for Lucia.

Four months later, there was devastating news. Tom's Uncle Alex had died at his Saranac Lake summer home in the Adirondacks. He had suffered for years from tuberculosis, and the previous fall he had been stricken by pneumonia, but he had appeared to be on the mend when the end came on June 20, 1929.

The front page of the *Yonkers Herald* was devoted to reporting the event: "The entire city was plunged into mourning. Flags on all public buildings and on most of the semi-public institutions, many of which had received generous contributions from Mr. Cochran, were placed at half-mast as soon as the word arrived."

The mayor hailed Alex Cochran as Yonkers's greatest benefactor and announced that the city's business would be suspended, with all city officials attending the funeral. A line of people which the police estimated at upwards of 5,000 formed a procession to view the open casket. The turnout was an astonishing tribute to a man who all his life had shunned publicity, done his own thing, asked no favors, made no show. Born to be successful, in success he was incredibly generous, more than anyone knew exactly, other than that he had given millions away in his lifetime, and now an additional $16 million to various charities and to hundreds of Alex Smith & Sons employees whom he regarded as his personal trust, in death as in life.

Probably no one was more affected than Tom Ewing. Uncle Alex had been his role model, his mentor, the anchor and inspiration of all he aspired to and believed about life, business, and family. Now he was gone.

As far as the outside world was concerned, the biggest tangible effect that Alex Cochran's death would have on Tom Ewing was made public four days later when the *New York Sun* ran a two-tier headline: "Young Ewing May Be Cochran Heir—Nephew Rumored as Chief Inheritor of Fortune." The true size of either the actual or residual estate became the subject of innumerable articles and speculations during the weeks that followed. But it was generally estimated that even after the hundreds of bequests specified in Alex Cochran's will had been made, Tom Ewing's inheritance would be somewhere in the millions and that he would probably be the next president of the carpet mills.

With this mantle now squarely on his shoulders, Tom was obliged to take a closer look at the way Alex Smith & Sons was being run. After a few initial consultations, he felt the first inklings of alarm and straightway gave orders that everything be temporarily closed ("a two-week suspension for inventory and repairs" was how it was reported in the papers) and that an exhaustive study of the entire Yonkers operation be done as rapidly as possible.

When the results came in, they presented an unnerving picture of an almost totally antiquated system. There was almost no efficiency in any department. The waste was shocking and promised only to get worse. Huge changes were needed quickly.

If only this task had begun ten years earlier, right after the war when the economy was on the upswing and business was booming, it might have been a wonderfully exciting challenge. But now, a decade later, the stock market, which had been reaching new heights through the first half of 1929, suddenly crashed that autumn, and the Great Depression was on.

Almost instantly, economic catastrophe struck the entire country. Workers were being laid off wholesale, sales were plummeting, and stores and plants were closing. At the mills in Yonkers, each month was worse than the last, with orders for new carpeting nose diving to a fraction of what they had been only a few months earlier.

Although conditions were critical and future prospects even grimmer, Tom tried not to talk about it much at home. Somehow he managed to keep his two worlds apart, and the joy he received in his private life strengthened his resolve to introduce changes at the mills that were not always popular but were the sole hope for the future.

It was unrelenting, painful work, but at the end of each day, he would gather himself together, tear home, and burst into the apartment, presenting himself as ready for fun and games with his son. Little Tommy would race to greet him at the door, and the great tumbling on the floor would begin.

Late that spring, there was stupendous news: Lucia was pregnant again. Tommy would be just two by the time there was another baby in the house. Lucia insisted she wanted several more, which was fine by Tom: the more the merrier.

That fall they moved to a much grander apartment at 720 Park Avenue. Their "palace in the sky" was a magnificent duplex on the fourteenth floor of a landmark building where they started a new home for themselves in high hopes they would never have to move again.

I was born in February 1931 and named Alexander Cochran after my great-uncle. Whereas my brother Tommy was dark-haired and rosy-cheeked, I (who was immediately nicknamed Sandy) was blond, very fair, and blue-eyed, thinner and smaller than my robust bouncing brother had been at the same age.

"Tommy was just like Tom," Lucia always used to say, the highest praise she could give, "whereas poor Sandy, I'm afraid he takes after me."

Tom was now president of the sprawling Alex Smith & Sons in Yonkers. Although he had managed to introduce prodigious physical improvements and new efficiencies into the overall operations, as a result of the nation-wide depression, the public appetite for fine carpeting, which for so many years had been insatiable, had practically shut off. Production was cut in half, then in half again, as Alex Smith & Sons underwent the greatest decline ever in its proud history. Salaries were being cut, and hundreds were being dismissed each month, until by year's end, over half of the Alex Smith workforce was laid off. With all eyes looking to him for help, Tom drove himself harder than ever.

Yet there was always that wondrous time at the end of the day when he could return home and Lucia would be there, lovely and loving, prepared to go out or stay quietly at home, exactly as he wished. And now there were "the boys," little Sandy toddling after an exuberant Tommy, who would shout, "Daddee's home!" the moment he stepped out of the elevator, and both of us would rush at him and grab hold, and we would all tussle and laugh and romp together down on the floor.

My father started a new game that we played every evening. While our mother would be taking her bath, we three Ewing men would line up outside her bathroom door and bump against it with our rear ends, one big and two very small, and my father and Tommy would announce loudly, "When you hear the signal, the time will be exactly seven fifteen and three-quarters!"

January 1933 brought still another burden when Tom was selected for jury duty. It was a murder trial and very demanding. Despite his ferocious daily schedule, he felt he had to serve. Added to that, near the end of the month, Lucia's uncle, Arthur Kimball, died, and they went up to Waterbury for the funeral. Tom, one of the pallbearers, was obliged to stand bare-headed in the cold rain for the service at the cemetery. Two days later, Tom's aunt, Eleanor Steward, died, and they had to go to her funeral in Washington.

Returning to New York, the following night they hosted an elaborate dinner at the apartment in honor of the opera star Antonio Scotti, who was then singing in New York. The party was still going on late in the evening when Tom appeared at Lucia's side and said he felt terrible. She told him to go upstairs to bed, but he said he couldn't while their guests were still there. It wasn't until an hour later that they all left and Lucia took his temperature. It was 102.

It was 104 the next morning. Lucia called the doctor, who came and talked about how others were suffering the same illness: it was the winter season, and flu was everywhere. But when the fever didn't go down that night, a nurse was hired. The doctor appeared around noon the following day, examined Tom again, and reported he had pneumonia.

On Monday morning, Tom's temperature was still 104. Lucia was told not to worry. It was perfectly all right for her to go out and keep to her sched-ule. However, just to be safe, the doctor suggested bringing in oxygen tanks and a tent, which arrived Tuesday after lunch. Tom was set up with the new equipment in the guest bedroom at the end of the hall.

He slept some, and the next morning his temperature went down a lit-tle. He told Lucia he felt better and joked with the nurse while he tried to shave himself in bed, but that afternoon he started feeling worse. The doctor came again. There were hurried consultations with a medical col-league. Lucia was allowed in and out, but it was deemed better not to admit others.

That night around eight o'clock, Tom Ewing suddenly suffered an embolism. The doctor came out into the hall and said quietly there was really nothing he could do. Thirty minutes later, my father died.

⟲

From head to foot, my arms and legs and every piece of me inside, I ache—a heavy ache, as though my blood were trying to burst through my veins.

I cannot think, I am still dazed—I cannot believe you will not come back. . . .

I cannot think it possible that I will not see you again.

The words are written in pencil on the opening page of a plain cloth-stitched copybook, and continue on for forty pages. My mother's handwriting, remarkably neat and clear from early childhood all through life, in this particular instance finally breaks down around the last ten pages, the words getting larger and almost scrawled across the page. Yet the narrative flows unbroken from start to finish, one long agonizing recapitulation:

It was Friday night, my sweet, Feb. 3rd, and just as always I was waiting to hear that elevator door open and your key in the lock and then You. I was lying down, and Tommy and Sandy were playing in the room, and we were all waiting to scream, "Daddee!"

We were all so happy. And then you told me, Sweetheart, that you had felt funny after lunch, and you were tired, and I told you to lie down awhile, and you did, but there wasn't much rest with Tommy and Sandy jumping all over you. And oh precious, I thought you were all right. . . . (Next day) at 7 a.m. your temp. was 104. I called Dr. Benson—"Flu"—and in bed for you. It was a mean day. In the afternoon I took the children down to F.A.O. Schwartz (toy store) and Tommy tried the tricycles so I could get the right size from us for his birthday

[On Monday] Things seemed about the same. Dr. Benson told me it would take a couple of days more and then you'd be better or—but I never heard the "or," or if I did, I'd have paid no attention because it wouldn't occur to me that there could be any question of not getting well in a day or two. . . . [On Tuesday] Coughing, and it was bloody and that scared me. I asked the Drs. if they were sure it wasn't TB, and they laughed and said oh no. They always seemed to be gone before I could find out anything. . . .

About 7 o'clock, Harry motioned to me to come downstairs, and there was your Mother on your blue chair in the library, almost collapsed. Dr.

Benson had telephoned her that morning [she was at St. Paul's School with Bayard who had just passed his crisis in bronchial pneumonia] and she had flown down from Boston. She had prayed all the way, and when she came in, she had fairly fallen into the apartment asking if it was too late! Even that didn't make me see how serious it was. . . . [On Wednesday] Woke up at 5:15. Went in to speak to you, and you said quietly, "I think I'm going to pull through," and I said, "Why of course you are, darling." Dawn was breaking when I was there with you, the pinkish light was on the buildings, and the room was so peaceful and sweet, just you and me together. All morning I wandered about in the hall just outside our room, jumping every time the nurses wanted anything, itching to do something more.

I was talking to Bill [Tom's brother] in Library when the nurse came: "Mr. Ewing wants to see you." It was 4:15. I was so relieved and glad, it was like letting me out of a cage, and I flew up the stairs. The nurses were in the hall and told me to stay "only a minute"—and oh how thrilled I was to see you, and you were so glad to see me, your precious brown eyes almost ate me up, and you wanted to know what was going on, and I tried to keep you from talking and talked fast myself and told you all the people that had telephoned. . . . You were so eager to hear it all, and I was so afraid of getting you excited or of staying too long that I said, "I must run down and say good-bye to Bill because he has to go to play tennis." You said, "You'll come back, won't you?" and I said, "Oh yes Darling," and I ran out. Oh sweetheart, had I known those were your last words to me, I'd have collapsed right then, or I'd have stayed on my knees at the door, praying. [I talked with Johnny Hanes downstairs.] Then Johnny left. It was almost 6, and as I came up upstairs, I saw Dr. Benson very busy hauling the ice in from the terrace, filling up the oxygen tank, and my heart stood still. A terror clutched me, though I still didn't know what it was. . . . I had a tray in the sewing room, but I couldn't eat, I was getting numb already. Mother telephoned at 8:10 and said both Dee and Eleanor had had oxygen. The telephone kept me running, and between calls I stood at the door. . . . At 8:30 Dr. Johnson said to me, "It doesn't look so good as it did." He had called Dr. Benson. My ears just heard but my brain didn't, it had gone under a cloud. [Called a third doctor.] At 8:40 he came. Hardly spoke to me, and the three doctors went in to see you. I wandered up and down in the hall, slowly, and when they came out and went into the guestroom and closed the door, they didn't speak to me. . . . The next minute Miss Simmonds came running from your room and rushed in to the doctors, and they all went in to you. My heart must have stopped.

And out came Miss Simmonds with her hand outstretched and such a look, and she led me in—and Dr. Benson said, "I'm sorry but there's nothing we can do."

I knelt down beside my beloved—they took away the tent and your eyes were almost closed, and you were breathing so slowly and quietly. I held your hand and pressed as close to you as I could and kept talking quietly to you, "Precious Tom, my own darling sweet Tom, my precious, dear Tom, my sweet. . . . He's looking at me." "But he doesn't see you, my dear," said Dr. B., and he closed your eyes.

I don't know how long I was there, but finally someone lifted me up and took me slowly into the guestroom, and I sat on a little straight chair, and your Mother was there, and Bill and Dr. Benson, but I had gone, darling. Half of me went with you when you went, and from then on I was only part of a person. . . . I don't know much what happened then. I remember Dr. Benson said, "You must relax." My back was as stiff as a ramrod, it was like iron, and I was numb from head to foot, but I heard him, and I thought I must do as I was told. Miss Simmonds gave me green pills and other things, and I did everything mechanically. I asked them to tell me just as soon as I could go back to you. People kept coming. Everyone that came I took in to you. I wandered in and out, I couldn't keep away. It was the only place for me. . . . Sometime they got me undressed. I remember being in bed, light on and door open, and Bill on the floor by me, trying to comfort me while I sobbed, as I'm sobbing now. . . .

I went off to oblivion, drugged by pills. Years later, it seemed, I began dreaming faraway, and there were voices singing. The voices got nearer and nearer and louder till everything broke in me and I was conscious. I had been asleep for years it seemed, and to my horror I was awake—everything was a cold light and queer and awful, and then I remembered—oh sweetheart, how could I wake up and have to live?

I had told Miss Simmonds the night before not to let anyone else tell Tommy. I wanted to be the one. I went in and took Tommy on my lap, and I told him, "Remember, darling, you said the other day there weren't any boy angels? Well you were wrong, darling—of course there are, and Daddee's an angel now. Poor Daddee was so very sick, and he died last night, and now he's an angel, but he'll always stay right near us, and even if we can't see him, we'll know he's right near." Tommy was very quiet and asked me why you had to die. Oh precious, why? I don't know why.

[Friday] Another day—stayed with you as long as they would let me.

Things began to go too fast. The coffin was there—oh God that hurt—People kept wanting to take me away, but I only wanted to be in the living room. . . .

The Bishop was there. I begged him to make the service as short as possible.

It was time. Mater and I held on to each other. A sea of faces, the living room banked with flowers . . . you, darling. . . .

Bill gently took me up—coats—elevator—people downstairs—in the car—snow all the way to Yonkers, the garden plot, the roses and you.

"All right, Bishop," Mater said. . . .

It was over. I fell on my knees by you. Bill pulled me up and got me in the car. Back. Absolutely numb. . . .

At 74th Street and Park I saw people walking along as though nothing had happened, but my world had gone. . . .

Oh God. Only my inside living from now on, where you are. Outside, oblivion.

2. The Mordkin Ballet

After Tom died, I was flat on my
face, but Mordkin made me go to
work. He made me stand up again.
—Lucia Chase

TIME PASSED, but for Lucia, there was no great release
from her grief. Everything reminded her of Tom. His clothes and shoes
in the closet. His books in the library. The checkbook with the latest stubs
in his handwriting. And most agonizing yet wonderful, Tommy and I were
in our rooms just down the hall. No matter how much our mother wanted
to bury herself, to withdraw and hide away from the rest of the world, she
could not ignore the two of us. She didn't want to, either. We were parts of
Tom still alive in the great emptiness surrounding her.

"Mater," Tom's mother, came closest to sharing Lucia's feelings of devastating loss, and Yonkers became Lucia's favorite destination—particularly
the hillside grove dedicated to the Ewing family at the Oakland Cemetery.
The two of them would go there together, usually carrying armfuls of roses
to place at Tom's grave. These little pilgrimages were heart-wrenching but
a great comfort to them both.

During the spring and fall of that first year, 1933, when Tommy was four
and I was just two, our little family would go to Kinross, the Ewing homestead in Yonkers, every weekend. There was always someone in the house
to watch over Tommy and me while our mother closeted herself alone

with her mother-in-law, sitting on her bed and talking for long periods at a time.

Late in June, we all went to Narragansett where Dad had played polo, met her, danced with her, proposed to her, and so much else. Once again Tom was everywhere, which in a way was good, but then it also could be agonizing.

"Last night was awful," she wrote in the journal she kept by her bedside:

> The weekend was too much, so many people and all of them in party spirit having such a good time, and all of the time my insides were screaming for you. Crowds at the train, and I left. I called out to you all the way home, and I tried to get you, and I fell on the bed and cried and cried and I couldn't move. It all went black inside me.

She would pull herself together, get her nerve up to try again. Just three days later:

> Darling thing, I played golf for the first time today, and it was as though I were playing with you. I hung on tight to you, my sweet, and I was doing quite well—it hurt, but it was sweet too, that tingling consciousness of you. But then, sweetheart, a caddy crossed the fairway in back of me on his way home, and I turned around and it was your caddy! Oh darling, I just burst— it just got me all over, a terrible ache rushed over me, I could hear you call him "Bobby," and the tears came.

She never knew when it was going to hit her:

> I think I'm getting stronger, and then the awful longing comes and I am gone again. All of me tingles and the tears come. I would gladly let skin be scraped off me, or any sort of torture, I would not hesitate, if it meant I could have a few minutes with you.

Back in New York, the summer over, the only place Lucia wanted to be was alone in the apartment, high up and far away from all the people and distractions of the city. She had stopped all her theater activity and no longer went to any classes. How could she sing when all the time she felt like crying, or throw herself into acting out a scene when everything about it seemed contrived, and life at home was the one reality? Even dancing, which had become her favorite activity back when life was fun and she was full of energy, now seemed like an escape when she didn't want to escape.

Each morning she would take Tommy to nursery school. There were afternoon walks with both of us boys in Central Park, supper in the dining room, then a quiet time together for all three of us, ending with a little prayer Mom wrote for us that we all said, and so to bed.

In one long entry—dated October 39–she describes Tommy's first day at school:

> We arrived about 8:40 and what a howling mob of parents and children. I shouldn't have blamed him for being overcome by it, but not at all, those big eyes took it all in . . . stood so straight and looked so dear, so serious, he was the image of you, my love.

At the start of the next year, a short letter from Lucia to her mother told of how she took Tommy to the Philharmonic in the morning and then to a classmate's birthday party. The letter goes on for another page and then ends up: "If there's sunshine tomorrow, I'm going to the country with the Mordkins."

Mikhail Mordkin had long been a celebrated figure in the dance world. A former principal dancer of the Bolshoi Ballet in Moscow, he left Russia in 1909 to join Diaghilev's Ballets Russes for its inaugural season in Paris and later that summer danced in a benefit at the Opera as partner to Anna Pavlova. Their performance so impressed Otto Kahn, chairman of the board of New York's Metropolitan Opera, that he invited them to dance a late-evening two-act version of *Coppelia* for five weeks at the Met and subsequently to make two tours of the United States in 1911 and 1912.

Returning to Russia, Mordkin was made ballet master of the Bolshoi company, but after the October Revolution of 1917, he had a difficult time under the new authorities. After seven years of Soviet dictatorship, he and his wife and son, Michael Jr., left Russia, this time for good, and came to America, where he lived the rest of his life.

The following year, Mordkin and a company he formed appeared in the Greenwich Village Follies in New York and then for two years toured the United States under the management of the impresario Morris Gest. Financially the tours were not a success, and the company disbanded. He made a second attempt in 1926–27 with a new troupe starring Vera Nemchinova and Pierre Vladimiroff from the Diaghilev company and a corps de ballet composed primarily of students from his own ballet school. However, once again its two tours were financial disasters. The company folded, and Mordkin opened his own ballet school in New York.

He called it the Mikhail Mordkin Studio of the Dance Arts. It was, in his words, "my long-dreamed-of International School of the Dance, where every art is fostered but where the art of the dance reigns supreme."

Lucia had also come to New York pursuing a dream. Years later, in a taped interview with Walter Terry, she said:

> I came to New York, to the Theatre Guild School, to be an actress, and then I met Mordkin. He was doing a small entertainment for the Junior League here, and I got the lead, so I started studying with him.

Never in her wildest dreams could Lucia have imagined where this association would eventually lead. Mordkin, on the other hand, was always on the lookout for anyone who might advance his ambitions. He was quick to boast about how Katharine Hepburn, while still in her early twenties, had studied for more than three years with him. Now in 1935, he was fifty-five years old, long past the age when a leading male dancer was expected to retire, yet his zeal to make a name for himself still burned as powerfully as ever.

Lucia Chase was only beginning serious training as a ballet dancer when she first turned up in his studio. Already in her twenties, she was almost totally lacking in classic ballet technique. Yet the story goes that on the very first day, when she crossed the floor of the studio to introduce herself, there was something about the way she walked that attracted Mordkin's attention. And after learning she came from a privileged background, he may have been even more convinced that this was one student who merited his special attention.

This helps explain the first part of a note Lucia wrote him back in March 1931 shortly after I was born:

> Dear Mr. Mordkin—It was dear of you to send me the sweet little roses and lilies of the valley. I was terribly pleased that you should think of sending them to me. The baby is fine and so am I, and we are going home today so I am very happy. I shall come back to class just as soon as I can, in about six weeks. Love to you, Lucia.

Studying with Mordkin was generally not simply a matter of taking his ballet class but a major commitment. Inside the studio and out, Mordkin was an exceptionally powerful figure, both physically and temperamentally, who combined a domineering personality with a colossal ego. While his fame was generally attributed to his having once been Anna Pavlova's partner, according to Mordkin it was Pavlova who had the good fortune to have danced with him: after all, he was the Bolshoi star back when she was only a soloist.

His description of himself in the program book for his Mordkin Ballet company was in the same self-congratulatory vein:

> He is not only remarkably handsome, not only a dancer with a beautiful leap, but also a master of mimicry, an actor of inspiration. Possessing an extraordinarily perfect technique, and knowing the art of Ballet in its classical purity, he achieved the art of dramatic mimicry as none of his predecessors had.

His classes reflected this exalted idea of himself. There was no question that this was his universe where his word was law, and anyone attending was expected to be subservient to him. Though a tyrant inside the studio, outside he could be very open and friendly as long as it was understood that he and his wishes came first.

Lucia was not put off by his domineering attitude. People who did not know her well often assumed that, like so many of the exceptional women who emerged as prominent leaders in their field, she must have been very assertive. But actually, quite the opposite was true. She was very much the kind of woman who liked it when men were making most of the decisions. Providing it didn't involve her having to abandon a transcendent goal, she had no problem deferring to a man. Ever since childhood when her father's word was absolute, a consistent quality throughout her life was the way she allowed herself to be ruled by men: Harry Zuckert (the Ewing/Cochran family's lawyer), John Wharton, who succeeded him as her longtime counselor, Oliver Smith, whom she pressed into service and insisted on his being her partner for thirty-five years, her brother-in-law Ed Carmody, her favorite choreographers, Fokine and Tudor, and most of all, her husband. Lucia not only did not mind but preferred it when men took command of her world.

Consequently, back in her early days in New York when she was just beginning her serious training as a dancer, Mordkin's imperious ways did not alienate her but instead provided reassurance that her career as an aspiring dancer was in strong capable hands. Following Tom's death and a year of annihilating grief, when the time came for Lucia to take her first exceedingly tentative steps back into the outside world, the door she chose to enter was not connected with the theater, or singing, but was Mordkin's morning ballet class.

There was something safe about the inflexible, impersonal, totally demanding routine of ballet class. Lucia would arrive early, allowing plenty of time to change into practice clothes. She never wore anything bright or outlandish that might attract attention. All she wanted was to be just another body at the barre, turning up at the appointed time in the standard garb, and once there to work hard, very hard, as hard as she possibly could, under Mordkin's piercing eye and fierce presence. Class over, she would quickly change and go back to the apartment, one more day successfully gotten through.

Mordkin's autocratic way was as welcome as the rigorous discipline of ballet class. Whatever Lucia's problems, there was no place for them either in his class or anywhere else she might find herself in the illustrious presence of the world-famous Mikhail Mordkin. With his proud bearing, his muscularity, his sudden unpredictable outbursts, he was like a magnificent animal that had to be accepted on his own terms.

In July 1935, three summers after Tom's death, Lucia invited Mordkin to Narragansett. As a four-year-old at the time, one of my earliest memories is seeing Mordkin striding confidently across the beach, clad in the briefest kind of bathing suit, a rubber bathing cap clamped on his head. He would sweep me up onto his shoulders and march out into the waves, way out to where the water reached high on his chest, almost to his chin, far beyond the point where I could stand or get back to shore if I fell. He would hold my shins in an iron grip and turn around, exulting, as if to say, "Look everyone, see how I, Mikhail Mordkin, have Lucia's boy way out here in the big surf. But not to worry! I'll bring him back safe to shore."

For the next two or three years in New York, Lucia each morning put herself in Mikhail Mordkin's hands and let him decide every move that she made for the next hour and a half. She was never going to be a classical ballet dancer in the traditional sense of the term. She had started much too late. Her body was too set, and her feet were strong but not beautifully shaped. She moved well, but not in the long-limbed, graceful way of a true ballerina. Her greatest asset was that she had an innate vibrancy, a spark that caught the eye. She might not have the beautiful technique, but people liked watching her onstage—she was interesting and fun.

Given her particular attributes and shortcomings, Mordkin was probably just the right person for her to study with. While he had won worldwide recognition as a *danseur noble,* his primary distinction was his dramatic power, the way he took on a role and imbued it with great strength and individuality. Where others might concentrate primarily on the dancing, his main interest was in the story, just the area where Lucia—more an actress than a dancer—was most able to absorb and put his instruction to her own use.

She still couldn't revert to being her old self or expose herself to the familiar faces and activities that had been so much a part of her life when Tom was alive. However, it was becoming just possible for her to enter gingerly into this essentially foreign world that was not Waterbury or Yale or Park Avenue but was totally focused on dance, where the dominant figure was Mordkin, the talk was all about ballet and Russia and blintzes, and the people were mostly émigrés or else young dancers who were poor and friendly and had no idea who Lucia was or where she came from.

Besides taking daily class at his studio, she started going out on special occasions to the Mordkins' house in New Jersey, to a grand Easter feast or a boisterous birthday party, everyone in a festive mood, eating and drinking and jabbering with each other in their mother tongue. Before long, Lucia acquired a certain facility in Russian and was able to join in the talk.

She also began taking an interest in Mordkin's school that went beyond simply attending his daily advanced ballet class. When the Brooklyn Academy of Music inquired what Mordkin would charge for an appearance with a company of dancers, the school secretary in New York forwarded the message on to Lucia in Narragansett, who wrote Mordkin back that in her opinion, his fee should be $500 with two pianos or $750 with a small orchestra. Her letter closed with three short but notable sentences: "Isn't it amazing the success the Fokine Ballet is having at the Stadium. I wish we had done it! Maybe we'll do some later anyway."

For Mordkin, these words must have been a call to action. His original school had by this time branched out to include another studio in the Roerich Museum on Riverside Drive, and he was also teaching in Great Neck, Long Island.

Lucia wrote him again the following summer. The first paragraph of her letter was written in Russian. Then, switching to English, she wrote: "I hope you don't mind if I tell you what I feel so sure of," and then said that in her opinion, he should give up the ancillary studios:

I am sure there is not enough money in them to make up for your time. If it is only because of using the [Roerich] stage, I promise to rent the stage any time you want it. . . . I will do everything I can to help.

In the same letter, she invited Mordkin to come back to Narragansett to do some concentrated coaching both for herself and for his latest protégé, Viola Essen.

The early accounts of Viola Essen tell of an astonishingly precocious artist whose career began when she was only two and a half and her mother took her to California for a children's dramatic test at Los Angeles. With 1,700 children competing, the first prize was awarded to "Baby Essen," who recited verses written by her mother. Changing her name to Beebee Essen, she spent the next three years doing dramatic sketches on the radio before returning to New York in 1930 and winning a scholarship (at the age of six!) in a Mikhail Mordkin Studio competition in dancing and music.

The little wunderkind was apparently equally talented as a pianist. At the age of nine, she won the piano scholarship offered by the New York Master Institute of United Arts and another prize at the Birch Walthen School for superior physical and mental excellence. Now eleven, her practice time was divided between studying dance with Mordkin and piano with the Russian Vladimir Drozdoff, all under the eagle eye of her very protective mother.

Lucia invited the Essens to spend the entire summer of 1935 in Narragansett, and early in July she wrote Mordkin from her house, High Tide, located on Taylor Street next to Miramar:

We are all settled here and everything is fine, but we miss you terribly and are waiting for you to come. Mrs. Essen and Viola are in my sister's house [Sans Souci] just next door, and they seem to be very happy. Viola is crazy about the water, had her first swimming lesson yesterday—when you come, you will find a swimming champion instead of a ballerina! She weighed 75.5 pounds last Saturday.

Mordkin did arrive a few weeks later for an extended visit, then returned to New York to begin working on several new projects, including a series of excerpts from *Sleeping Beauty*, a studio version of the venerable classic designed to give performing experience to the students of his school.

He also instituted a new corporation, Allied Arts Ballets Inc., whose express purpose was to present a reconstituted Mordkin Ballet company. The Allied Arts stationery, printed by the company of his old friend Rudolf Orthwine, listed Orthwine as managing director, Frank Cruikshank as general manager, and Mordkin's son as business director. Mordkin gave himself no official position but was represented on the letterhead by the bold caption "The Mordkin Ballet, Choreography and Direction— Mikhail Mordkin."

The new company's first public endeavor was a concert organized by Mordkin and Professor Drozdoff in the spring of 1936 at the St. Cecilia Auditorium in New Jersey. Listed in the program for six of the eight dance numbers was "L. Chase," performing two solos and also two duets with "V. Essen," all choreographed by Mordkin.

It was probably fortunate that this formal reentry of Lucia Chase into the public arena did not take place onstage in New York but inconspicuously out of town, for there is something slightly grotesque about a performance featuring two dancers when one of them, who is just starting out as a professional dancer at the advanced age of thirty-nine, is placed alongside the other who—regardless of her talent, which may have been considerable—is only a child. The theater world contains countless examples of aspiring actors and dancers who have gone on to become renowned figures in the arts but whose careers started out with ridiculous or disastrous initial experiences. What in the world was Mordkin thinking, pairing the two of them, the widow and the wunderkind?

Meanwhile, a much more ambitious program was beginning to take shape at Mordkin's studio. Never one to underestimate his own choreographic ability, Mordkin proposed to present what he termed the first full-length version of *Sleeping Beauty* ever to be performed in America. Originally choreographed in 1890 by the legendary Marius Petipa of the Russian Imperial Ballet, with a commissioned score of surpassing beauty by Tchaikovsky, it was premiered in St. Petersburg at the end of the nineteenth century and introduced to Western Europe by Diaghilev's Ballets Russes in the early 1920s. George Balanchine, who fifty years later inherited Petipa's mantle as the world's preeminent choreographer, went on record to describe *Sleeping Beauty* as "the highest achievement of the Russian Ballet." Now Mordkin planned to take the colossal step of introducing *Sleeping Beauty* to the United States, keeping Tchaikovsky's score but providing his own new choreography.

His one concession was to bring in a recognized professional, Dimitri Romanoff, to star as Prince Siegfried. Romanoff had performed the lead role in Max Reinhart's celebrated 1935 film of *A Midsummer Night's Dream* and had also been a principal dancer in the San Francisco Opera Ballet under veteran choreographer, dancer, and teacher Adolph Bolm. Romanoff was a true professional, but otherwise all the dancers for Mordkin's *Sleeping Beauty* were to be students at his school. The part of Bluebird, tradition-ally a pas de deux, was here assigned to his flighty protégée, Viola Essen, while Princess Aurora, the female lead who in Diaghilev's production of *Sleeping Beauty* was danced by the legendary Olga Spessivtzeva, was to be performed by Mordkin's other big discovery, Lucia Chase, whom he publi-cized as "the all-American Prima Ballerina." The site chosen for this land-mark performance was to be her hometown—Waterbury, Connecticut.

Sleeping Beauty represents an absolutely enormous undertaking for any ballet company at any time, comparable in its particular art form to such gi-ant works as Verdi's *Aida* or Shakespeare's *King Lear* or Beethoven's Ninth Symphony. It's hard to believe that Mordkin proposed performing *The Sleeping Beauty* with only one recognized professional dancer, with the leading female the completely unknown and totally inexperienced Lucia Chase, the fabulous Bluebird role given to little Viola Essen, and the rest of the cast drawn from the current ranks of his pupils, yet that was what was about to happen.

When summer came, Mordkin once again took to working on two fronts, in both New York and Rhode Island. In early July, Lucia wrote from Narragansett to tell him that Viola Essen was already there and was sched-uled to appear in a special outdoor charity performance to be held later that month at the Castle, a local landmark. Lucia had arranged to have a pianist come up to play Tchaikovsky's music for the outdoor event and promised in a letter to Mordkin "to keep her through next week while you are here, to work on *Giselle* or anything you say."

Judged from today's vantage point, when first-rate professional ballet companies are established in most major American cities and the compe-tition to be accepted into any one of them is ferocious, all this talk sur-rounding Mordkin's company sounds distressingly naïve. Similarly, sev-eral photographs—of Mordkin, Lucia, Viola Essen, and others—taken in Narragansett on the beach and out at Sunset Farm which appear in the Mordkin Ballet's souvenir program, all above a cheerful caption proclaim-ing "Playtime Is Practice Time with Mordkin Ballet Artists," seem more fitting for a family photo album than the visual record of preparations for a historic artistic undertaking.

Mordkin's production of the great Russian classic *Sleeping Beauty*, to

Tchaikovsky's immortal score, took place in Waterbury, Connecticut, on December 9, 1936. It was a performance that does not appear in most dance history books and might otherwise be totally forgotten, except that it marked the professional debut of Lucia Chase.

It's only natural to wonder today what Lucia thought about this undertaking and the principal part she was expected to play in it, artistically and also financially. Not that the cost of Mordkin's *Sleeping Beauty* was a prohibitive amount, certainly only a tiny fraction of what such a single performance would cost in New York. As principal heir of Tom's estate, Lucia had substantial wealth and very few outside obligations. Despite her household expenses, which were considerable, and the cost of raising two small boys in New York City, she was living well within her income and didn't mind putting a small part of her money into such a singular event.

Her reaction to the artistic implications is more difficult to assess. One might well conclude that this was simply a grandstand play by a rich woman to put herself in the limelight of her own hometown: if so, she would not have been the first glory-seeking patron to have done such a service for herself. Certainly Lucia had never been a shrinking violet, and she had cheerfully confessed on several previous occasions that when there was a lead role to be performed, she would go all out to win it for herself. Yet taking into account all that hindsight now provides us in terms of the good taste and professional modesty that Lucia Chase displayed throughout her long and distinguished life, one has to arrive at some reasonable conclusion about her acceptance of this outlandish project.

Probably the paramount fact to consider is that at this particular point in her life, Lucia thought of herself—and wanted to be considered by others—first and foremost as a dancer. As such, she was not in a position to make major artistic decisions or judgments but had subjugated herself to being directed by a very autocratic mentor and choreographer. Clearly, mounting a new *Sleeping Beauty* was Mordkin's ambition and not hers. He called all the shots, starting with the choice of the cast to perform it.

Furthermore, it is a cardinal rule in the ballet world that dancers do not question or contradict choreographers: the crux of their relationship is that the choreographer dictates and the dancer follows, very much like a doctor and an attending nurse. Lucia may have been delighted that Mordkin picked her for the leading role, but there can be little doubt that the decision was his and made by him alone. As for picking Waterbury as the site for the performance, Lucia and her hometown connections may well have played a large part in his thinking—she may even have advised and helped him with the arrangements—but again, it is only reasonable to assume that this was another of Mordkin's decisions. Unlike Lucia, who was not boastful and did not go out of the way to promote herself, no one ever attributed a great deal of modesty or exquisite taste to Mikhail Mordkin.

In any event, largely as a result of mounting *Sleeping Beauty*, the Mordkin Ballet was now off and running. Mordkin's company made its next public appearance four months later, under a new sponsoring organization, with four performances at the Majestic Theatre in New York in April 1937.

The poster announcing the opening-night performance read: "Advanced Arts Presents The Mordkin Ballet in *Giselle*, First Performance Since 1911 When Mikhail Mordkin as Ballet Master of the Imperial Russian Ballet Made Ballet History with Anna Pavlova as His Dancing Partner." Underneath the words "Cast of 50" there were four dancers named: Lucia Chase, Leon Varkas (a young American who frequently took roles formerly danced by Mordkin), Viola Essen, and Dimitri Romanoff. Choreography and direction were by Mikhail Mordkin, his name printed in giant type. Stretching down the entire right side of the poster was a line sketch of Giselle in her peasant costume, signed by the designer, Serge Soudeikine. The title role in this most popular of all classic ballets, still a favorite after nearly a century of performances throughout the world, was to be danced by Lucia Chase.

The undertaking was glowingly described in the inaugural souvenir program, printed by the Rudolf Orthwine Corp.:

> This curtain rises on another chapter of the great career of Mikhail Mordkin. May his ballet live on indefinitely as an American Institution, and presented by his disciples in all corners of the world.

The reaction from the press was considerably more guarded: "Mikhail Mordkin (in *Voices of Spring*) made his first appearance on the local stage in many years, and was greeted with all the enthusiasm such an occasion warranted," John Martin reported the following day in the *New York Times:*

> As a matter of fact, his miming of the role of the aged fisherman constituted by all odds the evening's highest point, for he brought to it the authority of his great experience and provided a fine flavor of comedy and a richly colored characterization.

Otherwise, this dean of dance critics found little to praise, glossed over the rest of the performance, and even went so far as to observe that "Lucia Chase is by no means an ideal Giselle."

As a New York company debut, the engagement could hardly be considered a success. Attendance was painfully small: only 105 tickets were sold, netting a gross of $161.50. The miniscule turnout was no doubt aggravated by the fact that only one performance was originally announced in the *New York Times,* and the subsequent three were not mentioned until after the opening night. Also, there was a competing attraction that same week at the larger, much more prestigious Metropolitan Opera House, where Colonel de Basil's Ballet Russe de Monte Carlo, presented under the colorful banner of impresario Sol Hurok, was scheduled to give five performances with an all-star cast featuring the three legendary "baby ballerinas"—Irina Baronova, Tamara Toumanova, and Tatiana Riabouchinska—and a celebrated repertory.

Although the Mordkin Ballet's mini-season in New York was a disaster, the company pressed on from New York to make a short tour to six cities—Newark, Scranton, Philadelphia, Wilmington, Baltimore, and Washington. Besides dancing the lead in all the performances of *Giselle,* Lucia's other principal dancing role on the tour was that of Lisette in *La Fille Mal Gardée,* the oldest ballet still being performed. Much less challenging than *Giselle* in its technical requirements, this role of a warm-hearted girl who outmaneuvers her mother and all other obstacles to win her true love was particularly suited for Lucia, who was totally engaging as the happy soubrette. Balanchine's *Complete Stories of the Great Ballets* even includes her among the outstanding Lisettes in the history of *La Fille Mal Gardée.*

Despite the exhilaration of performing as a principal dancer before public audiences, Lucia was not comfortable with her top billing in the Mordkin company. "I'm not good enough to hold the fort," she wrote Rudy Orthwine, Mordkin's managing director, at one point in the course of the tour. "Neither is Viola Essen. You can still use us both for many things, [but] we shall have to get two good ballerinas."

By 1937, the Mordkin Ballet was being presented by Advanced Productions Inc., a new corporation headed by Orthwine that had Michael Mordkin Jr. as its business director. Lucia was not listed on the letterhead, but she was the corporation's principal stockholder, and Orthwine understandably was inclined to pay attention to whatever she said. By the time the tour of eighteen cities ended in February 1938, Lucia was writing to her mother that Karen Conrad, a dancer from Philadelphia, had been hired and was working out very well: "She is very easy to get on with and will be excellent." That was the good news. The bad was that there had been a blow-up with Viola Essen. "It's a shame, but she seems to be quite impossible. I'm really very sorry, we need her."

> We close after tomorrow night and are not playing New York after all as they were too slow on making arrangements. . . . [The tour] is again a disappointment financially, arranged too quickly without proper publicity, but a wonderful reception everywhere and assurances of full houses next year. So we must go home and get set for next year with some good concert bureau—raise some money and get new ballets ready. I only hope this strange hysterical start we made this year will develop into a sane and healthy affair next year. Then this orgy will not have been in vain.

Now that Mordkin was devoting most of his time and attention to the company, also traveling with it on all of its out-of-town engagements, someone had to be found to stay at home and manage the Mordkin school. In November, during the company's brief stay in Chicago where it gave two performances at the Studebaker Theatre, Dimitri Romanoff introduced Lucia and Orthwine to a young man he had encountered out in California who he thought might take on the job of running the school.

Richard Pleasant was not exactly the type one might pick to look after and safeguard a disorganized New York ballet studio. His experience in dance was nil.

Born and raised in Colorado, he had come east to attend Princeton University, where he earned a degree with honors in architecture in 1932. However, due to the Depression, there were very few job openings for unknown, unsponsored young architects. So after graduating, Pleasant headed to California to try his luck in the film industry. He was equally unsuccessful finding steady employment there, but during his stay he met Dimitri Romanoff, who was just beginning to make his way as a dancer in the San Francisco Opera Ballet.

After spending nearly two years in California, Pleasant moved on to several other short-lived jobs while Romanoff came to New York to become one of the two leading male dancers of the Mordkin Ballet. Now late in 1937, when the Mordkin company was performing in Chicago, Pleasant again met Romanoff, who introduced him to Orthwine and Lucia Chase: together, they talked briefly about the possibility of his coming to work for the Mordkin organization in New York. A month passed before Orthwine followed up the initial meeting by sending Pleasant a telegram asking if he was still interested.

Pleasant's answer was affirmative:

> The possibility of working with the Mordkin company has interested me very much. However, I have never known whether the job you proposed was to be manager of the company while on tour, or of the Carnegie Hall Studio during Mr. Mordkin's absence.

The fact that Pleasant even posed the question was significant, for there had never been any thought or discussion of his becoming manager of the company but only of the ballet studio. Even that had been described in very vague and ambiguous terms, since Mordkin, like many Russian émigrés, was acutely suspicious, almost to the point of paranoia, of anyone who might infringe on his authority. Consequently, it was necessary that Pleasant be introduced into the Mordkin arena as little more than a receptionist, someone to open and close the studio and record class attendance during Mordkin's absence. Any mention of his also being associated in some capacity with the company had to be carefully avoided.

Yet apparently it was the company that had attracted Pleasant's interest. He replied: "With the split of the De Basil and the Massine-Blum companies and the increasing interest in ballet in the United States, this promises to be an excellent year. Whether I am with you or not, I wish you and the company prosperity and a big success."

This was a rather grand and far-fetched response to a modest little inquiry, but that was Pleasant's manner and might have constituted quite a clue of things to come had it been carefully analyzed with an eye to the future, which it wasn't.

With no further discussion of his being involved with the company, Pleasant was offered the opportunity to work for the Mikhail Mordkin School of the Dance and Mimo-Drama at Carnegie Hall at the munificent salary of $60 a week, and he straightway accepted. So it happened that when the Mordkin Ballet early in January 1939 set off on an extended tour of thirty-three cities, Richard Pleasant settled into his new studio job, which consisted mainly of taking attendance and answering the phone.

It wasn't long before Orthwine reported to Lucia and Harry Zuckert, the old-fashioned lawyer and guardian of the Cochran/Ewing dynasty, the welcome news that the school was beginning to run like clockwork, "so there are hopes that the boy will make a good man for us." The results Pleasant was getting were vastly better than those which Columbia Concerts Corporation, which had been hired to manage the Mordkin company's U.S. tour, was achieving out on the road.

A year earlier, Lucia had expressed high hopes for this new booking arrangement. "What a difference it will make," she had written her mother at the time the contract was being negotiated. "There's no better manager, and we will be 100 times more formidable. Everyone will sit up and take notice of us, and we'll really be on the map."

Another reason Lucia had for being so optimistic the year before was that Mordkin and Orthwine had heeded her advice and hired a recognized ballerina to head the company. For the past four years Patricia Bowman had been the popular and highly regarded leading dancer at Radio City and the Roxy Theatre; now she was working every morning with the Mordkin company, and everyone was very encouraged, particularly when Columbia Concerts was hired to manage the company the following year.

"Hip hip hurray," Lucia wrote home. "Now we don't have to worry about the tour etc. anymore. It is wonderful."

The public reception of the company was also a great improvement over the previous tour. "We are having the most tremendous success everywhere," Lucia wrote from Toronto. "Our Canada critics are wonderful. You never read such praise for ballet in general. What a big advance we've made in a year!"

Yet, although the agreement with Columbia Concerts had been reached half a year before the fall tour was to commence, it was still too late for Columbia to place the company on the powerful concert series it ran for all its contracted artists. Without this highly organized backing, the box office returns in one city after another were way below expectations, the tour was a financial disaster, and once it ended, in March 1939, the company was laid off and the dancers scattered. Despite all its frenzied activity over the previous two years, it was becoming clear to many that the costs of Mordkin's company were veering out of control and that there was little point in continuing to rejuvenate an organization that was now essentially defunct.

In the meantime, Richard Pleasant had come a long way from the moment little more than a year ago when he had begun his very modest job at the Mordkin studio. His commendable work there had led to his being appointed secretary of Advanced Arts Ballets Inc., and after the company set out in the fall, taking Mordkin and Lucia with it, Pleasant became the principal figure left on the home front. Because he was available, with extra time on his hands and eager to work, he was enlisted to arrange a brief engagement for the Mordkin Ballet in New York at the end of its tour, and he had accordingly booked the Hudson Theatre for the ill-fated series of four consecutive Sunday night performances in January 1939.

One might expect that the disastrous box office results of this effort, which was totally engineered by Pleasant, would have terminated any further association between him and the Mordkin organization, perhaps not with the ballet studio but at least with the ballet company, yet this did not happen. The Hudson Theatre engagement, pursued while everyone else was out of town, had the effect of elevating Dick Pleasant into the unarticulated but de facto position of managing the day-to-day affairs of the Mordkin Ballet company, a position he continued to maintain after the company went on the road again early in February 1939 for its final outing under Columbia Concerts. When this proved to be another financial disaster, the company disbanded and Harry Zuckert delivered his ultimatum . . . that except for whatever had already been committed, Lucia was not to be asked to underwrite any deficit-producing activity by the Mordkin Ballet, at least not for the remainder of the year.

Up to this point, the main financial supporter of the company, although not officially acknowledged or recognized outside very immediate circles, had been Allied Arts's principal stockholder, Lucia Chase. Yet when it seemed time to curb further spending, the dampening word came not from her but from Zuckert.

Zuckert had long been accustomed to carrying out any and all instructions from the presiding heads of the Yonkers-based family—originally Alex Cochran, then Tom Ewing, who had been named his residual heir. The current preoccupation of Tom Ewing's young widow with ballet was a matter of great concern to Zuckert. To begin with, the Mordkin Ballet was not a legally recognized charity: in fact, in Zuckert's opinion, it was even questionable whether dance represented an established and reputable art form in America, the way museums and many musical organizations like the Philharmonic or the Metropolitan Opera had managed to become. To Zuckert, the expenditure of good Alex Smith & Sons carpet money for dancers' tutus and empty theater seats was tantamount to fiscal sacrilege and violated all his cautionary canons.

He was in a position to speak out forcefully and be heard. First, Lucia Chase was his client, which to him meant far more than simply giving legal advice. The tragic shift of the family hierarchy due to the deaths of Alex Cochran and Tom Ewing in rapid succession had, according to Zuckert's fiduciary turn of mind, effectively entrusted Tom's widow to his abiding and scrupulous care. It was clear to him now that she was unhappy at the way she was constantly being asked for money when all she wanted was a chance to dance. He could understand why she was unwilling to assert herself when that meant exerting control over Mordkin, but Harry Zuckert had no compunctions about expressing his opinion. Besides being Lucia's lawyer and unofficial guardian, he had also been asked to serve as the treasurer of Advanced Arts Ballets Inc., the body currently responsible for providing support to the Mordkin Ballet. In Zuckert's eyes, that support was now threatening to exceed all proper limits, and duty called on him to put matters back on track.

Consequently, at the next meeting of the Advanced Arts board of directors in March 1939, Harry Zuckert announced that except for those expenses which were already irrevocably committed, no one should count on any further financial support from Miss Chase that year without first obtaining the approval of her advisors, which in effect meant himself.

Undoubtedly to Harry Zuckert's razor-sharp mind, his directive was clear and unequivocal: Lucia Chase's short but painfully expensive underwriting of the Mordkin Ballet had now come to an end, at least for the remainder of the current year, possibly forever. Yet words are always subject to interpretation and can mean different things to different ears.

What Zuckert didn't realize—nor did a great many others—was that Pleasant, after a yearlong close association with dancers through his job at the Mordkin school, had acquired a compelling, almost obsessive interest in ballet. His architect-trained mind had begun envisioning a totally different kind of company than the one bearing Mordkin's name. Pleasant had never entertained a very high opinion of Mordkin, either as an administrator or as a choreographer. In his abrupt and undiplomatic fashion, Pleasant had already expressed this in such clear and open terms that Mordkin's son, currently vice president and business manager of Advanced Arts Ballets Inc., refused to have any further dealings with him.

However, with the Mordkin Ballet at least temporarily disbanded, Pleasant was protected by the sheer ambiguity of his undefined position somewhere between the studio and company. Zuckert's pronouncement would no doubt have caused a drastic, possibly fatal curtailment of both Pleasant and the ballet company had the company remained in existence.

Instead, the Mordkin Ballet had quietly disbanded on its own, which was quite different from its being ordered to shut down.

All of which helps explain the memo to Orthwine that Pleasant soon had occasion to write: if he wasn't mistaken, he reasoned, the specific wording of Zuckert's statement was that Lucia "will bear the expenses of studio, accompanists, insurance, etc., and the retaining of 16 dancers between now and December 31, 1939, but that she cannot finance any other venture either in New York or on the road."

> We have, therefore, a plant, scenery, costumes, music and 16 dancers which will be given free for us to work into any plan or type of production . . . that much headstart toward a new venture.

New venture? What Harry Zuckert had been calling for was an almost total reduction of expenditures for the next nine months, including any new commitments that were not self-supporting. Virtually all activities of a ballet company—certainly all production and rehearsal expenses, and even most public performances—had since time immemorial unfailingly produced a deficit. Considering that, aside from Lucia, there didn't appear to be any other potential sponsor on the scene, Zuckert must have assumed that without her support, any future for the Mordkin Ballet had been effectively canceled.

Yet here was Pleasant hearing not a death knell but a bright sparkling overture for a great new venture once the curtain went up on the new year—providing, of course, that Lucia would go along with the grand vision that was now burgeoning in Pleasant's hyperactive imagination.

As Pleasant viewed the current situation, if there was any hope for matters to work out, a select core of the Mordkin dancers had to break free from the straitjacket that the existing company had become. The problem was that everything revolved around Mordkin. Somehow the new venture had to reach around and beyond Mordkin.

Pleasant did not have the ideal personal makeup to manage this delicate tactical maneuver. Sensitive, prickly, prone to feeling slighted, he gave the appearance of being stiff and aloof, certainly not the type who was likely to ingratiate himself with those who held different persuasions. He wasn't even inclined to try but was more apt to turn away at the first sign of skepticism or opposition and stride off, clinging jealously to his own opinions. Added to this was the fact that he was starting off in the ballet world as a complete outsider, a vagabond from the west with no great personal resources, few close friends, and virtually no important acquaintances. Essentially a loner by nature, he tended at particularly difficult moments to withdraw even further, subject to an increasing tendency toward sleepless nights and solitary drinking. In view of all these personal shortcomings, what this moody young idealist managed to accomplish during the next eighteen months is little short of incredible.

Few people had any suspicion of the grand ambition that was rapidly taking hold of Pleasant's imagination, a sweeping vision of a major ballet company of international stature. Zuckert would have considered his ambition preposterous; Orthwine, that it was just a youngster's pipedream, while the basic concept probably would never have entered Lucia's mind. As for Mordkin, he would have laughed at the idea of an American college boy from a cowboy state trying to put together a ballet company. Unless, of course, someone suggested to him that Pleasant intended to use the Mordkin Ballet as an initial stepping-stone for his grandiose project, in which case Mordkin would have become apoplectic with rage. But for the next few months, none of these central figures—Zuckert, Orthwine, Lucia, Mordkin—had much to do with Pleasant but kept interacting and maneuvering with each other in their own intricate little ballet as they all tried to control center stage.

As head of the company and the studio, both of which bore his name, Mordkin was ostensibly still in command. He was the teacher. He was the choreographer. He was the ultimate arbiter of all questions relating to production, performance, and artistic decisions. His authority continued to be unquestioned and absolute. And yet he sensed that his power was being usurped and he was being pushed aside. Although he became bitterly resentful, he didn't quite know what to do about it.

The main—in fact the only—problem to Mordkin's way of thinking was simply money. He didn't need all that much, nothing like Colonel W. de Basil's or Serge Denham's companies, but without at least some money, he couldn't run his new company. As he looked back over the last couple of years since the company had reemerged, it was clear to him that he had essentially formed it around and for Lucia Chase. None of this would have transpired if he hadn't first pulled her up out of her grief-filled seclusion and brought her back into the world, taught her (when she was nothing more than an aspiring actress) how to dance ballet, invited her into his home, coached her in the great principal roles of *Giselle, Sleeping Beauty,* and *La Fille Mal Gardée,* made her his leading ballerina, introduced her to the public, all this in return for a relatively small amount of money when she obviously had so much, possibly too much for her own good, certainly way too much for a dancer.

Yet here she was now suddenly pulling away or at least holding back, under orders issued by a cold-blooded fish of a lawyer who knew nothing at all about art, the two of them teaming up with Orthwine, who was supposed to be his friend, Russian like himself. Now they were all being misled and turned against him. And by whom? By the young upstart Richard Pleasant, who really had no business being involved with the company in the first place. Why wasn't he, Mordkin, the one who was making all the decisions? Weren't they his dancers, his ballets, his company? Just give him the money, and he could take care of everything.

Orthwine for his part found himself in a terrible quandary. As a successful businessman, he had seen firsthand that, when it came to money matters, his friend Mordkin was practically oblivious to any understanding and consideration of the dollar. Orthwine did not have any of Mikhail's artistic talent, but he did know how to put things together so that they worked. Therefore, wasn't it up to him to get behind Mordkin, stand up for him, and stop all this bickering? It shouldn't be as difficult as everyone was making it. He liked them all—Mikhail, Michael Mordkin Jr., Zuckert, Pleasant, Lucia. They should just sit down and talk like sensible people.

Pleasant had little, if any, of Orthwine's benign wisdom. All those months he had spent sitting at a desk in Mordkin's studio without a great deal to do had allowed him lots of time to think, and what had started out as a germ of an idea had gradually grown into a magnificent image: why not bring in as many good choreographers and dancers as possible under one roof and let them all work, each in his own way, taking here and giving there, ultimately forging a fantastic new repertory and a company like nothing that had ever been seen, at least certainly not in America.

The more he thought about it, the more the essential ingredients seemed to be all right there, a grand design just crying out to be drawn up and done. At last the haphazard, fruitless gypsy life he had led up to this point was starting to make sense. It almost appeared as though he had been specially groomed for the task, all those little jobs in the film industry and the brief contacts he had made there, eventually leading him back through Chicago and on to New York, the undisputed dance hub of the entire country, with a swirl of dancers constantly coming in and going out of the studio every day, while outside there were all those theaters and arts shops and dance talk and talent. New York was like a great web extending out over the Hudson into the vast country beyond or eastward to Europe and Russia. Everything was out there, ready and waiting to fall into place. Pleasant was beginning to see how it all could be done.

As for Lucia, she had no such sweeping vision or grand ambition. As she struggled to recover from a devastating grief, she simply wanted a chance to dance. Back in New York, Tommy and I were safe in Buckley School, and she had people at the apartment to take good care of us when she wasn't there, so she could devote herself almost totally to ballet.

If only she weren't always being asked to pay for everything. She didn't mind giving some money on the side. Things had to be paid for, she knew that, but not over and over again. As Irving Chase's daughter, she knew the value of a dollar, all one hundred cents, and she had been brought up to think you were supposed to keep track of every penny, not to be stingy but careful. That was just good New England frugality.

What made this money question extra painful was that she couldn't help thinking how it was really Tom's money. Not that he would have minded: he had always encouraged her and had loved to spend when it was for a fine time or a good cause. Zuckert obviously disapproved of her attachment to ballet: she hated having to keep going back to him and asking for additional funds.

She hoped that he had made everything clear to the others now. She would pay for the things Pleasant was stuck with, which was only fair, and he could even count on her for a little more to keep things going, which was the important thing. She just had to get through this year.

3. Richard Pleasant

I wonder if you can see your way
clear to finance the beginning of
the program. It will be, as always,
a gamble and a risk, but it will be a
magnificent venture.
—Richard Pleasant to Lucia Chase,
July 26, 1939

MIKHAIL MORDKIN was jealous to the point of being almost psychotic about his position as the sole leader and arbiter of all things bearing his name. All his close associates—particularly his friend Rudy Orthwine, who was named president of Advanced Arts, and Mordkin's son, Michael Jr., who was vice president and business manager—were careful to emphasize that no one other than Mordkin himself had the right to speak for the Mordkin company. Yet with so many conflicting ideas being pursued, someone had to make the regular daily decisions, both large and small, and this role fell almost by default to Richard Pleasant, the secretary of Advanced Arts who in effect became the general manager of the Mordkin Ballet.

This was not a particularly happy arrangement. Pleasant did not have the easygoing, self-effacing kind of personality that might have disarmed Mordkin's ever-lurking paranoia. He also made no effort to conceal the fact that he considered Mordkin unsuited to be an artistic director and even less qualified to serve as the company's sole choreographer. By the summer of 1939, the two men had ceased talking to one another, communicating only when absolutely necessary and then usually through a third party.

Meanwhile, Pleasant was becoming more and more intrigued with the idea of a second company, probably allied with but distinctly independent from the Mordkin Ballet. Having an extremely quick and active mind, plus a great deal of time on his hands, Pleasant began imagining one model after another until a master plan emerged. He could envisage how his dream company might work out. The only real obstacle, and it was the usual huge one, was how to pay for it.

Without confiding in any of the other officers or board members of Advanced Arts, Pleasant marshaled all the far-reaching hopes and ideas he had been nurturing for months and, early in July, set off for Narragansett to talk to Lucia Chase.

Despite her intelligence and common sense, Lucia was not by nature what might be termed an original thinker. Her customary way of working was to take all the elements at hand, no matter how numerous or how conflicting, and to sort through them, rearranging, adjusting, changing a little bit here and there, until a practical solution could be found. This was how she managed life on her home front, deftly organizing not only her own busy existence, particularly when she was often out on tour for long stretches at a time, but also that of her children, guests, staff, and everything to do with her various houses. Later on, this same skill enabled her to work out Ballet Theatre's exceedingly complex rehearsal schedules, balancing the various choreographers' usually exorbitant requests against the very limited number of hours, studio space, and dancers available on any one day. In contrast, what she was not particularly equipped to do was to conceive out of the abstract a totally new image or approach to a problem, some strikingly original solution completely outside the box of customary thinking, which was exactly what Dick Pleasant proposed to unfold for her on the porch of High Tide in Narragansett.

The critical question, of course, was money, but neither Lucia nor Pleasant would have enjoyed addressing that directly. Lucia was desperately anxious to be recognized and accepted as a dancer, not at all as a rich patron of dance. She believed that in the eyes of the world, one could not be both a professional dancer and a philanthropist. The fact that she had been just that combination for the past couple of years did not mean that she had to admit it. She would not have been very receptive to Pleasant's proposal if he had expressed it in terms of the money required.

Pleasant may have been inexperienced in the ways of the moneyed world, but he was no fool and could clearly read the warning signals that Lucia gave whenever the talk veered toward money. Although Pleasant was often judged to be aloof, distant, impersonal, he was actually extremely sensitive and perceptive, also someone who was very shy and reluctant to push for his own selfish interests. A more crass, unfeeling individual would have had little chance of gaining a favorable reaction from Lucia at this point, particularly so soon after she—or Harry Zuckert speaking for her—had ruled out her giving any additional money, at least for the rest of the current year.

Instead, the great appeal of Pleasant was that his primary interest wasn't money but a great burning idea, a concept so shining and compelling that he could talk about it for hours without ever descending to the mundane, distasteful level of dollars and cents. He was still very young, too young in Lucia's eyes to be a totally legitimate authority. Yet she couldn't help being impressed—and excited—by the daring scope of all that he was proposing to do. Also, there is something basically appealing, almost irresistible, in the air when a young man pours out his dream, his fondest hope, to a woman who is somewhat older but not beyond the stage of dreaming herself.

So for two days, Pleasant talked, and Lucia listened, about his vision of a new American ballet company, built not around a single person but one that incorporated the talents and styles of the leading choreographers of the United States, Russia, England, Denmark, Sweden, in fact anywhere in the world. By the time he left, her main reservations were not so much with his ambitious plan but with her role within it. She just didn't like the feeling of being the principal party. Couldn't he find some other people who would help, particularly financially?

He promised to work as hard as he could on finding other money, but once back in New York, he wrote a long letter asking her to confirm that he indeed had her permission to press ahead:

> From this point on out, the whole thing will begin to unravel again unless we act. Everything must be done almost simultaneously and quickly. The one thing that now holds us back is money.

The new company would have expenses of such proportions that he could understand if Lucia felt she couldn't assume them by herself. So far, he had been unable to find anyone else ready and willing to help. However, long term, he did entertain certain hopes of securing support from other benefactors, people like Laurence Rockefeller, who was a classmate when they were both at Princeton; Dwight Wiman, the well-known Broadway producer who had recently employed Vera Zorina, Balanchine's new wife, as the star in the hit musical *I Married an Angel;* also possibly Gordon Mendelssohn, who was the patron of prominent dancer Yurek Shabelevski. But for now, if Lucia could just help get his program off the ground . . .

She agreed and gave him the crucial go-ahead. Not a blank check—that was not the New England way she had learned from her father. She never relinquished her desire to follow the example Irving Chase set of being frugal, but she did promise to provide, through the remainder of the year, "up to $25,000" additional money so that he might proceed to take the most pressing first steps.

With that relatively modest amount of start-up money, Dick Pleasant went to work, and the wondrous story of Ballet Theatre began.

—❥—

One of the first people Pleasant contacted was Carmelita Maracci, a native of Uruguay who came to California and became known as a dancer and teacher who, in the 1930s, also began choreographing for her own small company. Pleasant wrote a letter inviting her to come east and bring whatever soloists she needed: "You would produce several ballets on your own, using your own key people and filling out with Mordkin-hired dancers; the Mordkin Ballet would do likewise, using your people in its own ballets. Each evening throughout the series, each company would give one or two of its own numbers."

This was quite an extraordinary proposal. The idea of lending Mordkin's own company dancers to another choreographer, in this case Maracci, then presenting her ballets—along with Mordkin's own works—as part of the same evening program, was something Mordkin had never been consulted about. He never would have accepted the idea, so he simply wasn't asked.

Pleasant sent another letter along the same lines to Ruth Page, former principal dancer and director of the Chicago Grand Opera Company and cofounder and director of the Page-Stone Ballet Company. For Page, Pleasant suggested that "an evening's bill might be one Mordkin ballet; one Page ballet with Page choreography; (also) artists, scenery and one ballet by the *X Ballet.* Possibly a reciprocal arrangement could be worked out whereby the X artists could appear in a Page ballet, the Page artists in a Mordkin ballet, etc."

Pleasant never discussed any of these ideas directly with Mordkin, who only heard about them by way of his son. Mordkin's reaction was immediate outrage. The only person Mordkin would ever consider collaborating with was Michel Fokine, generally regarded as the greatest living ballet chore-ographer in the world, and Fokine was currently working in Sweden and not available. Otherwise, he would collaborate with no one. Period.

Although Mordkin flatly rejected Pleasant's ideas, he was not in the least forthcoming about his own artistic plans. His disbanded company was officially scheduled to reassemble and commence rehearsals for a fall tour and possibly a New York season. Yet, as late as mid-July, there was no word from Mordkin about what ballets he intended to present or who would be cast to dance in each one.

While the absence at this late date of any definite commitment from Mordkin on either dancers or repertory posed a real problem for Pleasant, it also had its advantages. It meant that Pleasant was left to work on his own with an essentially clean slate. Beginning in early August, while Lucia was in Narragansett, Pleasant began implementing his grand plan, using the Mordkin Ballet as a nucleus but expanding to form an all-embracing organization designed to attract dancers, choreographers, and other artists from all over the country and the western world.

The list of people Pleasant contacted during the next thirty days was quite staggering and included practically all of ballet's most prominent dancers: ballerinas Irina Baronova, Alexandra Danilova, Alicia Markova, Margot Fonteyn, Nina Verchinina, Nana Gollner; also two of England's leading male dancers, Anton Dolin and Hugh Laing. Equally extensive were the invitations he sent to most of the leading choreographers on both sides of the Atlantic, starting with Fokine and including Frederick Ashton, Antony Tudor, Andrée Howard, Adolph Bolm, Bronislava Nijinska, George Balanchine, Agnes de Mille, Eugene Loring, Michael Kidd, and even Gene Kelly.

The immediate response was not encouraging. Most of those contacted already had other commitments or were concerned about the risks involved in accepting this unexpected and startling invitation. But as Pleasant continued his widespread campaigning through August, his ideas continued to develop. The fact that some refused, and others delayed or simply didn't answer, only intensified his efforts. For the first time in his life, he found himself entrusted with a mission, although with little or no help from anyone else. This might have daunted others, but it was just right for Pleasant, who was by nature a loner.

Up to now, during all the time Pleasant had been employed by the Mordkin organization in New York, there had been no official directive or incentive for him to exert himself beyond simply administering the ballet studio, and once he had this properly organized, it practically ran itself. Meanwhile, the parent ballet company was strictly and emphatically Mordkin's private territory. Yet Mordkin had abdicated, at least temporarily, and no one seemed to be interested in taking his place or doing anything with the company—except Dick Pleasant.

When his initial idea of getting two or three small dance groups to join with the Mordkin Ballet in a collaborative program under the all-embracing title of *America Dances* didn't produce results, he made a complete turnaround and focused on the idea of having two separate entities functioning at the same time: the Mordkin Ballet, which was expected to go out on a fall tour, and a second unit, temporarily called Ballet Theatre, designed to fulfill an unusually ambitious season in New York City.

Late that August, Rudy Orthwine undertook the ticklish assignment of summarizing Pleasant's plans for this second company to Mordkin, specifying in a lengthy letter the dancers who were to be hired and also who would be working with them:

> It is understood that there shall be more than one choreographer for The Ballet Theatre, but that no one choreographer shall be artistic director and that each shall be responsible for his own work and not that of any other.

As for Mordkin's role in this new amalgamation, Orthwine was careful to stress that Mordkin was not only being offered a contract that recognized him as head of his company, but also that the overall arrangement called for nine Mordkin ballets, in a majority of which Mordkin would appear as a leading dancer.

Mordkin's response was delivered by his son:

> He [Mordkin Sr.] heartily approves of all those principals and Corps de Ballet who are now under contract, but he wishes to exercise sole right selection of the balance of the company and casting.

Perhaps this could have been worked out, but a bigger complication occurred when the Embree Concert Service, the booking organization that had been contracted to arrange the Mordkin company's fall tour, announced that it was backing out. Mordkin's insistence that he, and only he, could select dancers and repertory was dwarfed by the much larger question now of what to do with the Mordkin Ballet, a company which suddenly had no definite future plans and whose de facto manager (Pleasant) was focusing all his attention on building another organization altogether.

While all this was taking place in New York, an infinitely larger and more disruptive struggle was rapidly coming to a head thousands of miles away on the other side of the Atlantic where an ominously well-armed Germany continued to threaten the shaky peace of the European continent. By the summer of 1939, it had become clear that a titanic storm was brewing, and there was little doubt, at least in Europe, that an awful conflict was about to erupt. On September 1, Hitler invaded Poland, and the war was on.

Rather than demolish all of Pleasant's simmering plans to create the new Ballet Theatre, the declaration of war amazingly had the reverse effect. A considerable number of the most influential figures in the ballet world, including many of the artists Pleasant had originally contacted but who had turned him down, were now suddenly anxious to leave Europe and find safe haven and employment in the United States.

First to respond, within a week of the declaration of war in Europe, was Michel Fokine, at the time generally considered the foremost ballet choreographer in the world. In his early years with Diaghilev's Ballets Russes, Fokine had created several masterpieces, including *Les Sylphides, Carnaval, Scheherazade, Firebird,* and *Petrouchka.* Fokine also had become recognized as a pivotal figure with the publication in the London *Times,* on July 6, 1914, of his *Five Principles,* which called for a more natural look for classic ballet and provided a new impetus that was still being felt a quarter of a century later. Fokine and his wife had lived in the United States for many years, beginning in 1923, and he had become a U.S. citizen in 1932. When contacted for the first time by Dick Pleasant, Fokine had been under contract with the Royal Swedish Ballet and had turned down the invitation. But suddenly the war's designation as a force majeure liberated him from his legal obligations to stay in Sweden and allowed him to start negotiating to join Ballet Theatre.

This was a cataclysmic development for Mordkin, who had always said that Fokine was the only choreographer he would ever even consider letting into his company's fold. Now the very likely possibility that Fokine would sign a contract with Ballet Theatre meant that soon there would be a new face on the scene eminently qualified—more than Mordkin him-self—to select dancers for whatever work was lined up for the forthcoming fall and winter seasons.

Suddenly, with artists anxious to escape the war, Pleasant was embold-ened to reach out to a great many more prominent figures in the dance world. The first week in September, once again he wrote Frederick Ashton, the highly esteemed resident choreographer of the Sadler's Wells Ballet in London, about the possibility of his coming to New York "to mount bal-lets for Ballet Theatre, a new organization which will absorb the Mordkin Ballet."

This statement constituted quite an additional leap:

> Now, with the declaration of war over last weekend, I don't know whether it will be totally impossible for you to leave the country or if by chance it might make you more available. We plan a great permanent organization in which there will be definitely a place for a person of your attainments.

It was a canny effort, but unfortunately it was not very well aimed: the letter was addressed to Harton Street, not Wharton Street where Ashton lived, and came back stamped "No such address. Return to sender." One has to wonder what might have been the result if Ashton, who went on to head Britain's Royal Ballet in its heyday and is now generally regarded as one of ballet's greatest choreographers, had been successfully contacted and brought in as one of the founding figures of Ballet Theatre.

Despite this mishap, Pleasant pressed on, undeterred even when he fol-lowed up on some earlier unsuccessful efforts and once again was rejected: George Balanchine sent word that he was unavailable for a number of reasons; Margot Fonteyn replied that she was bound by her contract with Sadler's Wells; Gene Kelly reported he had been cast in the upcoming play *Time of Your Life.*

Yet there were also some breakthrough successes, particularly a very im-portant British contingent: the dancer- choreographer Antony Tudor, who had already created a number of small works for England's Ballet Rambert but was still practically unknown in the United States; Hugh Laing, Tudor's close associate and a superb dancer; a third Rambert artist, Andrée Howard, who had choreographed two ballets that Pleasant hoped to include in Ballet Theatre's initial repertory; and Anton Dolin, one of the premier male danc-ers of the Western world and a recognized authority of classical ballet (who incidentally was well qualified to restage Mordkin's versions of both *Giselle* and *Swan Lake*). A few months earlier, none of these stand-out figures on the English dance scene had considered themselves available, but now that England had been placed on a war footing and their careers at home were in jeopardy, the twin lure of personal security and joining up with an exciting new company resulted in all four boarding the SS *Washington* and arriving in New York on October 12, just as rehearsals for the new Ballet Theatre were beginning.

In addition to Fokine and Dolin, soon there was also a third person to challenge Mordkin's position of choreographic authority: Bronislava Nijinska, sister of the legendary male dancer Vaslav Nijinsky and herself a former principal dancer and choreographer for the Diaghilev ballet. Pleasant hired her to restage *La Fille Mal Gardée*, another of Mordkin's productions, which had been a staple work for his company just the year before.

At this point, Mikhail Mordkin's fortunes began taking a downward turn so swift and extreme as to be hardly believable. Early in October, when the first contingent of dancers, most from Mordkin's old company, showed up to begin rehearsals, Pleasant delivered a note to Mordkin via messenger, enclosing a list of the company which to date had been hired:

> I had hoped to have you participate actively in auditioning and choosing the corps de ballet, and, as a courtesy, extended to you that privilege. Since according to our basic agreement with AGMA, our options had to be exercised by Saturday, September 30th, the corps de ballet as it now stands was selected by Mr. Fokine and Mr. Gavrilov. However, out of consideration for you, I did put in as many members of the Mordkin Ballet as was possible.

After that, one blow followed another in quick succession. On the first day of Mordkin's rehearsals for his ballet *Goldfish*, he heard the music of *Giselle* in the next studio and learned that his existing *Giselle* was being taken over by Dolin. Next, by registered mail: "We shall not require your services in rehearsing *Swan Lake*," which now stood also to be directed by Dolin. The same for Mordkin's production of *La Fille Mal Gardée*, which was handed to Nijinska. And in the midst of all this, Mordkin was informed that his studio would no longer be required for company rehearsals.

Before October was over, of the nine ballets that Mordkin had either created or revised for his company and which only two months earlier had been earmarked for the fall tour, now only one—*Voices of Spring*—was being rehearsed. With tremendous activity galvanizing around him, new faces at every turn, a crammed schedule of rehearsals posted on the board every day, suddenly he—Mikhail Mordkin, founder-director of the Mordkin Ballet, described in its own souvenir program as "the first great American Ballet . . . a company of stars such as America has never before had in one organization . . . the greatest repository of the past, the prophet of the future"—now found himself almost totally disinherited. Other than rehearsing one last ballet, there was nothing left for him to do but step out of the picture and retire back into his old school, minus company, performances, public attention, everything.

Small wonder that Mordkin ended up bitter. Besides Dick Pleasant, to whom he had refused to speak long ago and whom he regarded as thoroughly despicable, the person Mordkin blamed most was Lucia, who he imagined was behind it all. While perhaps this was quite understandable from his vantage point, the charge was way off the mark. Lucia would have had to be blind not to see that Mordkin was being pushed out of the picture. Yet she was most decidedly not the author of the early plans for Ballet Theatre, nor was she calling the critical shots. Other than providing the seed money for Pleasant to proceed with his grand design, Lucia had made a strict and unequivocal effort to stay out of management.

This decision was reinforced by the fact that Lucia Chase, the dancer, suddenly found herself in great demand in this jam-packed tumultuous rehearsal period, possibly the most complex and adventurous start-up ever to be attempted in the annals of dance. Although Lucia was not a trained ballerina in the classic sense, she had certain qualities that several of the most prominent choreographers in the early history of Ballet Theatre—particularly Fokine, Tudor, and Agnes de Mille—found particularly useful.

Lucia was a born actress and compelling figure onstage. Once handed a part, she put such an individual stamp on it that her performance invariably attracted public and critical attention. Roles such as the eldest sister in Tudor's *Pillar of Fire,* Lizzie Borden's stepmother in de Mille's *Fall River Legend,* Queen Clementine in Fokine's *Bluebeard,* the Greedy One in *Three Virgins and a Devil,* Minerva in *Judgment of Paris,* and the Queen Mother in *Swan Lake* all became indelibly associated with Lucia Chase. She danced some of these roles for ten, fifteen, even twenty years.

As a dancer in rehearsal, Lucia was attentive, eager, happy to take instruction, and practically tireless—all qualities particularly appreciated by choreographers working under crushing time schedules and harrowing emotional pressure. So for this first Ballet Theatre season, Lucia was constantly busy, rehearsing prominent parts in Fokine's *Les Sylphides*, Eugene Loring's *The Great American Goof*, Tudor's *Dark Elegies* and *Judgment of Paris*, and *La Fille Mal Gardée* as restaged by Nijinska.

Besides all these claims on her time emanating from the rehearsal studio, Lucia also had a singularly demanding schedule on the home front, overseeing a large household staff, attending to a constant succession of guests and family moving in and out of the Park Avenue apartment on a near-daily basis, and most of all, making herself available to Tommy and me, two very active boys—ages ten and eight—who, though busy in school each day, looked forward to seeing their mother once they came home, hopefully not just for a few minutes but right up to bedtime.

While there was little time to worry about Mordkin, he was on her conscience. After all, it was Mordkin who had brought her out of her soul-wrenching grief after Tom died and drawn her back into the world, Mordkin who had trained her to be a compelling dancer, Mordkin who had made a principal place for her in his company, launched her professional career, and brought her recognition as a legitimate artist. As long as she lived, Lucia would always be grateful to him.

Yet there was nothing she could do to repair their formerly close relationship, which was now devastated. Mordkin became more and more unapproachable. For a while he remained on the scene, teaching a single class each day and rehearsing his one ballet, which was still being readied for an anticipated New York season, but he gradually retired into a studio like a cornered animal, trapped and snarling. At one point, it was reputed he took to carrying a pistol with him that he would dramatically place on the piano each morning at the start of his one remaining ballet class. The friendship and cordial relations between Mordkin and Lucia were over: she could only leave things alone for others or the passage of time to work out.

There was one occasion, several years later, when she attempted to make amends. Without giving any prior notice, she went uptown to Mordkin's eastside apartment and rang the bell. Mrs. Mordkin opened the door. Seeing who was there, she drew herself up, took a deep breath, and spat in Lucia's face. Then, without saying a word, she slammed the door. As far as anyone knows, that was the last time Lucia ever saw or spoke to either of the Mordkins.

By the start of 1940, Mordkin had returned to teaching in his former

Carnegie Hall studio, but his life and hopes were shattered. Five years later, in July 1944, he died at his summer home in upstate New York, a sadly inconspicuous end for a flamboyant figure.

— ⁂ —

Back at Ballet Theatre's rehearsal studios, work continued at a furious pace throughout the fall of 1939. Dick Pleasant's master plan had swelled to the point that it now consisted of building a monumental repertory, representing every major period of ballet, all to be ready in time to open a major New York season, wherever and whenever that might be. In mid-November he began searching for a theater, but to his dismay, everything was booked. He tried everywhere, but there wasn't a single appropriate stage in New York that conceivably would become available before late spring.

Meanwhile, many of the most renowned figures in ballet were busily rehearsing every day: Fokine with *Les Sylphides* and *Carnaval;* Tudor on three separate works, *Jardin aux Lilas, Judgment of Paris*, and *Dark Elegies;* Dolin, besides being the company's leading male dancer, was mounting *Swan Lake* and *Giselle* and a new ballet, *Quintet,* to music by Raymond Scott; Adolph Bolm, also employed as a leading dancer, was rehearsing his *Mechanical Ballet* and an original production of *Peter and the Wolf;* Eugene Loring was creating a particularly ambitious new work entitled *The Great American Goof;* Bronislava Nijinska was reconstructing *La Fille Mal Gardée;* Andrée Howard was rehearsing her *Lady into Fox* and *Death and the Maiden;* and Yurek Shabelevski was polishing his *Ode to Glory.*

In addition to all these, two outside groups of dancers were brought in to perform two new pieces. The first, *Goyescas,* by Mexican-born Jose Fernandez, was created using twelve Spanish dancers. The other was a new work, *Black Ritual (Obeah),* which Agnes de Mille was commissioned to choreograph for sixteen African American dancers. However, it was not at all certain that de Mille could complete this in time, since she was simultaneously preparing for the opening of a new musical, *Swingin' the Dream,* which was scheduled to open in November in the Center Theatre at Radio City Music Hall.

The rehearsal scene was chaos. At any moment there were groups of dancers everywhere, in studios and hallways, on the stairs or out in the street, wherever there was an available space. Choreographers were on many occasions rendered apoplectic when dancers, who were supposed to be working on one ballet, were taken over by another. There was never enough time, music was a constant problem, the status of costumes or scenery was often a mystery, and on top of all this, without a specific theater in hand, it was impossible to arrange programs or to schedule exactly what would be performed when. Yet somewhere in the midst of the bedlam, giving a quick word here, a fleeting smile there, unruffled, slightly amused by the simmering hysteria, Pleasant, who had put the entire mad scene in motion, was quite pleased by all that was going on.

He still faced the problem, however, of finding the necessary money. Lucia back in July had promised as much as $25,000 through the end of the year. Considering all that had been activated since then, there was no way that limited amount was going to pay all the rehearsal and production costs of some sixty dancers, eleven choreographers, and eighteen ballets.

Payroll expenses alone were considerable, even though dancers' salaries—set by the American Guild of Musical Artists (AGMA)—were extremely low compared with today's standards. A dancer in the corps de ballet earned $30 a week for rehearsing, $40 a week for performing; soloists earned the same for rehearsing and $5 more for performing. The two outside groups were contracted at even lower levels: the Spanish dancers for $20 a week, both rehearsing and performing, the dancers for *Black Ritual* only half that amount. It's hard to believe that professional artists could be paid so little and still manage to survive in New York. Equally amazing was the fact that—considering the number of people involved, including the choreographers, accompanists, and dancers who worked practically around the clock—Lucia's original sum lasted through even the first month. By the end of October, total disbursements were reported to be $23,452.60.

After that, the financial crunch got much worse. November expenditures swelled to four times the total for October, with more expenses being added every week. Yet with everyone under contract and all productions being mounted at top speed for a still unspecified opening date, turning back or shutting down was not an option.

No new money had been found, and after making many attempts, Dick Pleasant had run out of prospects. Personally, he was dismayed, even sickened, by the expenses that his grand design had generated, but it was all he could do just to keep all the volatile tempers under control and everything moving ahead on schedule. When the end of each week rolled around, there was no one to turn to for money but the same source as always before.

Each time Pleasant took Lucia aside and told her the awful figures, she took a deep breath, promised she would come up with the money, and then quickly rushed away to lose herself with all the others rehearsing in the studios.

Harry Zuckert, on the other hand, was not quite so compliant. Only Lucia could call a complete halt to the spending, but he did the two things that were within his power. First, he arranged that the increased amounts that Lucia felt obliged to put up were submitted not as outright contributions but in the form of loans, given with the understanding that they were eventually to be repaid with any monies received from box office receipts or from other contributors.

Second, he issued a new directive stating that from then on, neither Pleasant nor Rudolf Orthwine could sign any more checks. In their place, all further outlay had to be first authorized by him in his capacity as the treasurer of Advanced Arts Ballets, which continued to be the presenting corporation.

At the same time that all this rehearsing and massive production of scenery and costumes were rushing to beat an impending deadline set for the end of the year, there was still no prospective theater where the inaugural season could take place. A large part of the problem was that there were very few performance spaces in New York that could accommodate such a colossal undertaking: eighteen separate ballets to be loaded in, then alternated from one night to the next while the remainder were stored backstage; also an orchestra pit big enough to fit more musicians than were required for most musicals; sufficient dressing rooms for sixty-plus dancers; and a huge seating capacity to allow for at least the possibility of substantial box office revenue. The few legitimate theaters in New York that could meet these requirements to any acceptable degree were all booked through the winter and well on into the spring.

And then the miracle occurred. There would be many others in the perilous history of Ballet Theatre, but this was the first: the musical *Swingin' the Dream*, with choreography by Agnes de Mille, opened in mid-November at the Center Theatre and, after garnering poor reviews, closed ten days later. The Center Theatre, located in the heart of Manhattan in the Radio City Music Hall complex, was the largest legitimate theater—nearly 3,500 seats—in New York and was ordinarily booked months and months in advance. In fact, *Swingin' the Dream* was only scheduled to stay for two months before it had to clear out to make room for Walt Disney's *Pinocchio* on February 4. This prime space was now available for a strictly limited interval that happened to be just the right moment and overall amount of time.

Pleasant leaped at the opportunity. He signed a lease agreement on December 11 and nine days later presented a $3,000 check, presumably authorized by Zuckert and with the funds and full approval from Lucia Chase, as a first deposit for Ballet Theatre to present an inaugural three-week season beginning January 11, 1940.

Two weeks before Christmas, Dick Pleasant sent Mikhail Mordkin a letter, along with the program copy for *The Goldfish* and *Voices of Spring*, asking him to proofread them and to give his preference for the cast of *Voices* on opening night. Mordkin did not answer.

The following week, Pleasant sent another letter, along with a check for $1,650, the full amount Mordkin was due under contract for conducting rehearsals calculated at $150 a week for eleven weeks, from October through December 16. The payment marked the final note of Mikhail Mordkin's association with the entire cadre of dancers, including Lucia Chase, that had constituted the company which he had founded, created ballets for, and directed for the past four years.

As a result, by the end of December 1939, the Mordkin Ballet ceased to exist and Ballet Theatre had taken its place.

Part 2

4. Debut of Ballet Theatre

New York has had many memorable
nights of ballet in its past, but never
any to match the extraordinary
success now crowding the Center
Theatre.
—*New York Herald Tribune* editorial,
January 1940

ALTHOUGH BALLET THEATRE as a company was still totally unknown, ballet enthusiasts showed up en masse in New York for the opening night of its inaugural season, filling the huge Center Theatre to capacity.

What made this massive turnout noteworthy was that there had been practically no advance time, and very little money, to publicize the event and help attract an audience. Word of the season didn't even get out until the Center Theatre was secured, barely three weeks before the first performance. There was no chance of selling any kind of subscriptions, ordering tickets by mail was impractical, and only the programs for the first week were announced, and these were termed "tentative." Nevertheless, thousands came on opening night, representing the avant-garde, the elite of New York society, and a mass of ballet loyalists, as well as hundreds of curiosity seekers.

They had little idea of what they were about to see. Many were familiar with the opening ballet, Fokine's *Les Sylphides*, from the old Diaghilev days or subsequent Ballets Russes productions, but Fokine had been working with Ballet Theatre for the past three months, an unprecedented stretch for the old master who was known to be highly organized and an unusually quick worker: what would he have done with *Les Sylphides* in all that time?

As for the rest of the opening night's program, the closing ballet–Mordkin's *Voices of Spring*–wouldn't have many surprises, but the middle work–*The Great American Goof*–had everyone buzzing. It was choreographed by Eugene Loring, who was known for several works created for the Ballet Caravan company, including *Yankee Clipper* and his signature piece, *Billy the Kid*. Yet *The Great American Goof*, a world premiere, promised to be most unusual, since Loring had chosen to collaborate with William Saroyan, the well-known author and playwright whose *Hearts in the Highlands* had just been produced by the Group Theatre.

Saroyan claimed that he had never seen a ballet before he wrote this one. His joint work with Loring was described in the Center Theatre program as "A Number of Absurd and Poetic Events in the Life of The Great American Goof, the native white hope of the human race":

> If a ballet is to tell a story at all, it must tell a very fundamental story; and if it is to have characters at all, they must be aspects of human character in general. . . . No one could possibly create anything more surrealistic and unbelievable than the world which everyone believes is real and is trying very hard to inhabit. Willy-nilly, the story of this ballet is on this theme.

Beyond that, little was known except that there were supposed to be speaking parts for the dancers, and the work was reputed to be altogether different from what Loring had ever attempted.

The combination of the dawning of a brand-new company, the great Fokine back working in New York, a world premiere of possibly a new kind of art form, with posters and window-cards appearing throughout the city proclaiming "The Greatest Ballets of All Times staged by the Greatest Collaboration in Ballet History," and now the excitement of a massive audience, with not an empty seat in the house: all these gave rise to the feeling that this was about to be an American dance event like none other had ever been. There was a special electricity in the air as everyone waited for the curtain to go up.

Meanwhile, backstage, everyone was transfixed by the magnitude of what was about to unfold. It was impossible to predict what the reaction of all the people out front would be. Would they like the new *Sylphides* when it didn't have the familiar setting of trees and moonlight of former productions but a startlingly different new set by Augustus Vincent Tack? And as for *Goof*–would it be laughed out of the house?

For the dancers, the pressure surrounding this event went far beyond just another opening night. In joining Ballet Theatre, they had put their careers on the line, betting on a whole package of unknowns. As the critical moment drew closer, a small group gathered downstairs and said a prayer together. Those standing in the wings touched each other, gave little nervous smiles before turning away to check their costume, their shoes, take deep breaths, then back to waiting, hoping, fearing, wishing it would start. Finally the ready word came from the production stage manager, the *Sylphides* cast took their places onstage, the orchestra played Chopin's familiar three opening chords, the curtain went up, and what happened after that is now ballet history.

"The finest performance of Fokine's *Les Sylphides* that New York has seen in many a season," proclaimed Walter Terry in the *New York Herald Tribune* the following day. "With the master himself in charge, *Les Sylphides* emerged the beautiful, breathtaking work that it has not been away from his guiding hand. . . . Karen Conrad walked off with the first honors as one of the soloists and won cheers and applause for her amazing elevation and the brilliance she brought to every one of her moments on the stage."

As for *The Great American Goof*, John Martin of the *New York Times* in his closing review of the season hailed it as being "certainly entitled to the season's laurels as the most significant contribution made by the new company." He wrote, "It is not the slickest or the loveliest or technically the showiest, but it dares . . . to strike out boldly in the direction of a new and authoritative idiom." He was slightly sardonic about Mordkin's *Voices of Spring*, "a version which was said to have been abbreviated but which still indicated that the vernal season in Vienna is a fairly protracted one."

Yet his verdict on the entire evening was exuberant: "With the opening of the Ballet Theatre at Center Theatre last night, New York acquired for the first time in its life a cosmopolitan company of its own. . . . If the plan seemed to be too good to be true in advance, there is no room whatever for skepticism this morning, for the beginning was no less than a brilliant success."

This high praise continued for all of the next three weeks. Reactions naturally varied from work to work, and each critic had his favorites: Walter Terry thought Dolin's revised version of *Swan Lake* "a work of great beauty and liveliness"; Anatole Chujoy in *Dance News* called Nijinska's version of *La Fille Mal Gardée* "one of the finest ballets given this season"; and virtually everyone found reasons to praise the young English choreographer Antony Tudor, who three months earlier had come to America unheralded and practically unknown to present three small works he had originally created for Ballet Rambert. For this, their first viewing in America, they were all eminently successful: *Judgment of Paris* was termed "a hilarious piece of ribaldry," *Dark Elegies* "sensitive and unusual . . . a distinguished effort," and *Jardin aux Lilas* "as near to perfection in its own category as any work that is likely to turn up."

But the praise was not just for Tudor or Fokine or certain stand-out programs. By the time the season ended, the highest accolades of the *New York Times*'s principal dance critic, John Martin, were focused on the entire undertaking:

> The success of the new Ballet Theatre has proved to be a welcome surprise all around. On paper the plans looked very like a beautiful pipe-dream, for they promised no less than the long-hoped-for establishment of the ballet in America in an organization of its own. That such a project could possibly be carried out without some glamorous European director at its head seemed incongruous, so provincial is our habitual thinking about the arts. Nevertheless, the impossible had happened, and the wiseacres (whose name, it must be confessed, was legion) had been confounded. The Ballet Theatre had laid the solidest foundation that had yet been laid for the development of the art of the ballet in America.

No one had more reason to cheer this ringing affirmation than Lucia herself. Already in her forties, a time in life when most dancers would already have retired, she had been a noteworthy performer in Ballet Theatre's landmark season. This was possible only because the roles she had been given—Minerva in Tudor's *Judgment of Paris,* Columbine in Fokine's *Carnaval,* the Little Girl in *The Great American Goof*—were all character parts that didn't require extraordinary technique but made the most of her considerable dramatic abilities.

As for being the company's primary financial backer, this distinction was for her a source of acute embarrassment, displeasure, even emotional agony, and would continue to be for many years to come. Yet there was some consolation this time in the fact that the inaugural season had been a colossal success, considerably greater by almost any measure than the amount of money she had been required to provide. Still, she hated the way time after time she was called upon for money.

One day in the early 1960s, I invited Dick Pleasant, who was working with Isadora Bennett and Don Duncan in their own theatrical publicity firm, to have lunch with me. Knowing his reluctance to talk about Ballet Theatre, we each had several drinks before I asked him what it had been like working with my mother during this pre-season spending spree. At first, he turned silent, and I wished I hadn't posed the question, but then looking off in the distance, as though he had just caught sight of someone coming through the door, he gave a rueful smile and recalled a little incident that occurred just minutes prior to a dress rehearsal at the Center Theatre.

Lucia was already in costume and had started to climb the little twisting iron stairway leading from her dressing room up to the stage when he rushed out and called up to her from the bottom step to say that several thousand dollars were needed that very moment. She stopped and seemed to give a little shudder. He heard her mutter, "All right, go ahead," without even turning around, then with her toe shoes pointed ducklike out on either side, she continued awkwardly up the steps and disappeared into the wings while he stood below, hating himself and their little unobserved encounter, yet greatly relieved that once more the dreaded shutdown had been averted.

In each of these fiscal emergencies, Lucia was theoretically free to refuse to pay anything more, thereby bringing everything to a halt, an action that would have meant letting Ballet Theatre go under. Yet in practice, she really didn't have a choice. Considering all the money that had been spent so far, each new deficit was only another small fraction of the total and brought them that much closer to opening night. The end result of each little confrontation was always the same: despite her resolve to stand firm, Lucia would feel obliged to ante up again, and again, then again once more.

But then what was perhaps most disturbing, the same painful pattern continued after the season started. Although thousands of new fans of

Ballet Theatre swarmed up to the box office windows to buy tickets, the total dollar returns were nowhere near as grand as was reported in the press, and there continued to be substantial weekly deficits. While exact tallies are difficult to compile now over half a century later, after all money was in and all bills had been received, the net expense between September 1939 through early February 1940 amounted to well over $200,000 and constituted a very large, bitter pill for Lucia to swallow.

And yet, when considered in terms of what had been accomplished, the return achieved on her money was astounding. Eleven choreographers had been hired to prepare eighteen separate ballets, and some eighty dancers had been paid to rehearse for three months before the Center Theatre season had even started. In addition, there were the costs of designing and building the sets and costumes and preparing the music for over a dozen new productions. Also, a great many other major items—the expense of renting the biggest legitimate theater in New York City, performing for three weeks with full orchestra and wardrobe and stage crew, all the advertising and publicity, special lighting and sound equipment, accompanists for the daily classes and rehearsal sessions, all the office and studio accounts—the list goes on and on. Yet it was all accomplished for something in the neighborhood of $250,000, which in today's terms would be considered quite a modest sum for just a single new production. If this were not exactly cause for Lucia to celebrate, still it did constitute the basis for a certain Yankee satisfaction over money very well spent.

However, such a massive outflow couldn't continue at this same profligate rate. Lucia had been left a substantial amount of money when her husband died, but it was nothing like the fortune that had once belonged to Alex Cochran or even the residual estate which in accordance with his will eventually passed on to his favorite nephew, Tom Ewing. In comparison to them, Lucia's inheritance was a distinctly finite amount, sufficient to provide an exceedingly comfortable private life but not of the Medici-level magnitude required to support all the many phases of ballet on a grand scale. Furthermore, the nation's economy, which had been drastically buffeted throughout the 1930s and was only slowly emerging from the Great Depression, had significantly diminished Lucia's capital funds.

Once again, the ever-solicitous Harry Zuckert intervened in an attempt to provide Lucia some protection. After overseeing the formation of a new corporation, Ballet Theatre Inc., he agreed to serve as its president and straightway put through a ruling that no further financial commitments for the Ballet Theatre company could be made, or expenditures incurred, without the approval and express permission of the corporation's president and six other directors. In other words, unless and until some additional sponsorship help was secured, all future deficit-producing activities for Ballet Theatre were to be put on hold.

5. Life at Home

She was a complex and extraordinary
woman, and she achieved an
enormous amount. She gave us one
of the world's greatest companies . . .
a company that was sustained longer
than any other non-state institution.
She has set her mark on this century.
—Agnes de Mille, October 1, 1992

IN FUTURE YEARS, Ballet Theatre would customarily follow
a New York season with extensive tours across the country and back, often returning for a second New York season late in the spring. For this
first year, the effort and expense of bringing the company into existence
precluded making any additional commitments for the period immediately
following the company's closing at the Center Theatre on February 4. After
four months of struggle, everyone was grateful for the chance to take a brief
rest while waiting for some future employment to be arranged.

For Lucia, the winter break must have been particularly welcome. What
few members of the company or the dance world ever fully realized was
that, besides her crammed schedule as a dancer with Ballet Theatre, there
was an equally demanding call on her heart, mind, and body on the home
front, especially from two young boys who were left totally dependent on

her after their father had died. Lucia Chase was generally viewed as a vivacious, wealthy, socially well connected public figure. Yet to understand Lucia, one must realize that she had two and only two interests, ballet and family, two opposite but equally passionate concerns which, day in and day out, dominated all of her thoughts and actions.

She went to considerable lengths to keep these two worlds separate, particularly during the early years of Ballet Theatre when Lucia Chase, the dancer, was intent on establishing herself as a legitimate performing member of the company. Her greatest worry was that if her private life—couched in a luxurious Park Avenue apartment replete with a full household staff, Alex Cochran's antique furniture and art works, and two growing sons—ever became common knowledge, it would stamp her as being irremediably different from all other dancers, both in and outside the company. Consequently, she made a point of keeping the image of Lucia Chase completely separate from that of Mrs. Thomas Ewing Jr., and she somehow managed to maintain both while assigning each to its own sphere.

Meanwhile, as Ballet Theatre was embarked on writing a new page in the history of dance in America, with Lucia Chase a prominent and indelible part of that process, life for Tommy and me continued to be centered around a mother who somehow managed to be available for our especially important moments—first day at school, most weekends, and always the great summer excursions to Sorrento, Maine, or Narragansett, Rhode Island, staying in one or the other or often both for weeks at a time.

The same duality of roles carried over into our normal day-to-day existence. No matter how late the previous night had been for Lucia Chase, the dancer, early the next morning, even if she were still asleep, Lucia Chase, my mother, insisted that Tommy and I wake her and talk with her before leaving for school. Likewise at the other end of most days, if there were no guests at the apartment, we would all three have supper together, or certainly we would have a chance to talk later on before going to bed.

Part of what made it possible for her to carry off this acrobatic split between her ballet and private life was that she employed a steady and absolutely dependable household staff. There was Harry Larssen, the massive Swedish butler whom Tom Ewing had spirited away from his mother's house in Yonkers: Harry had stayed on following my father's death to provide a man's muscle in the apartment and to be a rock-solid heroic figure for "the boys," as Harry called Tommy and me.

Then there was Ellen Swenson, the cook, also Swedish but a total oppo-site from Harry, a timid yet constant presence who rarely strayed from her position in the kitchen until the very end of the day after dinner was over and everything was cleared away. Ellen was so shy she seldom spoke, and when she did, it was barely more than a whisper. But she was an indelible presence as well as a cook whose hot roasted meats and rich desserts were famous in family circles.

Every day that my mother was at home, without fail, the same little do-mestic event would take place, to the great amusement of Tommy and me and everyone else in the family who witnessed it. Around 8 a.m., Ellen would tiptoe upstairs and furtively edge to the threshold—never an inch farther—of the bedroom door where my mother would be sitting in bed, having her breakfast. The conversation always went the same way:

"Good morning, Ellen," Mom would gaily start the interview off.

"Yes, vell, Mrs. Ewing, for dinner tonight . . . " Ellen's voice would trail off.

"Yes. Dinner tonight. Let's see. There'll be eight of us. What do you think we should have?"

"Ve could have chicken?" Ellen barely whispered.

"CHICKEN! That would be perfect," Mom would say, greatly relieved. But Ellen had not yet quite finished.

" . . . or roast beef . . . "

"Yes, Roast Beef. Let's have that!"

"Oh . . . you don't like my chicken?" Ellen would say in an anguished tone of voice. And so it unfolded, always at the start of each day, possi-bly the most difficult negotiating session that my mother, who otherwise battled zestfully with proud ballerinas and imperious choreographers, ever had to face. That was Ellen, who was an immutable part of the family for nearly twenty years.

There was also generally a third person—first Helen (who ended up marrying Harry Larssen, to our great astonishment and delight), then Lillian, and still later Aili and Sassa—who kept the house clean, took care of the guests, and in the beginning did double-duty when necessary as part-time watchers over Tommy and me. And for the first ten or twelve years, until the country was deep in the war and tight gasoline rationing was in effect, outside the apartment there was also Jerry Sylvester, ostensibly serv-ing as chauffeur but actually functioning much more as a sort of guardian-companion for us boys whenever we went out on the streets of New York.

These were all good, kind, caring people who were constantly around so there was rarely any prolonged loneliness in our childhood, even those times when our mother was away on tour with the company. But important as all this household help was, my mother was the dynamo who made the system work. My brother and I were scarcely aware that there was anything particularly unusual about the whole arrangement and enjoyed what we considered back then to be a perfectly normal home life. We had no problem accepting the fact that there was a new ballet company which often required our mother to be absent the greater part of most days and certain evenings as well, even sometimes out on tour for weeks at a time. We understood that this separation would only last until a certain day, well marked in advance, when suddenly Mom would be back and everything would be the same.

During this long-ago time, it was also my good fortune to get to know firsthand a number of memorable ballet personalities who used to come regularly to the apartment—people like Irina Baronova, Agnes de Mille, Alicia Alonso, Anton Dolin, Antony Tudor, Hugh Laing, Alicia Markova, Dimitri Romanoff, Nora Kaye, John Kriza—all celebrated performers. Plus Lucia Chase, the dancer and original member of Ballet Theatre, very much one of the group: how did she appear, at least to her son's eye, when she performed onstage?

For one thing, she could be very funny when a role called for humor, as in *Three Virgins and a Devil, Judgment of Paris,* or the queen in *Bluebeard.* She was also very winning as the ballerina in *Petrouchka*—perhaps not the best dancer ever to take the role, but certainly a wonderfully wide-eyed convincing doll. In a totally different mode, her interpretations of the stepmother in *Fall River Legend,* the eldest sister in *Pillar of Fire,* or the Queen Mother in *Swan Lake* have never been surpassed. And I for one never tired of hearing her voice at the beginning of *Peter and the Wolf,* inviting everyone to meet Peter, his friends the bird and the duck, and of course his old grandfather, the silly hunters, and the wolf. Lucia had a bright, friendly, beautifully modulated voice that was totally engaging, the kind that children respond to instantly and are happy to accompany any fine day out into the meadow.

At home, my mother might best be described as being "funny" in the Danish sense of the word, which is to say that she was fun to be around. Whether driving with her in the family car, or at a ballgame, or out riding waves in the surf, she was always a good sport and had a wonderfully infectious laugh. Regardless of who she was with, her spirits never flagged, and she always made a great effort to raise the level of people's enjoyment.

People often ask, didn't Lucia Chase have any romantic attachments after her beloved Tom died? After all, she was a widow for a full half-century. She certainly had a great many opportunities, and she continued to be an exceedingly attractive, buoyant, outgoing personality in grand health and full of vitality. Maybe her son would be the last to know, but the opinion from this corner is that there was one very special man for Lucia Chase in her life and only one. There came a time when, as an adult, I found myself wishing for my mother's sake that she would fall in love and marry again, even just have a romantic relationship. Yet unless someone testifies to the contrary, I do not believe, and there is no evidence, that Lucia ever turned her heart to another man after my father.

So what did she do after a busy New York season was over, or following a major tour, either at home or abroad? She came rushing home, and once there, she couldn't wait to tell everyone how she was just going to enjoy herself doing nothing. Very often she caught a cold, but that only lasted a couple of days. If it were winter and she was in New York, she would do a little shopping, particularly in the two months before Christmas when the other bed in her room would start getting covered with dozens of packages for family and ballet friends.

Nights after supper, she would often sit at her desk and pay bills so that the next morning there would be a pile of stamped envelopes out by the elevator door ready to be mailed. Weekends she would always go to Rose Hill, taking Tommy and me if we were not yet away at school. Sundays after church, she would invariably drive out to Middlebury to see her sister Dee and brother-in-law, Ed Carmody. Or if it was summer, the moment a tour ended, she would barely stop over in New York before heading straight for Narragansett, to stay there as long as possible, at least a few weeks, year after year without fail, as long as she lived.

For a person whose professional life pulled her thousands and thousands of miles around the world, a willing but nevertheless captive participant in Ballet Theatre's exhausting schedule, once she was unharnessed and away from the company, Lucia was a total creature of habit, a partisan of long-standing routines that never varied. Just as professionally she always performed all her roles onstage in exactly the same way, without the slightest variation, so that audiences came to expect and look forward to the way she would slide her finger down her cheek in her chilling portrayal of Lizzie

Borden's stepmother in *Fall River Legend,* or as the Queen Mother in *Swan Lake,* would benignly survey the bevy of young debs vying for her son's attention, always a royal presence but also unmistakably a mother, so in her private life, every action fitted into a totally familiar pattern, predetermined and undeviating, as fixed in its place as the green rotary phone by her bed whose numbers gradually wore away from years of dialing until they were indecipherable; or the tippy glazed ashtray I made in the second grade that sat, unused but treasured, in its place of honor on the right side of her desk; or the tradition she maintained every night of the summer of "cocktails at seven-fifteen on the porch." Nothing ever changed. That was the way our mother lived, back at the start of Ballet Theatre and ever after.

Meanwhile, in February 1940, after the historic debut season at the Center Theatre, Richard Pleasant did not take any time off but worked feverishly to keep Ballet Theatre together. If he hadn't, and the dancers had been allowed to disperse and scatter across the country, there might have been little hope of their regrouping and precipitating another monster rehearsal period in order to relearn the still brand-new repertory. Although ostensibly the postseason interlude was designated a quiet period, the situation was really quite desperate: unless some employment for the whole company could be arranged in the next few months, the "brilliant new venture" Pleasant had succeeded in launching would go down the drain.

He quickly managed to lease the George Blumenthal mansion on West 54th Street (later the home of the Theatre Guild and ultimately part of the Museum of Modern Art) to serve as an interim Ballet Theatre home. For most of the spring of 1940, Fokine, Tudor, de Mille, Dolin, Loring, and others rehearsed there and began several new works while Pleasant desperately sought performance outlets for the company.

Unfortunately, it was much too late in the season to come up with any significant engagements. A couple of Ballet Theatre appearances were contracted in connection with charity benefits, two outdoor performances took place at the Robin Hood Dell in Philadelphia, and four more occurred during the summer at Lewisohn Stadium in New York. However, no extended engagement could be secured until late in the fall when the Chicago Civic Opera was scheduled to hold its thirtieth anniversary. As part of its yearlong celebration, Pleasant managed to get Ballet Theatre hired to choreograph and dance in the Civic's operas during its six-week season beginning in early November.

It should have been a very good arrangement. Besides appearing in the operas, Ballet Theatre was given the opportunity to perform on its own for two evenings each week. For once, there was also a substantial dollar incentive because, in addition to a weekly guaranteed fee, the formal agreement allowed the ballet company a percentage of any profits. As a reward for having obtained this very favorable contract, Pleasant requested and was given permission by the board of Ballet Theatre Inc. to book the Majestic Theatre for a three-week season in New York, beginning February 11, 1941.

The Chicago engagement did not prove to be nearly as good as expected. The midwestern audiences did not flock to see ballet's sensational newcomer. In fact, attendance for the whole season was paltry, particularly for the strictly ballet nights, whose total costs added up to nearly $36,000, while receipts amounted to only $15,000. The final reckoning proved to be even worse: not only would there be no profits for Ballet Theatre to share with its host house, but the Civic Opera claimed that it ended the season with no funds at all and reneged even on paying the weekly fee that its contract with Ballet Theatre had guaranteed. The prospect of a major fall season in Chicago had effectively kept the company together throughout its first year, but at a considerable price that now became the responsibility of the board of Ballet Theatre Inc. to cover.

Lucia was never an officer of the corporation, but she was a member of its board of directors. More significant, she was still the principal financial supporter of the Ballet Theatre company, although back in the fall of 1940 she was joined by another member of the board, Dwight Deere Wiman, the Broadway producer and father of Anna Deere Wiman, a professional dancer and an original member of Ballet Theatre's corps de ballet. Now, after the Chicago fiasco, Wiman and his very astute lawyer, John Wharton, put together a new supporting organization, Ballet Presentations Inc., which was specifically designed to finance the upcoming New York season at the Majestic Theatre by selling shares to outside stockholders, much in the manner of standard Broadway show financing.

According to the new corporation's by-laws, if the forthcoming New York engagement proved to be unprofitable (as in fact the majority of such "angel" underwritings generally were), then it was deemed lawful and permissible for the original stockholders of Ballet Presentations to take their losses and claim them as business deductions against their regular income. Another advantage of financing through the new corporation was that it provided a potential investor with two possible approaches: he might make an outright purchase of the corporation's stock, or else he could advance his money in the form of a loan to the corporation. Later on, if the engagement turned out to be profitable, the loan would be repaid with interest, whereas if there was no profit and consequently no such reimbursement, then the loan could be written off like any other standard business loan that proved unsuccessful. The result was that having Ballet Presentations Inc. as a new option made the prospect of Ballet Theatre's upcoming season at the Majestic Theatre seem much less precarious, and several members of the board decided to join Lucia and Wiman by investing or lending their money to help support the venture.

In February 1941, one year after its sensational debut at the Center Theatre, Ballet Theatre's second New York season scored another resounding artistic success. The opening night program set the tone with two American premieres of works that had been created and performed in England but never before seen in the United States. In *Gala Performance*, Antony Tudor portrayed three haughty ballerinas—one Russian (Nora Kaye), one Italian (Nana Gollner), and the third French (Karen Conrad)— each one doing her best to dominate and upstage the other two. The competition was ferocious, with no holds barred, and the audience roared with laughter as Tudor showed just how spiteful three jealous prima donnas could become.

The other premiere that night was another comic work, *Three Virgins and a Devil*, choreographed by Agnes de Mille. This extraordinary woman had become involved with Ballet Theatre the previous year when she created *Black Ritual*, and she remained closely associated with the company until she died over half a century later. During all those years, Agnes and Lucia were locked together in a complex love/hate relationship that was endlessly entertaining to all onlookers but also highly productive. They were seasoned professionals who collaborated for four full decades, generally as compatriots but often as spitfire antagonists who at certain critical times would have cheerfully ordered the other one out of the picture if only that had been possible. Fortunately, it wasn't.

Agnes de Mille would become very well known as a ballet choreographer (*Rodeo, Fall River Legend, Tally-Ho,* and others), an author (*Dance to the Piper, And Promenade Home, To a Young Dancer, The Book of the Dance*), and particularly for her work creating dances for musicals (*One Touch of Venus, Bloomer Girl, Brigadoon, Carousel, Gentlemen Prefer Blondes, Oklahoma!*). Before 1940, she had studied dance with a host of great teachers, created several works (including *Three Virgins and a Devil*) for Ballet Rambert in England, and had given dance concerts in Europe and the United States. Yet for all her talent and success, Agnes was acutely envious of Lucia's place in the professional world. In Agnes's eyes, compared to herself, Lucia Chase had no proper credentials as a professional artist, only great social position and a lot of money.

Never one to mince words, and often deliciously wicked when she sharpened her pen, in an unpublished account written and sent to me for comment some fifty years later, de Mille gave the following reenactment of Lucia Chase's first encounter with Mordkin:

> I am not sure she had ever seen ballet dancing. Certainly she had never danced herself outside of the Charleston, the Black Bottom, or the One-Step, but she was healthy and straight limbed. She decided she would dance professionally. As she was used to going straight to the top, she decided she would begin by being a ballerina, and cost being of no consequence, she would buy herself a company. And she vigorously set about doing just this with all the dispatch of a rich customer ordering a new house.

For Agnes, it was galling that when Dick Pleasant invited her to join Ballet Theatre as a choreographer for its inaugural season, Lucia was already a principal soloist in the company and Tudor, in his *Dark Elegies,* had given Lucia the role that Agnes had created in London. And she was particularly irked the following year when, at the same time that Pleasant asked her to revive *Three Virgins and a Devil,* he specifically suggested that she include Lucia in the cast.

As Agnes, years later, described the whole scene, everything leading up to the American premiere of *Three Virgins* at the Majestic Theatre was a dreadful ordeal. She was only allowed two weeks to get everything ready, which she declared monstrously unfair and virtually impossible. Eugene Loring was put in the cast as the Devil, despite the fact that he despised the work and was only kept in it by Pleasant's specific orders. The rehearsal room they were given was very small, with no window, blank walls, and only an exhausted pianist as an audience, with the result that nothing seemed to be at all funny. The dress rehearsal was a nightmare. Everything pointed to a catastrophe.

Yet the following night, when the curtain went up for the first performance and everyone appeared onstage—Agnes as the Priggish One, Lucia as the Greedy One, Annabelle Lyon as the Lustful One, Loring as the Devil, and Robbins as the Youth—it was just the opposite:

We moved, and with the first long blanching stare that Lucia leveled at me, there was a roar of laughter. She flapped the ostrich feathers in her Cranach hat and there was another roar. "Goodness," I thought, "Lucia must have packed the house with her friends." At the end, as we took our bows with flowers, I said to Lucia, "You have friends out front." Lucia gave me one of her wide pale-eyed stares. "None of my friends come to the ballet. Not one. I don't ask them to." It was true. Lucia was a genuine comedian and had earned her laughter like any true professional. I should have had my mouth slapped hard. But I was taken by surprise: there had been no laughter in the empty rehearsal room. Lucia was an actress, no excuses were necessary for her in this field. She held her own with anybody one could name.

From then on, Agnes was a redoubtable presence in Lucia's life, and vice versa. They were like two cats who generally enjoyed each other's company, but there were times when they could turn on each other and battle with thinly veiled animosity. Yet beyond all their squabbles and often violent disagreements, they genuinely admired the other's talents, and in later years, whenever addressing the public, each became perhaps the foremost champion that the other ever had.

The entire second season by Ballet Theatre in New York won high praise. The dean of all dance critics at that time, John Martin of the *New York Times*, wrote:

> No other dance organization within memory has demonstrated more clearly its integrity of purpose as a non-commercial, public-spirited institution. . . . It has exhibited a sturdy sense of values and has defied tradition consistently in its creation of artistically important new works designed for the general public instead of the professional balletomane.

Martin did find a glaring weakness in the male side of the company where, in his opinion, no man except Anton Dolin was capable of carrying the classical roles. He also disapproved of the way some of the ballets had been underrehearsed, which he felt betrayed Ballet Theatre's self-imposed standard of excellence.

He was not alone in finding fault in this quarter: his opinion was shared by Dick Pleasant. Limited funds and rehearsal time had obliged him to cut corners and bring certain ballets to the stage that were not up to what he felt New York was entitled to receive.

Pleasant had his faults as a company director, but he did have a very discerning eye and a hunger for quality of the highest order. What he did not have, unfortunately, was the financial power to pay for the very high standards he set for Ballet Theatre performances. Nor was he able to find anyone else who could come up with the kind of money this required. He of all people was most mindful of the extremely large deficit that the Majestic Theatre season was running, and he also knew the cost would have been considerably greater if more time and money had been spent on rehearsing. Still, he felt his artistic creed was being violated when things were not done exactly right, and he let his dissatisfaction be heard all the way to the boardroom.

Those who had agreed to be backers and had put up money also felt considerable dissatisfaction with the way the season had turned out. While the performances had been praised, they had not been well attended, and ticket receipts were way down from the returns at the Center Theatre the year before. Although originally a longer run had been planned, the disappointing box office persuaded the board to cut short the season after one month. With no possibility of realizing a return on their money, the investors were left with no other recourse than to declare their contributions bad loans, deduct them from their income taxes, and even back out of Ballet Theatre Inc., which most proceeded to do. However, they didn't go alone. Dick Pleasant, as the man responsible for arranging the financial disaster, was also obliged to step down.

He might have stayed on if he had been more adroit or focused his efforts on protecting himself. But Dick Pleasant had never been the sort of person who went out of his way to advance his interests by self-adulation or by ingratiating himself with others. It just wasn't part of his lexicon to explain away past disasters, to make all sorts of promises for the future, or even just to duck when absolutely necessary. Such tactics were beneath his proud bearing. He envisioned Ballet Theatre in just one way, and that was at the highest level of excellence. Anything smacking of mediocrity was distasteful to him and unacceptable. So at this critical moment when a number of important individuals were unhappy and looking for someone to blame, he did not resort to defending himself but said he accepted full responsibility.

This he proceeded to do in his own characteristically abrupt style. Immediately after the curtain of the Majestic Theatre came down on closing night, he ordered the entire company to gather in the outside lounge. Once everyone was there, he gave a stiff little account of the situation and then announced that effective immediately, he was bowing out as director of Ballet Theatre.

It was all done in a matter of minutes: a few words, a half smile at the irony of it all, and a last little bow to the company he had worked day and night for over two years to build. And with that, Dick Pleasant stepped down and out of the picture forever.

He never went to any more Ballet Theatre functions, official or informal. He did not talk or write about what he had done or what had been done to him. As far as he was concerned, his part was over. He went on to become the manager and guiding light of the McCarter Theatre in New Jersey and then to partner a New York publicity office with Isadora Bennett. But his meteoric career in ballet had ended.

⌒

One personal memory: during the fall of 1939, just before Ballet Theatre burst on the scene at the Center Theatre and was in the midst of what was possibly the most hectic rehearsal period in the history of ballet, Dick Pleasant on his own initiative offered to take me, then age eight, on the ferry out to visit the Statue of Liberty.

I was thrilled. Usually such opportunities only came to my older brother, Tommy. It was a beautiful day. There was a little chill in the air, but that didn't matter. It was such a tremendously exciting adventure to have this almost-stranger all to myself, on a big boat plowing along across the dark blue water, then stepping out and going up to the very top of the statue where we could look out across the whole of New York harbor.

But then there was the problem of getting down. There was no elevator, just a steel-grill staircase, from the top of which you could look down through each of the steps a sickening distance, way down hundreds of feet. It was enough to cause panic, and to my shame, I was too scared to begin the awful first steps.

"No problem," said the man I was with. "We can just bump ourselves down." And sitting himself on the first step, he showed me how to get on down to the next and then the next—perfectly easy, in fact sort of fun. And that's the way it was done.

Dick Pleasant: distant, lonely man of great imagination and heart, founder and first director of Ballet Theatre. Ave atque vale—hail and farewell.

6. *Pillar of Fire*

When Americans want champagne,
they want French champagne. When
they want ballet, they want Russian
ballet.
—Sol Hurok

AFTER DICK PLEASANT left, Ballet Theatre was like a boat adrift, with no one at the helm, no fixed destination, and no strong wind blowing it in any particular direction.

The one person who might have taken command was Lucia, but this was the very last thing she wished to do, for a number of reasons, including that she had no firsthand experience in running a ballet company and didn't feel qualified to step in. Unlike Pleasant, who had a nose for scenting talent and a great curiosity and knowledge of all the arts, the only composers, writers, designers, painters, even most of the choreographers that Lucia knew were those who were brought by others into Ballet Theatre. She lacked the restless curiosity, the discerning eye, the encyclopedic acquaintance with the arts world that characterizes and motivates most ballet directors, both established and aspiring. The job of running Ballet Theatre was hers if she wanted it. No one stood in her way or would have withheld it from her, but she didn't want it because she didn't have any idea of what to do with a ballet company if she had taken control.

An even more compelling reason, as always, was her desire to be a dancer. This was particularly important in connection with the other members of Ballet Theatre. Lucia wanted to be one with them, no better or worse, just accepted as someone who had a legitimate position in the company roster. In return, she asked for no favors: quite the opposite, any little perk or indication of special privilege was anathema to her and emphatically ruled out. Instead, she insisted on being treated just like the rest of the company and set great store in doing the same little things that everyone else did—sharing a hotel room, signing and happily taking her miniscule dancer salary every week, darning her ballet shoes, washing her tights, carrying her own suitcase, riding the bus—they all helped confirm that she was a regular member of Ballet Theatre. Someone else could run the company. And at this particular moment, there happened to be someone who, unlike Lucia, did want very much to take on Ballet Theatre, not exactly as its director but to be formally associated with it in such a way as to control the way it was run.

Solomon Izrailevich Gurkov started out in life as a poor Russian Jew from Pogar (in his own words, "a town of no importance in the Ukraine"), who entered the United States in 1906 through Ellis Island where a customs official changed his last name from Gurkov to Hurok. When he was married two years later, he signed his marriage certificate Sam Hurok, but soon he came to be known locally, and in time celebrated internationally, as Sol Hurok.

The first few months of Hurok's life in America were spent in Philadelphia, where he is said to have had eighteen jobs, including cannery worker, pie baker, ice cream maker, bottle washer, hardware store clerk, and streetcar conductor. After half a year, he had made enough money to buy an $8 suit and a ticket to New York, where he would spend the rest of his life.

It wasn't long before he gained a position for himself as manager of the Brownsville Labor Lyceum in Brooklyn, where he was responsible for organizing and presenting various public events—banquets, rallies, lectures, concerts—usually imbued with a political or socialist tie-in to help increase public attendance. In 1913, he went out on his own and personally presented a young violinist, Efrem Zimbalist, at the New Palace Gardens in Brownsville for a Socialist Party benefit and netted $1,600 on that single performance, a very large amount for that kind of an event at that place in that time.

Two years later, he took a greater risk, hiring the New York Hippodrome, a gargantuan 5,200-seat performance hall occupying an entire block on Sixth Avenue between 43rd and 44th Streets, for a succession of Sunday night concerts featuring prominent artists. Entitled "Music for the Masses," each concert cost him $6,000, a sum that included a disproportionate $1,800 allocated for advertising. Tickets were offered at conspicuously low prices, from 50 cents to $2 for the most expensive. The entire series, which continued for several years, was especially designed to cater to the swelling population of immigrants who were swarming into the United States from all parts of Europe, particularly Russia, which was about to undergo a cataclysmic revolution. So many responded and became regular attendees that they became known as "the Hurok audience." Hurok is said to have cleared $40,000 on the Sunday night concerts alone and soon dropped everything else to concentrate on what would turn out to be a lifelong career of presenting artists in the dance and concert field.

Shrewd, calculating, daring, flamboyant, and dictatorial, Sol Hurok proved to be a genius at discerning and promoting artists, exhibiting such flair and merchandising skill that, by the mid-1930s, the words *S. Hurok presents* were like a Good Housekeeping seal of approval, just about the highest endorsement a performing artist or company could receive in America. Marian Anderson, Arthur Rubinstein, Mischa Elman, Anna Pavlova, Isadora Duncan, Richard Tucker, Isaac Stern, Gregor Piatigorsky, David Oistrakh, Andres Segovia, and Itzak Perlman are just a few of the celebrated figures presented by Hurok Attractions Inc. As Hurok's publicity department constantly reminded concert managers across the country, "No season is complete without the appearance in your city of at least one attraction from this star-clustered roster."

Of all the arts with which Hurok was involved, ballet was the one closest to his heart and for which he took the grandest, most self-congratulatory bow. Just the word *ballet,* coupled with *S. Hurok,* came to connote glamour, grande luxe, champagne, and caviar. Especially caviar, because that evoked the image of his native Russia, a country where ballet was generally considered to be the supreme expression of art. In the United States, Hurok had at various times throughout the 1930s represented both Ballet Russe companies—the Ballet Russe de Monte Carlo, directed by the Russian-American banker Serge Denham, and the Original Ballet Russes, directed by the former White Army officer Col. Wassily de Basil—and he had succeeded not only in making their names synonymous with ballet in America but also in promoting the converse, the idea that ballet in America by its very nature, almost by definition, had to be Russian and presented by S. Hurok.

When Ballet Theatre burst onto the scene in 1940, Hurok saw it as a personal as well as a professional challenge. His virtual monopoly of ballet in America was suddenly in danger of being questioned, even seriously threatened, by this American upstart. By the end of Ballet Theatre's inaugural season, Hurok's close friend and fellow Russian émigré, Anatole Chujoy, later editor of *Dance News,* had gone so far as to proclaim in print that Ballet Theatre's arrival constituted "a new page in the history of ballet in America." If this were true, and Ballet Theatre was really going to be leading the way, then Hurok felt he needed to be associated with it and cash in on the company's meteoric popularity. It was an ideal time for him to make such a move since, outside of New York, local theater managers around the country were starting to clamor for more ballet in their season offerings.

There was one major obstacle standing in his way. In 1940, Ballet Theatre was being managed by Richard Pleasant, a decidedly American, highly opinionated, instinctively uncooperative if not downright hostile in-house director who wanted to make all decisions and have everything proceed according to his grand design. This was not the S. Hurok way, not the Russian way, but a newfangled, distinctly American way. Dick Pleasant posed a most unpleasant problem for Hurok, and for over a year he was stymied. But then suddenly, at the end of Ballet Theatre's second season in New York, which again was proclaimed as a great success and left the company in greater favor than ever, Pleasant unexpectedly stepped down. Like a hawk, Hurok swooped in to grab hold of the hottest ballet company on the dance scene.

He had several great advantages over anyone else who might try to compete. Over the years, he had established connections in city after city throughout the United States with local managers who gave preference to Hurok because he controlled the big-name artists that their audiences wanted. For Ballet Theatre, which needed a massive amount of uninterrupted employment in order to remain intact, Hurok could guarantee the company ongoing work across the United States for several months at a time.

Besides having the inside track to most of the country's performing venues, Hurok also held the highest trump card of all, which was the Metropolitan Opera House in New York, the biggest, most glamorous theater in the country for a major ballet company. During the spring and fall every year, whenever the Metropolitan Opera wasn't performing on its own stage, Hurok had the exclusive lease on all the time that the house was vacant. And what made this license particularly valuable was that the years he had spent presenting high-powered attractions at the Met had enabled him to compile a Tiffany-quality mailing list of dedicated theatre-goers that practically guaranteed any Hurok-sponsored client a successful engagement. If Ballet Theatre wanted to perform in the Met Opera House, which it most desperately did, particularly after the depressing box office results of the Majestic Theatre, then Hurok held the key to the house.

He also had another ace in hand in the person of Gerald Sevastianov, the handsome, debonair Russian currently serving as his promotion manager who had previously worked for four years as executive secretary for Colonel de Basil, head of the Ballet Russe. This invaluable experience would have, by itself, qualified Sevastianov for the position of managing director of Ballet Theatre, vacant now that Dick Pleasant had left, and Hurok was more than willing to release Sevastianov in return for securing the rights to book Ballet Theatre, especially if it meant that his own man would be on the inside directing its activities. But Sevastianov's greatest distinction resided in the fact that he was married to Irina Baronova, one of the Ballet Russe's "baby ballerinas"—Baronova, Toumanova, and Riabouchinska— and one of the most exquisite and adored dancers of our time. Until very recently, Hurok had had a formal agreement to represent the Ballet Russe in all its booking arrangements, but when he had a falling-out with Colonel de Basil, Hurok had signed a separate contract with Baronova as one of the celebrated individual artists under his banner. Now the road to his goal was clear: Ballet Theatre wanted the Met, it needed an experienced company director, and it could have enlisted no greater ballerina into its ranks than Irina Baronova, all three of which resided under Hurok's control.

One very important element sparking Hurok's interest in Ballet Theatre was that the company appeared to have a dedicated patron in the person of Lucia Chase. Hurok truly enjoyed associating with great artists, and he particularly loved being connected with ballet companies, but first and foremost, he was in the concert management business to make money. The client contracts he had worked out over the years generally had him assuming a large part of the direct performing expenses but otherwise shielded him from all the other costs—the production and maintenance and overhead items that confronted all performing arts organizations and that often far exceeded the amounts spent in connection with the specific theater involved for each engagement. Running Ballet Theatre on a year-round basis was a very expensive proposition that Hurok most definitely did not wish to take upon himself but wanted, rather, to leave to Lucia Chase.

Although Hurok may not have been specifically aware of it at the time, Lucia had been anxious about the possibility of a drastic letdown following Ballet Theatre's great inaugural success at the Center Theatre, and she was looking for just the kind of help Hurok was in a prime position to offer. In a letter written a year earlier to her mother, she emphasized the need to add to the company roster: "I think things are coming along all right, but I don't know. Monday night Baronova and her husband [Gerry Sevastianov] and Anton Dolin were here. She is lovely, and it will be wonderful if she joins us. (Sh!)"

Nothing along this line had happened back then, but now the possibility of Baronova's joining Ballet Theatre was being proffered again. As Sevastianov smoothly informed Harry Zuckert and the board of Ballet Associates, if Ballet Theatre decided to hire him as its new manager, he would be delighted to arrange for his wife to join the company, providing that Ballet Theatre agreed to give S. Hurok exclusive rights to manage all its engagements, including its New York seasons.

There were those in and around Ballet Theatre who were not particularly enamored with the idea of signing the company over to Hurok. His taste and outlook were quite different from the objective Dick Pleasant had laid out, which was a company that, despite having many nationalities represented in its ranks, was nevertheless distinctly American in its approach and overall appearance. It certainly was not Russian, which was the only way Hurok saw or presented ballet.

Harry Zuckert, as president of Ballet Theatre Inc., was especially put off by the high-handed way Hurok had first exploited and then eventually discarded the Ballet Russe company. It took a couple of months of bargaining and maneuvering for the two parties to come to terms, but after Sevastianov was hired as managing director and Baronova joined the group of Ballet Theatre dancers who were rehearsing during the summer at Jacob's Pillow in Massachusetts, an agreement was reached in the fall of 1941 that authorized Hurok to represent the company and arrange all of its engagements for the next two years, with a further option for one additional year if he chose to exercise it. In return, besides taking on all expenses of transportation, publicity and advertising, and non-company salaries, Hurok guaranteed to provide Ballet Theatre a set weekly fee and fifteen full weeks of employment for the coming year, including at least nine performances in New York, and eighteen weeks at a higher fee the following year with at least eighteen performances in New York.

Lucia was greatly relieved. From the very limited contact with the company's business that she had allowed herself up to this point, she had developed a simple credo: that ballet company deficits resulted primarily from inexpert direction on the part of those handling how, when, and where the company was to perform. Since it was generally agreed that the master-booker for the arts in America at the moment was Hurok, she concluded that being under his banner would eliminate the awful fiscal emergencies that continually threatened Ballet Theatre's existence, destroyed her peace of mind, and had already cost her a small fortune. Now, with Sevastianov taking over internal operations and Hurok on the outside pulling all the right strings, she believed she could finally relax and simply be a dancer. Best of all, the new arrangement meant that the superbly talented, enchanting Irina Baronova was now going to be in the company.

Of all the dancers in the history of Ballet Theatre, Irina Baronova would soon become the warmest, most devoted, and most loyal friend Lucia ever had in the company. This allegiance developed despite several very considerable differences between them. For example, their ages: Lucia was already forty-four, twice as old as Baronova. Also their financial status: Lucia was wealthy, whereas Baronova, though well paid as a dancer, lived on her salary and had no extra money beyond that which she regularly earned. Finally, there was the huge disparity in their dancing ability. Yet the greatest compliment and gift Lucia ever received from another dancer was the way Irina Baronova, from the very first moment, always regarded Lucia Chase as her fellow artist. Throughout their short time together in the company, and then afterwards forevermore, their friendship was intimate and full of laughter, affection, and great good cheer.

The first engagement Ballet Theatre had under its new Sevastianov/Hurok management was a two-week season in the fall of 1941 at the prestigious Palacio de Bellas Artes opera house in Mexico City. Since the company's contract with Hurok called for at least two major ballerinas, Sevastianov hired—in addition to Baronova—the exquisitely classical and renowned

English ballerina Alicia Markova. As for repertory, Hurok had insisted on a clause in the contract that required Ballet Theatre to add two new major works each year. Accordingly, the long rehearsal period in New York and Jacob's Pillow resulted in producing the classic *Princess Aurora,* adapted by Dolin from *The Sleeping Beauty,* and a frothy entertainment piece, *Bluebeard,* by Fokine, which featured Dolin and Baronova in the lead roles and which also cast Lucia as a beguiling Queen Clementine. Both works were premiered in Mexico and given their first U.S. performances in the four-week season that Hurok arranged at the 44th Street Theatre immediately after the company's return to New York.

Although it had only been a half-year since Sevastianov had taken over as managing director, a definite change in the way the company presented itself for this third New York season was clearly apparent and provoked some disapproving comments in the press. According to the *New York Herald Tribune*'s Walter Terry,

> From the choreographic angle, the Europeans win out, for Eugene Loring and his American ballets are gone. In this I disagree with the new Ballet Theatre policy, for I believe that the lustiness of a *Billy the Kid* and the straightforward, emotionally adult and fresh movement invention of American choreographers would give added power to the Ballet Theatre repertory.

The *New York Times*'s John Martin was even more severe:

> This season the whole direction of the company has been altered, and the original purpose of the Ballet Theatre can be said to have been abandoned altogether. . . . The concept of a "museum of the living art of the ballet" as a permanent public institution has been put aside for the more familiar commercially sponsored privately subsidized Ballet Russe pattern. Such a change seems of questionable wisdom.

Obviously the new management was largely responsible for this transformation of the company along Ballet Russe lines. Yet the association with Hurok had its compensations. Compared with the situation confronting the company back in the spring when there was a critical absence of any bookings, now it could look forward to being employed for months at a time. And beginning the following spring, Hurok promised regular engagements at the Met, which was the best theater in all New York for showing off Ballet Theatre's prima ballerinas Baronova and Markova, as well as the glittering new productions that were being created especially for them.

Regarding this question of new productions, Sevastianov, as Ballet Theatre's new managing director, inherited right at the start what he feared might well turn out to be an awkward problem. Antony Tudor had been working on and off for over a year on a new ballet using some of the lesser figures in the company, particularly one dancer ranked eighth in the company roster, the strong but virtually unknown Nora Kaye. Tudor had, from the outset, chosen Kaye to have the lead in his new work, which was given the working title of *I Dedicate*. Also, for the other four major roles in the new work, Tudor, in defiance of custom, had bypassed the "stars" of Ballet Theatre—Baronova, Markova, Dolin—and assigned the parts to Lucia, Annabelle Lyon, Hugh Laing, and Tudor himself.

An inveterately private and painstakingly slow choreographer, Tudor had his own idiosyncratic way of working which he maintained regardless of any pressures or competition. Physically an extremely spare figure of a man, with sharp facial features and a bony head that seemed more like a skull than flesh and blood, both his voice and choice of words were equally sparse, pared down to the least amount that would suffice. Also, he never laughed outright but only now and then allowed himself a fleeting furtive smile, as though he had just caught sight of something quite humorous before it disappeared around the corner.

Antony Tudor tended to see things that others didn't, little quirks which interested and amused him and which given time, usually a great deal of time, he would reintroduce through his choreography to form a startling portrait of inner drama, a cold-blooded glimpse of the comedy of life. In like fashion, he selected dancers out of the company on the basis of puckish qualities and quirks in their inner nature, characteristics which others—often even they themselves—did not suspect.

Tudor made his dancers work out their interpretations by themselves. He knew, but rarely explained, exactly what it was that he wanted. He was much more apt to hold back and stare, at times somewhat amused but mostly just watching and waiting while the poor soul in front of him struggled to get it right.

He could be fiendishly difficult. According to Muriel Bentley, "With every class Tudor taught in the early days of Ballet Theatre, someone went out crying. . . . But we were all dying to be in the Tudor ballets. To be selected for one of his casts was a great honor. It made us nervous, too, because we felt the tremendous responsibility of living up to his expectations."

What made the dancers' task more difficult was that, unlike almost all other choreographers and their ballets up to this point in time, Tudor did not deal in known, recognizable movements, stringing together classic ballet steps performed by easily recognized characters working out time-honored plots. Rather than confining himself to ballet's traditional heroes and villains and princes, Tudor dealt with in-laws and tortured feelings and frustrated hopes. He gave ballet a new language, fascinating but not always straightforward or easy. Or widely popular, particularly with Hurok, who liked a good show, full of bright dancing and smiles and high kicks that brought lots of applause, sent people home happy, and translated into surging ticket sales. Hurok much preferred Ballet Russe's principal choreographer, Léonide Massine, and his ballets—like *Le Beau Danube*, *Gaîté Parisienne*, and *The Three-Cornered Hat*—to Tudor and his psychological dramas.

Sevastianov agreed. Despite the fact that three of Tudor's ballets—*Jardin aux Lilas*, *Dark Elegies*, and *Gala Performance*—had been widely praised, and that Tudor was already established as one of the artistic pillars of Ballet Theatre, Sevastianov (unlike Pleasant) was not eager to promote Tudor's work. When it came time to list the company's choreographers for the new souvenir program, he gave explicit instructions that Tudor was to be listed only after Fokine, Nijinsky, Dolin, and even Mordkin, whose *Voices of Spring* was kept as a possible alternate work to show off Irina Baronova.

However, Sevastianov had to tread carefully because Lucia had been working for months with Tudor on the role of the eldest sister in the new ballet, and she was keen on the idea of his new work. Although she made a point of staying out of the picture and leaving the management of the company completely up to the new general director, she was still paying most of the bills. In deference to her, and because he was a suave operator in dicey situations, Sevastianov signed a contract with Tudor authorizing his rehearsals to continue but not specifying any particular date for an opening performance. He didn't particularly care whether a new Tudor work ever appeared onstage; in fact, he rather preferred that it did not, but he refrained from coming right out and saying so.

The other dancers who were in *I Dedicate* felt, as did Lucia, that it was a supreme opportunity, and they cared a great deal that work on the ballet be allowed to continue.

Not that the rehearsals were particularly cheerful or pleasant. According to Maria Karnilova, "He was cruel and demanding," but he cared:

> Tudor never let you feel you were just a member of the corps. You were always an actress, a character. He worked as much on each minor role as he worked on the leads. Though he badgered us, he also gave us a feeling of our own importance.

As for Nora Kaye:

> He put me into *Dark Elegies*. That changed me as a dancer and as a person: it changed my life. *Elegies* was so absolutely marvelous. I had never before thought of people moving that way in ballet. Suddenly dance had a focus for me. I had no background then. Tudor and Laing did so much for me: they told me what to read, what to wear, what to think. They got me to read Proust—all six volumes. For years I was emotionally dependent on them.

With the 1942 spring season at the Met coming up, the question was whether this latest Tudor work should be offered as one of the company's featured new productions. By now it had been renamed *Pillar of Fire,* although Sevastianov and Hurok had taken to dubbing it *Pills of Fire.* The dark psychological piece was definitely not their Russian cup of tea: Nora Kaye in the lead figure was portrayed as a tense, tormented, sexually frustrated woman, her older sister (Lucia) as coldly disapproving, and her younger sister (Annabelle Lyon) as a flirtatious vamp—hardly personalities designed to be particularly appealing to the audience.

Nor was the way they danced exciting in the traditional sense of electrifying jumps, flashy turns, bravura balances, or gorgeous long extensions. While Tudor's choreography used movements derived from classic ballet, he was not interested in showing off extraordinary technique but rather in rendering inner psychological pressures through arresting gestures and actions that depicted someone in an anguished state.

Hugh Laing, Tudor's lifelong colleague and protagonist in all of his ballets, described how the technique of dancers cast in Tudor's ballets had to pass unnoticed:

> He may want—and expect you to be able to do—four pirouettes, but you can't let the preparation for the pirouettes show. The turns are part of a phrase that may be saying, "I love you, Juliet," and you must not interrupt that phrase to take a fourth position preparation, because then you are paying attention to yourself as a dancer and not to Juliet.

Nora Kaye described the highly unusual, exhaustive approach that Tudor would take in preparing those who were performing in his works:

> We knew where and how we lived, what our house was like, what clothes we wore, exactly what kind of people we were. We lived our characters before Tudor set a single step. Then, when he began to choreograph, it seemed perfectly natural to move that way.

None of this talk sounds the slightest bit like Sol Hurok or rang any bells for him. It really had nothing to do with Russian ballet, with ballerinas and premier danseurs, nor did it take into account box office returns, which were the principal concern of Hurok Attractions Inc. What *Pillar of Fire* did represent were many of the original ideas and aims of Dick Pleasant and the brash new ballet company that he had caused to spring up out of nowhere only two years earlier. Now, all by itself, Tudor's latest work appeared to contradict the very powerful efforts of Hurok and Sevastianov to remake Ballet Theatre into a Ballet Russe facsimile and to use Ballet Theatre as a vehicle to show off Markova and Baronova dancing in classics like *Giselle* or *Swan Lake,* or in the two new ballets created by Ballet Theatre in the past year, *Princess Aurora* and *Bluebeard.* Both had been smash hits in the company's recent Bellas Artes season in Mexico, and they were already attracting widespread attention in the United States as a result of color-picture spreads that appeared in *Life* and *Vogue.* Why now dampen all this public enthusiasm with Tudor's morbid portrait of a woman in sexual torment, performed by a virtually unknown dancer?

The only reason Hurok and Sevastianov even considered offering *Pillar* in the upcoming Met season was Lucia. In order not to offend or discourage her by an outright rejection of Tudor's new ballet, a special preview in a private studio was set up—to be attended by Hurok, Mae Froman (his executive secretary and most trusted advisor), and Sevastianov—as a sort of trial run to decide whether *Pillar* should be included in the Met season.

According to Charles Payne, whom Ballet Theatre had recently hired as an assistant manager, Lucia was called in after the run-through to confer with the other three from Hurok Associates in a nearby dressing room. The other dancers in the cast stayed outside. They had heard rumors that the ballet was about to be jettisoned, and they feared Lucia might fail to assert herself lest it appear that she was pressing only because the ballet provided her with a significant role. However, it wasn't too long before Sevastianov emerged to announce irritably to Payne that "Lucia insists it has to go on."

It was one of the few occasions, if not the only one, on which Lucia exercised her behind-the-scenes influence and directly overruled Sevastianov's management of the company.

On April 8, 1942, the third night of Ballet Theatre's first season at the Metropolitan Opera House, the world premiere of *Pillar of Fire* was unveiled.

At first, it appeared as though the public reaction would be distinctly unfavorable, for when the curtain came down, the audience sat for a long moment stunned into total silence. Then someone started to applaud, and excitement spread as the entire cast came out to take their bows before giving way to each of the principals, one after another. When it was Nora Kaye's turn, she stood for a moment staring out across the footlights, then went down on one knee, bowed her head, and the audience went wild. Everyone stood up. Next, Tudor came out, and the ovation intensified. Before it was over, Kaye had received twenty-seven curtain calls: the first one, followed by another, followed by another, and another. It must have taken nearly half an hour.

The review in the *New York Times* the following day described it all:

> It was a great night at the Met Opera House last night . . . as near perfection as can be asked. For once everybody on the stage seems to know what he is doing and what it means. . . . The work as a whole is a tremendous achievement, and last night's audience treated it accordingly. There were countless curtain calls, much full-voice cheering, and probably as many flowers as were ever heaped together on a single stage.

"A great ballet," echoed Terry in the *Herald Tribune,* "eloquent and stirring. Superlatives are inadequate. . . . It is gripping, frightening, and incredibly beautiful by turns. . . . Last night's capacity audience cheered itself hoarse in the loudest, longest ovation that any theatre dance has had within my memory."

It is hard to exaggerate the importance of *Pillar of Fire.* Almost everyone who saw it realized, even at the first viewing, that Tudor had taken ballet to an entirely new plane, a world where dancers were not portraying essentially standard set figures—princes and peasant girls—but starkly individual persons possessed and driven by private emotions. *Pillar* is certainly one of the two or three most significant original works ever produced by Ballet Theatre. Coming at a time when the company risked losing its original identity, overnight *Pillar of Fire* reestablished Ballet Theatre's image as a creative force on the world dance scene.

After years of stepping back and deferring, Lucia had finally taken a stand on a most admirable cause. At the absolutely critical moment, it was she who championed and succeeded in saving *Pillar of Fire*.

7. Touring in Wartime

We shan't have any time off now
because Massine arrives today and
Fokine next week, and we have
5 new ballets to prepare in the next
7 weeks!
—Lucia writing from Mexico to her
mother, July 2, 1942

FOLLOWING THE SPRING 1942 SEASON at the Met, Ballet
Theatre sorely needed to slow down and collect itself. Fortunately, just at
this moment, an invitation arrived from the Mexican government for the
company to spend ten to twelve weeks in Mexico City and its surroundings,
beginning late in the spring. For once there would be enough time to prepare an array of new works that could then be premiered at the resplendent
Palacio de Bellas Artes in Mexico City.

Foremost among many projects was for Fokine to revive *Petrouchka*,
one of his masterpieces from the Diaghilev era, and to create a new work,
Helen of Troy, to music by Jacques Offenbach. Léonide Massine, the longtime Ballets Russes choreographer with a reputation rivaling Fokine's, left
De Basil's company and came to work with Ballet Theatre to create two
ballets: *Aleko*, with scenery and costumes by the fabulous Russian-born
artist Marc Chagall; and *Don Domingo de Don Blas*, featuring Mexican
artists and themes. Although no one at the time was aware of its future

significance, another new work was also being conceived by a young dancer in the company, Jerome Robbins, which two years later would premiere as *Fancy Free* and become the all-time signature piece for Ballet Theatre.

Lucia had a number of problems to attend to at home before she could commit to spending the entire summer with the company in Mexico. Her main concern was to make arrangements for Tommy and me, now thirteen and eleven years old. She managed to find a summer camp for each of us, one in Massachusetts that specialized in sailing for Tommy, and an all-activity dawn-to-dusk bruiser called Camp Wallula for me in New Hampshire. For the remaining part of the summer, her older sister, Marjorie (our Aunt Marge), offered to take us to live in her spacious, rambling house, Spindrift, down by the edge of Narragansett Bay in Saunderstown, Rhode Island, just ten miles north of Narragansett. Reassured that we were in good hands, Lucia left New York in early June to spend the next three months with the company in Mexico.

This summer idyll in 1942 turned out to be a particularly memorable time artistically for Lucia, particularly with regard to Fokine and the ballets he was working on in Mexico. Although she was not in the first cast of *Petrouchka* (wherein the role of the Ballerina was given to Baronova), she did rehearse the part and later often performed it; in *Helen of Troy,* she was Athena/Baccis; she also rehearsed with Fokine the role of Queen Clementine in *Bluebeard,* which she had performed when the ballet was premiered at Bellas Artes in October 1941. As for Massine's ballets, she rehearsed the roles of the Fortune Teller in *Aleko* and Constanza in *Don Domingo.*

It was also especially pleasant because, for the first time in several years, she was not embroiled in Ballet Theatre's money troubles. And a further bonus, much as she enjoyed our home life, Lucia loved to travel, particularly where she had a chance to practice another language, eat other foods, meet new people. Perhaps best of all was the feeling she had, from the moment she arrived, of being totally involved and accepted as a bona fide member of the company. "We've worked very hard this week," she wrote on July 18 to her mother. "Mr. Fokine has done two acts of *Helen of Troy* out of 5. I have a very funny dance in *Helen,* a take-off on modern dancers, and I'm the Fortune Teller in Massine's [*Aleko*]. Only 5½ weeks now at work, and costumes all over the Bellas Artes—our season begins Aug. 26th."

Fokine was exceptionally busy, reenacting the very complicated crowd scenes and lead roles of *Petrouchka,* rehearsing his comic *Bluebeard,* and working with his usual methodical precision on a brand-new *Helen of Troy,* all this despite the fact that soon after his arrival in Mexico, he developed a thrombosis in his left leg and was forced to conduct all his rehearsals from a chair. There was no elevator in the building where they were working, and he couldn't manage the long flight of stairs up to the studio. But each day a team of dancers volunteered to carry him so that his rehearsals continued uninterrupted.

He finished composing the entire *Helen of Troy* on paper in his room, working out all the details in advance, including props, lighting, and other stage effects. *Helen* was to be his eighty-first ballet, and it was scheduled to be premiered in the Bellas Artes on September 10. Then one day early in August, he collapsed. Leaving the completion of *Helen* to former Ballets Russes dancer and choreographer David Lichine, Fokine checked into a hospital in New York. Once there, he was stricken with pleurisy, which soon developed into double pneumonia. On August 22, 1942, to the dismay of the entire dance world, Michel Fokine died.

It was an enormous loss for Lucia, who revered him and all his work. *Les Sylphides, Carnaval, Bluebeard,* the newly revised *Petrouchka,* and most recently *Helen of Troy* all contained prominent roles in which Fokine had personally taught and coached her during the past three years. Fokine was like a father to her, and no other choreographer ever quite filled his niche.

Despite Fokine's death, the company kept to its schedule and on August 26 began three weeks of performances at the Palacio de Bellas Artes in Mexico City. "Marvelous season," Lucia wrote to her mother at the end of the first week:

> Full house every performance. I'm dancing *Petrouchka* and *Helen of Troy.* . . . All this time Irina [Baronova] gets up at 6 a.m., works in her movie all day [a full-length feature film called *Clorinda*], then comes and does a knock-out performance at night! I don't know how she stands it. Mr. Hurok arrived Tuesday to see what was going on and all the new productions. (I think he's worried to see us in the midst of such success without him!) Mayor LaGuardia comes next week (from New York) and will probably do something with us. We're full of celebrities every performance, loads of flowers and all very gala. Everyone is beginning to realize how much we've done for Pan American goodwill.

Bluebeard, starring Markova, Dolin, and Baronova, was a big hit with the local audiences and provided Lucia with one of her favorite roles as

Queen Clementine. But the biggest success of the Bellas Artes season was Fokine's *Petrouchka*. Originally performed in Paris in 1911 by Diaghilev's Ballets Russes, with the renowned Nijinsky in the title role, the ballet had lost none of its impact in thirty years. According to the leading Mexican dance critic, although Fokine was dead and never saw this latest production onstage, Ballet Theatre's revival was an authoritative rendering "he would have been proud of." For Fokine to have, in just the past year, completed two such important additions to the active repertory took some of the sting out of his death, and all the dancers felt grateful to have had the privilege of working with the grand master in his final days.

This summer in Mexico turned out to be possibly the most pleasant and memorable time Lucia ever had in all her forty years with Ballet Theatre. Underlying everything else, it was in Mexico that she felt that she had finally been accepted as a dancer. Until then, there had always been an unspoken but definite sense—in the studio and hallway, backstage in the wings, out front in the audience—that the reason Lucia Chase was prominent in the company was because she had a lot of money.

This habit people had—of focusing on her personal wealth and privileged social position, often over and above everything else she was or did—infuriated her. "I get as mad as blazes when they ask me, 'Why should you work so hard when you don't have to,' or when they say that I can be famous through money. I don't want fame that way." Yet the more Lucia tried to hide this part of her life, taking care to make all her gifts and loans under the table rather than out in the open, always keeping anonymous as a patron, and steadfastly refusing to answer any and all questions relating to her money, the more inquisitive people became.

Not so in Mexico. The gossip, the snide remarks, the rumor mongers stayed home in the States. All that summer, if any fresh money was needed for incidental or ongoing expenses, the payments were made, privately and completely out of sight, and Lucia was left free simply to enjoy the way her name appeared prominently on every rehearsal schedule posted each day on the board. She took class with the rest of the company, attended every meal either in the hotel or a nearby restaurant, and went to all the late-night parties for Ballet Theatre. At the age of forty-three, about the last moment it could have happened to her in her ballet career, Lucia Chase was recognized as a professional dancer.

The biggest advantage that Ballet Theatre gained from its new partnership with Hurok was that it provided employment for the company during the greater part of each year, including—at least once and often twice a year—a season of several weeks at the Met in New York. There were also extended bookings, varying from several days to a week or more, in a number of major cities, including Los Angeles, San Francisco, Chicago, Toronto, Boston, and Washington. Still, the greatest part of each year's performing schedule was derived from the wide-ranging cross-country tours that carried Ballet Theatre to scores of towns and smaller cities across the United States.

Ballet Theatre was not the first large ballet company to undertake such a massive venture. Throughout the 1930s, when Hurok had contracts with both Ballet Russe companies, he made a practice of offering them, alternately or sometimes both in the same year, to local theater managers as feature attractions in their annual concert series. By the time Ballet Theatre came along, a nationwide network of organized audiences had been built up.

Viewed in retrospect, these transcontinental excursions have a glamorous ring to them. Like a Norman Rockwell magazine cover, a Hurok tour was sheer Americana with just a slightly Russian twist, a troupe of young artists performing in old vaudeville theaters and converted movie houses in homespun locations like Sioux City, Iowa, or Joplin, Missouri. Yet the reality was not particularly glamorous. The greater part of most tours consisted of a series of quick in-and-out appearances with a lot of travel in between, a relentless succession of back-to-back cities, week after week, with hardly a break of even a single day in which to unpack or do laundry or simply to rest. The distances between stops were often considerable, sometimes many hundreds of miles, which meant that much of the traveling was done overnight, beginning after midnight following a performance and continuing on most of the next day, or else spending a few hours in a local hotel before setting off early the next morning, racing to reach the next city in time to check in, grab a bite to eat, then rush to the local hall or high school, wherever the stage was, in order to warm up, get into costume, put on makeup, and be ready when the curtain went up for that evening's performance.

Complicating what was already a very demanding schedule and itinerary was the overriding fact that throughout the years 1942–45, the country was at war. Military transportation—troops and supplies—had top priority and constantly disrupted everything else. Most of Ballet Theatre's travel was necessarily by train, which was a cumbersome and totally unpredictable experience, full of detours and delays that could mean waiting for hours in stations or being diverted into sidings along the way. And always crowded conditions, soldiers everywhere, most of the seats taken all of the time, so there was no place for the company dancers to move around or stretch overworked muscles or comfortably rest.

Rank had no privilege. Everyone was the same, the young and the not-so-young, from newest member of the corps to prima ballerina, along with the wardrobe mistress, orchestra conductor, ballet master, accompanist, company manager and other staff and crew—everyone jammed in together, all the way across the wide expanses of midwestern and prairie states as far as the Pacific, then up and down the west coast before heading back, a resolute band of extraordinary dancers dedicated to practicing their art, bringing ballet to the hinterlands.

The stories of what it was like to be on a typical Ballet Theatre tour during the 1940s are colorful, touching, and often hilarious. It was a time of deep friendships and romances, of quarrels and reconciliations, jealousies but also heartfelt respect that often bordered on veneration, and out of the whole conglomeration of experiences and feelings came a bonding from having been part of a fabulous adventure which for many constituted the greatest experience of their entire life.

Michael Kidd, choreographer of the ballet *On Stage* and a member of Ballet Theatre from 1942 until 1947, recalled in a 1942 interview with Sidney Fields what it was like:

> We had it down to a system. The old railroad cars had seats where you could pull the backs out. You brought a small suitcase which you laid between the two seats at just the right height, so you pulled the back off, laid it across the suitcase, and stretched out there. When you came onto a train after not having much sleep the night before, you immediately stripped the car. I remember the look of astonishment on the conductor when he walked in and saw this whole car virtually demolished and everyone stretched out asleep.

Shortages of equipment, troop transfers, and unexpected delays meant there was no way of telling when the company would finally arrive in the next city. John Taras, another dancer and choreographer of Ballet Theatre during the war, recounted how for an 8 p.m. performance, they might get to the theater at 8:30 or 9: "Mr. Dolin [Anton Dolin, Ballet Theatre's leading male dancer], who was performing that night, would come out in his dressing gown and talk to the audience, trying to keep them calm while we were getting ready."

Sono Osato, in her autobiography *Distant Dances,* wrote about the company's first tour under Hurok in 1943:

When trains were unavailable, we traveled in buses which were even worse than the crowded Pullmans. We felt trapped in our seats with nowhere to walk, no space in which to straighten our aching legs as the hours passed. . . . [Nicholas] Orloff scrambled up into the overhead luggage rack and stretched out to sleep among the suitcases. Many nights I sat upright on the long seat across the back of the bus, wedged between Nora Kaye and Dorati [Antal Dorati, Ballet Theatre's conductor]. By morning, we were always grimy, cranky, and stiff-necked from continuous drafts.

Whether traveling by train or by bus, the biggest concern was always to arrive in the next town in time for the performance. Sometimes the dancers made it, but the costumes and scenery did not, in which case *Princess Aurora* would not be performed with Karinska's sumptuous robes designed by Bakst but in practice clothes on a bare stage.

Again Sono Osato:

One night we sped into Savannah, Georgia, several hours behind schedule, to find the audience passing the time by singing endless choruses of "Roll Out the Barrel." We danced that night on the shiny varnished floor of a basketball court in a large gymnasium. While the audience sat in the bleachers belting out one chorus after another, we frantically slapped on our makeup. Still pulling our straps, tugging at our wigs, and yanking ornery hats and feathers, we hurried to our places as the music began. . . . The performance ended that night at 1:30 a.m. We straggled into the streets to find something to eat and to wait for the bus. Alicia Markova lay down on a pile of overcoats, her head resting on her hatbox. Close by, Jerry Robbins slept on a bed of suitcases. . . . Less than 24 hours later, we were dancing in Miami.

As Sono Osato observed, none of the hardships appeared to bother Lucia:

Day after day she sat with Irina in the front seat of the bus, smiling and chatting cheerfully. You could never tell from looking at her that she bore the heavy financial burden of the company as well as dancing every night with the rest of us.

Others made similar observations, and there's little doubt that Lucia genuinely loved touring: "We've had some hard traveling this week," Lucia wrote her mother from Detroit, "but you get used to it and sleep it off after. . . . One night from Lansing to Kalamazoo, it was 12:20–4:30 with an hour-and-a-half wait at a junction, but the next day we had breakfast at 4:15 p.m.! The night we left Washington, we slept five in a drawing room! Usually we have only coaches, so that was a great luxury."

Her letters from out on tour are invariably cheerful. From Quebec, February 1, 1942:

Played Friday and twice Saturday. . . . A glorious snowstorm, and we walked home from the theater and romped on the skating rink in snow up to our knees. We had a wonderful time there—it has been like a pleasure trip—and we keep on having marvelous reviews. I did *Peter and the Wolf* in French yesterday at the matinee—now I've done it in 3 languages. . . . Hurok comes tomorrow to confer with Jerry [Sevastianov] and Charlie [Payne] about the future. It seems there is some doubt about Chicago, so maybe we'll have a layoff even sooner than we expected. I hope not. If it weren't for the war work would be easy, but as it is, I guess they have a hard time arranging places to go.

The company's 1942–43 tour under Hurok began early in November and continued through March, out to the west coast and back. "We had a marvelous opening last night," Lucia wrote home from Seattle. "The opera house is beautiful, and there were 3,500 with many standing—jammed to capacity—This is a very exciting week of our tour, it's such a good public here, and Los Angeles will be, too."

Six days later she wrote again:

Our week in San F. was marvelous. Most performances were sold out, and there were crowds of standees at all of them. It was really terrific. Mr. Hurok came out to see our first appearance on the west coast and had a big smile on his face. . . . We're not due back in NY till March 29th—booked for Canada 15th–29th, but I shall have to play hookey and go home March 20 for at least 4 days between Toronto and Montreal. Tommy's vacation is March 19 to April 1. I hate to miss a min. of it. Luckily we'll be at the Met in April and home May & June.

Private life and professional career are constantly intermingled in the letters she writes to her mother. On Biltmore Hotel stationery, Los Angeles, February 17, 1943:

Dearest Mumsie, You were so sweet to send me the lovely yellow roses and pansies last week. I was terribly pleased that you remembered and were thinking of my beloved Tom. It doesn't seem it could be 10 years ago since he had to go. But he seems just as close and alive as ever, and I still think I was the most fortunate girl in the world to have him for over 6 precious years. It was happiness enough to last a lifetime. . . .

We had a wonderful season in LA with terrific success. Now we are on a sleeper 3 hours later from Tucson—we'll only arrive just in time for the performance. . . . I called Sandy Sun a.m. and everything seemed to be fine. It feels pretty good to be starting towards home again though we're still a long way off.

Out on the road now for four months, in her next letter—this one to both her parents—she sounds just as fresh and chipper as when she started out.

(February 28, 1943): Happy Anniversary! It's a happy one for us 5 daughters because though we didn't have much to say about it, we couldn't have picked better possibly, and we're mighty fortunate to be blessed with such a mother and father. There isn't a day I don't thank my lucky stars and bless you both for my background and training. The training is a help every hour of the day, and in this business especially, I find it most helpful.

The tour ended up in eastern Canada, with an entire week spent in Toronto where reviews were ecstatic. "Great Art Achieved by Ballet Theatre. NY Group Reaches New Heights in Toronto Performance" was the headline in the *Toronto Star*.

Next thing to a miracle transformed Royal Alexandra last night into a temple of incredible magic. The Ballet Theatre from New York is a thing of beauty, a revel of colors, a parade of enchantments, a scenario of splendid music . . . not a mere ensemble, it's a marvelous, humanized mechanism whose productions last night were miracles of consummate perfection.

The headline in the *Evening Telegram* two days later sounded the same note: "Ballet Found Near Perfect in Two Shows." "Closest to perfection in ballet that this reviewer ever hopes to see. . . . One would be hard put to find flaws in the grace and precision of the present ensemble."

Robertson Davies summed up the opinion of most Canadians:

Ballet Theatre is now the foremost ballet company in the Americas and presumably in the world. . . . If you have not already seen the Ballet Theatre, do not neglect to do so, for you will reproach yourself otherwise. This is ballet as it ought to be.

Hurok came for a few days near the end to check up on the condition of this company, which he had booked to perform for five weeks at the Met, beginning April 1. In the course of his visit, Lucia heard that she probably would be dancing the first performance of *Petrouchka* on the company's second night in the Met. Igor Stravinsky, who composed the music, was scheduled to be guest conductor, which meant it would be a big event.

That was the good news. The bad news was that the reason Lucia was dancing the part of the Ballerina in *Petrouchka* was that the previous month Irina Baronova had fallen ill and had to be hospitalized. No one took the news too seriously at first, including Lucia, who always had difficulty accepting the fact that everyone wasn't as tough and resilient as herself. However, Baronova was very much of a trouper, and when she didn't turn up to dance in either San Francisco or Los Angeles, the company's two major California engagements, people started to wonder whether she would recover soon enough to rejoin the company for its season at the Met, now only two weeks away.

"My Darling Lucia," Baronova wrote early in February:

I got out of the hospital yesterday, but I am still in bed and do not feel much better. I am so depressed, so weak, I wish I could die!! . . . I think I will never go on the stage again, it will be the best for everybody! I hope you are fine, but then you are always fine. You are a wonderful person, really wonderful in all respects! One cannot help but admire you!

Baronova's news one week later was, if anything, worse. There was a distressing note of finality in the apologies she kept making to Lucia for the breakdown in her health:

You have been so good to me, I will never forget that, and I am sorry that I brought so much trouble with me and that I cannot stick now to the end. I will love you always.

Soon after that, a letter from Baronova to Harry Zuckert as president of Ballet Theatre Inc. enclosed a report from her doctor confirming the worst.

Irina Baronova has been under my observation and treatment since 2/22/43. She is suffering from acute Pharyngitis, acute Sciatica of the right leg, secondary Anemia in the advanced stage, and complete physical and nervous exhaustion due primarily to overwork. I referred her to Park East Hospital where she remained until March 2. . . . She needs prolonged office treatment of an undetermined period. At the present time, she is absolutely unfit to work.

And lest there still remained any cause to dispute his report, Baronova added her own postscript: "Dr. Sylberstein is a doctor of good standing and, in fact, is the physician to Mr. Hurok."

With Baronova absent, Lucia lost her closest friend in the company and her best touring companion. It was one more reason, after nearly five months on the road, that she was glad finally to settle down at home, where Tommy and I were on spring vacation and very glad indeed to welcome her home.

Lucia's mother, Elizabeth Kellogg Chase, a remarkable woman who ran the Chase household, took an active interest in everything that her five daughters (and sixteen grandchildren) did, and steadfastly gave her approval and support to Lucia throughout her ballet career.

Lucia's father, Irving Chase, president of the Waterbury Clock Company and beloved pater familias. His granddaughter Louise wrote, "The family is still repeating his injunctions like old unchangeable laws."

Irving Chase and his five daughters (left to right): Dorothy (Mrs. Edward Carmody), Elizabeth Irving (Mrs. John Griffith-Davies), "Popsie," Marjorie (Mrs. James Sheldon), Eleanor (Mrs. Charles Taft), and Lucia (Mrs. Thomas Ewing Jr.). Photo by Carl Klein.

Lucia in leading role of Clyde Finch's play *The Lion and the Mouse*, which her Bryn Mawr class of 1917 produced and performed at the college in 1914. Courtesy of Jerome Robbins Dance Division, the New York Public Library for the Performing Arts, Astor, Lenos, and Tilden Foundations.

Tom Ewing, Lucia's husband and my father. Ten years after he died, Lucia wrote her mother, "I still think I was the most fortunate girl in the world to have him for over six precious years. It was happiness enough to last a lifetime."

Lucia and Tom's wedding photo. They were married December 29, 1926, at St. John's Episcopal Church in Waterbury. More than 500 guests attended the wedding dinner at Rose Hill.

Lucia and Tom on vacation in Aiken, S.C., where they stayed in a small cottage that Tom bought from his uncle, Alex Cochran.

My brother, Tommy, and I, ages five and three, in my room in our family's New York apartment.

My brother, Thomas Ewing III, at age twenty-eight in Cambridge, where he attended Harvard Law School. After graduation, he joined the law firm of Debevoise, Plimpton, Lyons, and Gates, where he worked for five years before he died in a sailing accident off the coast of Watch Hill, R.I.

Lucia as the Ballerina in Michel Fokine's *Petrouchka,* created in 1911 for Serge Diaghilev's Ballets Russes. The original cast included Tamara Karsavina as the Ballerina
and Nijinsky as Petrouchka. Fokine personally staged the Ballet Theatre production
that premiered in Mexico City in 1942 with Irina Baronova as the Ballerina.

Anton Dolin as Red Coat and Lucia as Khivria in David Lichine's *Fair at Sorochinsk*, which Ballet Theatre premiered October 14, 1943, at the Metropolitan Opera House.

Lucia as the Greedy Virgin in Ballet Theatre's production of Agnes de Mille's ballet *Three Virgins and a Devil*, first performed in the company's second New York season at the Majestic Theatre, February 11, 1941. Others in the cast were Agnes de Mille (Priggish One), Annabelle Lyon (Lustful One), Eugene Loring (Devil), and Jerome Robbins (Youth). Photo by Walter E. Owen.

Lucia as Queen Clementine in Michel Fokine's *Bluebeard*, which he choreographed for Ballet Theatre and premiered at the Palacio de Bellas Artes in Mexico City in October 1941. Others in the cast included Anton Dolin as Bluebeard, Alicia Markova, Irina Baronova, and Antony Tudor. Photo by Annette and Basil Zarov, Montréal.

8. Jerome Robbins and *Fancy Free*

I do think it has gotten beyond the
point where Mr. Z [Zuckert] has to
worry about annoying Mr. Hurok
and with your backing can fight for
and insist upon Ballet Theatre's
becoming and remaining the kind
of company we all want it to be, not
a company that becomes more and
more old-time Russian every year.
—Charles Payne, letter to Lucia,
    May 7, 1943

IN MARCH 1943, as its five-month U.S. tour came to an end
and Ballet Theatre headed for its three-week spring season at the Met, the
contract between the company and Hurok Associates was still in its initial
phase with another six months to go. Yet several contentious points had
already cropped up.

Like Lucia, Hurok was greatly distressed by Baronova's illness. He had
been receiving complaints from theater managers all along Ballet Theatre's
tour route when the company arrived in town and performed without her.
Even more upsetting was the recently confirmed news that she would not

be able to dance in the upcoming Met season. Ballet Theatre was as strong, perhaps even stronger, than it had ever been, with at least two brilliant emerging ballerinas in Nora Kaye and Alicia Alonso. But in Hurok's eyes, they did not qualify as the kind of internationally renowned big-name performers, most of them Russian, like Baronova, Toumanova, and Danilova, who had a marked impact on the box office. He constantly pressed Ballet Theatre to bring in prominent guest artists to bolster the company's regular ranks.

The same kind of disagreement developed regarding new productions. Hurok believed the prospect of seeing an exciting new work was a great attendance booster, and he had insisted on a clause in the contract requiring Ballet Theatre to provide and pay for at least two major fresh works each season. Ballet Theatre was allowed to choose which ballets would be done, but Hurok had reserved for himself the right of final approval. The problem was that he and the company had conflicting viewpoints: Ballet Theatre, always strapped for cash, favored smaller, less expensive works that provided a number of challenging new roles for the company; Hurok preferred lavish, splashy, colorful productions that filled the stage and were guaranteed to send people home happy.

There were other serious issues. A hot dispute erupted in the Canadian portion of the tour when Hurok proposed paying the company's weekly fee in Canadian dollars, which amounted to a 20 percent reduction and was clearly contrary to the basic contract Ballet Theatre had with AGMA, the dancers' union.

Also, Ballet Theatre resented the way Hurok persisted in presenting the company as an essentially Russian attraction, despite the fact that the overwhelming nationality of the dancers was American. A typical example of the publicity he put out was the ad that appeared in the *Seattle Star* on August 3 announcing the company's upcoming performances: the banner headline read, "S. Hurok presents the greatest in Russian Ballet by the Ballet Theatre." So much for Dick Pleasant and his dream of creating a contemporary American ballet company.

Probably the biggest complaint Ballet Theatre had was with the way the income from the performances was divided. According to the contract, every week that the company was on tour Hurok Attractions had agreed to pay Ballet Theatre a fee of slightly more than $5,000, an amount that barely covered the dancers' payroll and left nothing for all the other running expenses the company had to assume on the road and back at home. As a result, Ballet Theatre was afflicted with a sizable deficit week after week, while Hurok was reaping a handsome profit.

It was around this time that Gerry Sevastianov, the suave, worldly, incredibly handsome husband of Baronova and former Hurok assistant, was suddenly declared eligible for the draft. The root of the problem dated back to when Sevastianov, already in his thirties, was wooing Baronova, a star in the Ballet Russe but still only a teenager. To allay the concern that she, or particularly her parents, felt about his being so considerably older, Sevastianov falsified his age in applying for a U.S. passport, claiming to be several years younger than he actually was. Now that the government was reaching out to draft all able-bodied men up to a certain age, Sevastianov's sworn statement as recorded in government files made him eligible to be called up for military service.

Early in May, despite his desperate protests, Sevastianov was taken into the U.S. Army, leaving Ballet Theatre once again without a managing director. Fortunately, this time there had been advance warning and considerable scouting around for his replacement. The leading candidate was John Alden Talbot, a semiretired New Jersey real estate magnate and a member of the Ballet Associates board and the Met Opera Guild.

There were two problems about his appointment: in marked contrast with Sevastianov, he had very little theatrical experience; also, Talbot wasn't particularly eager to take on a job that promised to have him living a good part of the year out of a suitcase. Just as the company was due to leave for California, where Hurok had booked it for six weeks on the West Coast, Talbot relented and on June 28 accepted what promised to be a very ticklish assignment.

Immediately upon his arrival in California, Talbot ran into the familiar issue over new productions. Looking ahead to the company's fall season at the Met, public attention was focused on two new works, *Fair at Sorochinsk* by David Lichine and *Tally-Ho* by Agnes de Mille, although there were several problems with the de Mille work, principal of which was a long silence from the choreographer. Finally, in early July 1943, de Mille wrote from Hobbs, New Mexico:

Dear Lucia . . . I'm a pig not to have answered you sooner, but getting married I find is a highly engrossing experience. And the war doesn't make things easier. . . . Of course when I was told that Antony [Tudor] planned a Mozart ballet for the autumn, I suspended work on mine immediately. I thought that he had simply stolen the jump on me. When Mr. Talbot a couple of weeks ago asked for my Gluck scenario, nothing naturally was ready. I don't think I can be blamed for this, but this week I have done a scenario and am mailing it with full details. . . .

As to rehearsing, I work very fast, providing I'm working with people who know how to play comedy. And very economically.

This was the gospel according to Agnes de Mille, but not according to Alden Talbot, who a few weeks later wrote from California to Harry Zuckert in New York:

The de Mille ballet is going to take up a lot of money this week, as she is another one who thinks she is a little dictator. We are going to have to work out some way of curing our choreographers, just how I am at a loss to know at the present. . . . Lucia is really being a brick about the whole thing, and I must say that my stay here in California has increased my admiration and affection for her very much. . . . She deserves better treatment than she gets a good part of the time, and she certainly is a good trouper.

Zuckert responded by way of a curt note of advice sent to Lucia: "If you persist in showing your enthusiasm for a new ballet before the funds are on hand with which to produce it, you will be stuck with the costs."

More sympathetic words came to her from Charlie Payne, who, after two years with the company as executive manager, was about to go out on a career of his own. "Name me a choreographer who isn't impossible," he wrote Lucia near the end of summer, "and you can have him. In fact, you can have him without naming him."

He went on with his typically wry humor:

The kids seemed to be very excited about Lichine's ballet [*Fair at Sorochinsk*] and they all said you have a wonderful part and are doing it beautifully. They seemed particularly entranced with the way you vomit all over the stage. Do you think Mr. Zuckert will approve? A lady, you know, never vomits.

Nor did a lady, a true lady, at that time ever talk about her money, and Lucia never did. But privately she was becoming progressively more involved in a tax dispute over her ballet contributions with the Internal Revenue Service. Hearings associated with the case revealed that her ongoing support of the company was colossal by any standards: just the 1942–43 season cost her close to $200,000, an astounding amount for those times when theater tickets, for example, were one-tenth of what they cost today.

This uncontrolled outpouring of family money ran totally against her upbringing and essential nature. Although Lucia appeared to live in a grand style, personally she had surprisingly simple habits and tastes. She was famous in the ballet world for wearing the same old leopard winter coat for nearly thirty years; she darned her own toe shoes and washed her own tights; and as a dyed-in-the-wool New Yorker, she was most apt to ride the bus or simply walk instead of taking a taxicab. Paying out thousands of dollars in regular weekly increments seemed like tossing masses of dollar bills out the train window every time they left one town and went on to another.

Although the predicament she found herself in was intolerable, it was also proving to be inescapable. Whenever the next money crisis came up, she could have—at least theoretically—just stepped back and let Ballet Theatre go under. Yet after so much had been already spent over so long a period, her decision at that particular moment was inevitably the same: she wrote the check. So the pattern continued, but pressure was building and her patience was running out.

Ballet Theatre's fall 1943 season at the Met was a mixture of tribulation and achievement. There were several injuries and illnesses, most notably Markova, who took sick and was out for the entire season. Yet, in her absence, other dancers took on a greater prominence, most noticeably Alicia Alonso, whose Giselle set the entire dance world talking.

For Lucia, there was a happy little incident at the outset of the engagement when a note was delivered backstage to her from Anton Dolin, premier danseur and original member of Ballet Theatre:

Dear Lucia—Tonight starts again what I hope and feel sure will be another great season of our beloved Ballet Theatre. Outwardly you take, or even care to have, mighty little credit for this undertaking. However, my deep affection and tremendous admiration for you both as an artist and a person does not blind me to the fact that a great debt is due to you, for the work you do, seen and unseen. My love, as always, Anton.

There was a card added to the note that read, "You looked very happy in the performance of *Bluebeard,* even tho there were so many men condemned to die for the love of you. A."

And then at the end of the season, there was another happy note when John Martin on November 15, 1943, gave his final verdict in the *New York Times:*

No matter how carefully one may weigh superlatives, it is difficult to come to any other conclusion than that this is the finest ballet company that has yet been seen in America. . . . Its crowning glories are of course Alicia Markova and the choreography of Antony Tudor. But even crowning glories are not enough unless they have something to crown, and in this case they find a magnificent ensemble and a fabulous roster of individual talent.

Allured by the company's continuing eminence, Hurok early in the fall picked up his option to manage Ballet Theatre for another two years. After finishing up at the Met, the very next day the company took off again on another massive Hurok- booked tour.

Lucia traveled and performed with the company practically the entire time on each of its tours, yet while she was away from home, her household continued to run smoothly with a steady stream of family and other visitors coming and going.

Tommy and I were day students at Buckley, a demanding school with an extensive sports program and a heavy load of homework that took up most of our evenings. We also took piano lessons from the Russian-émigré Drozdoff family, which made for a full and very busy schedule. Still, it was great, suddenly much better, when a tour was over and Mom blew in the door, breathless and excited and laughing and hugging, with Skippy, our Norwich terrier, barking madly and running full-speed down the hall and back into her bedroom where he would go around and around in circles. Later on, there'd be candles and peppermints on the table for dinner.

During the times she was at home, our weekday routine remained the same, but weekends would be spent at Kinross, full of Ewing cousins and dogs and gardens and pebbled paths, with Granny Ewing presiding at the upper half of the dinner table, Grandpa at the other end (always bounded by children) telling stories of the Old West.

Late in June, the New York apartment would be closed, and everyone— Mom, Tommy, and I, the entire household staff, along with Skippy—moved into High Tide, with my grandmother and various other members of the Chase family right next door in Miramar.

My mother's life in Narragansett was the same as it had always been since earliest childhood. Mornings would generally be spent at the beach. "You can't imagine how wonderful it is just to be relaxing here, doing nothing," she would tell any casual acquaintance who stopped her along the way to her daily swim in the ocean. Her afternoons might include family doubles on the tennis courts of Point Judith, driving to nearby Wakefield to purchase sundry items for the new tenants who had just moved into Sea Shell or Sans Souci, circling around to stop in at Sunset Farm to bring back fresh eggs and vegetables, ending up late in the day back in her own house, with "drinks on the porch at 7:15" for whatever family or guests were staying in the house or just coming for dinner. The table was always full, the meals were delicious, and the conversation was lively night after night, with my mother sparking the festivity from her end of the table.

Tommy had taken up sailing and spent a great deal of time in nearby Saunderstown, where a small fleet of Lawley 15s raced against each other in Narragansett Bay. I generally headed to Point Judith on my trusty blue bike, racquet in hand, seeking anyone of any age, sex, or ability who was available to play tennis. Inevitably, there would be the day when out would come the little red suitcase our mother always took on tour. We would have a hurried breakfast downstairs, then a last-minute rush off to the train station at nearby Kingston. Tears on the platform, last kisses, and Mom was off, waving from the train window, once again Lucia Chase en route to rejoin Ballet Theatre in New York or California or some far-off port. Soon handwritten letters and postcards would start arriving, full of ballet talk and asking for news about all the family.

Hers was an absolutely full, fast-paced, sometimes almost frenetic schedule as she raced back and forth between her two worlds of ballet and family that were often thousands of miles apart. What was most surprising, there was nothing else in between. She never went any other place, with any other people, for any reason: no pleasure jaunts to fashionable resorts somewhere else in the country or away in Europe, no visits to friends' houses, no retreats off by herself, no diversions for any purpose to see anyone or do anything apart from the ballet company and her family. A world-traveler when Ballet Theatre was on tour, spending more time in more different places in more countries than most workaholic business executives, at all other times she was the most home-oriented, housebound, rooted individual imaginable. Although she was rich, attractive, inexhaustible, irrepressible, and—if she had wanted to be—totally independent, she clung to a path that was totally circumscribed by two circles and only two: ballet and family. Whichever one she was in at the moment, the other was never absent from her mind or farther away than the nearest telephone.

The 1943–44 U.S. tour was one of the longest and most wide-ranging ever booked for Ballet Theatre, covering seventy-three cities, with forty-eight of the engagements just single performances. There was little time for anything except to travel, perform, rest in a hurry if and when possible, then move on to the next city.

With such a relentless schedule, the challenge of tackling the creation of a new work during this frenetic period was formidable. Also, as Alden Talbot had written to Harry Zuckert many months earlier, working with Agnes de Mille was difficult, progress on *Tally-Ho* was slow, and its scenery and costumes were elaborate and costly. Nevertheless, it was completed midway through the tour and premiered in February in Los Angeles. At last, Hurok had a lavish new work to publicize Ballet Theatre's spring engagement at the Met.

The original plan for the season had called for de Mille to do two new ballets. However, when she didn't have time to finish the second, a small, unheralded and quite inconspicuous other new production, one which had been in process for some time and which was finally completed in the course of this most recent tour, was substituted in its place. It was introduced without fanfare or any great advance expectations, just a fledgling endeavor choreographed by a rising but still relatively unknown dancer in the company, Jerome Robbins, who called his new offering *Fancy Free.*

The piece had originated two years earlier when the company was in Mexico. I remember being at summer camp in New Hampshire and receiving a postcard from my mother in Guadalajara saying she could hear typing in the room next door where Jerry Robbins was working on what she thought was a story for a new ballet.

Most choreographers start out with a germ of an idea that may lead them to do considerable research beforehand, but they generally wait to be in a studio with dancers before they begin formally working. But Robbins took the novel approach of writing everything down first, working out on paper exactly what would take place in each miniature segment, who would be dancing what and for how long, how the characters would look and act in relation to each other, and describing every movement in such intimate detail that later on, after seeing the ballet, to read the written script was like watching a rerun of everything that took place onstage.

But then everything about *Fancy Free* was unusual. The three leading parts were all for male dancers, which was hardly the norm in ballet. The men Robbins picked were not principals of the company but drawn from the second tier—John Kriza, Harold Lang, and Robbins himself. As for the rest of the small cast, there was no ballerina: the three subordinate female roles went to Janet Reed, Muriel Bentley, and Shirley Eckl, all new to the company. Also, the two other artists working on the set and the music were as young as Robbins and no better known than he was. Oliver Smith was a twenty-six-year-old theater artist who had only just begun to make a name for himself six months earlier by designing the sets for Agnes de Mille's *Rodeo* for the Ballet Russe de Monte Carlo. As for the music, the commission for an original score was turned down first by Morton Gould and then by Vincent Persichetti before being offered to and accepted by a still barely known composer and conductor named Leonard Bernstein.

Perhaps the most unusual aspect of *Fancy Free* was that the protagonists depicted by Robbins did not fall within ballet's time-honored precincts of princes and peasants. Instead, it featured three footloose American sailors on shore leave in New York who were batting around town looking for a little fun. It was the same scene as the one that was going on night after night around Times Square in 1942 when *Fancy Free* was being conceived: just a trio of sailors, ordinary guys doing ordinary things—chewing gum, drinking beer, looking for girls. Nothing could have been more commonplace.

When the ballet opens, the three chums have nothing particular to do. Two girls come along, and they all wind up together in a bar where each of the three gobs tries to impress the gals by dancing a solo, a friendly but intense rivalry. When the competition gets a little rough, the girls leave, and the sailors find themselves alone again, but then a third girl saunters by and they race off to catch up with her . . . end of ballet. But what great fun: the camaraderie; the three sensational solos, each trying to outdo the other; the winsome girls; the familiar scenery showing the street and the bar, with stools for the sailors to jump up and off; the tension set up by the grouping, always three sailors vying for two girls; and through it all, from the opening blast of music to the mad race at the end, Bernstein's great jazzy score.

From the beginning, *Fancy Free* faced all sorts of problems. When Robbins first submitted the script to the Ballet Theatre office back in May 1943, Sevastianov had just been drafted, Alden Talbot had not yet been hired, and there was no general director making decisions. There was also no money at hand to pay for a new ballet, particularly by an unknown choreographer. Robbins was asking for an immediate go-ahead and to have his work included in the Met season the following spring, a terrific gamble considering there was nothing to see or go by except the script. There was still no music. In fact, there was not even a composer, nor would there be by the time the company left for the west coast two months later.

From then on, there was never any formal authorization given for Robbins to proceed, no officially scheduled rehearsal time, no general agreement on what was to happen if and when the work was ever finished. One can imagine what Hurok's reaction would have been if he had been asked whether this unpretentious little work could qualify as one of the two major ballets he would approve for the 1943–44 season. There was understandably a good deal of attention being paid to Agnes de Mille's *Tally-Ho* But *Fancy Free* flew in under the radar, with no budget or place on the official agenda of things to be done.

Instead of being part of the company's regular rehearsal schedule, Robbins would call impromptu rehearsals in any space he could find and whenever the dancers had a spare moment. The ballet was literally conceived on the road—in hotel lobbies or someone's hotel room, on the train, in the street, in any nook or cubbyhole that was available. Somehow Robbins and Smith and Bernstein pulled it all together. The set was built for $250, the music was finished on March 30, and Robbins completed his own variation on April 3, six days before the start of the Met season. Meanwhile, there were regular performances every night of the week, with four on the weekend. *Fancy Free* was scheduled to premiere, ready or not, eight days later.

It was second on the program. During the intermission before *Fancy Free*, just minutes before the curtain went up, it was discovered that there was no phonograph onstage to provide the blaring "canned music" from the barroom's jukebox that Bernstein and Robbins had decided should be the opening notes of the ballet. By the greatest good fortune, Betty Comden and Adolph Green, friends of Bernstein who, the following year, would write the lyrics and book for the musical *On the Town*, which was inspired by *Fancy Free*, happened to be sitting in the audience. When they heard about the crisis onstage over the missing phonograph, they left their seats and rushed to a nearby apartment for a portable record player, getting back just in time to deliver it backstage.

Robbins was in the wings still working on his solo when he broke the zipper on his pants and required a desperate last-minute repair. Another near-catastrophe occurred, after the curtain was up and the ballet had started, when the rung on one of the barstools broke just as Robbins leapt off it, so that he nearly lost his balance in midair and risked having a serious accident right in the middle of his solo.

No matter—rarely in ballet history has there ever been such an instantaneous roaring success. Harold Lang's solo absolutely stopped the show, and the audience demanded the unheard of—that he perform an immediate encore of the entire solo—before the ballet could go on. At the end, there were at least two dozen full curtain calls when the six dumbfounded young dancers came out to take their bows at center stage of the Metropolitan Opera House.

Agnes de Mille recounted what it was like:

While the audience gave itself to applause, I rushed backstage and discovered Robbins sweating and startled, leaning against a wall. His eyes moved about almost in terror. His mouth was open. He kept giggling in short mirthless gasps. I didn't think he could have taken in what I said, but I kept talking anyhow. I held him tight. I told him he was safe and need never be frightened again.

The critical verdict was delivered the following day in the opening words of John Martin's review in the *New York Times:*

To come right to the point, without any ifs, ands, or buts, Jerome Robbins's *Fancy Free* is a smash hit. This is Robbins's first go at choreography, and the only thing he has to worry about is how in the world he is going to make his second one any better. . . . Indeed, the whole ballet, performance included, is just exactly ten degrees north of terrific.

Despite Lucia's extremely limited involvement with this new work, she was especially thrilled and exultant over *Fancy Free*. It made up for so much: the money she had consistently been forced to pay out for every new production, the constant laments of choreographers hired to work for Ballet Theatre that they were never given enough time, complaints from all the other choreographers who were upset about not being asked in the first place, the occasional savage criticism leveled directly at Lucia that certain ballets only were commissioned because she had a principal part in them, and always the pressure from Hurok for more new productions, preferably bigger and more expensive.

Lucia generally tried her best to stay clear of these and all other management decisions, but more and more it seemed that everyone ended up coming to her asking for this or for that, but not so this time. Robbins, Bernstein, and Oliver Smith had worked everything out essentially on their own, with virtually no involvement on her part. As a matter of fact, the first time she ever met and talked to Oliver Smith is said to have been at a final dress rehearsal of *Fancy Free.*

As for how she related to Jerry Robbins, it can truly be said that Lucia felt a special kinship with all the dancers who ever joined the company. Besides a deep and abiding love for a few closest friends, like Baronova and Alonso and Kriza, she felt real affection for practically everyone. But up to this point, Jerry Robbins had never been a particular favorite of hers. She found him cocky, brash, opinionated, and self-important—all qualities she tended to dislike. Yet, for the rest of her life, despite the demon that Robbins would become at certain critical moments, toward herself personally and for her fond hopes and plans for Ballet Theatre, she never afterwards talked badly or turned against him, even when she had every right to, because back when it really mattered—when both she and Ballet Theatre desperately needed an uplift—Jerry Robbins gave her and the company *Fancy Free.*

‿❧‿

On the surface, the first half of 1944 appears to be one of the brightest periods in the history of Ballet Theatre.

On March 20, *Life* magazine came out with an issue showing Nana Gollner and the words "THE BALLET" on its cover; inside was a twelve-page article almost entirely about Ballet Theatre, including two half-page photos of *Three Virgins and a Devil* and *Pillar of Fire* showing Lucia as a principal in each of the casts. The only criticism of the article she had was that, in the caption for the *Three Virgins* photo, Lucia Chase was identified as the "carpet-fortune widow whose money has helped support Ballet Theatre."

"Of course I was livid they had to label me again," she wrote her mother. "I wish they'd mind their own business and leave me alone."

Overall, the Met season, highlighted by the sensational debut of *Fancy Free,* was the most successful the company had yet enjoyed in New York, breaking the Met's box office records for a dance attraction and resulting in the engagement's being extended an extra week to total twenty-four performances. Once again, though, by far the greatest share of the box office went to Hurok, while Ballet Theatre ran up a substantial deficit which as usual had to be picked up almost entirely by Lucia.

The same problem continued on into the summer when the company spent six weeks touring out on the West Coast, bringing a big smile to Hurok's face but causing Lucia to feel more and more victimized by the uneven division of spoils: "[David Lichine] said he thought I was the biggest sucker he'd ever seen, and I agreed with him. I believe my brain is clearing, and I hope the 'biggest sucker' is not permanent."

Yet once back in New York, the predicament she found herself in was, if anything, worse than ever. After yet another unproductive board meeting, Lucia vented her frustration in an uncharacteristic letter of complaint to a member of the board:

> Money flows. I signed for $10M ($10,000) last week, but they need more. Money was never mentioned today. One meeting in three months, and we must repeat for two hours everything that was discussed in the Executive meeting. No word was mentioned of pushing Ballet Associates to raise money. I think the whole setup is idiotic. I can pour in money, but so as not to hurt Alden's feelings, hours and hours are spent and we get nowhere.

Her principal dispute with Alden Talbot was precipitated by the now familiar issue of having to add another ballet to the repertory for the 1945 spring season at the Met. Talbot, a sensitive and very decent man, was caught square in the middle between Hurok's demand for new ballets and Lucia's reluctance to pay for them. It didn't help matters when an article appeared in *Variety* near the end of the summer announcing that for the nine performances of Ballet Theatre at the Hollywood Bowl, the gross revenue was $124,000, which was split 50/50 between Hurok and the local manager:

> So he got $62,000 and magnanimously paid us $6,000 for those nine performances while we lost plenty of money. Has anyone else looked into that or worried about it? In 7 months I had "loaned" $52,000; in 8 months, I have "loaned" $72,000.

Lucia finally tried to call a halt, stating that she would pay for Tudor's projected new ballet *Undertow* and provide up to $25,000 more, but that was all for the rest of the 1944–45 season.

It was an impossible quandary for Talbot, and at the next directors' meeting, held in October 1944, he announced that he either had to be able to arrange for Ballet Theatre to function legally and effectively—which, in effect, meant Lucia's backing down from her ultimatum—or he would resign, a move that caused dancers in the company to sign a petition requesting that he be kept on in his position as managing director.

The financial stand-off continued unresolved. On November 6, Lucia (probably acting on the advice of her lawyer) wrote Alden Talbot that she had now paid the $25,000 she had previously offered and also had, to this point, covered a cumulative deficit amounting to over $132,000. For this 1944–45 season, she could do no more.

No action was taken, and at the next meeting of the trustees in December, Talbot restated his position: unless Lucia agreed to meet all the company's operating expenses, including the cost of producing *Undertow*, he would resign. In fact, he announced that he would resign anyway after the annual meeting on April 1, 1945.

The board clearly was in no position to step in and take any meaningful responsibility, either for *Undertow* or any other significant expenses. The sad fact was that for the entire year up to this point, with only three weeks still to go, the total amount that the Ballet Associates had managed to raise was $3,375. It was suggested by the chairman that perhaps before the end of the year, it might be possible to raise another $700: other than that, nothing was resolved and the problem was tabled, to be taken up again at the next meeting.

On January 3, 1945, the board met again, and the same argument between Talbot and Lucia took up most of the discussion. Talbot repeated his ultimatum: he would resign unless Lucia withdrew her refusal to offer any financial support. Lucia responded by turning the question around and saying that if Talbot would take full responsibility for the future finances of the company, she herself was willing to resign and turn her hand to trying something else, like possibly working with Oliver Smith to underwrite Broadway shows, a rather shocking suggestion that led to a resolution to elect the same Mr. Smith to be a member of the Ballet Theatre board.

This was at least one positive step forward, but otherwise Lucia found little to cheer about. As she related to Charlie Payne, "I came out of the meeting as usual looking like a G.D. fool."

After all the squabbling and backing and filling, the fact remained that Ballet Theatre still was obligated to produce two major ballets for the coming year, a point on which Hurok was absolutely adamant. Accordingly, on

January 18, Talbot telegraphed Lucia, who was out on tour with the company in Spokane, Washington, that he thought he could get *Concerto Barocco,* a beautiful abstract ballet by George Balanchine set to Bach's *Concerto for Two Violins,* for $6,000.

This was quite a bargain and became even greater when Talbot wired three days later that Hurok had agreed to pay half the cost. Lucia, still smarting from previous confrontations, wired back that *Concerto Barocco* was a fine idea and that Talbot should go ahead as long as he could find a way of paying for it, but as she had already said several times, she had reached her limit. Talbot was aghast and indignant at the way he had been led to believe that she had fully approved of *Concerto* and had meant for him to go ahead. He sent back a terse letter, suggesting that henceforth she should keep copies of what she told people so there wouldn't be such misunderstandings in the future.

This was not the way to maintain cordial relations with Lucia Chase, and from then on, he was left to fend as best he could. He made several efforts to gain some financial backing for the company but was unsuccessful. At the annual meeting in April, true to his word, he resigned his position as managing director and became just a member of the board and treasurer of Ballet Associates. Meanwhile there was nothing definite planned for the next five months. Something had to be done, and consequently, at the same meeting—April 21, 1945—the board voted to make Lucia Chase and Oliver Smith administrative directors of Ballet Theatre.

The appointment surprised many of the board members who had grown accustomed to Lucia's always insisting that she didn't wish to get involved in the business affairs of the company. "I only wanted to be known as a dancer," Lucia often said, and they believed her. But finally her patience and forbearance had given out.

At the time, both she and Oliver thought that their appointment would only persist for a year or two at the most, until they managed to get things sorted out to their liking and could set up a permanent management team. But this was not to be: as things turned out, they were the one and only "team" that was to run Ballet Theatre for the next thirty-five years.

9. Covent Garden

Month of May would be much better
than August at Covent Garden. If
you come in May, is it necessary that
Hurok manages or not?
—Letter from E.I., July 9, 1945

BESIDES HER FATHER AND MOTHER and two sons, the two
people closest to Lucia and whom she cherished above all others were her
two younger sisters, E.I. (Elizabeth Irving) and Dee (Dorothy).

Early in her adult life, E.I., the older of the two, had gone to live in
England and before long was as British as the Union Jack, but she remained fiercely loyal to her American roots, particularly her family. Small,
dark-haired, with flashing eyes and at times an irrepressible giggle, she was
a spunky personality with a hot temper who didn't mind fighting for any
cause she believed in. During the war, instead of coming home to safety
in the States, she stayed in the center of London and drove an ambulance
through all the terrifying nights of bombs and shells falling indiscriminately
out of the skies.

When I recall E.I. now, some twenty years since she died in her eighties
in England, close to her beloved Greystones Farm in Gloucestershire, my
first thought is her deep and abiding love of animals, all types of four-legged
creatures, from the prize Ayreshire dairy cattle she raised and tended and
showed in small-town fairs all over England, to the ongoing parade of semi-

domesticated pets—cats of any number, always a dog or two, and even a piglet who was allowed full range of the house. Her heart went out to anybody that crossed her path: if it needed help or just a touch of caring and love, E.I. would be there. Despite being separated by the Atlantic Ocean, she and my mother were extremely close, with hardly a week going by that they didn't talk at least once by phone as well as maintain a constant exchange of letters and postcards.

In June 1945. Lucia wrote to tell E.I. in strictest confidence that Lord Keynes, the ruling arbiter of Covent Garden in London, had sent a vaguely worded invitation of sorts about Ballet Theatre's coming the following summer, and what did E.I. think about the whole idea? E.I. was passionately interested in her sister's ballet career and made a habit of coming back to the States every year in order to attend one of Ballet Theatre's seasons in New York. Now the possibility of reversing this and having the company come to London was thrilling, and she wrote back full of excitement, saying she thought the month of May would definitely be the best time. "In August, everyone ('tout le monde') goes to Scotland or Europe, nothing but Americans in London. Hard to have a brilliant season at that time." She also advised moving fast: "I'm afraid Ballet Russe will come in May, and it's important to come before them." And then she added a cryptic question about whether it was necessary to come under Hurok's management.

It was a very interesting point. Whereas summers were not included in Hurok's agreement with Ballet Theatre, he had just signed a contract to present Ballet Theatre for the coming two months on the west coast, and the normal assumption would have been that the same arrangement might take place the following year. Yet something in Lucia's letter, or its tone, intimated that Ballet Theatre might begin charting its own course, and E.I. had picked up on the idea, although nothing more was said at the time.

Meanwhile, relations between Hurok and the Ballet Theatre office, already strained, were about to be further aggravated over the issue of what new production Ballet Theatre would mount for its upcoming fall 1945 season at the Met.

The first indication of trouble came in early April. *Undertow*, an imaginative but controversial new work by Antony Tudor, had been scheduled to be premiered at the Met on April 10. However, Hurok sent a letter to Ballet Theatre several days prior to its opening performance, stating that he could not accept *Undertow* as the major new work that Ballet Theatre was required by contract to provide before the end of the year. Hurok suggested that the company select either Fokine's *Scheherazade* or a new version of *Firebird* to Stravinsky's great score, both ballets that had already been produced and performed by other companies. It turned out there were problems that eliminated *Scheherazade*, but *Firebird* seemed to be an acceptable choice. The one proviso was that Ballet Theatre had to be willing to work on it during the summer in order for it to be ready in time for the Met season in October.

For once, Ballet Theatre had some bargaining power, owing to the fact that Hurok had already committed to providing a ballet company that summer out on the west coast but still hadn't secured one. Now he was being pressured by California managers to specify to them which company he would send. His preference was Ballet Theatre, but when he insisted—as part of the agreement—that *Firebird* had to be produced for the Met, Ballet Theatre countered that it could only pay up to $15,000, which was then estimated to be the ballet's probable cost. Any amount over that figure would have to be assumed by Hurok. Since it didn't seem as though any overage would be more than a couple of thousand dollars, and because Hurok was anxious to have an enticing new work to publicize for the fall season, he agreed. Having gone this far, he then contacted Stravinsky about revising the score, hiring Adolph Bolm to do the choreography, and having Nicholas Remisoff, the designer of *The Fair at Sorochinsk*, do the sets and costumes.

Lucia knew about all this, and at one point in the following month, after she and Oliver Smith were appointed administrative directors of Ballet Theatre, she wrote Remisoff that she and Oliver would be coming out to the west coast in midsummer and could go over his scenery and costume sketches at that time. However, when Smith arrived in California and sat down with Lucia to review Remisoff's designs, he felt they were not particularly distinguished and declared that the job should be assigned instead to the eminent Russian artist Marc Chagall. Although switching meant a slight delay and probably also some increase in the original budget, it was a bold and exciting proposal, and since Chagall was a compatriot of Hurok's (they even came from the same small village in Russia), Hurok agreed to the change, and work proceeded in a rush to have *Firebird* ready for the fall.

Time passed. One by one, bills for everything to do with *Firebird* were presented to Ballet Theatre. By now, the total cost of the production had gone way past the original $15,000 and in fact added up to $34,000, of which not one cent had yet been paid by Hurok. With the October 24 premiere of *Firebird* little more than two weeks away, an invoice for $19,000 (the total amount over the original estimate of $15,000) was sent to Hurok's office but elicited no response.

On October 7, the Met season started, but Hurok continued to pay nothing, confident that, in the end, Lucia Chase would pick up the tab as she always had. The day before *Firebird*'s opening, a formal letter was delivered to Hurok from Ballet Theatre's office detailing bills on hand totaling $11,825 and over $7,000 of already committed expenses that were owed by Hurok and were as yet unpaid:

> We must therefore insist that there be in our hands not later than tomorrow morning (Wed. Oct. 24) a remittance from you to pay the above stated obligations, or else the first performance, scheduled for tomorrow evening, will have to be postponed until such payment has been made.

The decision to use Chagall, which in turn had caused the huge increase over the original estimate, had been Oliver's, but the problem of preparing *Firebird* for its Met premiere had become Lucia's, and in her new capacity as codirector and acting head of the company, she was not about to be bullied any longer by Hurok. At the conclusion of the company's evening program on the 23rd, one night before *Firebird* was scheduled to open, she went backstage and, speaking in the very tight, carefully enunciated tone of voice she used in difficult situations, she instructed the production stage manager that on no account was the curtain to go up the following night on *Firebird* unless and until she gave the word.

It was a phenomenal ultimatum, rare in the theater world, but even more than that, it was unprecedented from a company under Mr. Hurok's management. Especially in the Met, which was Hurok's house, his little kingdom. Yet the order delivered backstage by Ballet Theatre's new top-gun director had been clear and emphatic: without official clearance from her, there would be no *Firebird* tomorrow night.

The deadlock was resolved just before noon the next day when a check from the Hurok office was delivered to Ballet Theatre for the full amount owed. The curtain went up on time that night, and the evening program proceeded as though nothing had happened.

Firebird was not a tremendous hit, nothing approaching the tumultuous success of *Fancy Free* or even *Tally-Ho* the previous year. Adolph Bolm's choreography was called conventional and unimaginative, and Stravinsky's ravishing score, specially revised for the new production, was apparently not played particularly well. The one redeeming feature was the extraordinary set, as reported the following day by Edwin Denby in the *New York Herald Tribune:*

> Marc Chagall's décor for the new version of *Firebird* is as wonderful a gift to the season as a big Christmas present to a child. It is heartwarming and scintillating, it is touching and beautiful. One sits before it in childlike enchantment. . . . *Firebird* is mere nonsense if you should go expecting a ballet. But since the décor is so beautiful a work of art, one hopes Ballet Theatre will, out of respect for Chagall's genius and Stravinsky's too, get a first-rate choreographer to reset it completely. It could be a glorious ballet.

This qualified praise was not enough to placate Hurok. For him, the overpowering fact was that he had been ordered in no uncertain terms to pay up, and in the end he had no choice but to comply. This was something that just did not happen in the great impresario's world. Up to this point, there had been all sorts of disagreements between him and Ballet Theatre, but they could be characterized as just the usual bickering between booker and client, which Hurok was accustomed to and rather relished. But to be defied and forced to give in completely, as Lucia Chase had made him do with *Firebird,* that was a different matter entirely, an affront he could not forgive or forget.

From that moment on, it was clear to both parties that their professional relationship had been irreparably blasted. Technically, their contract extended through October 1947, and until then neither party was free to negotiate with anyone else. With communication broken down between them, the dispute was handed over to their respective lawyers, with instructions to work out terms of a permanent release as quickly as possible.

A final agreement was reached in April 1946, midway through Ballet Theatre's five-week engagement at the Met. Hurok was awarded the sets and costumes of *Firebird* and three other ballets, Ballet Theatre was released from its subservience to Hurok Associates, and the two immediately started scrambling to pick from the various possibilities they had each been surreptitiously probing for the past three or four months.

It was only a few weeks later that Sir David Webster, general administrator of the Covent Garden Opera Trust, flew to New York to discuss a summer engagement by Ballet Theatre of at least six weeks at the Royal Opera House in London.

This opportunity for Ballet Theatre to perform at Covent Garden had materialized in the past few days like a godsend, perfectly filling the frightening employment gap looming directly ahead as a result of Ballet Theatre's having severed all ties with Hurok. Providing that a satisfactory agreement could be reached, Ballet Theatre would be the first American dance company to tour in England since the Littlefield Ballet from Philadelphia had visited in 1937.

There wasn't much time to decide all the complicated questions of money, repertory, individual programs, personnel, sets and costumes, rehearsal schedules, and so much else. Yet both sides were so eager for the engagement to take place that problems were quickly sorted out, and only six weeks later, on June 20, an eye-catching contingent of fifty Ballet Theatre dancers boarded the *Queen Mary* in New York and headed out past the Statue of Liberty, bound for Southampton and from there to London.

Even for a seasoned company used to traveling, it was the grandest of adventures. The trip started with six days of superb weather. During the war, the magnificent *Queen Mary* had served as a troopship and hadn't yet been converted back to a luxury liner, so the dancers were crowded together in cabins sleeping eight to twelve in multilevel bunks. Still, it was a thrilling experience, particularly for newcomers to the company, some of whom were barely twenty years old and had never been out of the country. London was a transfixing spectacle, wartime devastation still being cleared away, the double-decker buses, the food and flower market that was Covent Garden, and best of all, the Royal Opera House, home of the world-renowned Sadler's Wells Ballet (soon to be renamed simply the Royal Ballet).

Lucia, in her new capacity as codirector of Ballet Theatre, was on her own, Oliver Smith being obliged to stay behind in New York. Bringing Ballet Theatre to London—home base of Margot Fonteyn, Frederick Ashton, Ninette de Valois, one of the world's major ballet companies and schools, and a repertory of new ballets as well as the only repository of late nineteenth-century Russian works outside of Russia—was a formidable challenge. Furthermore, the English, especially their dance critics, had long been recognized as being very particular about how ballet is executed, meaning according to the standards prescribed by their august Royal Academy of Dance. A dancer might perform prodigious feats, soar through the air in defiance of gravity, spin like a top, or dance so beautifully as to bring tears to the eyes of the audience. But if the arms were not at all times placed exactly right, any such momentary lapse was apt to be considered paramount and unforgivable.

For the opening night, Lucia chose an all-star program of proven favorites—*Les Sylphides, Fancy Free*, the Black Swan pas de deux, and *Bluebeard*. The audience at the beginning was respectful and attentive, until Nora Kaye, dancing as the black swan, advanced to center stage and tossed off, in quick succession, thirty-two perfect rapid-fire fouettés, at which point people went wild and Ballet Theatre won its way into British hearts.

At first, the critics still tended to be reserved in their praise. Regarding *Les Sylphides,* Ballet Theatre's traditional choice to impress a new audience, it was observed that "while their footwork was admirable, their arms were lacking in becoming grace." Another labeled *Fancy Free,* the company's trademark work, as "music hall," and *Bluebeard* as "little more than a farce comedy." Still, the writer for the *Observer* concluded his review of the opening performance by saying, "They gave us an unusually exciting evening, they had a tremendous success, and if their other 17 ballets live up to the first night, nobody with any taste for the art should miss Covent Garden now."

Lucia was ecstatic about being in England and performing at the Royal Opera House. She wrote her father from the Savoy Hotel three days after the opening:

> Here I am just around the corner from Covent Garden, the most lovely theatre I have ever been in. Isn't it exciting? We are a huge success and the talk of the town. They gave us a rousing reception our first night, and our 2nd program Friday was just as big a success. Now we have 13 more ballets to put on, a new program twice a week for the next four weeks, and they must all be equally good, so we are rehearsing like mad. The whole thing is much better than I ever dreamed.

This was really her first all-out experience as Ballet Theatre's director, and it was one of the most successful she and the company would ever spend. Night after night, a huge crowd would turn up to fill all the seats in the spacious opera house. Princess Elizabeth and Princess Margaret came several times, as Lucia excitedly reported back to the assembled family in Narragansett, Rhode Island. The entire engagement of "Ballet Theatre—New York" (as it was called for this first appearance in England) had originally been scheduled for six weeks, but it proved so successful that it was extended another two, by far the longest run the company had ever performed in a single city.

"If it is a young company," the *Dancing Times* commented at the end, "it is full of enthusiasm, exuberance, and vigour combined with a fine sense of theatre."

And Arnold Haskell, one of England's leading dance critics and very much a ballet enthusiast, wrote, "Here was a company with a marked personality of its own: vital, stylish, finely trained and essentially forthcoming and generous. The strength of Ballet Theatre lies in the fact that it comes to us as a company, something organic. . . . Managers and impresarios should realize that names mean very little as compared with good work, and that we enjoy discovering our own favorites."

Besides the heady pleasure of two months with her beloved sister E.I., who came into London from her farm in Gloucestershire almost every night to attend Ballet Theatre's performances, Lucia also had a special dividend at the end of the engagement when a notable personal honor was bestowed on her by the Royal Academy of Dancing. Chartered by King George V and headquartered in London, this was the ultimate voice in the English world of dance, and there could be no greater award given than when Lucia Chase became not only the first American but the first foreigner ever to be elected a member of the RAD.

Ballet Theatre's season at Covent Garden was a great success on many counts: it reinforced the image and reputation of Ballet Theatre as one of the preeminent ballet companies of the world; the dancers loved spending eight weeks in one place, especially when it was the grand city of London; and the venture accomplished the very welcome action of getting Ballet Theatre out of Hurok's territory and impressively off on its own, confounding all the skeptics who thought that without Hurok's guiding hand, the company would flounder and quickly fold.

Lucia, although unquestionably at the helm of Ballet Theatre, had only agreed to serve as director of the company on the condition that Oliver Smith could partner with her. She was aware from the outset that he would continue to be preoccupied with his work as a scenic artist, a field where he would become renowned as the designer for such Broadway shows as *On the Town, Brigadoon, High Button Shoes, My Fair Lady, West Side Story, Sound of Music,* and *Camelot,* the operas *La Traviata* and *Martha* for the Metropolitan Opera, and the motion pictures of *Guys and Dolls, Porgy and Bess,* and *Oklahoma!* It wasn't the greater part of his time and attention that Lucia wanted from him: that was what she proposed to give to the company and their partnership. It's quite possible that she would have been more than mildly displeased if, after having subordinated herself to Dick Pleasant, Gerry Sevastianov, Alden Talbot, and, most recently, Hurok, she now had to rein herself in and share the driver's seat with anyone else. At least insofar as the strictly ballet side—the dancers, programs, performances—of the Ballet Theatre organization was concerned, Lucia wanted to be both the field commander and final authority for the company.

However, there were other aspects of the business, such as arranging tours, booking theaters, running the office, heading the board of directors, and raising funds, where she had no experience and was happy to have others take over. And then, in addition, there was also a third area, centering around the selection and production of new ballets for the repertory, where Lucia felt ill-equipped to make the big decisions: it was here that she wanted Oliver to stand by her side and be her partner.

Despite his young age, Oliver Smith was a remarkably erudite and astute judge when it came to recognizing what was not only beautiful but also workable and valid. He knew the people who were currently doing impressive work. He could talk to them in their terms and they to him, something that Lucia never felt comfortable about attempting by herself. If only to fill this gap, Oliver Smith was invaluable to her.

In a great many ways, he was the exact opposite of Lucia. Where she was small (five foot three), he was tall, well over six feet, and because he was thin, his height was all the more noticeable. Whereas Lucia didn't look even close to her true age (only one year short of fifty), Oliver was only twenty-six. Lucia was vibrant, vivacious, always on the move, while Oliver was languid. His usual pose was sitting down, his long legs languorously crossed, at ease and slightly bemused at the hustling scene he surveyed from the comfort of his chair. Lucia was wealthy, whereas Oliver, at least in his early years, never had much money, certainly not enough to support the elegant lifestyle he aspired to adopt.

But Oliver was genuinely and deeply fond of Lucia (as she was of him). He approved of who she was and what she did, the kind of life she led, the household she managed. He was fascinated by and truly enjoyed being with her family, particularly her sisters E.I. and Dee. Most of all, he was never in the slightest bit bored with or tired of Lucia's company. In any setting or under any circumstances, he felt entirely at ease and at peace with her.

However improbable a combination they seemed, they were ideally suited to work together, which they did until their retirement together in 1980. It was a rare partnership, for the theater or any other world, and they both treasured it as much the last day as the first.

Late in August 1946, just as the engagement at Covent Garden was coming to an end, Ballet Theatre announced that the company was returning to its original 1940 credo, to serve as a permanent institution, international in scope but distinctly American in character, and that henceforth it intended to build from within its own ranks, "thus rigidly eschewing the invidious guest-star system and giving its own young, predominantly American dancers a chance at stardom." The new directors wanted to make it perfectly clear that there would be no more emphasis on Russian ballet and that big-name stars would no longer be brought in as guests for a single season unless they agreed to sign on as regular members of the company. At least for the near future, the majority of principal dancers would come right out of the company, true stalwarts of Ballet Theatre like Alicia Alonso, Nora Kaye, Hugh Laing, Muriel Bentley, Diana Adams, John Kriza, Melissa Hayden, and Igor Youskevitch.

Regarding the artistic committee that had been formed two years earlier to oversee and help guide the future course of the company, the original group of five members—Lucia Chase, Oliver Smith, Agnes de Mille, Jerome Robbins, and Antony Tudor—was now expanded to seven to include the composer Aaron Copland and the arts curator Henry Clifford, with a new position and title of "artistic administrator" bestowed on Antony Tudor. With this new team in place and fresh from the exhilarating success at Covent Garden, the company returned to New York and at the end of September opened a five-week season at the Broadway Theatre.

It wasn't long before some of the grim realities of its newfound freedom began to make themselves known. Hurok, as usual, had the first option to lease the Met whenever it was available, and for this fall—partly for profit but also out of spite—he had renewed old ties with Colonel W. de Basil and was presenting the Original Ballet Russe at the Met in direct competition with Ballet Theatre.

That alone would have made a financially successful engagement for Ballet Theatre extremely difficult, but there were other problems as well. While the Broadway was the largest commercial theater in New York, it had only half the seating capacity of the Met, which meant the company's potential revenue was drastically reduced. Also, having up to this point always been presented by Hurok, Ballet Theatre had no experience in promoting a major New York season. All the essentials were missing: no master file like the giant list of names Hurok had compiled of people who, over the years, had bought tickets to the ballet; no in-house publicity staff trained at turning out a steady stream of press releases or an effective advertising campaign; and because money for anything outside the company's own immediate artistic needs was, as usual, practically nonexistent, there was a niggardly amount allocated toward "selling" the house.

The result of these critical shortcomings was that the audience attendance for the Broadway Theatre engagement was dismally small. Less than 50 percent of the seats were sold, a shocking figure that can best be appreciated by realizing that theoretically this meant that every other seat—the one immediately to the right and left of every spectator at every performance—was empty. In terms of dollars, out of a potential revenue of $272,000, Ballet Theatre grossed only $140,000, and out of this it netted barely half for itself, or a mere $87,000 for the entire five weeks. Meanwhile, in its new independent status, the company now had to pay all the ancillary expenses that Hurok had formerly covered, such as orchestra, wardrobe, advertising, loading in and out, and all stage expenses throughout the course of the season. The awful final reckoning showed this to have been probably the most expensive engagement the company had ever experienced.

As for the artistic quality of the season, it was a mixed story. Frederick Ashton's ballet *Les Patineurs*, seen for the first time in New York, won high praise from the critics, as did the revival of Tudor's *Dark Elegies.* There was much exceptional dancing, most notably an absolutely stand-out performance by Alicia Alonso and André Eglevsky in *Giselle,* but also a number of other highlights. Walter Terry in the *New York Herald Tribune* wrote, "The dance virtuosity of Miss Kaye and Mr. Youskevitch is without equal in these parts." Alonso and Youskevitch in *Swan Lake* caused John Martin to remark on how "almost for the first time, the opening scene becomes a love scene. One had almost forgotten indeed that it was supposed to be one."

Balancing these positive comments, there was also some extremely adverse criticism, particularly a withering reaction to *Facsimile,* the new ballet choreographed by Jerome Robbins.

After the fabulous success of *Fancy Free,* Ballet Theatre had followed it up the following year by adopting another Robbins work, *Interplay,* a modest but engaging ballet that would prove to be extremely useful and popular for years to come. As a result of these back-to-back winning efforts, Lucia asked Robbins to work on creating a third new ballet for the company and very quickly learned that Ballet Theatre's original informal working relationship with Robbins had drastically changed. No longer a neophyte choreographer, Robbins was beginning to get enticing offers from Broadway after the runaway success of the musical *On the Town,* and Lucia was obliged to accept some quite extraordinary demands, including an exorbitant allotment of 138 hours rehearsal time for a 19-minute ballet.

Facsimile did not pan out like Robbins's previous two winners, and the first performance received some of the most scathing reviews of any work the company had ever presented: "If you find out what *Facsimile* is about," Robert Garland remarked in the *Journal-American,* "write and tell me: I promise not to make it public."

Robert Sylvester went to greater lengths in the *World Telegram:*

First Nora Kaye wanders around the stage swinging a rose on a string. Or maybe it was a lobster. Then Jerome Robbins bounces in. He's swinging a red shawl. . . . Robbins kisses Nora's hand. He kisses her on the kisser. She kisses back. He kisses her knee. She jumps around and falls down. He kisses her foot. She gets coy. He sulks. She kisses the back of his neck. Then they both fall down and play dead for a while. In comes John Kriza, in red underwear. Everybody gets all mixed up, kissing Nora some more, until at one point Kriza nearly kisses Robbins. Then Robbins kisses Nora's foot while Kriza kisses her on the kisser and runs her around Robbins like he was a Maypole. . . . A minute or so before the finale, after the boys have tied her in a tight knot, dumped her on the floor and then fallen on her head, Miss Kaye raises her voice in agonizing appeal: Stop!' she cries plaintively. Ballet Theatre should have listened to her at the first rehearsal.

These reviews, entertaining to read now, were exceedingly painful at the time. *Facsimile* had been an expensive undertaking, and it had so monopolized the available studio and rehearsal time that it became necessary to cancel Agnes de Mille's *Harvest Reel,* a new work that had been planned as a second world premiere for the Broadway Theatre season. Lucia had authorized both the exceptional rehearsal time for *Facsimile* and the cancellation of *Harvest Reel* in hopes of gaining another popular Robbins hit to add to the repertory. The result, ridiculed in the press, was a bitter reward, particularly since she had not only to accept the responsibility for *Facsimile* but, as usual, to put up the money to pay for it

Yet as far as the reputation of Ballet Theatre was concerned, the

Broadway Theatre engagement was no artistic disaster. Well-wishers who feared that the separation from Hurok might prove to be a mortal blow instead found the company wonderfully intact, with Igor Youskevitch, its leading male dancer, an outstanding addition. There was an unmistakable ardor onstage when he and Alicia Alonso danced together.

Edwin Denby, writing at the end of the season, gave what was perhaps the fairest critique:

> Ballet Theatre's season was a very pleasant one as a whole, though distinctly uneven. . . . Though smaller and not quite so strong as once, it is still as pretty a company and, despite overwork, it managed generally to look fresh and crisp. The management has restored the company's collective harmony and morale.

All in all, since the company set sail for England on June 20, it had been either traveling, rehearsing, or performing for nearly five solid months and now might have expected at least a brief respite in order to rest and renew itself. Instead, two days after closing in New York, it set out again, this time on a U.S. tour booked by MCA (Music Corporation of America), which would last twenty-three weeks or nearly half a year more.

Right away it was evident that MCA was no Hurok when it came to booking a ballet company. After being only two weeks out on the road, Lucia wrote a discouraging letter to Agnes de Mille, who had expressed an interest in doing another ballet:

> Philadelphia and Boston have proven a very expensive beginning, and I seriously considered whether we should continue or not. However our [board of] directors feel that we must keep on and finish this experimental year. We expect things to be better after Boston, and I hear that the west coast business is much better than the east. Under the circumstances, I can tell you nothing of our future plans. Our directors will meet again at Christmas, and maybe I can tell you something further at that time.

The problem, of course, was the same as usual: the company was losing money every week, and there was nobody around willing and able to keep it going week after week except Lucia. Charlie Payne, out of the Navy now and back in New York, on the board of Ballet Theatre and working for a publicist, wrote Lucia, who was on tour with the company:

> In thinking over what you, Mr. Z. [Zuckert], and John Wharton have said, it seems to me you are faced with 3 distinct problems:

1) how to survive through April 1947;

2) how to carry on during the summer of 1947;

3) how to finance a 1947–48 season.

I feel confident Ballet Theatre will not operate at a loss during the 1947–48 season. However, plans must be made now and contracts signed. [The board] does not feel justified in making such plans and signing such contracts unless it knows that funds are available to meet all obligations and any possible losses. Ballet Theatre must have $100,000 to underwrite the summer and 47–48 season.

This was not the first time that Lucia had been confronted with the prospect of a deficit on the scale of $100,000 (equivalent in today's dollars to at least ten times as much, or over $1 million), although up to this point, the cash demands made on her usually did not come all at once in a giant lump sum but rather in a succession of lesser challenges, one every two or three weeks. Yet, however the deficits came, she was never quite willing to concede, even to herself, that she would, in the end, cover whatever amount was needed. At least this time, with the plain facts spelled out in advance, clearly something had to be done to try to reach a long-range solution.

"As I see it," Charlie Payne wrote early in the new year, "Ballet Theatre cannot avoid an annual deficit. You cannot continue to make up the deficit. Therefore Ballet Theatre needs financial aid."

Part of the problem was that, up to this point, there had never been a proper fund-raising vehicle in place, one that was set up to receive donations and in return could offer contributors a partial deduction on their federal income taxes. This was something that should have been instituted years earlier, back when it first became clear that Ballet Theatre would be obliged to raise outside funds in order to keep going. The absence of an approved 501 C3 nonprofit tax-exempt status was just another indication of the notably deficient business practices that had characterized the organization from the very beginning. Not until May 1947, when the Ballet Theatre Foundation was officially incorporated, would this particular oversight be corrected.

Meanwhile, on a different front, overtures were being made to Ballet Theatre to form an alliance with the Ballet Institute, an outside organization headed by Tom Fisher, a Chicago lawyer and husband of the choreographer Ruth Page. The Institute offered to raise $150,000 for Ballet Theatre, and in return, receive all of Ballet Theatre's assets, with the understanding that it would continue to lease these same assets back to Ballet Theatre for a nominal fee as long as the company remained in existence.

Lucia was understandably reluctant to enter into any such relationship that required handing over the sets and costumes of the entire Ballet Theatre repertory to an outside party. Another reason she was less than totally happy with the proposal was that the sum of money Ballet Institute was pledging to raise—$150,000—was not all that considerable, representing roughly the annual amounts Lucia had been contributing every year for each of the past seven years. And, most important, ultimately her instincts were lined up against ever relinquishing control of Ballet Theatre, her pride and joy, to any outside party, even though Tom Fisher took pains to claim he was on her side and working for her: "We believe in the policies followed by Lucia Chase and Oliver Smith," he wrote Ballet Theatre's board, "believe they have the knowledge, experience, and taste to direct a ballet company, and [we] are willing to give them financial assistance so they can keep Ballet Theatre alive and maintain it as the best, most progressive of the ballet companies."

But Fisher did feel that at least one big adjustment had to be made: "To raise the entire $150,000, it will undoubtedly be necessary to go out of the circle of ballet lovers, to approach public-spirited persons who up to now have had no particular interest in ballet. All the money you have raised thus far has been from balletomanes with a sentimental interest in ballet."

While this may have been largely true, it did not address the fundamental problem, which was that fund-raising had never been a principal concern of the Ballet Theatre organization. While there was always agreement that cash was desperately needed, there had been no concerted attempt to study how the deficit problem could be effectively addressed, no plan for a comprehensive fund-raising campaign, and no move to begin assembling an expert permanent staff to carry out the work. The idea of turning everything over to Tom Fisher and the Ballet Institute appeared to be just another of the haphazard solutions that sprang up whenever the company's finances became particularly desperate. At the root of it all was the fact that dealing with an acute ongoing financial problem requires granting the power to make tough decisions, and Lucia did not like the idea of giving anyone else the ability to decide exactly what should and should not be done.

Meanwhile, the company continued to undergo twenty-three solid weeks of touring, a great part of which consisted, as usual, of performing one-night stands. By the time the tour ended, the last week of April 1947, everyone was exhausted and in need of a rest. But two days after arriving back in New York, the company opened a three-week engagement at City Center.

This time there were no new productions scheduled, yet for once this didn't seem to matter: the public was just glad to welcome the company back. As explained by John Martin in the *New York Times:*

> Up to the end of last week, it looked as if the ballet around here was a dead duck, or at least a seriously sick one. The artistic accomplishments [of other attractions] have fallen to a new low, and there have been more empty seats at every company's performance than ever before. It looked like pernicious anemia on both sides of the footlights.
>
> Now Ballet Theatre has come back to town, and the whole situation has become suddenly brighter. This company, which managed to contribute its full share to the general debility in its fall season, has pulled itself into wonderful shape during its tour. . . . Whatever differences one may have with its behavior from time to time, there is no denying that it is a superb company, with great distinction of style, backed by substantial technical skill, personal pulchritude, and awareness of the theatre and a sense of artistic responsibility.

His review, while very complimentary to the new direction given the company, still had a few barbs for Lucia personally:

> Lucia Chase should not dance in *Sylphides, Pas de Quatre, Petrouchka*. To dance in the classic idiom simply for the fun of it, and to underestimate her genuine artistic contributions in such things as *Pillar, Three Virgins, Judgement, Tally-Ho*, is to exhibit a curious sense of values. Against the positive achievements and the general standards of the organization, these reservations are relatively unimportant. There would be reservations about a ballet company that came directly to us from the Elysian Fields. Ballet Theatre is unquestionably the nearest thing we have to such a company at the moment.

Another positive note: attendance, which at the Broadway Theatre in the fall had been only 55 percent of capacity, now six months later, in the considerably larger City Center, had increased to 75 percent.

Part of the improved attendance figures may have been due to the exceptionally low prices charged for tickets at City Center. Yet it was also painfully clear that City Center was not the elegant Metropolitan Opera House but rather, in Martin's words, "a makeshift theater, with a cramped and inadequate stage and no facilities whatever for creating the peculiar magic that makes the theater really a theatre."

In short, although Ballet Theatre had new direction, appeared to be dancing well, and had developed a loyal following of fans in New York, it still had the same old problems: too little money and no home of its own.

10. Ballet Theatre Closes Down

> Poor Lucia! She had his [Tudor's]
> threats, and they were major ones,
> for breakfast. She had my hysteria
> for lunch, and various stars' tantrums
> around the clock. And while we were
> rehearsing, she was struggling with
> the lawyers and bankers.
> —Agnes de Mille, writing in *Lizzie*
> *Borden: A Dance of Death*

IN THE NEW YORK theater world, the New Year does not start on January 1, or on July 1 like many fiscal years, but shortly after Labor Day, when summer vacations are over and the city gears up for the excitement of a new fall season. For Ballet Theatre, 1947–48 began when the company set out late in September on its sixth major U.S. tour in as many years. After eight weeks of performances in the Northeast and Midwest, the tour was interrupted at midpoint to allow for a four-week season at City Center.

There was every reason to expect that this return appearance at City Center would be a lackluster event. The grand eight-week engagement at Covent Garden in England back in the summer of 1946 was by now a distant memory, and the company's schedule since then had been grueling and almost unremitting: first, six weeks at the Broadway Theatre; then, two days after the closing, twenty-three weeks of touring under MCA's management all the way across the United States and back; then, arriving in New York, the company immediately began three weeks at City Center; ten days later, it went to Cuba for a week's engagement in Havana; then it set out in the fall for eight more weeks of touring before beginning, the very next day, this latest season at City Center.

Most of Ballet Theatre's performers were both young and in superb physical condition; otherwise, they could never have maintained this schedule. What was more remarkable was the way that Lucia, now fifty years old, kept up the same grueling pace. Perpetually cheerful and well dressed, she was among the first on the bus in the morning, working while she was traveling the entire day, often dancing in the night's performance, yet always ready to organize and lead the way to a private party given to honor Ballet Theatre after the evening performance. As far as anyone can remember, she never voiced a single word of fatigue or complaint.

Considering the schedule and touring conditions, the company's morale remained amazingly high and the quality of the performances still consistently impressive. Perhaps the biggest surprise came during the second week of the City Center season with the world premiere of *Theme and Variations,* choreographed by George Balanchine during one of the company's busiest stretches, a period when there was no spare time and dancers were rarely available for anything except emergency rehearsals. Yet Balanchine somehow managed to carve out, from September until its premiere on November 26, a major new work, a neoclassical ballet that was just what was needed in New York to show off the company and particularly the brilliant, ardent partnership of Alicia Alonso and Igor Youskevitch.

Despite its bland title, *Theme and Variations* was anything but dull. Quite the opposite, it was beautiful and exciting to watch, very challenging for the dancers and particularly the two leading principal dancers, an ideal work to open a program, perhaps even better as a closing number. Brought in at the last moment before the company left town in early September, Balanchine proved to be a wonderfully accommodating and efficient choreographer.

The speed with which he put together his new piece is particularly striking when compared with Jerome Robbins and Antony Tudor. One year earlier, when Robbins was creating *Facsimile* to premiere during the company's Broadway Theatre season, he required 138 hours of rehearsal to complete the 19-minute ballet, and even after being given all that time, he complained of being unfairly rushed. Tudor, a notoriously slow worker, sought and was given 52 hours of precious rehearsal time simply to polish up his ballet *Undertow*, which had already been in performance for most of the past year. In contrast, Balanchine, in September 1947, had only 7 hours with the company before it left on tour, yet he managed to complete the entire first movement, then rejoined the company in the middle of its fall tour, worked at spare moments whenever there were dancers available, and ultimately spent only 39 hours to complete the entire 32 minutes of *Theme and Variations*.

While the amount of time an artist spends to create a new work of any sort is ultimately immaterial, and the only thing that matters is the quality of the finished piece, in ballet the number of hours allotted to conceive a new work is a critical concern because, for most of the time that a ballet is being created, the choreographer requires the physical presence and collaboration of dancers in the studio. A composer doesn't need to have the musicians who are going to play his composition on hand to assist him as he writes his symphony or opera, nor does a playwright need actors to stand by: not only would that make the preliminary creative part of the process inordinately expensive, but just to have professional performers standing around waiting for their notes or words to be written so that they could begin learning their parts would impose a horrendous additional burden on the person doing the creating. But that is the condition under which a choreographer does his creative work and helps explain why creating a new ballet is particularly difficult and expensive. A further problem intrinsic to producing new ballets is that after they have been created, they are almost impossible to record in a permanent, accurate, relatively inexpensive format. As a result, even long-established dance works are easily forgotten or simply lost soon after they are not actually being performed.

As artistic director of the company, Lucia possessed a number of personal attributes that, time and again, would prove invaluable to Ballet Theatre. She had a commanding presence, was forceful yet likeable, had great energy, was resolutely optimistic, and never buckled in the face of adversity. Yet unlike other notable company directors–Balanchine, Robert Joffrey, Martha Graham, Paul Taylor, Merce Cunningham, Alvin Ailey–she was not artistically creative. Nor was she particularly good at discovering and attracting other artists, in the manner of Diaghilev or Ninette de Valois or Marie Rambert, and she had almost nothing illuminating or inspiring to say to authors, composers, painters, or even to choreographers. Left to her own dogged, strenuous, but essentially workaday talents, she was not equipped to keep coming up with the new works Ballet Theatre needed to produce. Her only hope was that others, particularly her colleague Oliver Smith, might do this commissioning work for her while she attended to all the other duties that went into running a company.

In the case of *Theme and Variations,* it was Max Goberman, Ballet Theatre's music director, who suggested combining the final movement of Tchaikovsky's Suite no. 3 with Balanchine as choreographer to give Ballet Theatre a classical ballet that would particularly show off the dancing skills of Igor Youskevitch. Unfortunately, in the years to come, there were not many such inspired suggestions from other outside sources, and the extended failure to produce a succession of fine new works to enrich the company's repertory would come to be the greatest single criticism leveled against Lucia Chase.

Besides new ballets, the other most critical need facing the company was to secure a working home for itself. New York was certainly Ballet Theatre's home base. It was also the one and only locale Lucia ever claimed as a permanent address. For her, as for most of the inhabitants of this greatest American metropolis, there is New York and then there is everywhere else. Although Connecticut-born and essentially a New Englander in terms of her upbringing and most of her values, she couldn't imagine either herself or her ballet company in residence anywhere else.

The word *home,* when applied to a ballet company, can mean several things. It can be a single building or several spaces. It can include the company's office, one or several dance studios, a place to store costumes and scenery, any or all of these, either grouped together or scattered around town. In the case of Ballet Theatre, a home ultimately meant a place where the company could count on performing once or twice a year in an appropriate setting for a significant number of weeks at a time.

This was a hard order to fill. To be a proper home for Ballet Theatre, a theater needed to have a big stage, a sizable orchestra pit, and also a seating capacity that conceivably could provide enough revenue to cover at least the company's immediate running costs.

The largest and most aesthetically appropriate space was unquestionably the Metropolitan Opera House. However, it was reserved for the Met Opera throughout its lengthy annual season, and all other times it was under lease to Hurok, who, after his battle with the company over *Firebird,* was not inclined to release it to Ballet Theatre, at least not for the time being.

The next best choice after the Met was New York's City Center on 55th Street. It did have an adequate orchestra pit and a considerably larger seating capacity than any other legitimate theater. However, the greatest number of seats were located upstairs in the two distant balconies above and beyond the dress circle. Also, since City Center was maintained by the city as a public theater, ticket prices were scaled down substantially, which meant that the potential gross revenue was seriously diminished.

City Center had two other shortcomings: the stage was quite small, with almost no extra space in the wings on either side; and the building (which was mosque in design and formerly known as Mecca Temple) was cavernous and rather drab, not a particularly inviting place to call home. Nevertheless, it existed and, despite its obvious faults, did offer several enticing features: ample studio space for rehearsal, extremely low-cost operating expenses, and a growing nucleus of enthusiastic theater-goers.

At one point, an invitation for Ballet Theatre to take up residence in City Center did come from Morton Baum, the canny lawyer and power figure in New York City affairs who served not only as special tax counsel to the city but also as the behind-the-scenes director of its public theater. If the decision had been left to someone other than Lucia Chase, Baum's offer might well have been accepted. (In fact, it was soon afterwards accepted by Lincoln Kirstein, who was seeking a performance outlet for Balanchine and assorted Ballet Society ventures that eventually developed into the New York City Ballet.) But Lucia loved the grandeur and all the trappings of the Met. She wanted the uplift that comes from entering a beautiful theater, even before the curtain goes up, whereas in City Center, she felt the architecture and interior did not enliven but, if anything, dampened the spirits of those entering the house.

From an emotional or aesthetic viewpoint, her rejection of Morton Baum's offer was understandable. However, in the next twelve months, the hard, cold realities of Ballet Theatre's restless rootless existence would make it practically impossible for the company to continue on in the same costly, exhausting, and ultimately unproductive way.

After closing at City Center on December 17, the company had one week off before setting out again on the second half of a five-month tour across the United States.

Lucia would rejoin it several days later in Chicago. Meanwhile, though, it was Christmas, and although she was prepared at all other times of the year to drop everything in order to be with the company, her two exceptions were Thanksgiving and Christmas, which she always tried to celebrate in Waterbury at Rose Hill.

She also made a special effort to make Christmas in her ancestral home seem the same as it had been since her childhood days: the same furnishings, pictures on the wall, carpets on the floor, the same familiar slightly musty smell, and, at least for Thanksgiving or Christmas, the house always filled with family, assorted Taft or Sheldon cousins, or whoever else in the family was around for the holidays.

Besides everyone staying in the house, which always included Tommy and me, Lucia's sister Dee, her husband, Edward Carmody, and their two children, Deirdre and Basil, would come from their house in nearby Middlebury; often one or more Sheldons, sometimes accompanied by a visiting friend or two from school or college; and, no matter who else, Dimitri Romanoff.

Like my mother, Dimitri Romanoff had been in the Mordkin Ballet back in the late 1930s. He went on to become regisseur at Ballet Theatre for the next forty years. Dimitri was like a member of the family, a kind and familiar face who came to Rose Hill every Thanksgiving and Christmas throughout my childhood and later on for the early years of my children's lives. His presence gave a Chekhovian quality to the entire setting, which otherwise might have been just a roomful of chattering Chases. Dimitri would sit quietly with his glass of vodka, a little outside the central hubbub, happy to talk to anyone who came up but otherwise a calm presence almost from another world, in contrast to my mother, who never sat still but scooted about the living room, talking to everyone, pausing only to check that lunch was being readied in the kitchen and that everything was proceeding on schedule.

When the big moment came and my mother would announce that lunch was ready, invariably Dimitri, from his chair, would call out, almost plaintively, "Looshia, please could I have another vodka?" at which point she would check herself, a little startled but perfectly willing, and cheerfully answer, "Why, of course, Dimitri," and hurry to refill his glass. Then he and everyone else would stand up and go into lunch.

The annual Chase family party took place the day after Christmas. Late in the afternoon, car after car would drive up the steep driveway from Prospect Street, stop under the porte- cochere by the front door to let everyone out, then pull ahead to park out on the lawn. Sometimes as many as 100 relatives from all over New York and New England would pile into Rose Hill. It was like a living version of the first act of *Nutcracker,* the arrivals all freshly scrubbed, beautifully dressed, and excited to be seeing each other. Inside, in the midst of the hubbub and din, Popsie–"Uncle Irving" to most of the family–could be counted on to be sitting in his chair in the living room, and at the appointed time everyone would crowd around, children on the floor at his feet, watching as he would take out the little gold music box with the tiny jeweled bird inside, carefully wind it up, and press a switch, at which point the top opened and the bird would twitter and turn from side to side, beating its wings until suddenly it stopped and the top would snap down.

"Tweet tweet kaboom," Popsie never failed to say, explaining how that was what little Tommy Ewing once said at the age of three, and my brother's words were repeated religiously every year from then on whenever the box with the little bird was brought out.

There were also various games going on in different rooms, always a Blind Man's Bluff and a fiercely contested Charades, constant food streaming out from the kitchen, carols at the piano, lots of running around and screaming, gently controlled bedlam. And presiding over it all, was Lucia–"Lolo" to her immediate nieces and nephews, "Aunt Lucia" to all the rest–the cheery hostess on her home stage, laughing, talking, spilling the latest news about Ballet Theatre to young and old alike who listened breathlessly with eager faces and admiring eyes, year after year the same scene inside Rose Hill at the Chase family Christmas party.

⊙

The company began 1948 with two weeks in Chicago, then remained out on the road for eleven more weeks of touring. All-engrossing as this was, the tour was only a preamble to April, when Ballet Theatre miraculously managed to schedule a full month of performances for itself at the Met.

Hurok still held the lease. Yet this one time, his ability to seek out and sign other dance attractions to perform at the Met ran out, and Lucia's fondest hope of performing again in New York's grandest setting suddenly materialized. For the company to be on its own and to present itself at the Met constituted a huge challenge, particularly coming as it did at the end of two years of unremitting travel and performance, but Lucia didn't hesitate to take the gamble.

One thing was certain: for such a momentous engagement in such a mammoth auditorium, the company would have to present at least two compelling new works. Never an innovator, Lucia hardly reached out at all. She called on Ballet Theatre's two principal in-house choreographers–Antony Tudor and Agnes de Mille–to create, each one, a major new work.

Of the two, Tudor was unquestionably the most distinguished, with a matchless series of notable ballets–*Pillar of Fire, Jardin aux Lilas, Judgment of Paris, Dark Elegies, Gala Performance, Romeo and Juliet, Undertow*–all still part of Ballet Theatre's active repertory. From his newly appointed position as artistic administrator, Tudor had the inside track when it came to asserting his priority as a choreographer, and once again he demanded an inordinate amount of rehearsal time for a new ballet, *Shadow of the Wind.*

From the outset, Tudor's latest work was conceived in big terms, with music from one of Mahler's most moving scores, *Das Lied von der Erde,* scenery and costumes by Broadway designer Jo Melziner; and a glittering cast that included most of Ballet Theatre's stars, including Alonso and Youskevitch, Hugh Laing, John Kriza, Diana Adams, Nana Gollner, Dimitri Romanoff, and Ruth Ann Koesun. Tudor was known to be an extremely slow worker, and for *Shadow* he demanded more time with the dancers than ever, an astonishing total of 358 hours, most of them crammed into the busy tour days between January and the world premiere on April 14, 1948.

The ballet imposed a horrific drain on Ballet Theatre's already strained resources. Mahler's score required a full symphony orchestra, considerably more than the company's usual number of forty musicians, plus vocal soloists. It also used practically the entire roster of dancers, which meant scores of costumes. Although it is impossible now to assess exactly, it reputedly cost more than any previously attempted new work for Ballet Theatre and if attempted today would constitute somewhere close to $1 million. While there were several beautiful passages in it, it was probably too complex and ahead of its time. The audience never warmed to it, and for the entire five-week Met season, *Shadow of the Wind* was performed only five times, the last of which was for an audience that only occupied 24 percent of the house.

The other featured new work fared much better. Agnes de Mille, with her unerring instinct for the dramatic, had picked for her subject the story of Lizzie Borden, the New England spinster who, in 1892, reputedly "took an axe, And gave her mother forty whacks; When she saw what she had done, She gave her father forty-one." Staging the complex action was difficult, and there were innumerable problems getting it ready on time for its premiere, which was scheduled for April 22. As de Mille put it:

I was to have three weeks to mount a fifty-minute work. Simultaneously, Antony Tudor was to rehearse a sixty-one-minute magnum opus to Mahler's *Lied von der Erde.* It was hoped he would have a lot of it done on the road, since he was traveling with them.

On the return, we were to work morning, noon, and night, using the same dancers but staggering their time. There were not to be three hours' margin for choreographic hesitation or creative mistake. There were to be two hours of lighting, costume, scenery, and orchestra rehearsal for each work. We were to open cold in New York at the Metropolitan Opera House, with the entire New York press assembled and a first-night full-dress ballet audience.

Because of the exceedingly tight schedule, de Mille recruited a group of dancers from her Broadway shows and began actually choreographing on them while Ballet Theatre was still out on tour. Dania Krupska, who had been the leading dancer in the road show of *Oklahoma!,* worked with de Mille on the principal role of Lizzie Borden until the company returned, at which point the part was handed over to Nora Kaye.

The entire production evolved spasmodically under the enormous pressure of having too much to accomplish in much too little time. Morton Gould had only a couple of weeks to finish composing the original score. Oliver Smith's marvelously ingenious set, one side of which was Lizzie Borden's house and the back side a New England church, all against a lurid backdrop of a bloody rug and three chairs floating under clouds, had to be painted and constructed in a matter of days. Meanwhile, Tudor was taking a disproportionate amount of the available rehearsal time, monopolizing many of the dancers who were cast in both new works. Despite all this, de Mille's ballet was nearing conclusion with only one week still to go when Nora Kaye, who was cast in the horrendously challenging lead role of Lizzie Borden, fell deathly sick with viral pneumonia and was rushed to the hospital.

There was no possibility of her recovering in time to dance the opening night as scheduled. The only question was whether or not the premiere would now have to be pushed back to a later date, possibly even to another season. Lucia declared that any postponement was out of the question: *Fall River Legend* had been programmed to open April 22, people had bought tickets believing that was what they would be seeing that night, and so they would. After very heated bickering, it was decided that Lizzie's role would be performed by Alicia Alonso (who also had a major part in *Shadow of the Wind*); that Dania Krupska, to compensate her for all her heroic work, would be given the opportunity to dance one performance the following week; and now would everyone, including de Mille, please stop disputing and work together to get the show on.

Alonso did the seemingly impossible, not only somehow learning and managing to get through the entire fifty minutes that Lizzie Borden was on stage but, according to most observers, including de Mille, also dancing brilliantly. The following day in the *New York Times,* John Martin began his review, "To come to the point at once, Ballet Theatre has a new hit on its hands."

Fall River was not a tumultuous crowd-pleaser as *Fancy Free* had been, but artistically it was one of the few truly successful original creations commissioned by Ballet Theatre in the course of the company's early career. It also established the reputation of Nora Kaye (once she recovered in a couple of weeks and assumed the leading role) as being the outstanding dramatic ballerina of her time. To quote de Mille regarding Nora Kaye's performance:

> Without seeming to move, with the barest turn of a hand, with the lowering of her eyes, great emotional chasms were revealed, the terrible progress from fear to fear, to helpless remorse, and the most heartbreaking of all human experiences, the acceptance of doom. . . . Nora was a woman in agony and helpless. In the scene with the dead mother, as she began the repetitive head-shaking, crushing from her unclosing eyes tears of blood, I began to cry, and as her hands moved in the idiot compulsions of despair, I put my handkerchief up to stifle sobs–I, who had watched all this every day for three months. Her Lizzie was century, and everyone knew it. The applause rolled to her feet like the seas, and it was to do this around the world for fourteen years.

Besides the change of Nora Kaye in place of Alonso, a second major switch in the original cast was made later on. The role of Abby Borden, Lizzie's domineering stepmother, originally danced by Muriel Bentley, was given to Lucia, whose performance, according to de Mille, was "hideously believable."

Bentley had played the woman's eccentricities; Lucia played her normalcy, and this turned out to be the more frightening approach because for one thing, she was so usual. One could meet her on every fifth porch in New England. One felt she would, with the best intention, take over the earth, like moss when life had stopped. Against such suffocating reasonableness, one longed for insanity: it seemed Lizzie's only path.

With Lucia's characterization, the ballet was to take on another dimension. Lucia has missed only two performances in seventeen years. There is always nominally an understudy, but the opportunity is not embraced with any great expectancy. It is Lucia's role, and I hope it will always be. Young dancers who can whirl and levitate and twitter on toe take one good look at the woman who cannot and their blood freezes, because she brings to the stage a power not learned at the barre, a power they cannot hope to evoke.

Fall River Legend, along with the dancing of Alonso and Youskevitch, was the high-water mark of the 1948 Met season, the long-anticipated engagement that hopefully would set Ballet Theatre on a new pedestal of artistic eminence and financial stability.

The company did succeed quite well with the first of these two goals. But regarding the second, the five weeks at the Met were a financial disaster. For assorted reasons, audiences throughout the five weeks were devastatingly small: overall total attendance for the first time fell below the 50 percent mark, to only 47 percent of capacity. Only on three Saturday nights did the company come close to selling out.

By the end of the Met season, the financial condition of the company was beyond perilous, which it had often been before. This time, the fiscal problems that loomed on the immediate horizon appeared insurmountable, considerably more than Lucia, who was still the principal source of rescue funds, could possibly provide. The only fortunate element in the otherwise dire picture was that, unlike other years when new contracts with all the dancers would have been negotiated during the course of the spring season, this time, because of an unresolved controversy between Alicia Alonso and Nora Kaye over which one was to be given the top billing for the following year, neither of them nor any other of the principal dancers in the company had as yet been signed to new contracts. Similarly, arrangements for a fall season, which had been tentatively booked at City Center and for a subsequent national tour, were both deemed to be nonbinding, so it was possible to cancel them and temporarily lay off the company without risking an additional financial penalty.

Accordingly, in July, an official letter on Ballet Theatre stationery was sent out to the entire company. "Dear _____," it began:

> I want to let you know immediately of the decision reached today on Ballet Theatre's fall season. Together we have built Ballet Theatre into the best ballet company in America, but in the process we have discovered that it cannot operate at its best without substantial preliminary financing. After the last season, both the directors of Ballet Theatre and the Governing Trustees of Ballet Theatre Foundation decided that performances should not be resumed until enough money had been raised to assure permanence and strength to Ballet Theatre. Since we closed at the Metropolitan, we have concentrated on raising the necessary funds but have found that this is taking longer than we anticipated. We all feel that sufficient money can be raised by January 1st to permit the resumption of operations at that time. I hoped until the last minute that it would be possible to keep to our October schedule and assure you that I have done my utmost, realizing how much it means to you. I have every confidence that this comparatively short delay will result in a healthier and stronger Ballet Theatre. I cannot thank you enough for your wonderful loyalty, and I hope that when we start forth again it will be possible for you to be with us.
>
> If there is anything that I can do to help you find something in the meantime, I shall be only too happy to do anything I can.
> Lucia

Part 3

11. Troubles with the IRS

It is an axiom that a ballet company's character is determined by the personality of its director. However many collaborators Miss Chase may have on paper, Ballet Theatre is and will remain her baby. . . . She pays the piper, and the organization will dance to her melody.

—Sol Hurok

THE NEWS THAT the company was closing down, at least for the remainder of 1948, came as a devastating shock to the dancers. Ballet Theatre was not just their place of work and their livelihood but in many ways was more like a home than any apartment they might temporarily return to when they weren't out on tour. They had sacrificed so much to become professional dancers, and now, at this stage in their lives, there was no other field readily available that held out the prospect of decent immediate employment, much less any sense of personal fulfillment.

Although there was the possibility that the company would start up again in six months after the first of the year, most were obliged to scramble to find another paying job as quickly as possible. The sooner the company was back in business, the more members would be likely to return, but there would inevitably be some who would have taken jobs in the interim that they couldn't abruptly leave, and their places would have to be given to newcomers. If there were a considerable number of them, the preliminary rehearsal period would have to be much longer and more expensive than usual.

Apart from the money issue, a long layoff could create a problem of resurrecting certain ballets in the repertory. Choreographers are often not particularly good at remembering their own works, and most ballets rely on the memory of dancers to remain intact and be passed on. The longer a work goes unperformed, the harder it is to find people who remember exactly how it had proceeded, from beginning to end.

Lucia recognized all this, yet she had encountered a personal financial problem. Only Harry Zuckert and John Wharton, her lawyers and close confidants, had any clear idea of how much money she had been putting into Ballet Theatre over the years. They also were the only members of Lucia's inner circle of family, friends, and professional associates who knew that she was currently involved in major litigation brought by the Internal Revenue Service for the "loans" or business losses to Ballet Theatre which she had claimed on her annual income tax returns.

The issue originated in 1937–39, the last three years of the Mordkin Ballet, when Lucia had reportedly spent in the neighborhood of $500,000 overall in support of Mordkin's company. On her personal tax returns for these years, she did not claim the entire amount as deductions against her income but only about 60 percent, or some $300,000. Since these original filings, she had continued to claim deductions each year for her contributions to Ballet Theatre, a practice that the IRS had consistently disputed. However, each time the question came up, a formal court hearing had been postponed–until October 1946, when the deductions Lucia had claimed for the years 1939, 1940, and 1941 were contested in U.S. Tax Court.

After hearing arguments from both sides, the verdict in this initial encounter was that the deductions should be allowed, although the judge found that the case presented "a most unusual picture to say the least":

A woman, who is herself a danseuse working for a company at a salary of $75 a week, had advanced to a corporation for the promotion and development of the ballet in America a sum considerably in excess of $400,000 in three years. . . . Such disposition of money could only be accounted for on the basis of an abnormal and excessive enthusiasm for the object of the loan and an exceptionally optimistic belief in the value of the project for which the loan was made.

Yet the judge concluded that, however ill-advised and indefensible the monetary advances might appear to be from a business point of view, the government's claim that they were patently imprudent investments in an obviously unprofitable venture was not relevant. The only material question was whether the person advancing the money thought at the time that there was a good possibility of being repaid.

Looking back now over half a century later at this initial period in Ballet Theatre's history when the company kept producing deficits that steadily increased year after year, it is difficult to imagine how Lucia could have continued to think that the company might ever show a profit and be able to pay back at least some of her money. Yet that was what she claimed, and her testimony at the time, delivered under oath, still rings true:

(Question): Will you tell the Court reasons you thought you would make a profit?

(Lucia): This was the first large American company of ballet performing in this country. Foreign companies were well known, and ballet was very popular in the foreign countries. I felt sure, as many others did, that this company would draw a big public and be very successful.

(Question): Did you pin your hope of profit on the Hurok contract?

(Lucia): Very much. Mr. Hurok had always been known for taking successful ventures. We had great faith that just the fact of Hurok's making the contract—that in his opinion it would be a success—meant it would be a successful venture.

(Question): What in general did Mr. Pleasant tell you about the prospects of profit?

(Lucia): Mr. Pleasant was very hopeful. He was very confident of profit in the first season of 1940.

(Question): Did he tell you that?

(Lucia): Yes, indeed.

(Question): Did that influence you?

(Lucia) Oh, yes. I wouldn't have gone into it if he hadn't thought there would be a profit. Mr. Payne also had worked on budgets and estimates, and he also was hopeful there would be a profit.

(Question): Who was your legal advisor?

(Lucia): Mr. John F. Wharton.

(Question): Did you have any conversations with Mr. Wharton?

(Lucia): Yes, I had many. Mr. Wharton believed also we would make a profit in that year.

(Question): Is that what he said to you?

(Lucia) Yes.

(Question): Has Mr. Wharton any particular experience in connection with the theater?

(Lucia): I don't know of any lawyer who has any more experience than Mr. Wharton.

The jury concluded unanimously in Lucia's favor, ruling that her advances to Ballet Theatre were bona fide loans or short-term investments, no different from those of anyone who invested in Broadway theater ventures: as long as the person doing the investing thought there was a chance that the show (or in this case, the ballet company) could in time become financially self-sustaining, the deductions were deemed legitimate. This favorable judgment was a great relief to Lucia, who otherwise would have been required to make very considerable back payments plus interest on the tax returns she had submitted five to seven years earlier.

However, that initial decision represented only the opening phase of an ongoing dispute with the Internal Revenue Service. Still to come up were the tax returns and deductions made from 1942 to 1948, all of which continued to be rigorously examined and contested by the IRS. During this period, the cash advances to Ballet Theatre that Lucia had been called on to make had increased in size and frequency, averaging close to $300,000 for each of the three most recent years, the period 1946–48, when the company had broken with Hurok and operated under the direction of Lucia Chase and Oliver Smith.

The entire tax case was bound to come up again. Lucia's position had become particularly difficult to defend, since the constant and ever-increasing deficits made the likelihood of repayment seem more and more implausible. There was good reason to believe that the next hearing, covering much greater amounts, might cause the court to rule against her and could result in a huge penalty payment, including interest on tax returns going all the way back to 1941. This was the main reason that Lucia felt she had no choice, at least in the near future, but to lay the company off and in the interim hope for the best.

The biggest reason for her to have hope took the form of Blevins Davis, an exuberant, well-connected, and ostensibly wealthy native of Kansas City who had just come breezing into the small closed business world of Ballet Theatre like a whirlwind out of the Midwest.

Several years earlier, Davis had married the widow of the grandson of James Hill, founder of the Great Northern Railroad. Davis also had other important connections, as he was not in the least reluctant to admit. Back when he worked as a high school superintendent in Independence, Missouri, he had become a close friend of Bess Truman, wife of Harry S. Truman. Later on, when Davis was scheduled to be married, Truman had been elected president of the United States, and the Davis wedding took place in Washington, followed by a dinner at the White House.

Since then, Blevins Davis had gained considerable renown in theatrical circles when he organized, presented, and paid for a notable production of *Hamlet* at Elsinore Castle in Denmark. And just before that, he had almost single-handedly arranged a major tour throughout Europe of Gershwin's monumental *Porgy and Bess,* somehow managing to get the U.S. Army Air Force to take care of transporting the company and all its extravagant scenery and costumes.

A big man, physically hefty, massive, and fleshy without being fat, full of energy and constantly talking in a high-pitched, somewhat effeminate but always forceful tone of voice, Davis was an undeniable presence. His ideas were as big as his physique. One example was his vision of establishing a "university of the world" somewhere in Kansas. According to this bold and extravagant concept, each campus building was to be devoted to a particular country, with only that nation's native language allowed to be spoken, that country's food served in the dining room, and all classes devoted exclusively to that land's history and literature and culture. The governing idea was to offer students a complete immersion in the geographical locale of their choice, as though they were not in Kansas but actually living in the foreign country. Such a university of the world was an intellectual breakthrough in the field of education back in the years just following World War II.

Now, in 1947, practically out of nowhere, this genial titan had catapulted himself onto the New York scene, openly professing a keen interest in promoting the fortunes of Ballet Theatre. He was quickly elected a governing trustee, and the following year—when the company was just entering what was probably its most critical financial season ever—Davis was promising Lucia he could raise $100,000, either with his own money or through others he knew. He also was convinced he could arrange a European tour for the company along the lines of what he had done for *Porgy and Bess,* again assuming complete financial responsibility.

On top of all this, he had a third prize to offer. While in Denmark with *Hamlet,* he had seen a young dancer named Erik Bruhn who was on the verge of becoming a star in the Danish Royal Ballet. Going backstage to meet Bruhn, Davis had been utterly captivated by him and had invited him on the spot to come perform in America. In the next couple of weeks, he managed to persuade Lucia to draw up a contract for Bruhn and straightway returned to Europe where, without any prior assurance that Bruhn would be coming to Paris, he left the signed contract waiting at his hotel in Paris for Bruhn to pick up on the chance that he might happen to be passing through. By an amazing twist of fortune, Bruhn soon did exactly that. A few days later, Davis arranged to bring the budding Danish star back with him across the Atlantic, a beautifully trained and tremendous new talent all signed, sealed, delivered, and ready to perform as soon as Ballet Theatre was back in operation.

To Lucia, Blevins Davis seemed almost unreal. He was so confident that anything was possible. Whenever she talked about him and his ideas to others, she prefaced her remarks with a disbelieving little chuckle, as though recognizing that no one could be so foolish as to accept all that Davis said, and yet she so desperately wanted to believe him. Here, certainly, was a reason for anticipating the "substantial preliminary financing" that, in her letter to Ballet Theatre's dancers, she had said was essential for the resumption of the company. If only a part of what Davis claimed to be able to do were true, that was already considerably more than anyone else had ever offered.

Meanwhile, others at Ballet Theatre were doing what they could to bring the company back. As noted in the latest Ballet Theatre souvenir program, "In 1947, a group of men and women deeply interested in the future of the arts in America organized a foundation whose aim is to establish ballet as a permanent institution in the cultural life of this country."

This was not the first time a new organization had been formed to help deal with the company's financial plight. Starting with Advanced Arts Ballet when the company was first formed in 1940, there had been Ballet Associates, Ballet Presentations, High Time Promotions, Hillbright Enterprises Inc., Ballet Theatre Inc., and now this new instrument, Ballet Theatre Foundation Inc. The one signal difference between this one and all its predecessors was that, as a duly authorized nonprofit tax-exempt foundation, it offered donors the opportunity to write off their contributions to Ballet Theatre as charitable deductions, instead of relying on the "loan" category that Lucia had employed, which was now in jeopardy of being overruled by the IRS.

Otherwise, the basic fiscal plight of the company remained the same, including what was ironically perhaps the principal problem, Lucia Chase herself. As long as Lucia headed up the company and remained apparently willing, however reluctantly, to pay for any deficit, others were inclined to leave the big financial problem to her. Consequently, although she continued to talk endlessly about wanting to get people to help, up to this point nobody had been employed at Ballet Theatre's office to organize and direct fund-raising efforts, nor had any steps been taken to establish a budget or recruit a staff to do the massive amount of work such an objective entailed. The board of governing trustees was expanded slightly from nine to twelve and now included some powerful moneyed names, such as A. Conger Goodyear, Mrs. S. Hallock du Pont, and Dwight Deere Wiman, but whether they would take much responsibility for turning the company's fortunes around was extremely problematical.

A statement by Lucia and Oliver, as administrative directors, in the new Ballet Theatre souvenir program under the heading "Tenth Anniversary Season 1949" covered all that at the time could truthfully be said:

> Prospects for financial security in the near future are bright as Blevins Davis, President of the Ballet Theatre Foundation, is determined that, through the Foundation, the company eventually shall be established as a non-profit but financially self-sufficient organization.

Whether or not this would actually happen was anyone's bet. Only time would tell.

⟶

Between the layoff in June 1948 and early 1949, when there was no company and little positive to hold onto, the absolutely vital ingredient that Lucia provided was her fierce insistence that Ballet Theatre not be left to die. She had promised the dancers, in writing, signed with her name, that they would be invited back by the start of the new year, and according to her particular set of beliefs and the way she was brought up, she would be *nada*–no good, worthless as a human being–if she did not somehow manage to keep her word. Others might term this hopelessly old-fashioned, nothing more than sheer stubborn selfish New England pride. No matter, she was not going to give in or give up.

It was a depressing and scary time for her: suddenly no company to be with or even to be briefly away from, no emergencies to overcome, no stormy confrontations in the office, no long bus rides, no cheering audiences or parties after a performance, no standing in the wings in full costume waiting to go onstage . . . no anything.

She rarely mentioned the layoff and gave no hint that all was not well. Instead, she was eager to pass on glowing reports to anyone who expressed the slightest interest. "Gracious, the way everyone danced last season at the Met–Igor and Alicia, of course, and our wonderful Johnny Kriza, and Nora in *Fall River Legend,* you just have to come see it"–the same words came bubbling out to everyone she encountered or who crossed her path. Lucia lobbied them all. To this lady of the theater, keeping up appearances and putting on a good show were as important in everyday life as performing a role onstage.

"Like New England granite," Agnes de Mille used to say of her. Once Lucia took a position, she never conceded an inch, and her message never varied or wavered. Yet that summer, spent in Narragansett as usual, behind the scenes–whenever she was out of sight or earshot, which meant the better part of each morning or midafternoon when everyone else was out of the house–she was either on the phone or at her desk, calling Florence Pettan or John Onysko, the two stalwarts at the office in New York, to find out what was going on, who had called, and if they had any news from any of the dancers. Often there would be long conversations with Oliver, if and when she could reach him: best with Oliver not to try too early in the morning. Or John Wharton or Charlie Payne. The phone was kept busy from shortly after breakfast until she rushed out of the house at the last minute to join her family and guests down at the beach.

There are no traces of the countless phone calls she made, but they were virtually all connected with Ballet Theatre and little else. The little pile of letters that went out every day, handwritten in her neat St. Margaret's School script, were sent without any copies that could be uncovered later, either at home or at the office. One might imagine that another woman in her place could have spent a good deal of her time at the hairdresser or shopping or reading books, except that Lucia rarely did any of these, nor did she indulge in any other pastime. Instead, she focused on the problem of reviving Ballet Theatre, working all by herself, without much of a system and to a large degree ineffectively. Yet she kept at it. I know, because having just graduated from St. Paul's School in New Hampshire and about to enter Yale University in the fall, I was in and out of the house various times throughout that summer.

And, in time, little things did start to happen. An old friend she had written might send back a check, $100 or occasionally maybe even $1,000. Now and then a new contact was persuaded to join the board of governing trustees. And then there was Blevins Davis, running back and forth between Kansas and New York and Washington, totally unpredictable, popping up like a gigantic bunny out of a hole with another of his brainstorms or startling bulletins. The European tour he had promised might have to be delayed for a year, but not to worry, thanks to his special connections with the Air Force, he was sure he could arrange it. Also, Lucia could count on some money next year, either from him or a few of his good friends. Everything was going to work out fine.

Months later, back in New York, enough had come together that it seemed she might soon be able to keep her word. One by one, the members of the board of the Ballet Theatre Foundation had managed to attract an initial hardy set of "associate trustees," individuals who were willing to give or pledge $1,000 or more, so that the total now was close to $20,000. There were also some sixty "founder members" who had given $100 or more. This still wasn't the "substantial preliminary financing" Lucia had cited in her letter as being essential to the company's reopening, but at least it marked a distinct improvement over last July.

Time was becoming a critical factor. The longer the delay, the greater the risk of losing dancers who were standing by, waiting to be called back. Midway through the fall, just when it was starting to become a question of now or never, the word went out: come the New Year, Ballet Theatre would be starting up again, so would all company members please contact the office for more information about the upcoming season.

"I hope that when we start forth again, it will be possible for you to be with us," Lucia had written in her letter to the company dancers. What happened was more than even a dyed-in-the-wool optimist like Lucia could have reasonably expected. Except for Alicia Alonso and her husband, Fernando, who returned to their native Cuba to start what would become a national ballet company, and Maria Karnilova, who was snatched up by a Broadway show, all the other leading dancers returned—fifteen out of eighteen! Along with them came fifteen other members of the old company, making thirty in all who, on short notice, found their way back to Ballet Theatre.

Even with this tremendous return, the amount of work involved in preparing a respectable repertory for three weeks at the Metropolitan Opera House was enormous. So were the expenses. Rehearsing the twenty-four separate works and twenty-two new dancers; getting all the costumes out of storage and having them cleaned, refitted, and repaired; dealing with scenery, music, and lights; churning out reams of publicity and advertising to alert the public that Ballet Theatre was back: in many ways, reorganizing was tantamount to starting fresh all over again, only much faster.

There was no time, or money, to attempt a new work or two for the Met season, which was scheduled for April. Just the return of the company would have to be excitement enough. However, the loss of Alicia Alonso couldn't be brushed over, and finding another recognized ballerina to go alongside Nora Kaye and Nana Gollner was imperative. The problem was covered by signing Maria Tallchief (in private life the wife of George Balanchine), who had been five years with the Ballet Russe de Monte Carlo and most recently with Ballet Society, forerunner of the New York City Ballet.

The company mood was euphoric. After a short tour as a sort of warm-up, for everyone to be back together again in New York, dancing at the Met, with talk of a gala tenth anniversary season next year, also possibly a big European tour, there was excitement in the air which carried out over the footlights into the audience.

When it was still midseason, John Martin wrote:

After its year of dispersal, it is not in its most poised or stable state. Its ensemble is not yet as strong as it should be, (and any company is only as good as its corps de ballet), the repertoire is without novelties.

Yet whether it has been thoroughly reassembled or not, it is still the most rewarding of all ballet companies to watch. It has wonderful artists, beautiful taste, a style all its own, and a genuine desire to carry on its high tradition and be something. Just to see John Kriza and Harold Lang along with Muriel Bentley and Janet Reed together again onstage in *Fancy Free*, Nora Kaye and Tudor and Hugh Laing in *Pillar of Fire*, Igor Youskevitch (probably the greatest Albrecht of our days) in *Giselle,* was to know that Ballet Theatre was back on its feet.

And then, to his great credit, Martin ended his review recognizing one man who, along with Lucia, had been in Ballet Theatre (and the Mordkin Ballet before that) longer than any member of the company, and who, as regisseur for the past eight years, had the titanic responsibility of maintaining the company's repertory:

> Dimitri Romanoff should, one of these nights, be brought on stage at the end of a performance and crowned with laurels, for nobody works harder and gets less recognition for it.

It was a short and simple tribute, yet it was not offered in an offhand manner but rightly commemorated one person's extraordinary service whose loyalty, phenomenal memory, and artistic taste left an indelible mark in the history of Ballet Theatre.

After its successful rebound at the Met, the company had to keep moving just to stay in existence, which meant making another national tour as soon as possible. This one began in November and continued on to the end of March 1950, nearly eighteen consecutive weeks, a killer pace that was bound to take its toll on both dancers and productions.

The climax of this gargantuan effort was ending up with another big season in New York, especially since the spring of 1950 represented the tenth anniversary of Ballet Theatre, which called for a special celebration. Yet Hurok still held first option on the Met whenever it was not being used by the opera company, and he had booked the Ballet Russe to perform there for the entire month of April, knocking out any hopes Ballet Theatre had of performing at the grand and venerable opera house. Dwight Deere Wiman, the prominent theatrical producer and member of Ballet Theatre's board whose major contribution of $25,000 the previous year had helped bring the company back into existence, suggested booking the Winter Garden Theatre in direct competition with Hurok and the Ballet Russe. But after much talk back and forth, in the end the Winter Garden proved not to be available.

There was one other intriguing possibility: the old Center Theatre at Rockefeller Center, which ten years earlier had served as the birthplace of Ballet Theatre. The Center Theatre had since then been reconstructed to provide for presentations of ice skating, and part of the rink extended past the orchestra pit out into the first few rows of seats. Still, it was workable and practically the only solution to the theater problem. Consequently, it was booked for three weeks, beginning in late April, and the hectic work began to make a blockbuster season featuring four new works, including another by Antony Tudor entitled *Nimbus.*

Whether it was attempting too much, had too little time, not enough money, or a combination of all three, the tenth anniversary season of Ballet Theatre was not a great success. Two of the new works, *Caprichos* by Herbert Ross and *Designs with Strings* by John Taras, did enter the company repertory, but Tudor's ballet, the last one he was to create for Ballet Theatre for the next twenty-one years, did not. The critical judgment on the whole engagement was generally not favorable, and in some quarters it was distinctly negative. According to *Dance News,* "The tenth season was singularly dull, uninspiring, cold," while another critic accused Ballet Theatre of having allowed the classic works in its repertory to slide into neglect. Only twelve months after its return to operations, it appeared that the company was heading back into a troubled state again.

It was about to experience a powerful antidote. Blevins Davis, newly elected president of the Foundation board, had been good to his word about arranging a foreign tour for the company, and he had persuaded the State Department to lend its cooperation and provide the transportation overseas. The result was an unprecedented government-sponsored tour of seven European countries–Germany, England, Switzerland, Italy, Holland, Brussels, and France–and the Edinburgh Festival. While officially presented under the auspices of the U.S. Cultural Exchange Program and with the sponsorship of the American National Theatre and Academy (ANTA), it was Davis who guaranteed the tour and ultimately picked up most of its uncovered costs.

This was the first of a series of official expeditions outside the country that Ballet Theatre was to make in years to come. They were all memorable events, particularly for the dancers, many of whom had never been outside the United States before. They were also extraordinary because they all seemed to be highlighted by unforeseen and highly dramatic incidents. According to soloist (and later principal dancer) Ruth Ann Koesun, Ballet Theatre in time was nicknamed the "powder-keg company" because it became involved in so many international crises, none of which were its own doing but all of which directly affected, and in some cases seriously threatened, not just the company's well-being but its very existence.

This first European tour in 1950 established the pattern. In June, only a few weeks before the company's scheduled departure, the Korean War broke out. Although the Air Force had officially agreed to provide the transatlantic travel, suddenly all government planes were diverted to the Pacific. The company took off instead on a commercial flight to Brussels, then proceeded on to Frankfurt where army buses transported them to Wiesbaden for their first performances. When it came time a few days later to fly behind the Iron Curtain to Berlin, an outpost city occupied by the four Allied powers, the approach into Tempelhof Airport had to be made through "the corridor," a narrow strip between Russian gun emplacements. The Russian government, in order to prevent spying on the surrounding sector that it controlled, required all arriving flights to come in at a frighteningly low altitude, and the dancers were told to don heavy parachutes for the flight into Berlin.

As recounted by Charles Payne, then editor and publisher of the *Ballet Theatre Annual*, the company was flown "in a transport plane equipped with bucket seats suspended from the inner walls, with parachute tracks leading to the escape hatches." Understandably, everything was much less formal than a standard commercial flight. The pilot even invited the dancers to visit the cockpit a few at a time, and at one point Nora Kaye emerged from up front, greenish-white in the face, to scream back at the others, "Do you know who's flying this plane? Alicia Alonso! Do something about it!"

After a matinee and an evening performance in Berlin and a night spent in the Air Force barracks, the company flew back to Frankfurt and then went on to perform for the next four months throughout Europe. For Lucia, besides the pleasure of seeing her sister E.I. in London, another particularly welcome part of the tour was the week in Paris where the reaction of the sophisticated audience at the Palais de Chaillot was as enthusiastic as the one the company had received at Covent Garden four years earlier: "It is an absolutely remarkable company," reported *Le Presse*. "It is impossible to imagine a troupe of fifty dancers with more poise, more distinction, and more perfect technique."

It would have been best if the tour had ended then and there, but it was scheduled to return to Berlin to perform for three days at the Titania Palast. Once again the entire troupe flew through the narrow air corridor and was able to complete this last engagement of the tour, but then there was a problem trying to get out. The Korean War had claimed all available planes, and the company found itself stranded in Berlin, still a drab postwar city surrounded by Russian-occupied territory. For an entire week, everyone was obliged to stay in Berlin until a chartered flight out could be arranged, and the net deficit for the tour was nearly doubled, from its original estimate of $50,000 to $98,000, all of which was borne by Blevins Davis.

If it had not been for his willingness to act forcefully and generously at this very critical time, Ballet Theatre might never have gotten beyond its tenth anniversary year. Instead, this first European tour was spectacularly successful, both artistically and as an international gesture of goodwill. Following its visit to the Netherlands, the American ambassador, Selden Chapin, cabled the U.S. secretary of state:

> Visit of American Ballet Theatre in Netherlands undoubtedly significant contribution . . . audiences and critics wildly enthusiastic. General public and Embassy impressed by naturalness, simplicity of entire ballet cast. Consider them real ambassadors.

His opinion was echoed after the company visited France, and a Paris paper carried the headline "Ballets of Ballet Theatre Make Us Love America."

12. Revolution in Argentina

As the American Ballet Theatre this
year sets forth for Latin America,
I hope its tour will increase understanding abroad of our cultural
heritage and fortify the friendship
which exists between our nation and
our neighbor Republics to the south.
—President Dwight D. Eisenhower,
   June 9, 1955

BALLET THEATRE'S career throughout the early 1950s
was a heroic record of endurance and achievement. The dancers braved all
kinds of weather and performed in every type of theater. Their efforts and
sacrifices did not go unappreciated. In many of the smaller cities across the
country, a Ballet Theatre performance was the outstanding cultural event
of the year. Along with the Ballet Russe de Monte Carlo, Ballet Theatre was
the principal influence in the development, through the 1940s and 1950s,
of a large, knowledgeable, enthusiastic audience for ballet. Ballet schools
began cropping up all over, and by the early 1950s, ballet stopped being
regarded as strictly a Russian import but came to be considered an indig-
enous form of American art.

For Lucia, perhaps the high point of the four-and-a-half- month tour of 1954–55 was three appearances that came near the end, in Albuquerque, New Mexico, Burlington, Vermont, and Manchester, New Hampshire. "These performances assume an importance in the Ballet Theatre history," she stated in the 1955–56 souvenir program, "because they mean that the company has now performed in all forty-eight of the States of the Union and has earned the undisputed right to be called the national American ballet company."

One month later, the company returned to the Met for yet another three-week season. To celebrate the company's fifteenth anniversary, twenty-six illustrious alumni—including Muriel Bentley, Patricia Bowman, Anton Dolin, Viola Essen, Maria Karnilova, David Lichine, Annabelle Lyon, Alicia Markova, Mary Ellen Moylan, Sono Osato, Donald Saddler, Agnes de Mille, and Antony Tudor—were invited back to perform thirty works chosen from Ballet Theatre's repertory. Doris Hering in *Dance* magazine described the entire turnout as a "triumph of programming, performing, and repertoire."

Naturally, in a season punctuated with guest stars and hastily restaged works, there were bound to be occasional lacunae. Yet one cannot but applaud Ballet Theatre's management for making a prodigal and in many ways audacious gesture, the kind of gesture that inevitably produces exciting theatre.

There were a number of highlights singled out for special mention: Nora Kaye's performance of *Swan Lake* was said by John Martin to be one of the richest and most completely realized of contemporary presentations; he also remarked that "Youskevitch never danced better in his life." Lupe Serrano made a tremendous impression as the latest star ballerina of the company. And this was the season when Erik Bruhn was widely recognized as one of the world's great male classical dancers.

According to P. W. Manchester, writing in the June *Dance News* about Bruhn's performance as Albrecht in *Giselle*:

No one who did not know could possibly have guessed that Bruhn had never danced the role before. If his dancing was magnificent, and it was, his partnering of Markova was no less so. Between them they shaped such a performance as only themselves, dancing again together in this ballet, will be able to match and surpass, perhaps in our time.

It seemed as if, practically overnight, the company had turned itself around and become once again the resplendent Ballet Theatre of old. One indication of how far it had come was that Hurok expressed an interest in representing it again, and soon after the Met season, Ballet Theatre signed a contract with him to book the company for the next three years. This time the terms were distinctly different from previous contracts: amongst other concessions, the company was granted the right to receive a commission on all of his bookings. Also, unlike previous arrangements in which Hurok had very considerable managerial prerogatives, this time it was specified that insofar as artistic policies were concerned, he would act solely as a consultant.

Another principal event was that Ballet Theatre was selected to make another tour for the State Department's International Exchange Program, this time to South America. As the first all- airlift operation ever undertaken by a ballet company, the itinerary called for 121 performances in fifteen cities of eleven Latin American countries before an estimated audience of 295,000. Sixty-four dancers and staff, along with fifteen tons of scenery and costumes, were involved in the tour, which covered 14,500 miles or the equivalent of nearly five coast-to-coast trips across the United States.

It was one of the most far-reaching and challenging ventures that Ballet Theatre had ever undertaken, and the dancers were understandably excited by the prospect. As they prepared to start out, they had no idea of just how much excitement was in store for them south of the border.

The tour began in Mexico with two weeks of performances, including one before 25,000 people in a giant outdoor stadium.

In Costa Rica, the president came to four out of the five performances. Also, a local editor there found the U.S. Exchange Program to have monumental significance:

> When American dance, American thought, American theater, music, painting, poetry, opera, and American teaching have captivated the imagination of the peoples of the rest of the hemisphere and become part of its cultural store and its spiritual formation, then the United States will be, without dispute, the lighthouse which was once France; it will become the new home of man. Now the United States has found the best way to talk to the spirit. Keep it up, because in the south, arms are open to receive it.

In Colombia, where the company was scheduled to spend three weeks, the nation's president came to the opening night performance, despite the fact that the government was under attack and there were guards lining the streets and surrounding the theater. Five days later, a curfew was declared in Bogota, and no one was allowed out. When the dancers of Ballet Theatre looked out their hotel windows, they saw tanks, red flares, and planes flying low overhead. There was considerable shooting and no electricity for half an hour, but the situation turned quiet at last shortly after midnight.

Despite the civil unrest, Ballet Theatre's visit was considered to be a memorable success, particularly when, at one point in the second week, a free performance was given for children crippled with polio: apparently no one had ever thought of giving a free performance before, and there wasn't one empty seat in the house. Another night, before *Theme and Variations,* Lucia came out in front of the curtain and gave a speech in Spanish to the audience, thanking them for the fine reception they gave the company. And for the last performance, tickets were completely sold out, the theater was packed with standees, while outside, crowds were fighting to get in.

After three days in Ecuador, the company arrived in Peru and was confronted with a different sort of crisis: although the tour was only halfway along, apparently the money budgeted by the State Department for the entire trip had run out, and the company was directed to return home. Lucia, in desperation, dashed off a personal letter, in pencil on lined yellow paper, to Bob Dowling, the president of ANTA, which was officially sponsoring the tour.

"Dear Bob," she began:

I believe as it now stands, another $25M ($25,000) would get us through and home, but as it is, we cannot go beyond Lima and save enough to get home. The company has done a magnificent job in Mex, Guat, Costa Rica, Panama, and now here in Bogota. I feel sure we could get the same results wherever we can play. It seems a crime to think of this big troupe being so near Chile and Argentina, countries so far away. . . . Would that I had funds myself but alas I have had to take care of bills and operations in NY and even on this tour. We are due in Santiago Sept. 1st, and the fatal day will be on us before long when we will have to burst the bombshell of returning unless some funds are found somewhere. . . . I can only hope, I suppose vainly, that the reports of our mission will melt hearts in Washington or somewhere to help us realize this marvelous opportunity we have of spreading the goodwill in these far-off countries.

Apparently her plea to Dowling, along with a series of frantic phone calls to Blevins Davis, secured the funds to enable the tour to continue. However, the company's troubles were not over.

In Argentina, the company gave its opening night performance in Buenos Aires before a sold-out house and a very enthusiastic audience. But the next day, amid rumors of a pending revolution, everything was suddenly shut down and all future performances were canceled until further notice. As Lucia described it in a diary:

> 9/16: Back to hotel for lunch. Discovered there was trouble—fighting in suburbs, all shops closed after lunch, banks already closed. Finally theaters ordered closed at night. 9/17: Hoped there would be one performance at 6, but gathered about downstairs and finally heard all theaters and everything closed. Walked to Plaza and around. Everything quiet and deserted. Nothing open. Good we are all 68 in one hotel.

Claridge Hotel was located only ten blocks from the waterfront and squarely in the district that was now suddenly restricted. There was a curfew imposed for 8 p.m. Bars were placed on outside doors, police patrolled the streets, tanks rolled by continuously, and two battleships lay in the harbor with guns pointing.

Ruth Ann Koesun told of how one evening, while a storm was raging outside, several of the company were relaxing with Lucia in the lounge right off the main lobby:

> Most of us had our noses buried in a book or magazine. Some were playing cards, and it was quiet except for the thunder and lightning. Suddenly there was a big boom! Sallie Wilson looked up and said, "I don't think that was thunder." Lucia said, "Don't start rumors, Sallie," and went back to her writing.

The next day the company was told that the secret police headquarters two blocks from the hotel had been attacked. With the city in turmoil, Ballet Theatre was isolated off in the hotel, its performance schedule on hold. Koesun described the situation:

> One afternoon, when we couldn't leave the hotel, a group of us went to Lucia's room to see what was going on down in the streets. She had a room with a rooflike terrace, and a bunch of us were out there when the shooting

started up again. The bullets started to ricochet off the façade of the hotel, above and below us. Well, you think you have seen dancers move fast? We dove through those French doors in a split second, and Lucia's hair was frizzier than ever after that experience.

Lucia's diary entries for the same time were short and amazingly matter-of-fact, especially considering that instead of spending days rehearsing and shopping in Buenos Aires's elegant boutiques and each night performing in the magnificent Teatro de Colon, she and the company were huddled up in the hotel, doors barred, listening to the tanks and shooting outside:

9/18 Could hear anti-aircraft guns at 7. Everything still closed tight. Stood around with everyone—ships in harbor, everyone waiting. Up to room and wrote Sandy. Wanted to walk but not supposed to.
9/19 Heard big guns. No—it was thunder! Everyone listened to radio. Bombing still possible.
9/20 Today no breakfast, no service. No one knows anything. Peron on Paraguayan boat. Junta discussing. Waited around. At 1:15 Randy [Brooks, stage manager] said, "That's not thunder!" Collected quickly in lobby, then all to shelter of basement! Wore Fernand's coat while knees trembled. Everyone behaved well. Manager down and reported it was not a bombarding but police and tanks shooting Allianza Hdqrs. 2 blocks away. Someone reported you could see fire from 13th floor. Nora [Kaye] and I went up—blaze of Allianza Hdqrs. Jaime, Chuck, Leo on terrace. Nora at window, just putting leg out to go when whistle of a bullet whizzed. All in and down! Finally went up at quarter to 9—collected things and laid out clothes etc., just in case! What a day.

It was nearly a week before the city returned to normal and Ballet Theatre's performances resumed.

The opening ballet, the old-time favorite *La Fille Mal Gardée*, occasioned another totally unexpected surprise. Near the beginning of the ballet, at one point the orchestra stops playing and waits while the male dancer throws a wide, powder-blue ribbon to his partner: the moment she catches it is the cue for the conductor to start the music again. Ruth Ann Koesun, who was dancing the pas de deux onstage with John Kriza that night, described what it was like when he tossed her the blue ribbon:

In that split second, the whole audience started to cheer and yell, throwing programs, hats, whatever was in their hands into the air, and jumping up and down creating a thunderous sound. We were so startled and couldn't imagine what was happening. All of the dancers came running up to stage level and into the wings to see what was going on. The roar was overwhelming and lasted until the end of the pas de deux. When the whole ballet was over, we learned that the audience thought we purposely used a powder-blue ribbon to honor them since the Argentine flag is powder-blue and white."

Ballet Theatre went on to complete the engagement in Argentina with no further surprises and great acclaim as popular survivors of the revolution. However, Lucia, ever a true New Englander, preferred not to focus too much on the dangers they had encountered. Afterwards, on one occasion back in the States when she talked about the South American tour to a women's club, she summed up the whole adventure by saying, "It's three weeks we won't forget. It was interesting, and we learned a lot about Argentine history."

13. Adverse U.S. Tax Court Verdict

> Regardless of the artistic appreci-
> ation one may have for the ballet
> or other arts, Congress has not
> seen fit to permit deductions for
> contributions made to support them
> unless it is clear that the taxpayer
> had a business purpose in mind.
> —Opinion of Judge Opper, U.S. Tax
> Court, August 1, 1956

WHEN BALLET THEATRE, suddenly very much in the international limelight as the cultural ambassador of the United States to the southern hemisphere, became stranded in Peru, it must have been difficult for Lucia to admit to Robert Dowling, president of ANTA, that it wasn't possible for her to provide quickly and discreetly the $25,000 that would have rescued sixty prominent artists from being abandoned thousands of miles away from home.

Lucia didn't like to talk about money. She never publicly admitted she was supporting Ballet Theatre, and no one in the ballet world had any idea of how much she had been contributing to the company over the years. However, her donations, and particularly the manner in which they were given, had been disputed by the Internal Revenue Service since the very beginning of Ballet Theatre back in 1939–40, and now suddenly, fifteen years later, the issue between them had come to a head.

After a series of delays, a preliminary trial was held in April 1953 (U.S. Tax Court, Lucia Chase Ewing, Petitioner v. Commissioner of Internal Revenue, Respondent), at which the judge reversed the original 1946 jury decision, which had been in Lucia's favor. In his summary statement, the judge declared that, after carefully reviewing all the evidence, it was apparent to him that the principal reason the petitioner (Lucia) kept advancing large sums to Ballet Theatre was not in hopes of making money but rather to satisfy her desire to see the ballet flourish in some form as an art in America.

> Despite the continued losses, the petitioner apparently gave little or no attention to the business management of The Ballet Theatre Inc., and we cannot find sufficient indication that she made the inquiries which would have been made as a matter of course if her primary interest was financial gain. In reaching the conclusion . . . we have kept in mind the fact that circumstances which would lead a reasonable businessman to conclude that a theatrical enterprise of this character had no reasonable chance of success might not have that effect on an enthusiast of the ballet; and in this proceeding, we are not testing the petitioner's motive or intent by asking what a reasonable man would have done. But even when the transaction is viewed from the petitioner's standpoint, we think the record at best merely establishes that she hoped for a profit . . . [and] even that hope must have become faint when the continuing losses did not diminish but actually tended to increase.

The verdict was appealed, and the case was referred to the U.S. Court of Appeals, 2nd Circuit, where it was argued in May 1954 before a panel of three judges (Hand, Clark, and Medina). For this all-important appeal, Randolph Paul, the distinguished senior partner of Paul Weiss Wharton Rifkind and Garrison, led the lawyers representing Lucia, and H. Brian Holland, assistant attorney general for the commissioner of Internal Revenue, headed the prosecution. At issue was the same central question: whether certain "losses" suffered by the taxpayer and claimed as deductions on her tax returns were losses incurred in "a transaction entered into for profit," in which case they were legitimate and should be allowed, or was the money originally advanced for some other reason rather than for profit.

On May 28, 1954, the three-judge panel, in an opinion by Judge Hand, upheld the tax court's prior finding that Lucia's primary purpose, perhaps sole purpose, in making these loans was the enhancement of American ballet as an art:

> Congress, by taxing gifts and limiting charitable deductions to qualified organizations, did not intend to allow a taxpayer to pour money into an artistic venture to satisfy only a personal desire.

Although this verdict related solely to losses Lucia had incurred from 1941 to 1943, it represented a severe setback and appeared to be most ominous when the time came to decide the 1944–49 tax returns also in dispute, which were still waiting to be brought before the tax court.

The decision in this climactic trial was handed down two years later, in August 1956, only ten months after the company returned from its daunting but resoundingly successful tour in South America. The court's "findings of fact" provide a lengthy and detailed account of Ballet Theatre's activities for each of the eight years from 1942 to 1949, including the amounts of total revenue, company losses, and the deductions Lucia claimed on her tax returns. More than anything else, it is a sad picture, one grim annual income statement of Ballet Theatre after another, with Lucia always picking up the tab for larger and larger amounts.

Viewed in terms of income (gross revenue returns), the total dollars generated by Ballet Theatre's performances are surprisingly great, particularly considering that this was still a relatively new company in a field of art that was only starting to become popular in the United States. For example, after signing a contract with Hurok Associates to manage all its bookings, Ballet Theatre in its 1943–44 season amassed over $750,000 in fees and ticket sales. The following year, this figure increased by 25 percent, close to $1 million, which at the time was an astounding amount for a ballet company to earn. However, the problem for Ballet Theatre was that, because of the way the contract was written, the greatest part by far of all the money went to S. Hurok Associates: from the 1944 Met season alone, Hurok received nearly 80 percent of the total revenue, or $743,540, while the company's share amounted to only $186,393.

When Ballet Theatre finally broke away from Hurok and began running its own business in the 1945–46 season, it was able to claim a much greater percentage of the overall proceeds. However, without the benefit of Hurok's managerial expertise, the gross revenues fell drastically, amounting to 40 percent less than the previous year. Overall, except for his first Ballet Theatre season when he only took the company on at the last minute, Hurok had succeeded in making a profit every year. In contrast, when Ballet Theatre took to managing its own affairs in 1946–47, its gross revenues went from $1,159,000 to $540,000, its net share of these total proceeds only amounted to $327,000, and its losses for the year totaled $431,950.

The fiscal consequences of these deficit-ridden years enormously reduced Lucia's personal resources. Between 1943 and 1948, the period covered by the third tax trial in 1956, the losses she reported and claimed as deductions in her federal income tax returns totaled over $1.5 million. In addition, throughout the latter half of 1955 when the company was on tour in South America, there continued to be the specter of a gargantuan penalty that an unfavorable verdict by the U.S. Court of Appeals in 1956 could exact, not only denying all the deductions Lucia had taken but also requiring interest to be paid on all these amounts, and not just for the six years in question but for the entire period of fourteen years that the loan issue had been in dispute.

To evaluate the cost of Lucia's support of Ballet Theatre in terms of today's dollar, a medium-priced new car in 1950 sold, on average, for a couple of thousand dollars or less than one-tenth of its price fifty years later. Same for theater tickets: an orchestra seat might cost $8 that today would sell for $80, whereas some items (like a college education) increased considerably more than that. In summary, it would not be unreasonable to reckon the amount of money Lucia originally paid in loans, plus the additional penalties exacted as a consequence of her losing her case on appeal, to be in the vicinity of ten times the amount represented in 1950s dollars, or somewhere between $25 to $30 million.

In some ways, the psychological implications for Lucia of this massive outlay were even more crushing than the dollar figure. The personal fortune that she controlled had originally come to her by way of inheritance. It was the fruit of a long and distinguished Cochran/Ewing family dynasty. It was not money that Lucia Chase or her family back in Waterbury, Connecticut, had made. If it had been, she might have looked at it as being much more hers, by blood or birthright. Instead, it was Tom's inheritance, which continued to be watched over by the Ewing family's hawklike lawyer, Harry Zuckert, until he retired.

In recent years, owing to Lucia's involvement and obsessive interest in Ballet Theatre, funds had been hemorrhaging. The only mitigating factor in this enormous outlay was the partial relief gained by writing off each year the amounts she contributed as a business loss and claiming them as a deduction on her income tax return. Now the U.S. Tax Court and Court of Appeals 2nd Circuit had ruled against her and delivered a devastating verdict, establishing beyond all doubt that there was no tax reprieve whatsoever for all the Cochran-Ewing money that, over the past sixteen years, she had given away . . . as though she had taken the greatest part of the money Tom had left her and simply tossed it out the window.

Nothing could have been more contrary to the New England standards with which she had been brought up and that continued to govern the way she conducted herself in all phases of life except for this one overpowering attachment to Ballet Theatre. For years, she had felt angry but helpless at being caught in a financial squeeze she could neither control nor walk away from. Now, after the courts' crushing verdicts compounded the dollar figures, she was more ashamed than ever of having squandered so much of the family fortune.

The entire topic was something Lucia would never talk about. Reporters over the years kept plying her with questions about the money she spent on Ballet Theatre, but she always curtly refused to enter into any discussion about her financial dealings. Nor did she confide her money problems even with those closest to her heart—her parents, her sisters, or her two sons. Especially not her two sons, who personified exactly what hurt her most, that she had somehow betrayed the trust—both fiscal and dynastic—that had been left for her to keep. Still, without ever hearing from her lips more than an occasional fleeting reference, first about some legal trouble she was having, later on perhaps a wry admission now and then about how things hadn't turned out as well as she had hoped, Tommy and I both knew that she had been drastically and bitterly hurt.

Up to this point in our lives, we had been essentially bystanders to the intensely close relationship between our mother and Ballet Theatre, witnessing it first from inside our home, then later on from farther off when we were away at school or college. But whether at home or away, we never actively participated. The glamorous, dramatic, perilous career of our mother's ballet company was an intimate part of our lives, yet at the same time, we were kept distinctly apart from it because that was what she wanted and the way she arranged her life and ours from the very beginning of Ballet Theatre.

By the mid-1950s, we had graduated from Yale, two years apart, and had gone our separate ways. Tommy had chosen to go into law, passed his bar exams, and was working at Debevoise, Plimpton, Lyons and Gates, one of New York's most prestigious legal firms. My inclinations were more literary or journalistic and had led to a short stint at Time Inc. and two associations as a cub reporter with medium-sized newspapers in Massachusetts and New Jersey. These had been rewarding experiences, but more and more, it had become inescapable to me that Ballet Theatre had run into serious trouble and desperately needed help.

Partly due to a deep-seated feeling of love, sympathy, even pity for my mother who suddenly seemed to be all alone and partly because I sensed that my continuing to work for newspapers was really of scant importance compared with rescuing a great ballet company, I decided to take on the challenge myself.

And so, with all the innocence and bravado of the very young, in the early fall of 1956, I went to work for Ballet Theatre in the belief that I just might help engineer a turnaround in the company's fortunes and convert a looming disaster into a long-awaited and well-deserved triumph.

14. Alex Ewing at Ballet Theatre

The organization [Ballet Theatre] as
it stands possesses no real and firm
basis for sound artistic achievement,
progress, or permanence . . .
no indication whatsoever of the
destination towards which the
vehicle is bound.
—Sol Hurok

E ARLY IN THE FALL OF 1956, I strode into the Ballet
Theatre office, ebullient and hell-bent to get a rescue mission started.

Ballet Theatre's office back in the 1950s bore little resemblance to what one might have expected as the headquarters of a nationally prominent arts institution. Essentially an oversized hotel suite, it consisted of a long narrow hallway connecting four or five rooms, each with a closet and a bureau or armoire, and lacking only a bed to be more of a living space than a place of business. The atmosphere was old-fashioned and subdued, totally different from the bustle and hubbub of the company's rehearsal studios or ballet school. There were no clattering typewriters, no cubbyhole workstations, no raised voices or people rushing around.

Even more disconcerting to me than its domestic appearance was the discovery that Ballet Theatre's regular office staff consisted essentially of only four people: Lucia, who was on the road with the company for a great part of the year; Florence Pettan, who for over thirty years served as my mother's lovely and scrupulously loyal secretary; John Onysko, the diligent, overburdened comptroller/business manager for both the Foundation and the company; and Terry Orlin, Onysko's assistant, who transcribed most of the official correspondence, kept the files, and answered the phones.

On the other side of the scale, counterbalancing the business staff of Ballet Theatre, was the artistic counterpart of the company, a core group of at least fifty dancers (not counting guest artists) and a permanent staff that included a musical director, conductor, regisseur, ballet master, company manager, production and stage manager, wardrobe mistress and assistant, press representative, and at least one or two rehearsal pianists. An additional complement was added whenever the company was performing that included the orchestra, stagehands, wardrobe personnel, and drivers for the company buses and trucks, in all probably 100 people, at times even more. Their combined activity generated a veritable flood of data, all to be checked, recorded, and dealt with: salaries and taxes, contracts, box office statements, information regarding costumes, scenery, music, everything to do with legal issues, accounting, advertising, publicity, booking, storage, insurance, and a host of other items, all poured into the ill-equipped little New York office. Even a total novice like myself, an English major just a few years out of college with practically no business or management experience, could immediately see drastic shortcomings in the support side of the company.

It didn't take long to discover another equally disturbing problem: beyond the jumbled mass of material concerned with the immediate situation, there was no long-range planning for more distant projects or even a strategy for the company's future. Meanwhile, dominating every issue that came under discussion was the ever-present question of how to raise extra money to pay for it. During this period in the mid-1950s, the picture was not quite as bleak as it had been a decade earlier when Ballet Theatre's entire board of directors consisted of just seven people. Now, at least, there was the new Ballet Theatre Foundation in place, with Blevins Davis as its president and a board of twenty-nine governing trustees, including several notable figures who either possessed or had ready access to big money.

There were also signs that some fund-raising had taken place. In the past year, the Foundation had enlisted nearly forty "founder members," individuals who had contributed $1,000 or more, as well as nearly 200 other sponsors and donors. While this represented a significant advance, the total amount raised from these outside contributors represented a very small fraction, certainly less than one-quarter, of the company's annual dollar shortfall. A major part of the problem was that the trustees had never been pressured to take on any meaningful responsibility for the company, financial or otherwise, and consequently the newly expanded Foundation board was still happy to leave final responsibility for all company operations in Lucia's hands, as well as all deficits to her checkbook. Nevertheless, Ballet Theatre as an institution in 1956 was better off than it had ever been previously, and now, with my arrival, there was a new bundle of energy on board to help.

With typical enthusiasm, Lucia hastened to establish exactly how this new face and element in Ballet Theatre's picture should be construed by everyone else. From the very first moment, she made a big point of introducing me around as "Alex Ewing," definitely not as "Sandy," the way people knew me as the younger of Lucia's two boys. The obvious fact that now I was man-sized immediately caused others to wonder how old that made my mother, a very worrisome question for Lucia Chase the dancer.

Instead of acknowledging any connection between us, she carefully explained that Alex Ewing was taking on the role and title of executive secretary of the Ballet Theatre Foundation. In the same breath, she went on to say how I would be involved in "all sorts of good things—fund-raising, developing new Ballet Theatre chapters around the country, working with the Foundation board—which we've always wanted to do but never had the time or the opportunity to take on ourselves. Now there'll be someone to do them all. I'm just tickled to death."

From the outset, she and I both recognized that this new working relationship was apt to be difficult, particularly since I wasn't her other son, Tommy, whose basic nature was to take things as they came, who readily accepted authority, and who from earliest childhood had existed on a totally harmonious wavelength with our mother.

"Tommy is just like Tom," Lucia used to say, which was her highest form of praise, "whereas Sandy," she added with a little self-deprecating laugh, "poor Sandy is very much like me." Not all that bad, but there was no denying that both Lucia and I (she would remain "Mom" at home but henceforth "Lucia" in the ballet world) could be a little stubborn at times. Complicating matters was a strong feeling that we both shared, which was that we didn't want our working relationship to smack of any sort of nepotism. The slightest hint that Ballet Theatre's director was bringing in her son to help feather the family nest would have been anathema to the image of Lucia Chase that she had worked so hard to maintain, whereas I for my part wanted it perfectly clear that my coming to work for Ballet Theatre was not due to a mother's indulgence but rather was my own decision. In our minds, this was going to be a strictly professional arrangement.

At least in the beginning, there was no question that the most fundamental and pressing problem facing Ballet Theatre was to get more people to contribute money to the Foundation and thereby diminish the crushing deficits that undermined everything. Lucia had already made a concerted attempt to start local chapters in some of the principal cities where the company had performed every year, and now there was finally someone new on the scene to work at organizing groups of loyal supporters outside New York City. I spent the better part of my first few months lining up contacts and making initial visits to Cincinnati, Cleveland, Denver, and Detroit to coordinate local citizens willing to work on Ballet Theatre's behalf, particularly when the company came to their hometown. However, it wasn't long before my work on building chapters was disrupted by two other major issues.

The first concerned a monumental event about to take place in New York. A gigantic construction project, to be called Lincoln Center for the Performing Arts, was already in the advanced planning stages of assembling in one place the city's leading institutions of opera, music, dance, and drama, plus a library for all the arts. There had never been anything quite like it in New York: the Metropolitan Opera, the New York Philharmonic, the New York Public Library's combined arts divisions, the Juilliard School, and a repertory theater were all slated to become Lincoln Center constituents. Also, the New York City Ballet was preparing to leave its current quarters at the City Center of Music and Drama on 55th Street and, along with the New York City Opera, move over to Lincoln Center, where they would share a new theater that was soon to be under construction. The new building, to be called the New York State Theater, was designed by the eminent architect Philip Johnson, with considerable input from George Balanchine and impetus from Lincoln Kirstein and Nelson Rockefeller, then governor of New York, close friend of Kirstein's, and brother of John D. Rockefeller III, president of the entire Lincoln Center complex.

The colossal project had been in the news for some time and had understandably attracted an enormous amount of attention, particularly in New York City, where it promised to transform the status of the performing arts in general and of the various participants in particular. Somehow this extraordinary development had totally ignored Ballet Theatre, and vice versa. Yet there appeared to be no justification, at least not to my admittedly partisan eyes, for Lincoln Center to have focused exclusively on the New York City Ballet and to have bypassed the country's senior dance company, which had performed one or two extended seasons in New York every year since 1940 and which had developed into an international organization of major proportions and importance.

It was also an obvious and well-publicized fact that American Ballet Theatre (the "American" had been added to its title after the last State Department tour) had been struggling for years to find a permanent home for itself in the city. Now for the New York City Ballet, which already had a performing base in City Center, to be rewarded with a new home at Lincoln Center while Ballet Theatre was completely left out was rapidly becoming a reality that could have devastating consequences.

In the fall of 1956, it appeared that it might not be too late to get the company included. At least my initial inquiry indicated that the door was not yet definitely and finally shut. If this indeed were true, then it seemed that getting American Ballet Theatre accepted into the new complex was more important than any other single goal that could be achieved at this particular time, and I started a desperate last-minute campaign to correct this oversight.

The powers at Lincoln Center were understandably reluctant even to entertain the possibility of adding another constituent to their gargantuan project, but after many appeals, our case was finally granted a hearing. Accompanied by Victor Bator, one of the most dedicated of all Ballet Theatre trustees, I met face-to-face with the Lincoln Center executive committee member designated to rule definitively on all participants.

What we didn't realize at the time was that this was as far as our terribly tardy initiative could have possibly taken us. Lincoln Center was essentially the power elite of New York's cultural hierarchy, with no outsiders invited or allowed to push their way in. Lucia Chase and American Ballet Theatre never had a chance. After weeks of maneuvering and cajoling, at this one-and-only direct encounter, we were kindly but unequivocally told that final arrangements had effectively been made, and that nothing could be done to accommodate the American Ballet Theatre, worthy though the company was conceded to be. It was crushing news that clearly had to be accepted, but the disappointment and consequences were great and lasted a long time.

At about this same moment, another imperative of a totally different nature appeared also to require immediate attention. To appreciate its urgency, it is helpful to recall the words of Dick Pleasant, the founder of Ballet Theatre, written after the astounding success of the company's first season in 1940 at the old Center Theatre:

> A true ballet theatre [company] cannot stop with being a collector. Its duty to the present is to be a contemporary Lorenzo di Medici to choreographers, designers, composers who require as material a company for creating the classics of tomorrow.

During its early years, Ballet Theatre astounded the dance world by producing a succession of brilliant works. However, this creative onslaught all took place during the first decade of the company. In the next five years, there had been many new productions, a few commendable failures, but nothing of lasting significance. The shining light that Ballet Theatre had initially cast across the dance stage had grown so dim that it had practically disappeared, and with it had gone the excitement, the originating purpose, the justification in many people's minds for the company's very existence.

Part of this appalling lapse could be attributed to its inability to secure a home base for itself. According to *New York Times* critic John Martin, a traveling showcase can do no more than present samples to prospective customers along the road; it cannot manufacture anything, create anything, or deliver anything. It can only become increasingly bedraggled.

As artistic director of Ballet Theatre, Lucia was being increasingly blamed for the company's protracted failure to produce any new work of lasting significance. It was the one aspect of running the company where she felt inept and ill at ease. Oliver Smith, vastly less involved than Lucia but at least a titular codirector of the company, did not share her inhibitions and was ideally equipped to conceive new production projects. However, as one of the most prolific and successful scenic designers of his era, he was rarely available.

Left on her own, Lucia knew surprisingly few choreographers besides those who had actually worked for Ballet Theatre. When it came to considering who might be commissioned to do a new ballet, her first instinct was to turn to the tried-and-true trio of Agnes de Mille, Jerry Robbins, and

Antony Tudor. Whether it was simply coincidence or because they found more interesting opportunities elsewhere, all three around this time deserted the company, de Mille for Broadway, Robbins for the New York City Ballet, and Tudor to be ballet master of the Metropolitan Opera and director of its ballet school. With them gone, Lucia was essentially at a loss when it came to lining up other candidates to choreograph for Ballet Theatre.

After the spring 1956 season at the Met, she did make one attempt to develop new works in the form of a single performance at the Phoenix Theatre down in Greenwich Village. In what was termed a "Ballet Theatre Workshop," four small ballets were presented, using plain costumes, no scenery, and only recorded music in order to minimize production expenses and focus attention solely on their choreography. Two of the works on that program, both by Robert Joffrey, had been created prior to the workshop and were performed by dancers in his mini-company, while a third piece, choreographed by Katharine Litz, employed Litz's own dancers. The result wasn't so much a Ballet Theatre Workshop as it was a special event arranged and presented by Ballet Theatre to show off the talents of assorted choreographers who, it was felt, deserved a public showing.

Four months later, while the company was embarked on another European tour for the State Department, Lucia chanced to meet Kenneth MacMillan, a young Scottish dancer and novice choreographer. Years later he would become artistic director of The Royal Ballet and a Knight of the British Empire, but at the time he was just beginning to work with the English company when Lucia persuaded him to try his hand at creating a new work for American Ballet Theatre.

The resulting ballet, entitled *Winter's Eve* and based on a story by Carson McCullers, was premiered in Lisbon in January 1957, and the following month, after the company had returned to New York, served as the basis for a single night's performance by American Ballet Theatre at the Met. Although MacMillan's new work did provide Nora Kaye with a highly dramatic leading role that won her considerable praise, *Winter's Eve* was only moderately successful and did little to fill the company's long-standing creative gap. From my personal standpoint, though, it was a distinct success in that I was able to get its entire cost paid by the Doris Duke Foundation, the first such underwriting (except all those paid for ex post facto by Lucia Chase!) in the company's history. Getting it commissioned, performed, and totally financed was probably the high-water mark of the entire time that the two of us, mother and son, worked at Ballet Theatre together.

Following the first Ballet Theatre Workshop and the extremely limited success of *Winter's Eve,* I proposed a much more ambitious idea that was to schedule in May not one but four successive Monday evening performances at the same Phoenix Theatre where the first workshop was held, this time with at least four brand-new works to be introduced on each of the four programs. Lucia was intrigued but from the very beginning somewhat leery of the idea. This new project called for better-known choreographers and more ambitious undertakings than before: two works by Agnes de Mille, a second effort by Kenneth MacMillan, and contributions from Erik Bruhn, John Butler, Robert Joffrey, Enrique Martinez, Fernand Nault, Valentina Pereyaslavec, Alfred Rodriguez, Herbert Ross, Don Saddler, Job Sanders, and Anna Sokolow. These workshop performances were cast as a series of creative rehearsals in process, again with minimal assistance in terms of costumes, scenery, or special effects, but with virtuoso dancing throughout by some of American Ballet Theatre's most brilliant artists. The underlying purpose was to transform the exceedingly risky and expensive traditional method of introducing new ballets to the public into modest workshop presentations without sacrificing the excitement or artistry of a superb major company.

This groundbreaking Ballet Theatre Workshop project quickly came to be regarded as a historic event. New York's ballet fanatics jammed the compact Phoenix Theatre to capacity, with all four evenings completely sold out. And while the overall level of choreography was uneven, some of the offerings were compelling, particularly MacMillan's *Journey* to a challenging Bartok score, de Mille's *Sebastian,* and Herbert Ross's *The Maids,* which cast two men in the roles that Genet originally wrote for women. Yet for my part, reacting with what was probably excessive pride of authorship and impossibly high expectations, I found the result of so much hard work and colossal talent to be very slight, even depressing in its mediocrity.

Being young and impulsive, I did not hesitate to express my feelings to Lucia, bluntly and in writing, so there could be no mistaking the disillusion I felt. Essentially, the question I posed and pressed her to answer was whether it made any sense to keep the company going at such a colossal expense when the ballets being created on and for it had so little real significance. Instead, I had now come to believe that Ballet Theatre should straightway adopt a radically different approach and establish, as a separate adjunct of the Foundation, a totally experimental wing, an ongoing, independent Ballet Theatre Workshop employing artists from other fields working with choreographers and dancers in a collaborative fashion, all to be set up on a permanent basis in New York. And, in what was probably for Lucia the most objectionable aspect of the entire proposal, I urged that the principal responsibility for running this new enterprise be assigned to Larry Arrick, a young theater director I had recently brought into the Ballet Theatre office.

"Perhaps this won't work," I concluded in the formal letter I wrote to her proposing the project. "I have often felt that suggestions were too often regarded as intrusions, and there was a general reluctance to delegate any authority. . . . Yet this is a million-dollar business and cannot be run as a private affair."

Reviewing my words now, many years later, they sound unforgivably arrogant and presumptuous. Yet I meant well at the time and was simply voicing my dismay at the way no one around the Ballet Theatre office seemed to be interested in any adventurous ideas. Instead, there continued to be a deep-seated preference for the traditional way, which in this case meant trying to create new ballets almost as an extracurricular activity, not undertaken as a principal end in itself but relegated to squeezing in a few extra hours into an already overloaded rehearsal period. And then, of course, underlying the entire proposal I was championing was a not too thinly veiled criticism of an artistic director who appeared to have no specific intellectual or aesthetic principles when it came to enriching the company's repertory. The obvious solution was to establish a new species of workshop, to be run by someone who had the time, inclination, and potential to be more creative than the current management, which was totally preoccupied with the daily operations of the company.

To Lucia's great credit, she did not take offense at my intemperate remarks but straightway wrote back, actually thanking me for my "clear and very wonderful letter":

> I agree with so many of your criticisms . . . also agree there were many mistakes. We prepared this Festival in too short a time. If it is done next year, we can start now to find better themes as you say. There is no reason you cannot find and select themes which you, Oliver, and I could discuss and agree on before any new work is considered. [However,] I believe the Workshop would be a very mediocre affair attracting a bevy of untalented people, dozens of dreadful choreographers on your neck demanding your attention. I do not think Larry Arrick is equipped to run a workshop, could

not give my approval, and do not feel at this time it is a step in the right direction.

I should have backed off at this point, but being young and headstrong, I didn't. Instead, several weeks later, I took up the cudgel again, claiming that a workshop need not necessarily be mediocre, as she had claimed, and that since she admitted to being too busy to deal with it, she shouldn't mind others trying: it was not healthy for the management of any organization to shut itself off from new ideas, and that was essentially what I felt was being done then.

Things had reached the point where the discussion needed to cool off, especially since our disagreement had been aggravated by my setting everything down in writing. Deep in our hearts, the familiar strong relationship remained between mother and son who continued to love each other. But within the confines of the Ballet Theatre office, it became impossible to submerge all personal feelings and intimate awareness of each other's idiosyncrasies so that we could revert to working together in a purely professional manner.

Fortunately, about this same time, love of a different sort invaded my world. While working at Ballet Theatre, I had also been ardently pursuing a beautiful young woman, Carol Sonne, to whom I had quite lost my heart. Finally, after nearly two years of courtship, I persuaded her to be my wife. In February 1958, we married and went off on a monthlong honeymoon to Mexico.

When I came back to New York and Ballet Theatre, everything seemed like past history, and it was obviously time for me to move on. I spent a couple of months cleaning things up at the office, then resigned late in the spring, probably (and understandably) to Lucia's vast relief.

15. Disastrous Cannes Fire

Morale is high, possessions low.
—Lucia's wire to New York office,
August 19, 1958

O N AUGUST 18, 1958, in Cannes, France, the telephone rang in the hotel room of Jeannot Cerrone, American Ballet Theatre's company manager. It was before dawn. Cerrone lifted the phone and heard a gruff voice informing him that the truck had gone up in flames.

Mumbling "Merci," he went back to sleep. Minutes later, he woke again with a rush and realized what he had heard. The call had come from the driver of the twelve-ton truck on its way from Cannes to Geneva carrying all of the American Ballet Theatre's equipment for the current European tour. Everything had been lost—the scenery, costumes, and props of twelve full productions; the orchestra music for four ballets, along with several musical instruments; thousands of ballet and pointe shoes; and the personal trunks of the dancers, with all their clothes and possessions. Total disaster.

At this very moment, Lucia was on her way from New York to Cannes to rejoin the company when her plane developed engine trouble. For a brief time, it seemed that ditching the aircraft would be necessary, but the pilot managed to make an emergency stop at Gander, leaving her and all the other passengers stranded on the ground in Newfoundland. After several hours, another plane was made available, and she flew on to Cannes, where she was met at the airport with news of the fire.

Always best in a crisis, Lucia took charge the moment she arrived at the hotel in Cannes. Her first decision had to do with the fact that, in five days, American Ballet Theatre was scheduled to open the brand-new U.S. Pavilion at the World's Fair in Brussels and then perform an entire week of three separate programs as America's feature presentation in the international jubilee. Despite the catastrophic loss in the fire of practically everything the company was carrying on tour, she immediately notified the State Department that the opening in Brussels would take place. Then she gave orders for a company rehearsal to begin early that afternoon. Since most of the dancers had lost almost everything except the contents of their small suitcases, they had to rehearse in bathing suits and bare feet, but at least they were soon no longer lingering stunned and aimless about the hotel.

Meanwhile, as news of the fire circulated, rescue efforts began pouring in from all quarters of the dance world. England's Royal Ballet in London sent complete costumes for two ballets. The Royal Danish Ballet, following a phone call from Erik Bruhn, immediately dispatched *Graduation Ball* costumes and shoes. Margot Fonteyn sent Nora Kaye her black swan tutu for *Swan Lake*. Claude Bessy of the Paris Opera suddenly appeared in Cannes with a load of tutus, tunics, and music. Ballet Rambert in England sent the musical score of *Giselle* in the Foreign Office's diplomatic pouch. Covent Garden set fifteen girls to work pressing a pile of *Sylphides* costumes.

"Morale is high, possessions low," Lucia wired the office in New York. As a top priority, a huge consignment of shoes, enough to resupply each one of the company's dancers in their special custom sizes, was ordered from Capezio, filled on the rush, and airlifted to Belgium in two days.

Most of the smaller specialty stores in Paris were closed for the summer holiday, but the company made a stopover on the way to Brussels, and even though it was Sunday, the theatrical shops opened up to give the dancers an opportunity to obtain makeup and other dressing room essentials. At the Brussels airport, a box heavily taped and marked "URGENT" aroused suspicion and was held up by customs officials, until the company stage manager warned, "If we don't get those athletic supporters soon, I'm going to call the American ambassador." The customs office quickly released the package.

In the days immediately following, while the full implications of the disaster were still emerging, it was clear that almost everything scheduled to be performed over the course of the summer had been lost. *Billy the*

Kid and *Fancy Free* had gone on ahead in a separate truck, but otherwise virtually the entire repertory selected for the tour had been wiped out. (Ironically, the only exception was *Pillar of Fire,* which had not been programmed for any of the previous stops on the tour and had been sent directly from New York to Brussels for the World's Fair.)

Only five days after the fire, on August 22, which was opening night at the U.S. Pavilion in Brussels, the theater curtain went up on time and as planned, with *Theme and Variations* as the first ballet. The only wayward notes, which most in the audience did not notice, was that the women on stage were all wearing white tutus designed for *Les Sylphides,* the men were in tights that had just arrived from New York, and the scenery was not the *Theme* set, designed by Woodman Thompson, but the backdrop from *Gala Performance.*

"We were all in borrowed costumes," Sallie Wilson remembered. "It was so funny, so exciting. It was like we all came out of the fire. The joke of the first performance was that there were only two dance belts for the whole company, so the boy who did the lead in the first ballet, in *Theme,* had to take off the wet dance belt and hand it to the boy who had the lead in the next ballet."

And so it went, with improvisations for every work and nothing onstage quite as it was originally conceived. Yet, despite having its entire active repertory wiped out in a single hour, the company's commitment to open the U.S. Pavilion was heroically kept, the European tour was acclaimed a success, and the gratitude of the U.S. government was confirmed when Lucia received word from the State Department that it was ready to send American Ballet Theatre on another international tour whenever the company reported back to Washington that it was available.

One gigantic challenge still remained before year's end: a long-scheduled, much-anticipated three-week season at the Metropolitan Opera House.

Instead of being sadly debilitated by the catastrophe it had just endured, the company came out in great spirit and fine form. Opening night was like a celebration, and three days later, the New York premiere of Birgit Cullberg's *Miss Julie,* with Erik Bruhn and Violette Verdy as the passion-driven lovers, was an immediate hit.

"This was easily both the best and the most successful season American Ballet Theatre has enjoyed in New York for many years," was the verdict in *Dance News.*

The dancers were especially praised. John Martin of the *New York Times,* who often could be very caustic, wrote:

> The recent season of the American Ballet Theatre at the Met Opera House turned out surprisingly well on the whole. . . . The box office was unusually good, surpassing even the company's fifteenth anniversary season three years ago. Better than that, the dancers themselves behaved with exemplary spirit and devotion.

He singled out several of the company for special praise: Nora Kaye, "as gifted and wholehearted an artist as there is in the field"; Erik Bruhn, "certainly the outstanding danseur noble in the picture"; also Violette Verdy, Scott Douglas, and Lupe Serrano. After finding some fault with Markova, Kriza, and Alicia Alonso, he went on:

> To end this survey of personnel on a happier note, it would be both blind and unjust to exclude Lucia Chase herself from the list of outstanding performers. Her stepmother in *Fall River Legend* is a masterpiece of forceful and economical playing; her older sister in *Pillar of Fire* is almost equally as strong and quite as admirably characterized; her weary old trollop in *Judgment of Paris* is hilarious and pitiful and performed with wonderful authority. How fine it would be if every company had a few mimes of this standard.

Lucia must have been gratified to read these encouraging words about herself and the company. However, the fire—a grievous shock to the company and personally to the dancers who all lost their personal possessions—was especially disheartening for her. She had personally paid for most of the sets and costumes that were reduced to ashes in the truck. Amazing adjustments had been made in order to carry out the Met season, but afterwards there remained grim realities that could not be ignored or quickly overcome. The problem of resurrecting the company repertory required, at the very least, a substantial timeout. Fortunately, the company had no immediate bookings for the months ahead; also, the dancers' contracts were about to run out and had not yet been renegotiated.

Unencumbered by any formal obligations, following the end of the Met season, Ballet Theatre—for the second time in its short career—closed down.

"Now I'm going to go out to get money to do something solid, something more lasting than this year-to-year struggle to keep alive," Lucia announced in a press interview late that fall. Since the primary problem that had faced Ballet Theatre from the very beginning, at least in Lucia's eyes, was essentially financial, the solution now was clear: get more money for Ballet Theatre. This was going to be her main objective for the months ahead. She was spurred on by the fact that, providing her efforts were successful and the company could be resurrected, the following year would mark the company's twentieth anniversary.

Fund-raising, long-range planning, and institutional reorganization were not tasks that particularly suited Lucia's personal talents. She had no big-business experience, nor had she ever been closely associated with ranking corporate executives who knew how to plan and implement emergency rescue missions. Even when it was simply a question of direct, one-on-one fund-raising, Lucia did not like soliciting others for contributions. She would have much preferred that someone else raised the money and left her down in the trenches, coping with the day-to-day problems of running the company.

But there was no "someone else." The most likely source of help logically would have been the Ballet Theatre Foundation's board of trustees. However, the board as a whole still held back from taking direct responsibility for the actions or finances of the company. Members were willing to come to meetings when they could fit them into their schedules, to listen and advise and lend their moral support, even to donate or help raise a little cash, but other than that, the board continued to leave most problems to Lucia.

Although no major overhaul of the business side of the organization was attempted, there were some innovations adopted during the next fifteen months while the company was laid off. A Women's Auxiliary was organized, which staged an inaugural Ballet Theatre benefit at the Waldorf and netted $10,000 for the Foundation. Not a princely sum, even back then, but it nevertheless was a start.

There were other promising developments that Lucia was happy to recount in a series of little talks she gave to attract new donors: "an important Men's committee is going to work on a gala opening night"; "a prospectus is being prepared to present our story to foundations and corporations"; "we are forming chapters in as many cities as possible."

Also, at some point in each of the small informal gatherings, she would always include a reminder that "our goal, of course, is a home." It was a time-worn refrain, but early in 1959, it appeared to have been finally achieved when the Met Opera invited Ballet Theatre to move in and take charge of mounting all the dance sequences in its operas. Lucia promptly accepted and seized on the invitation as a sign of better days to come.

"So at last we now have a rehearsal home where the company can rehearse in peace," she would cheerfully recount, "instead of having to run around town, one hour here and one hour there, to noisy, inadequate, rented studios." Although the Met studios were almost entirely devoted to opera rehearsals, and the opera house was not at all a practical workspace for a major ballet company, Lucia was never one to dwell on the negative. It was much more her style to focus on the company's achievements, as she did before a group of women who gathered at the fashionable River Club on East 52nd Street in Manhattan to hear Lucia Chase tell the story of Ballet Theatre:

> We played 48 states, Canada, Mexico and Cuba, and Covent Garden our first ten years. In 1950 we were the first American company of any kind to tour the continent of Europe, and since then we have played in thirty-three countries. I believe we have covered more countries and more miles than any other attraction under the President's Program.

On top of all that, her latest piece of big news was that Ballet Theatre had just been asked by the State Department to tour the Soviet Union. The trip was scheduled to take place the following summer and would mark the first time that American dancers had ever been invited to perform in Russia, long considered the birthplace and home of classical ballet. More than anything else, it confirmed what Lucia had been claiming for years: that Ballet Theatre had earned the right to call itself America's national company.

The invitation to perform in Russia couldn't have come at a better time, just when the company was about to be called back from its yearlong hiatus to celebrate, in April, its twentieth anniversary with a three-week season at the Met. That in itself was a massive challenge, but now it was to be followed by a four-month tour of Europe with a grand finale in Russia. Ever since the devastating fire had practically wiped out the Ballet Theatre repertory and seriously threatened the very existence of the company, Lucia had staunchly kept the faith against all the naysayers and prophets of doom. Now after fifteen long, harrowing months of inactivity, suddenly a bright future seemed about to open and provide a great chance to prove them all wrong.

The year 1960 started with a gargantuan rehearsal period of eight full weeks. There were to be twenty-one productions offered in the much-heralded three-week rebirth of the company at the Met, including two premieres—Birgit Cullberg's *Lady from the Sea* and Herb Ross's *Dialogues (Serenade for 7)*. All the principal choreographers still alive who had helped build the company's renowned repertory were invited back to revive their most celebrated works. (All except Tudor, who was in charge of the Met Opera's recent collaboration with Ballet Theatre and was heading up the Met's new ballet school.)

As for the dancers, besides featuring a stellar roster of returning principals—Nora Kaye, Lupe Serrano, Ruth Ann Koesun, Erik Bruhn, John Kriza, Scott Douglas, Royes Fernandez—a veritable brigade of guest artists was also invited to take part, including Alicia Markova, Alicia Alonso, Claude Bessy, Igor Youskevitch, Muriel Bentley, Maria Karnilova, Eric Braun, and Agnes de Mille in the dual capacity of choreographer and dancer. Everything that might help prepare for a grand anniversary celebration was worked into the schedule, often at very great expense.

Yet the Met season was not a success. On opening night, William Dollar's *Constantia* was judged to be a tepid work: even though it was beautifully danced, it did not offer the kind of excitement necessary to highlight a gala. *Lady from the Sea* won only mild approval. Even Walter Terry, dance critic for the *Herald Tribune,* who was usually one of the company's most fervent admirers, admitted that he was disappointed by Ross's *Dialogues:*

> It has moments of tenderness in it, lusty bursts of movement bravado and some bits of antic humor. But the whole seems to be a collection of dislocations, nothing hangs together, and we are faced with a work which goes nowhere.

So much work and expense had gone into preparing for the big anniversary that in the end there was understandably a certain letdown from the high expectations that had opened the season. Yet nothing prepared the dance world for the bombshell that John Martin delivered in the *Times* on May 15 at the end of the season:

> If the American Ballet Theatre actually goes to the Soviet Union (which heaven forbid!), it will be a profound national humiliation. . . . American

Ballet Theatre was once a vital and brilliant company, but it has burnt itself out. In its recent engagement at the Met, it virtually collapsed before our eyes. . . . This is not a surprising development. Its devoted, determined, and wrong-headed director Lucia Chase has never seen the necessity for an artistic director. She has concentrated on financial support and patronage—women's committees, men's committees, chapters in various cities—which is all very good in its way; but because she herself is in no way qualified to direct the artistic activity of a company, and does not seem to be aware of the fact, she has allowed a once-distinguished repertory to age and shrivel, a once-great company to dwindle away. . . .

Between now and September when the first Russian dates are supposed to be played, there is no earthly possibility of making a company where none now exists. Who, in the name of reason, would make it? Miss Chase? She has had twenty years to try."

Lucia was exceptionally tough, and for years she had weathered the most insulting, scathing remarks that a legion of dancers, choreographers, company and theater managers, Hurok, and even her own son had leveled at her. Somehow she had always managed to maintain her dignity and poise and to remain calm, never seeming to mind or to hold a grudge for anything that anyone ever said. (Once, when she was asked how she could possibly endure so much hostile criticism, she laughingly explained how "each morning I just get up and dust off my shoulders.") But this attack in the city's most important paper by the dean of dance critics was more than she could dust off. She could not even talk about it. Nor could most of her friends or associates. Martin's critique was so personal and devastating that it left everyone stunned.

Everyone, that is, except for E.I., Lucia's fiercely loyal younger sibling. Shortly after the article appeared, E.I. spotted John Martin on his way into the theater and strode across the lobby to confront him. With all five feet three inches of her compact frame quivering with indignation, she reached up and slapped him square in the face, declaring in a voice that everyone could hear, "How dare you write such things about my sister!" It was not exactly the approved way to handle a powerful representative of the press, but E.I. was never one to hold back her feelings. Her outburst, however intemperate and injudicious, must have been a considerable solace to Lucia.

Much as the personal criticism hurt, the most devastating part of Martin's comments was where he assailed the State Department's plan to send the

American Ballet Theatre to Russia and called for an immediate cancellation of the tour. There was probably nothing in the dance world that meant more to Lucia than this opportunity for the company—one might almost say *her company*. It vindicated so much of all that she had worked for. The past year and a half had been particularly tough. It would have been easy to become demoralized and give up, but Lucia had never lost her spirit and contemplated defeat. Now just one critic's comments had thrown the company's grandest opportunity into limbo, perhaps even killed it.

As matters eventually turned out, Ballet Theatre's European tour was not canceled but was allowed to proceed as originally scheduled. However, even after the company was abroad and already receiving consistently favorable reviews, the final portion covering the visit to the USSR was still left waiting for final official confirmation by the controlling powers in Russia. A special representative of the Bolshoi Ballet made a command inspection of the company's performance in the Netherlands and sent back a favorable report, but that was followed by a further four-week period of agonizing silence. Finally, at the very last possible moment, when it seemed that the company would be obliged to call a halt and return home, formal permission was granted and contracts were signed authorizing it to proceed from Bucharest to Moscow and to commence its historic six-week engagement.

It wouldn't have been a genuine "powder-keg company" without at least one more hair-raising crisis. In this instance, all the sets and costumes to be used in Russia had been shipped well in advance, but somehow they didn't arrive at the Moscow theater until the afternoon before the scheduled opening. There was just barely enough time to unload and hang the scenery, and no chance to have even a rudimentary dress rehearsal in the totally unfamiliar theater, with a crew that spoke no English and had never seen any of the repertory.

Yet the opening night in the Stanislavsky Theater was a grand occasion, with Premier Nikita Khrushchev's wife and high Soviet dignitaries attending along with a great many of Russia's leading dancers and choreographers. For the next two weeks, Moscow audiences were consistently enthusiastic, sometimes wildly approving, as when Lupe Serrano had to repeat her variation in *Don Quixote* before the orchestra could continue, or when Erik Bruhn was bombarded with flowers after dancing the Black Swan pas de deux.

From the capital, the company went on to perform another two weeks in Tbilisi, the capital of Georgia, eleven days in Leningrad, where it had the warmest reception of the entire tour, then five days in Kiev before return-ing to Moscow for five final performances at the Lenin Sports Palace, an enormous hall seating 10,000 people similar to New York's Madison Square Garden.

For the last night, without any prior notice, Premier Khrushchev made a surprise appearance, accompanied by the minister of culture, three mem-bers of the Central Committee, and several deputy ministers. Afterwards Khrushchev hosted a party in a private dining room on the upper floor of the sports palace for the entire company, an occasion that rated front-page coverage by *Pravda* the following day.

The official word on the tour was delivered by a Russian critic, Natalia Roslavleva:

> The visit was definitely successful. . . . The dancers worked very hard on the preceding European tour and came to Moscow in much better form than when they left home ground. Moreover, contact with the friendly Soviet audiences had the effect of a life potion on the company. The performances were on the whole presented at a very high level, and the company definitely gave of its best with every appearance.

It almost seemed as though she was writing to refute the article in the *New York Times*.

***

After returning home (and making a three-month cross-country tour that included some forty one-night stands!), the company opened a two-week season at the Broadway Theatre.

Although American Ballet Theatre had been very well received in Europe and on its national tour, New York was always a special challenge, particularly this time after having been so savagely lambasted by the city's leading dance critic at the end of its last home season one year earlier. The big question on everyone's mind was what John Martin would choose to say.

His reaction was surprisingly favorable, particularly regarding Lupe Serrano and Erik Bruhn, the company's two principal dancers:

> [Bruhn] is magnificent. If there is another male dancer in the field who is his peer, it would be worth a great deal to know his name and where he is to be seen. . . . As to Lupe Serrano, something about her success in Russia

must have given her a new sense of her art, for she has returned in every way finer and more exciting than before. . . . Here is a new name to add to the top line of our ballerinas.

Yet Martin couldn't resist ending his review of the season with one more jab:

This brings us to considerations of the organization as a whole, its policies, and its shortcomings. Since that subject was covered here with reasonable completeness just before the visit to the Soviet Union, there is no point in going into it again. Suffice it to say that it is still exactly the same company. It has come back to us a year later running more smoothly and rehearsed to the gills, but still directed not at all.

There was nothing for Lucia to do but to dust off her shoulders and go back out on the fund-raising trail to tell her version of how the company was faring. In Texas, holding six pages of notes composed in her habitually neat handwriting, she addressed the new Ballet Theatre chapter in Houston:

If you could see the impression we have made on Iron Curtain coun-tries—two years ago in Poland, this past summer in Bulgaria, Russia most important of all—you would realize that the American Ballet Theatre is a wonderful expression of life and culture in a free country, and their interest in us and respect for our art is a tremendous asset.

Six days later, she spoke to another gathering at the Westover School in Connecticut, saying, "We hope to have ten chapters this year, including Cincinnati, Indianapolis, Providence, Waterbury, and Wilmington. . . . You are part of us."

These small, informal talks were where Lucia appeared at her best, friendly and cheerful, never in the least boastful or superior but sound-ing plain and simple, just like anyone in the audience. But of course she wasn't: she was Lucia Chase, celebrated dancer and company director, just back from an epochal five-month tour of Europe and the Soviet Union. She was small, trim, and erect in her chic suit, talking about how much fun and how worthwhile slogging around Russia had been. There was no art or showmanship nor tricks of any kind in what she said or how she said it, just a bright straightforward account of the gospel according to Lucia, and it always worked. People were enchanted to have her come talk to them, and sometimes—most times—a good many of them even gave money. Not a great deal, but it was more than had ever been given up to then.

She never gave up, delivering the same engaging line over and over again, that the company was a national treasure that should be everyone's concern. As for herself, although she never came right out and said as much, it was clear to anyone listening to her that for Lucia Chase, American Ballet Theatre was a living, breathing body that she valued and cherished above everything else in her world.

It would take something awful to happen to prove this wasn't entirely true.

16. A Second Tragedy

The Navy and Coast Guard launched
a search yesterday morning for a
blue sloop with two New Yorkers
aboard off the Rhode Island–
Connecticut coast.
—*Waterbury American,* November
15, 1962

THE FIRST WORD CAME AROUND NOON on Tuesday, November 13, 1962.

Lucia was in Ballet Theatre's office when someone called from the law firm of Debevoise Plimpton, Lyons & Gates to say that Tom Ewing had not turned up for work that morning and no one seemed to know where he was. Did she?

She didn't. Nor did I. Nor did Lucia's sister Dee in Middlebury, where Tommy often went when he was not working in New York. Nor did Dee's daughter, Deirdre, who worked at the *New York Times* and was a particularly close member of our family.

Everyone remembered how at the big party for family and friends that my mother had given the week before, Tommy had talked ruefully about the way bad weather the past two weekends had postponed his plan to sail his boat, *Kria,* down from Rhode Island to its winter quarters in Essex, Connecticut. Basil Carmody, our cousin and Deirdre's brother, had signed up to go with him both times, but now he couldn't arrange it for the coming weekend.

At one point during the party, Tommy had asked me whether I could go, but I couldn't either. Nor could his old Yale roommate and Rhode Island chum, Eric Smith, who had recently broken his arm. Nor could Deirdre or a girlfriend, Ann Chambers. Finally, a fellow law associate at Debevoise Plimpton, David Evans, agreed to step in as crew, and they had reputedly set off after work Friday for Rhode Island.

Since then, no one had heard anything or thought much more about their expedition that weekend. Monday was Armistice Day, when many at the law office didn't come in to work. But now it was Tuesday, and when neither Tom nor Dave Evans showed up, someone at their office phoned Lucia. When she said she knew nothing, the caller from Debevoise said it was probably nothing, but still they would phone around and then call her back.

In an instant, all other thoughts and concerns left Lucia's mind, and she sat numb and alone by the phone, just waiting for it to ring again.

Edna Lindberg, owner of the marina at Snug Harbor, Rhode Island, reported that the sky had been clear and the outlook good last Saturday when the two young men sailed out of Salt Pond late that morning heading south. The Coast Guard confirmed that a strong wind had been blowing and the water was quite rough, but probably not enough to cause them to turn back. However, it was estimated that by mid-afternoon they would have begun to encounter gale-force winds and exceptionally heavy seas.

Around 4:30 p.m. that same Saturday, the crew at the Watch Hill lighthouse spotted the *Kria,* sailing under just a jib, a short distance offshore. The boat reportedly passed the lighthouse in fine form, but then it appeared to be heading too far south toward some dangerous reefs.

Although it was practically dark, the full moon meant that the man on watch could still see the sloop continuing on the same course about half a mile farther before it appeared that the running and stern lights went out. A flashlight blinked directly at the lighthouse several times, causing him to leave his post to call the nearest Coast Guard rescue station at New London. When he returned minutes later, he could still see a light, which indicated to him that the boat was proceeding slowly toward the entrance into Little Narragansett Bay and Stonington Harbor.

Two cutters from New London arrived within twenty minutes and searched the surrounding waters for several hours but found nothing. Since there had been no report of a missing boat, it was assumed there had been no accident, and consequently there was no search conducted on Sunday.

Nor on Monday, Armistice Day. It was only on Tuesday morning that anyone began to worry. Both the Coast Guard and Navy were contacted shortly after noon, but because it was November, there were not sufficient daylight hours remaining for planes to fly out that day. All that was known by late Tuesday was that the *Kria* was still missing but that no wreckage had been reported along the nearby beaches.

Lucia stayed in the office all that afternoon, sitting quietly at her desk. She didn't want to be away from the phone even for a few minutes.

I had spent that afternoon downtown in Greenwich Village. When I returned home, my wife, Carol, told me that Tommy had been reported missing. I called our uncle, Bayard Ewing, in Rhode Island. He had already spoken to Senator John O. Pastore, who had asked the Naval Air Station at Quonset to begin a search at dawn the following day. I left immediately and drove up to Bayard's house in North Kingston to join the search.

In New York, George Adams, Dick Pendleton, and Dave Smalley, law associates at Debevoise Plimpton, worked all night to organize a second search from the New York area, while Lucia and Deirdre Carmody set up the first of three 24-hour vigils at the apartment, Tommy's old home.

By early Wednesday morning, the entire coastline and offshore area from New York to Massachusetts were being covered by Coast Guard cutters and planes, a helicopter and planes and boats of the Navy, and a private plane with me, Uncle Bayard, and cousin Irving Sheldon aboard.

It seemed inconceivable at the time that the *Kria* could have been destroyed without leaving any traces. By the end of the day, there was still no conclusive evidence of disaster.

The search was expanded Thursday when the Fram Corporation and Livermore & Knight each donated planes to supplement the efforts of the Coast Guard and Navy. Fishing boats were kept constantly on alert by marine operators in Boston and New York. The Oceanographic Laboratory at Woods Hole, Massachusetts, provided detailed advice on currents, and the shore line of Block Island, Fisher's Island, and all land far down the coast below Watch Hill was inspected on foot. The entire firm of Debevoise Plimpton, senior partners and switchboard operators alike, dedicated themselves to the search. It was a consolation for everyone to be involved in some form of action.

But then, late Friday afternoon, some gear and pieces of a sailboat were found on Sandy Point near Stonington Harbor. I called home to tell Carol that Bayard, Eric Smith, and I were driving down the coast to Watch Hill to find out whether the items that had been discovered were from the *Kria*. Carol said she would go over to the apartment to sit with Lucia, Deirdre, and Dee.

As fate would have it, an old cherished friend of the family had just arrived from Italy to stay at the apartment and chose to join them all for dinner that night. Lucia made the others promise not to say one word about Tommy's being missing. According to Deirdre, each time his name came up and the Italian friend asked how he was doing, the subject was changed, and Lucia would hastily start talking about Alex, who happened to be off in Rhode Island for a couple of days, but he and Carol had the two most wonderful children: she just couldn't get over how fast they were growing and how bright they were—Carol must make a point of bringing them over to show them off. The conversation went on like that for all three courses without a hint that anything else might be on all their minds.

Very shortly after dinner, Lucia exclaimed how tired the friend from Italy must have been after her long trip, and she was hustled off upstairs to bed. It was only a quarter of an hour later that I phoned . . . to tell my mother that the remains of the *Kria* had washed ashore and that Tommy was dead.

All that night, Lucia sobbed and talked wildly. There was no consoling her. "Don't worry," she told the three of them sitting in her bedroom. "I won't do again what I did when Tom died. Just let me tonight."

She was back on her feet the next day when I arrived from Rhode Island. I went straight to the apartment and rode up in the elevator to where she was waiting, and I hugged her as tightly as I could.

Two days later, my mother, with all our family and friends, and lawyers of Debevoise Plimpton massed behind us, stood ramrod straight in the front pew at the memorial service held at St. James Church around the corner from the apartment.

On November 30, Tommy's body came ashore on the north side of Napatree Point. At a small private service, he was buried next to his father and grandparents in the family plot at Oakland Cemetery in Yonkers.

Part 4

17. *Les Noces*

We are doing this kind of season to
prove what we could do if we had
money.
—Statement by Lucia Chase in the
Saturday Review of Literature,
February 27, 1965

T HE SAME DAY THAT THE first pieces of the wreckage of
Tommy's boat were found on the low-lying island of Sandy Point near
Stonington Harbor, a headline in the *New York Times* announced, "Ballet
Theatre Moves to Capital."

According to the accompanying article, the actual move wouldn't take
place for another ten days, with the first performance of the company
scheduled to take place December 10.

On that harrowing night I had phoned from Rhode Island to attest
that the *Kria* had gone down and taken Tommy with it, Lucia had promised those in the apartment trying to comfort her that she would not give
way this time to the same overwhelming grief that half a lifetime ago had
afflicted her when her husband, Tom, had died. Somehow she managed to
keep her word, and on December 4, directly after a burial service was held
for my brother in Yonkers, she went down to Washington where to the dis-
belief and awe of everyone (including Jackie Kennedy, honorary chairman
of the Washington Ballet Foundation, who commented later that she could

only barely imagine what Lucia was going through), she met the company backstage and then took her place in the audience in Lisner Auditorium for American Ballet Theatre's inaugural performance as the new resident ballet company in the nation's capital.

Despite being awarded a new home, ABT was going through a particularly hard time artistically and had received a disturbing number of bad notices in the press.

In June 1961, the English critic Mary Clarke had written in the *New York Times:*

> The American Ballet Theatre has lost that company flavor, or personality, that once made it so endearing. Fine dancers are there in plenty, but so far as I could see, the repertory contains neither the new works of genius that sustains the New York City Ballet nor the full-length classics (old and new) on which our Royal Ballet so securely rests.

Four months later, on October 15, Walter Sorell in the *Providence Sunday Journal* warned that ABT was, in many ways, in danger of losing ground and should return to its original conception of being a ballet company that did not hire ballerinas and choreographers but created them.

Now in January 1963, one of the most influential voices in the dance world, Claudia Cassidy, commented in the *Chicago Tribune:*

> At its best, this company is fair to middling. At its worst, it is an embarrassment. A home would help. Money could help. But without taste and talent in a compulsive (renewed) drive toward quality, it will not be worth saving.

The following month, the leading dance critic in the company's new home base in Washington, D.C., sounded off after seeing a Ballet Theatre workshop performance in Roosevelt High School Auditorium: "One wonders how many such auditoriums the company encounters on its tours, and whether it always compromises its standards so readily."

More serious than all these negative comments was the way it didn't take long for the Washington Ballet Guild to discover that its first effort at underwriting the company had cost nearly twice the amount it had budgeted, and that the longtime responsibility of sponsoring the American Ballet Theatre was a considerably more expensive proposition than it could possibly afford. In April 1963, exactly six months after offering an official new home for the company, the Guild called off all future arrangements. Faced with the prospect of living in the capital without a local sponsor, at the end of May, Ballet Theatre Foundation announced that its Washington connection would cease, that the Foundation would reassume full responsibility for the company, and that it was already in the process of making plans for a restricted tour for 1963–64.

For once, the company's fortunes were not paramount in Lucia's heart and mind. At the first opportunity that presented itself, she broke away and made a special trip to Rhode Island to talk to the lighthouse keeper at Watch Hill who had first reported seeing *Kria* in the throes of the November storm. It was the first of many visits she would make to that fateful place.

She spent most of the summer of 1963 in Narragansett. Often, late in the afternoon, she would drive by herself down the coast to the spot in Watch Hill where the *Kria* was last seen and sit there for an hour or more on the lawn near the lighthouse or on the rocks, staring out at the water, then slowly return home to rejoin the family, never mentioning where she had been.

Uppermost in her mind that summer was a yearning to do something that would help preserve the memory of Tommy, and she developed two projects that soon became consuming interests. The first was to have privately published the handwritten notes Tommy had compiled to record the far-flung motorcycle trip he and George Ford, a friend from school and college days, had taken eight years earlier through much of the Middle East and on through India and Pakistan.

The other, more elaborate project was to build a small house in Tommy's memory just across the street from High Tide on a vacant lot that looked out from slightly elevated ground over a broad expanse of the Atlantic Ocean. Her idea was to fill the house with all the furniture, pictures, and various memorabilia from Tommy's New York apartment and then to maintain it as a summer place where his friends could come spend a few days (or as long as they wished, the longer the better) just the way they used to when he was alive. The cottage was to be named Moonraker after the first small boat Tommy had sailed and raced years earlier out of Saunderstown.

The little house became Lucia's paramount interest for most of the following year. It was the kind of task that required lots of small decisions, notes jotted at night on a yellow pad placed by her bedside, a multitude of telephone calls and local errands to choose fabrics and wallpapers and hardware, just the kind of ongoing detail work she had become accustomed to and was very good at doing for Ballet Theatre.

In May 1964, *Journal* by Thomas Ewing III was published, and Moonraker was nearing completion. Soon three years had passed since the company's last season in New York (at the 54th Street Theater).

Even without Lucia's direct involvement, the combined staff, with some direction from Oliver Smith, had kept ABT functioning. Late in the summer of 1964, there were ten weeks of performances throughout Central and South America, the third such tour sponsored by the State Department, ending up with a whirlwind trip back through the southern United States, mostly one-night appearances except for slightly extended stays in San Antonio, Houston, and New Orleans. Yet despite this activity, there were times when it seemed as though the company was just marking time, waiting for the captain to come back.

As the year neared its end, ABT gradually reasserted its inexorable hold on Lucia Chase because 1965 would mark its twenty-fifth anniversary. Lucia had never let it go under, and now her tenacity ("good old New England stubbornness," Agnes de Mille called it) made it all but impossible for her to remain on the sidelines while the company gradually slid into nothingness. The challenge was formidable, especially the cost of bringing everything back to the highest level. Working closely with Oliver Smith, she started laying the groundwork for the grand anniversary event.

It would take place at the New York State Theater, which had just opened at Lincoln Center. The absolute prerequisite to accomplish all that was being envisioned was a mammoth twelve-week full-company rehearsal. Plans called for six new works, along with seventeen others to be revived. Most of the choreographers still alive were contracted to personally conduct their own rehearsals. Harald Lander, after the successful remounting of his ballet *Etudes* for the company in 1961, was commissioned to mount the two-act Danish classic *La Sylphide*, which had been originally choreographed in 1836 by August Bournonville at the Royal Theater in Copenhagen. The modern dancer and choreographer Glen Tetley was engaged to direct the U.S. premiere of his ballet *Sargasso*, which had just been created for the Netherlands Dance Theatre. Two new works, *The Wind in the Mountains* and *The Four Marys*, were to be created by Agnes de Mille, as well as a greatly revised version of her earlier *Tally-Ho*. In addition, she was engaged personally to rehearse her *Fall River Legend*, as was Herbert Ross for *Caprichos* and Tudor for *Jardin aux Lilas* and *Dark Elegies*.

Before rehearsals started, Lucia was asked in an interview whether she herself would return to dance the Eldest Sister in Tudor's *Pillar of Fire.*

"Heavens!" she replied, "I haven't been on pointe in five years. I don't even know whether I could get up there. But if Mr. Tudor wants me to tackle a third performance of *Pillar,* maybe I'll try." When it came to her part as Lizzie Borden's stepmother in *Fall River Legend,* she was willing to do that too, saying, "It's not a dancing role, it just needs the meanest-looking woman around."

But none of these individual projects compared, in terms of cost or public excitement or sheer artistic risk, with the endeavor that Lucia precipitated when she asked Jerome Robbins to return to Ballet Theatre in order to create a new ballet.

Robbins was very reluctant. His work for Broadway, Hollywood, and the New York City Ballet (where he had worked alongside Balanchine as associate artistic director from 1949 until 1958, then left to form his own Ballets U.S.A.) kept him incredibly busy. He didn't have the time, nor did he need the work or the money.

Lucia was relentless. To her way of thinking, no twenty-fifth anniversary of American Ballet Theatre would be complete, or even conceivable, without a new ballet by Jerry Robbins.

There was only one idea that Robbins would even consider— *Les Noces,* to the music of the same name by Stravinsky. The same theme and music had been created in 1923 for Diaghilev's Ballets Russes by Bronislava Nijinska, the sister of Nijinsky, a celebrated choreographer in her own right and an early participant of Ballet Theatre. Robbins had never seen her version of *Les Noces* . . . fortunately, according to a statement he made some time afterwards, or he might never have tried it.

His conception for *Les Noces* was so considerably different from his other works, and was so complex in its rhythms and themes and highly charged patterns, that he felt he had set himself a challenge that was almost bound to fail—if it ever made it to the stage at all, he was quick to add. He did practically everything he could to duck the assignment, setting almost prohibitive requirements in his contract. One demand was that he be "allotted four hours of rehearsal time on each working day," a condition that was practically impossible to meet, considering the number of other choreographers, the very limited amount of studio space available, and the scheduling problem involved when each dancer cast in *Les Noces* was also in many other works being prepared in the same rehearsal period.

In another clause, Robbins insisted on having expressly stated in his contract that "it was understood that if, at any point, even at the last moment before the premiere, either his creative inspiration flagged or rehearsals did not proceed well and according to schedule, the entire project would have to be canceled."

It was foolhardy to agree to either of these conditions, but Lucia persisted. Tudor, de Mille, and Robbins represented vintage Ballet Theatre. They were Lucia's sanctified trinity, and having already garnered the other two, she was willing to go to any lengths to ensure that Robbins would also participate.

In an article in the *New York Times* before the ballet opened, Robbins wrote:

> I am deeply grateful to Lucia Chase. . . . I've told her over and over the tree is slippery and the height tremendous, but nothing will avail. "Forward!" she cries. "Danger!" yell I. "Onward," she prods. So here we go.

Like the rehearsal requirements, the financial demands for producing and performing *Les Noces* were extraordinary. Although most theaters were equipped and willing to provide one grand piano, for playing his score of *Les Noces* Stravinsky specified that four grand pianos had to be onstage. There also had to be four sets of tympani and a full singing chorus, which in this case was to be the American Concert Choir, also positioned onstage to render the full impact of Stravinsky's magnificently barbaric score. The combination of this special instrumentation and the full-sized chorus made it absolutely certain that no matter how popular *Les Noces* proved to be, and regardless of how many tickets the public bought to see it, no performance could ever hope to pay even its immediate expenses.

On top of all this were the demands placed on the dancers. According to Robbins:

> They must count continuously, unerringly, and with unceasing concentration. Once the music starts, nothing can stop it. You push a button and this terrifying machine begins to scream, launching into lamentations and incessant chattering, shocking you with unexpected outbursts and hypnotic murmuring. . . . a montage or Joycean stream of Russian folk songs and poems, pieces of wedding conversations, toasts, taunts, prayers, ribald folk symbols and fertility images expressed in terms of animals and all nature.

All this was to be combined in a single work that would never have the chance to be tried out on the road but would continue to be assembled right up to the moment it went on. At the same time, a huge set with massive drops, designed in a couple of weeks by Oliver Smith, was being painted in a rush and would be delivered at the last minute for the dress rehearsal, along with the four pianos and tympani and full chorus onstage, with Leonard Bernstein himself in the pit to conduct the opening performance.

Jerry Robbins, Oliver Smith, and Leonard Bernstein, the original neophyte trio who had created *Fancy Free* twenty-one years earlier, were now each celebrated artists in their own fields, back together one more (and last) time. Despite all the fearful expenses, rehearsal pressures, and production complexities, any one of which might have nullified the project and all of which made proceeding with *Les Noces* seemingly insane, still Lucia would not be deterred. As reported in "Ballet Theatre at Twenty-five," an article by Emily Coleman that appeared on February 27, 1965, in the *Saturday Review of Literature,* Lucia stated:

> We always knew we had to have new works each year, but we couldn't afford it. Now we have made the extra effort. It was simply a question of whether to give up or have the twenty-fifth anniversary the way we wanted it.

It remained to be seen whether all the money and heartache and herculean work would turn out to be a grand success or a colossal extravagance prompted primarily by ego and in the end showing little of any enduring worth.

18. A Full-Length *Swan Lake*

We had to go on or go out with
colors flying. The year before had
been a "down" year, and I just
couldn't let Ballet Theatre go out
that way.
—Lucia Chase, from a 1965 interview
with Walter Terry

L*IFE* MAGAZINE said it most succinctly: "The American Ballet Theatre, in its most successful season ever, bowled everybody over." The success was all the more striking, considering that this inaugural engagement in the New York State Theater at Lincoln Center could also very well have marked the demise of the company. Instead, as Lillian Moore, noted dance critic, historian, and teacher, reported in May 1965 in a summary review for the *Dancing Times:*

> In recent years Ballet Theatre has failed to put its best foot forward during its brief seasons in New York, and its status close to the top of the list of American dance companies has seemed in jeopardy. . . . Now, in four weeks of magnificent dancing in the most varied and truly comprehensive repertoire of any ballet ensemble on this side of the Atlantic, it has firmly reestablished its high position. The American Ballet Theatre has never been in more splendid form.

High praise was showered on one dancer after another: Walter Terry wrote, "In Lupe Serrano, the American Ballet Theatre possesses one of the major ballerinas of our day. . . . Royes Fernandez is at the peak of his career." Doris Hering, reviewing *Études* in *Dance* magazine, observed that "the real surprise was Scott Douglas. He has always been a precise and skillful dancer, but now there is richness as he reaches into space, boldness and a touch of abandon as he accentuates a rhythm." P. W. Manchester, covering Glen Tetley's *Sargasso* in *Dance News*, wrote, "The work is another triumph for Sallie Wilson, who was triumphing all over the place throughout the season." And Allan Hughes in the *Times* even included a salute to Lucia: "It was especially good to see Miss Chase back on the stage, because she is a character actress who can project wonderfully just by the bearing of her walk or the tilt of her chin."

The supreme test of the entire season was understandably Robbins's *Les Noces*. The night of the premiere, with Leonard Bernstein in the pit and the chorus massed in back, the curtain went up to reveal Oliver Smith's stupendous monolithic set, huge robed monastic figures that immediately established a majestic, brooding ecclesiastical atmosphere. Meanwhile, the action that proceeded to explode onstage was as vigorous, throbbing, gut-wrenching as ever performed by a professional ballet company. Whether people immediately warmed to what they were seeing was somehow beside the point. There was no doubt that they had just witnessed a stupendous theatrical achievement.

The dancers in *Les Noces* felt the same way. Forty years later, participants in the early performances are emphatic that it was one of the most exciting and fulfilling challenges that they ever experienced. Frank Smith, who performed the role of the Matchmaker, still remembers how physically draining Robbins's choreography was, how the dancers' eyes used to fill with tears and joy and emotion, and how the whole company would hug each other onstage each night after the curtain came down.

The initial reviews, for the most part, were either cautiously worded, begrudging in their praise, or in one case even distinctly critical:

Robbins's translation of the complicated and fascinating score into dance terms is masterly (Lillian Moore). It would seem that Robbins has not yet evolved certain key gestures which would give individuality to the principal characters (Doris Hering). The whole ballet is characteristically neat, slick as wax, the dancers watchable as monkeys . . . [but] ultimately it misses completely, either as abstract drama or as extended rhythmic configuration (Arlene Croce).

Yet writing months afterwards in the *New York Times,* Clive Barnes called *Les Noces* "unquestionably one of the most important ballets to be created in recent years":

> It is breathtaking in its imagery, in the power of its dancing, in its sense of human compassion, and in its sheer beauty of craftsmanship and imaginative grasp. . . . This *Les Noces* is a masterpiece.

It was also a huge extravagance. *Fancy Free,* Robbins's pioneer effort for Ballet Theatre twenty-one years earlier, had been performed everywhere under every conceivable set of conditions, from the Metropolitan Opera House to the lowliest high school gym, including a Las Vegas nightclub, the ballroom of the Waldorf Astoria, the steps of the New York Public Library, even once on the deck of a U.S. Navy aircraft carrier. *Les Noces,* on the other hand, was practically impossible to perform anywhere outside of New York. Furthermore, while nights with *Les Noces* on the program generally attracted an unusually large audience, they also inevitably produced a deficit, even when the theater was sold out.

Yet Robbins had provided just the excitement, the daring, the towering artistry that had recently seemed to be so lacking in Ballet Theatre. Despite its total impracticality, *Les Noces* gave an exclamation point to the entire anniversary season. The enthusiastic public response mirrored the sensational debut of the company twenty-five years earlier, a triumph generally attributed to Dick Pleasant. This triumph Lucia could claim. Although a great many other people contributed to what was a tremendous team effort, it could never have occurred if she had not willed it into action, hounded each participant, and set a constant example of confidence and determination. Faced with the daunting financial implications of all that the anniversary season entailed, she never flinched.

The critical significance of the occasion was pointed out on the eve of the season's opening in a lengthy article by Emily Coleman, "Ballet Theatre at Twenty-five," which appeared in the *Saturday Review of Literature:*

> Here, then, is a company with a distinguished, if spotty past, and with a present potential that could restore much of its old luster. The company has, after all, a record of pulling its own chestnuts out of the fire. In 1960, after the twentieth-anniversary debacle, [when] ABT was the first American bal-

let to tour the Soviet Union, somehow a predicted disaster was turned into a smashing success. It will have to turn the trick again. But what if it does? The same old problems remain: the company will still have no permanent home . . . and it will still, it is assumed, retain its indecisive leadership and haphazard business operations.

The assessment is harsh and yet hard to refute. Even while attributing enormous credit to Lucia Chase for the way time and again she rescued American Ballet Theatre from extinction, a large part of the constantly precarious state of the company was Lucia's own doing—or at least the result of things she did not do.

Perhaps not at the very beginning. Back in the early 1940s, when ballet was not a popular art form in the United States and Ballet Theatre was plowing essentially new ground, whoever took the lead probably had to do it single-handedly, including, when necessary, paying the cost of getting a ballet company established. But once the company was firmly in existence, it was critical that major steps be taken as early as possible to build an effective support system to ensure its survival.

Lucia never faced up to this fact. On the rare occasions when she had a spare moment in the office, she might use it to dictate a fund-raising letter to her secretary, Florence Pettan, or even more likely pick up her pen and write a personal message to an old friend or relative, even someone she had just met, requesting help for Ballet Theatre. "Doing my homework" was what she called it. For twenty-five years now she had done this, not happily or as a top priority but as a rather painful duty she grudgingly accepted as another part of her job.

It had long been the habit of anyone who became involved with Ballet Theatre to applaud Lucia's spirit, the way she carried on regardless of all adversity. But there was a problem arising from her unmitigating support of the company: in order to allow for building an effective infrastructure that would undertake to ensure Ballet Theatre's continuity, Lucia Chase had to be willing to give up her total control of all aspects of the company and hand the reins for running the business over to someone or some group of people other than herself. As long as she continued to make all the critical decisions, particularly those involving how much money was to be spent on what items and when, no one was going to take the fiscal burden off her shoulders.

This had been true ever since Dick Pleasant had originated Ballet

Theatre. Early in the second year, when it became apparent that he could not raise the funds to pay for his high-cost ambitions, he was obliged to resign. The same pattern repeated itself during Alden Talbot's tenure when a conflict arose over who was to meet all the current and projected operating costs of the company: to no one's surprise, Talbot said he wasn't willing or able to do this and accordingly stepped down. As Lucia's lawyer, John Wharton, wryly used to observe, "The hand that pays the piper calls the tune," and for Ballet Theatre, that hand always belonged to Lucia.

This is not to say that in each of those early situations, Lucia wasn't right to keep firm hold of the reins. Pleasant couldn't be depended on to keep costs under control; Talbot was businesslike and well meaning but not totally committed. Yet at some point in the course of more than two decades, Lucia either should have seen to it or pleaded with others to arrange for her that the authority for running the business side of the company was transferred away from her into appropriate and competent new hands.

The most logical candidate would have been a general manager or director, hired and supervised by the board of trustees of the Ballet Theatre Foundation. Yet ever since the Foundation was instituted, nearly twenty years earlier, whenever there was a board meeting, there might be considerable discussion about various critical issues facing the company, but in the end everyone always voted for whatever Lucia wanted. This was understandable, since the alternative was for the board to accept responsibility on the spot for what could amount to possibly hundreds of thousands of dollars.

The result was that, as a governing body, the board of trustees was totally ineffective. As late as 1965, a quarter of a century since the birth of Ballet Theatre, in addition to Lucia and Oliver, longtime associate Charlie Payne, and Charles Taft (Lucia's brother-in-law in Cincinnati, who had married her sister Eleanor), the board consisted of just nine other people, a distressingly small group composed primarily of kindhearted social figures or businessmen who were willing to spend a few hours and perhaps a few thousand dollars to help poor Lucia but not to take the ultimate responsibility for the company out of her hands and into their own.

In 1965, the chairman, who had held the position for the past five years, was Byam Stevens, a distinguished stockbroker with impeccable personal credentials. Among other qualities to make him particularly acceptable to Lucia, he was a graduate of St. Paul's School and Yale, in the class exactly between her two sons. Stevens was also the most committed, the best informed about ballet matters, and the most businesslike of all the chairmen that the Foundation had experienced up to this time.

However, although he was chairman, Stevens was in no way mandated to determine the future course of the company. Shortly after he came into office in 1960, the question arose of whether the company should follow its triumphant visit to Russia and subsequent U.S. tour with an additional two-week engagement at the Broadway Theatre. Stevens had come out strongly against the idea. It was his considered opinion that attempting a seriously constricted New York season in a commercial theater immediately following the other two major performing stints just didn't make good business sense. "But she did it anyway," he recalled with a rueful little laugh.

After all the highly publicized seasons in New York, with a couple of thousand people on average attending every performance, plus annual cross-country tours which, together, had reached over 200 cities, now there were large audiences in all the major municipalities. Yet, at the same time, there were only twenty-five donors—the equivalent of just one new person garnered each year of the company's existence—who gave $1,000 or more to help secure Ballet Theatre's future.

While this degree of financial support was drastically inadequate, it was what might be expected, considering that the entire full-time business staff in the company's New York office consisted of a business manager, a public relations person, a secretary, and a bookkeeper. The idea of developing a substantial organization capable of conducting highly organized fund-raising to cope with the cost of Ballet Theatre's ongoing operations was obviously a very low, if not an almost nonexistent, priority. This deficiency, harsh as it may seem to say so, has to be attributed to Lucia, since she still retained all the power and had the last word about everything that went on in Ballet Theatre.

At the beginning of the 1965–66 season, Ballet Theatre had only $150,000 available. Meanwhile, it was estimated that at least $300,000 was needed to set out on a new year of activities.

"We should have closed right there," Lucia admitted, "but we went on a short summer tour." This wasn't just another tour, at least not in her eyes. It constituted a landmark event in the company's career, since Alaska and Hawaii were among the states covered, which meant that by the end of the tour, American Ballet Theatre could boast of having performed in all fifty states. Historic achievements like that, while insignificant in terms of the company's survival, meant a great deal to Lucia. Similarly, by the end of the tour, she was often recounting how, in Honolulu, she bought what she called "my Lincoln Center opening-night dress." As she would explain, "It was a gesture to boost company morale."

Deciding to press forward to conduct one more Lincoln Center season was a tremendous gamble. Despite her unfailing optimism, Lucia recognized that without substantial help, the company would have to close. Already in the course of the past year, applications had been submitted to about twenty large foundations, but they had garnered nothing in return. By the end of the summer, most possibilities had been exhausted, and there was very little hope in sight.

Just at that critical moment, on September 5, 1965, a full-page article entitled "Dance" written by Agnes de Mille appeared in the *New York Herald Tribune,* announcing in characteristically dramatic Agnes de Mille language that "this autumn, Ballet Theatre faces the imminent prospect of extinction."

The reason the company was in danger, de Mille insisted, was due not to its own failings but to the inordinately high costs of a noncommercial artistic institution like American Ballet Theatre. Actually, de Mille pointed out, the company in its most recent New York season did very impressive business, grossing $90,000 in each of the last two weeks, including $13,000 just for the final performance. This was quite an impressive figure considering that the top-priced ticket was a mere $6. The problem was that the multitude of essential expenses far exceeded the potential income available through the box office.

De Mille went on to enumerate all that had gone into the total season: six new works mounted and premiered, seventeen old works revived, necessitating twelve weeks of full-company rehearsal at $11,000 a week or over $130,000, all prior to any production or actual performance expenses. The costume bill alone was nearly $50,000, the orchestra rehearsals over $90,000, the rental of the theater $88,000, and crew costs nearly $90,000.

Meanwhile, Ballet Theatre had received no state help and no big foundation grants, which, de Mille claimed, had been withheld on the totally unfair charge that Ballet Theatre had no proper artistic direction:

This is an odd contention in view of the record: in its 25 years of existence, Ballet Theatre has produced as many masterpieces as any contemporary company in the world, and discovered more creative talents. And how, pray, did the fabulous last season get on? By accident?

Having laid the groundwork to rage against the iniquity of it all, de Mille's protest soared:

> Here stands ready a company with the world's greatest repertory, a fortune in sets and costumes, a first-class trained complement of dancers, a roster of choreographers unmatched. With the gigantic funds at the disposal of foundations for non-profit organizations, is it not possible for monies to be diverted to this use? Where better? Yet the business men hesitate. There is no time for hesitation. We are in famine. The cry of disaster has been heard before in relation to Ballet Theatre, and each time Lucia Chase with incredible generosity has rescued the enterprise. But she has at last come to the end of her resources, and although she has struggled to maintain the company until such time as popular or state recognition would bring help, she can do so no longer. . . . If the funds are not forthcoming immediately, the company will be obliterated. Given our very great wealth, our enormous creativity, our enthusiasm and zest, this would be unpardonable. We are face to face with a national disgrace, and a very real national loss.

Very powerful words, printed prominently in a major newspaper, written by a highly respected and formidable dance authority. Yet time was running out. The upcoming New York season, scheduled for late January, was only four months away. About the same time that de Mille wrote her letter, Ballet Theatre's board of trustees met and reluctantly concluded that, unless some undefined, unanticipated, and thoroughly unlikely stroke of good fortune materialized in the next few months, all future business should be concluded and the company disbanded after February 16, 1966, the date of the last performance at the New York State Theater.

As ABT's artistic director, principal supporter, and one of the three vice presidents of the Foundation's board of trustees, Lucia must have given at least grudging support to this formal resolution passed by the board. Nevertheless, it did not deter her from choosing this moment, of all times, to launch the most challenging creative venture any ballet company might undertake: a full-scale version of the nineteenth century's greatest classic ballet, *Swan Lake*.

The mere idea of attempting a full-length *Swan Lake* under the current circumstances boggles the mind. First of all, it necessitated enlarging the current ABT roster of fifty dancers by at least another ten dancers only a few months before the company was due to be permanently dissolved.

A second major problem involved the principal roles of Odette/Odile and Siegfried, two of the most demanding assignments in all ballet. The company had an outstanding pair of dancers in Lupe Serrano and Royes Fernandez, both certainly qualified to head up one cast. However, the need to safeguard against any excessive fatigue or accidents required adding at least a second pair of stars and preferably also a third. This meant not only a considerable expense but also contradicted one of Ballet Theatre's basic tenets, that of being a body of dancers who were all regularly employed members, without a separate category of guest stars brought in as featured attractions whenever they were needed.

There were also lavish costumes, grand-scale scenery, and a prodigious number of extra rehearsal hours. Considered from almost any angle, the idea of adding *Swan Lake* to the twenty-nine other works, including three premieres already scheduled, flew in the face of plain common sense.

Despite all these considerations, Lucia pressed ahead, giving no indication to the company that *Swan Lake* might very well turn out to be ABT's swan song. Her only concession was to recognize that attempting the entire full-length ballet in one great swoop was too great a challenge in the time allowed. Accordingly, for the upcoming New York season, it was decided to present just act 2, or about half of the full-evening work, with the full version of the great Russian classic—the first ever to be attempted by an American company—to be completed at the earliest possible future date.

Meanwhile, on the financial front, nothing had happened to ameliorate the dire financial straits confronting the company. All the major foundations in the country had been contacted and the requests turned down. By early fall, there was only one possibility left, a brand-new but still inoperative federal agency entitled the National Endowment for the Arts.

The origins of the NEA dated back several years to when Lyndon B. Johnson was president. A government commission, established under the aegis of August Hecksher, had recommended that a new organization be instituted to deal with the arts, and action had been under way for some time in Washington to establish the machinery to allow federal support of the arts. However, getting the required legislation approved by a Congress that was traditionally leery of professional artists and the arts was like marching across a minefield.

Fortunately, the man appointed to head the effort and to be the NEA's first chairman was Roger Stevens, a consummate expert in both the theater world and the Washington scene who was not intimidated by the very considerable skepticism and often downright opposition he faced. Livingston

Biddle, who helped draft the crucial legislation for the Endowment and served early on as deputy chairman, recounted a pivotal exchange between Stevens and a rural member of the important House appropriations sub-committee. After asking to go temporarily off the record, the congressional representative proceeded:

"Mr. Stevens, isn't it true that most of the so-called male dancers in these companies you're talking about, isn't it true that most of them are—well—homosexuals?"

According to Biddle, Stevens "gazed with those blue eyes back at him across the table."

"It may be true in a few instances," he said without raising his voice, "but I guarantee you this, Mr. Congressman. If any male dancer happened by right now, he'd be strong enough to pick you up by the waist and put you over his head and throw you straight out that window."

That was enough to put an end to that particular line of questioning. But there were still a great many hurdles and bureaucratic procedures to get by before any tangible financial help could be distributed. Yet, only nine days later, the House of Representatives quite incredibly passed House Resolution 478, which cleared the way for a vote on whether or not to es-tablish a national foundation for the arts. The measure passed the following day in the House, was approved early in the evening of September 16, 1965, in the Senate, and was signed into law by President Johnson on September 29.

Ballet Theatre immediately applied for emergency assistance. By then it was mid-October, and the National Council, executive committee for the NEA, had not yet held its first meeting. That the embryo staff of the NEA somehow managed to get all the Council members together and had the most crucial of the first batch of applications ready for them to consider be-fore the end of the year was considered astounding at the time and seems even more miraculous today.

At this initial meeting of the National Council, held on December 11, the issue of Ballet Theatre's possible demise, as described by de Mille in her impassioned September article in the *New York Herald Tribune,* was taken up as a crisis of national proportions requiring immediate consider-ation. In the absence of any dissension or disagreement, the Council, as one of its first official actions, voted a special emergency grant of $100,000 to American Ballet Theatre, with a commitment of a second grant of $250,000 to follow.

It was a historic occasion, virtually the first time in the country's history that the federal government had given its direct financial support to a performing organization in the arts. The total amount approved was especially noteworthy in that it amounted to 14 percent of the NEA's entire original budget.

And so it happened, at this very last moment when Ballet Theatre faced extinction once again, coupled with the fact that the IRS had just exacted huge penalties against Lucia Chase so that, for the first time in Ballet Theatre's twenty-five years of perilous survival, the company could no longer be rescued by its perpetual guardian, on December 20, 1965, Vice President Hubert Humphrey presented a check for $100,000 to Dr. Harold Taylor, president of the Ballet Theatre Foundation.

"Did Miss Chase see the check?" someone was heard to ask.

"See it?" Lucia replied. "I kissed it."

⏤◎⏤

"Sweet, effortless, and splendid history," Clive Barnes proclaimed in the *New York Times* the day after the opening at the State Theater. "Miss Chase, in a print brocade gown from Honolulu, was everywhere greeting everyone."

The opening night audience was a glittering show in itself, with Gregory Peck, Richard Rodgers, and Museum of Modern Art president René d'Harnoncourt attending, alongside leading political figures headed by Humphrey, New York senator Jacob Javits, New York City mayor John Lindsay, and distinguished members of the National Council on the Arts.

The whole evening, according to Barnes, was a stunning night to remember. *Les Noces,* in his opinion, was nothing less than a masterpiece, one of the most important ballets to be created in recent years, and after *Études* closed the program, "a roar came from the audience that could put Shea Stadium to shame." But it was the opening work that received most of his attention, "a sensitive new production of the second act of *Swan Lake* which marks a milestone in American ballet." While it still had not achieved a completely cohesive style, it surely was "a first stage marvelously well surmounted. . . . Good already, clearly it will be better later."

Possibly the most far-reaching part of the entire evening occurred afterwards at a post-performance party that Lucia hosted at her apartment for the entire company and guests. A full elevator carried new arrivals up to the fourteenth floor. Off to the right, in the already crowded living room, with Lindsay and Javits standing on either side of the marble fireplace, Humphrey gave a short speech and then presented a second federal check to Lucia. This time the amount was for $250,000. As Humphrey said, speaking on behalf of the president and Congress, this new grant aimed at nothing less than to make it possible for the American Ballet Theatre to carry on.

"Now we can plan a year ahead," Lucia exclaimed, giving a radiant smile as she accepted the life-saving check. "This promises a real future. Tomorrows, not just todays."

19. Attempted Coup d'Etat

Lucia has great resiliency in the
face of disaster. She can handle
any problem. She can handle
temperament and never show her
own, unless you know how to read
the signs—a rigid smile appears, or
sometimes her speech gets very fast
when she's mad, or else she is very
quiet.
—Oliver Smith

THE SHUTDOWN OF American Ballet Theatre was averted
once again, yet in its place was a grave new problem. It was too late to book
a tour in the upcoming months and too soon to think about holding another
season at home in New York. The company was all dressed up and ready
to go, but there was nothing for it to do. It was the same old story: another
desperate situation, and then once again, as had so often happened, a totally fortuitous event came to the company's rescue.

The Soviet Union and the U.S. State Department had arranged for
Moscow's Bolshoi Ballet to perform in New York, and in 1964 the Russian
company had enjoyed an astounding financial success, selling out Madison
Square Garden for all its fourteen performances. According to the terms

of the International Exchange Program, in return for the Bolshoi's visit, an American dance company was to be invited to perform in Russia. Exactly which company would be chosen had not been specified. Now, early in 1966, the American Ballet Theatre had been fully reconstituted and, having just concluded a most successful New York season, emerged as the most obvious candidate. The only trouble was persuading the Russian authorities to give their final approval. The cold war was on, and cooperation between the two governments was at a low point. Without giving any explanation for the prolonged delay, authorities in Moscow continued to hold everything in abeyance.

Weeks passed. Lucia had promised all the dancers that they would have definite word about summer plans by the end of the New York season in mid-February, but this deadline came and went. By the end of April, it was necessary, according to union contracts, to give company members notice of when they could count on being employed for the remainder of the year. The Russian tour was still supposedly on, but since there was no official contract, the only notification she could give the dancers was a hopeful "maybe."

Agnes de Mille, who eventually went on the trip and later wrote about her experience in *Dance Perspectives,* described the agonizing impasse:

> Throughout this hell of indecision and suspense, Lucia Chase never wavered. "We'll go," she said quietly. Anyone with a sense of reality would have broken under the strain. Lucia did not break.

Instead, she kept reminding the State Department that the tour had been agreed upon; that she had necessarily spoken to the company; and that she, for her part, had kept it available and ready. Now, months later, it must be given the go-ahead. The deadlock continued up to the very last moment when it became a question of either signing contracts with the dancers or else letting them go to find other work. Finally, the State Department reluctantly agreed to allow the company to leave for Moscow, even though the Russians had not yet officially complied.

There were still a host of problems which had been discussed back and forth during the standoff, issues such as which ballets would be performed, the makeup of programs night after night for the entire engagement, daily schedules for dancers and crew, program copy, casting, advertising, billing, and dressing rooms. The whole gamut was still up in the air even as the company was in flight to Moscow.

Agnes described what it was like on the plane:

Lucia, the professional traveler, who in the course of her duties must go yearly one and a half times around the world, changed immediately into a pretty and comfortable robe, settled down with her aperitif and dinner, and then quietly turned to me in the honeyed tones she prefers when broaching disaster: "I may as well tell you now: the Russians have decided that *Rodeo* (de Mille's ballet) will end the program. It can't go on as a middle ballet as I agreed and promised." I was aghast. *Rodeo* has to be middle to make its best effect. She had promised that it would be in the middle to induce me to revive it.

Agnes: "Had you told me yesterday, I would not be on this plane."

Lucia: "In that case, I'm glad I did not tell you."

I began to bleed at the nose. But Lucia was so busy explaining unrelated matters that she didn't notice. It was no good arguing. She never stopped talking. She did not intend to listen. The decisions had been made.

When hearing some time later that Agnes had given this rendition of their conversation and her resultant bloody nose, Lucia laughed and said, "Don't be silly—she picked her nose until it bled."

Unlike Ballet Theatre's groundbreaking tour in Russia six years earlier, this second visit was not a happy experience. The Russian government was very uncooperative and imposed all sorts of conditions. Some of the most difficult happened to involve *Rodeo* and how it should be introduced to the Russian public.

De Mille had been adamant from the very beginning about the necessity of having a description of what the ballet was about in the house program. She had written the explanatory notes herself and had always insisted on having them included whenever and wherever *Rodeo* was performed. For this particular tour, she was more than ever convinced that her words in the house program were essential if Russian audiences were ever going to understand *Rodeo*. But now there would be no notes. Apparently Lucia had been obliged to bargain with the Russian presenters: no notes in the printed programs in exchange for the right to perform *Fancy Free* and *Billy the Kid,* two Ballet Theatre classics that the Russians had attempted to reject from the Russian tour repertory.

Again from de Mille:

She didn't tell me about this deal, allowing me to go on badgering all the authorities and to write out version after version of text. . . . Lucia's patience is inexhaustible. I would have taken a stand and had us all deported within forty-eight hours.

De Mille was upset about a good deal more in the course of her Russian sojourn. Her written account is full of complaints about the brutally inartistic treatment she was subjected to, and her irritation is sharpened by her awareness that much more was being unloaded on Lucia, who somehow kept her dignity and composure no matter what she faced. It was all much more than de Mille could have endured, and as she later frankly admitted, she was glad to leave several weeks before the tour was over:

> I departed before the company was really up and about, but as I was getting into the taxi, Lucia appeared, hastily dressed, hair astraggle and unmade-up, and threw her arms around me. "I couldn't let you get away without a good-bye." She almost never sleeps. She tends to everything. Personal matters—social relations and loving kindness—she tends to more than all others.

High praise from Agnes de Mille, who could be really spiteful when she wished.

This other, vindictive side of Agnes de Mille revealed itself in an extraordinary confrontation that occurred very shortly after the Russian tour.

The entire proceeding began quite innocuously back in 1965, prompted by a switch in Ballet Theatre personnel. Byam Stevens, head of the Ballet Theatre Foundation, had decided to retire, leaving the board of trustees without an official leader. At de Mille's suggestion, the trustees voted to elect as the new president Dr. Harold Taylor, a prominent figure in academic circles who had made quite a name for himself as the innovative president of Sarah Lawrence College in Bronxville, New York. In recommending Dr. Taylor, de Mille claimed that the presence of such an authoritative and highly articulate person would be an invaluable asset when it came to attracting money from the growing number of corporate, foundation, and government sources beginning to show support for the arts.

Taylor quickly formulated a comprehensive new image of ABT as an institution of unusual, but until now unappreciated, educational capabilities. Whether or not this was particularly accurate, it was an attractive concept that may well have helped garner the life-saving grant to American Ballet Theatre from the National Endowment for the Arts.

As a second step in filling out his new image for Ballet Theatre, Taylor proposed revising the artistic authority currently directing the company by establishing a new Policy and Planning Committee. The committee, which was to be composed of Lucia Chase, Oliver Smith, Dr. Taylor (ex-officio as president), Agnes de Mille, and Jerome Robbins, was set up to function like an executive committee to the board of trustees and was empowered to consider and decide questions related to the nature and direction of the ballet company. In a footnote to his memo proposing the committee, Dr. Taylor explained why the committee was essential:

> The artistic policy of the Company, the School, and the Workshop must take into account so many new factors and possibilities that it no longer can be dealt with by a single person, no matter how gifted that person may be.

Neither Lucia nor Oliver, as artistic directors of the company, voiced any objections. Instead, they were quite positive about the idea, since it seemed to promise that both Robbins and de Mille would henceforth take a more active interest in American Ballet Theatre, an arrangement which, in time, might well lead to their creating several new works for the company's repertory. Yet very soon, a follow-up memo to the board from Dr. Taylor revealed that what the two choreographers had in mind—with the new president's strong backing—were a number of draconian conditions that completely changed the existing artistic structure of the company.

According to this revised model, a new artistic staff was to be appointed to replace the staff that Lucia Chase had put into place. Furthermore, it was clearly stated that Lucia was not to be allowed to play any part in choosing her staff's replacements. The proposed change went even beyond that, specifying that Lucia Chase would no longer be authorized to supervise company rehearsals and performances. Instead, this responsibility was handed over to Nora Kaye, Ballet Theatre's former star dancer, whom Lucia and Oliver had appointed the previous year to work with them as assistant artistic director.

Speaking on behalf of the committee, Dr. Taylor further reported "that Chase should not be permitted to speak directly with the dancers but that all communication should be carried on through Kaye." In addition, Robbins and de Mille were granted authority to choose any new dancers they wished to bring into the company, as well as to dismiss some already in the company.

There was one final stipulation: the production of the full-length *Swan Lake* was to be shelved in order to reserve all funds for the production of new works.

To no one's surprise, Lucia hotly objected to all these suggestions, which were clearly aimed at undercutting her position as artistic director. The dispute carried on for the remainder of 1966, during which time Lucia continued to schedule further work on *Swan Lake*, over the vigorous objections of Robbins and de Mille, who were principals on the committee but who currently were not employed by the company. As long as there were no rehearsals scheduled for their ballets, there was nothing taking place either onstage or in the studio where they could effectively enforce their objections. However, soon it would come time to start preparations for the projected New York season, which was slated to begin in April 1967. As both Robbins and de Mille clearly (if indirectly) intimated, either their ideas would be respected or they might very well pull their ballets out of the ABT repertory.

The dispute finally came to a head in early January 1967 when a summary report, signed by Taylor and purporting to represent the findings of the Artistic Committee, was delivered to the board of trustees. As related in Charles Payne's *American Ballet Theatre*, the report stipulated that "no Foundation funds should be diverted to *Swan Lake*." Furthermore, if Lucia persisted in her plans, "there would be insufficient time to prepare for the New York spring season, and, accordingly, this entire engagement should be canceled or in any case not be financed with foundation funds."

For Dr. Taylor, who was new on the scene and to ballet in general, the committee's verdict may have seemed like a reasonable business decision. However, both Robbins and de Mille must have realized that this was a drastic reversal of the way artistic questions involving the company had always been decided. Also, as they (if perhaps not Dr. Taylor) were well aware, after all their years of association with Ballet Theatre, this kind of preemptive ultimatum was not apt to dissuade Lucia Chase. One might as well confront a mother bear and attempt to take away her cub as expect Lucia to comply with the new directives and meekly step aside.

In moments of personal crisis, Lucia had always relied on a handful of people whom she absolutely trusted and would heed no matter what others might ask or expect her to do. An increasingly important member of this sacrosanct circle was John Wharton, one of the senior partners of the powerful law firm Paul, Weiss, Wharton, Rifkind & Garrison and possibly the most respected legal figure in the entire theatrical world. John Wharton had taken over from Harry Zuckert the mantle of responsibility—both legal and personal—for Lucia's well-being, a role that went far beyond a lawyer's normal area of concern and was much closer to being like a father-protector. It was only natural now that Lucia would turn to John Wharton to ask what she should do about the Committee's recommendations.

Wharton responded in the scrupulously formal manner of a master negotiator by writing a memorandum to the entire Ballet Theatre board of trustees that began by stating that, in his considered opinion, if the forthcoming New York State Theater engagement were canceled and if the company were laid off for any extended period of time, it might prove to be the end of Ballet Theatre. With the recent advent of government subsidies, he urged that the company be kept going, even if this involved Lucia's once again assuming the ultimate financial responsibility for the season.

As for the prohibitions against *Swan Lake*, Wharton expressed no opinion in regard to the merits of continuing on with the production. Instead, he posed the question of whether the report was tantamount to usurping the authority of the company's two artistic directors. Was the committee, in fact, planning a takeover? The situation, he advised, needed to be clarified.

Dr. Taylor, de Mille, and Robbins claimed to be insulted by the very suggestion that they could be involved in any attempted takeover, and all three submitted hurt letters of resignation. As quickly as that, the battle over leadership was over. A few detached questions, a hasty retreat, and suddenly everything was back as it had always been.

The projected spring season at the New York State Theater would now be held as scheduled, with *Swan Lake* as its central feature, the first of many full-length ballets that Ballet Theatre would mount in the next few years. Others would include *Giselle, Coppelia, La Sylphide, La Bayadere, The Sleeping Beauty,* and *The Nutcracker.* What this meant was that all of ABT's subsequent major seasons would feature several consecutive performances—sometimes even an entire week—of a single full-length "classic," with prominent guest artists from other companies brought in to alternate with principals from within the company, an intramural competition that attracted packed houses of enthusiasts who came to cheer for their favorite star—a far different scene from the early glory days of Ballet Theatre, of *Fancy Free* and *Pillar of Fire* and *Fall River Legend,* of Alonso and Youskevitch and Hugh Laing and John Kriza and Nora Kaye, when the company was smaller and closer-knit, the ballets shorter, and—truth be told—the audiences much smaller. *Swan Lake* marked the start of a new era for American Ballet Theatre, with the company bigger, more classically oriented, enhanced with illustrious guest stars, and generally more powerful and able to mount longer and better-attended seasons, which greatly increased its chances for long-term survival. All in all, it was a drastic change that traced directly back to *Swan Lake,* an extremely risky and contentious issue championed by Lucia when the company appeared more than likely once again to shut down and disappear.

20. Balanchine and the New York City Ballet

She's very strong-willed, thank God,
but she's so used to handling all
policies herself, it was difficult to
make a larger structure, an effective
board, that she could work with.
—Harold Taylor, after resigning as
president of Ballet Theatre

L UCIA HAD WON OUT. She had kept control of the company; she had managed, despite vigorous opposition, to produce a full-length *Swan Lake* that Clive Barnes in the *New York Times* had hailed as "the best version of the ballet to be found anywhere"; and the critics, who only a short time ago had been harping on the shabby condition of the repertory and the prolonged absence of any creativity, were now generally full of praise, viewing the recently concluded spring 1967 season at the New York State Theater as being very good, in fact one of the best.

There were more principal dancers than ever, and they all appeared to be in top form. Lupe Serrano, recently returned from maternity leave, was hailed as an indisputably great ballerina, incredibly strong in her technique, striking and fiery in her attack, and increasingly mature in her dramatic ability. Erik Bruhn was generally conceded to be the greatest male classical dancer in the world, and to add to his allure, Lucia had garnered for him a new partner, Carla Fracci, from La Scala in Milan, who by the end of the season was hailed by Barnes as "surely the most purely romantic ballerina of this generation." Fracci and Bruhn danced a *Giselle* together that became one of those legendary performances that, years later, people continued to talk about.

Besides Serrano, Bruhn, and Fracci, Cynthia Gregory had become a star practically overnight; Sallie Wilson was following in Nora Kaye's footsteps and winning praise for her interpretations of one Tudor ballet after another; Ted Kivett was reported to have reached new and dazzling heights, and others attracting high praise included Toni Lander, Royes Fernandez, Ruth Ann Koesun, Eleanor D'Antuono, Bruce Marks, and Gayle Young. Rarely had so many members of the company, or of any company, been individually singled out for special mention.

This remarkable strength in dancers was reflected in the season's box office returns. Although the Royal Ballet from Covent Garden was performing at the exact same time at the new Met, less than 100 yards away from American Ballet Theatre at the New York State Theater, ABT's ticket sales did not suffer but seemed to benefit from the competition. It became the rage for avid New York theater buffs to fasten on the great dancing going on at Lincoln Center, with some fanatics even racing across the plaza during intermission in order to be able to take in both companies on the same night. The result for Ballet Theatre was the most munificent season yet, with the company playing to 90 percent of capacity.

Perhaps the most startling single feature of the season occurred four days after the company's opening when a new ballet had its New York premiere. The choreographer, Eliot Feld, was a young soloist in the company who had attracted widespread attention with his distinctive presence and dramatic performing style onstage, but he was completely unknown as a choreographer. Like Jerome Robbins's *Fancy Free* nearly a quarter of a century earlier, *Harbinger* was Feld's first complete ballet. Also like *Fancy Free*, the entire cast was chosen from lesser members of the company; and another similarity was that, as a new work, it had not been given top preferential status during the winter rehearsal period, and the final portions had been worked out *sub rosa* during random free moments while the company was on tour. The first official performance had taken place six weeks earlier in Miami, where it enjoyed considerable success with the audience, but advance word had only trickled back to New York where neither Eliot Feld nor *Harbinger* were highly publicized or considered to be prime attractions.

Up to this point, Ballet Theatre's recent record of putting on new ballets had been rather dismal. In the past nine years, ABT had produced twenty-seven new works, yet practically none of them survived their first year or two to become regular ballets in the repertory. According to Arlene Croce, writing in *Ballet Review*, "Since 1950, Ballet Theatre has not commissioned one ballet of lasting merit, and by that I mean a piece that doesn't yield up all its secrets after two or three viewings." While some might wince at the severity of this judgment, particularly the way it denigrated *Les Noces*, still it had been years since Ballet Theatre had commissioned an original work that could justly be called a popular hit.

Eliot Feld was not the type Lucia would have been inclined to pick as a new favorite son for the company. She tended to favor cheerful, enthusiastic, respectful associates, whereas Eliot Feld could be what Lucia would term "a little difficult."

She was not constitutionally averse to those who often caused her trouble: Antony Tudor, Jerry Robbins, and Agnes de Mille, Lucia's picks when it came to creative associates, were some of the most accomplished makers of trouble in the entire dance world. But Eliot Feld was still a young dancer, just barely out of the corps, and she found him to be often a trifle impertinent and overly demanding, especially considering he hadn't done anything yet. At least that was the way she felt before *Harbinger* hit New York the night of May 11, 1967.

As Barnes related in the *New York Times* the following day:

> Choreographers are seldom born—they explode. One exploded last night. Apparently the audience knew it for what it was—a new phase in American dance. It received 17 curtain calls, but numbers hardly give the feeling of the house. There is a special wind that blows when a choreographer emerges, and that special wind was blowing. . . . Here is the most important indigenous talent in classic ballet since Jerome Robbins.

At last there was a new creative light in Ballet Theatre's firmament, and no one could have been more relieved, if slightly nonplussed, than Lucia Chase.

The emergence of Eliot Feld as a new choreographer for Ballet Theatre was particularly noteworthy, since he was not someone borrowed from another American company or brought in from overseas but came right out of the company's own ranks. And the initial excitement over *Harbinger* was intensified later in the year when a second original work by Feld, *At Midnight,* again created on and for American Ballet Theatre, was premiered in the company's two-week December season at City Center.

Both of Feld's offerings were small-scaled intimate works. They used relatively few dancers, and their scenery and costumes were simple. Nevertheless, the result had great impact. As Deborah Jowitt noted on December 21, 1967, in *The Village Voice,* Feld had a distinctive style and displayed great control:

> What I like is its fragmentary quality, the way everything ends on enormously difficult poses. The movement keeps changing its course and surprising you with shifts that have the rhythm of a caught breath. The girls are suddenly on their pointes without any preparation or effort.

All this was sweet music to Lucia. To have, in a single year, two brand-new works by a young, relatively unknown choreographer who was also a dancer in the company was a brilliant reversal of what had been publicly noted as an embarrassing dearth of imagination and competence on the part of the company's management.

In the December 16, 1967, issue of the *Saturday Review*, Walter Terry wrote, "The feeling was one of exhilaration."

> Was "exhilarating" the *mot juste*? Yes, for its deepest roots mean "gladdening" and also "cheering." The superlative repertory—unmatched by any other ballet troupe in the world—and the exuberant dancing of a remarkable *corps de ballet* and a heady roster of principals gladdened the hearts of all dance lovers.

This came after Clive Barnes had summarized his report on the earlier spring season at the New York State Theater with:

> Suddenly the company looked like a genuinely creative artistic organization. This year may go down in the history of American Ballet Theatre as the year its luck turned.

There was still another reason for Lucia Chase to feel particularly gratified: the company's new full-length *Swan Lake* offered her a last great performance opportunity, as the Queen Mother of the young Prince Siegfried.

The role of the Queen Mother had never been particularly sought after up to this time. Although required by the plot, it was traditionally little more than a walk-through part that often fell to any dancer who was available. In fact, according to Lucia, this was how it initially became her assignment. "Someone had to do it," she once remarked, "and *Swan Lake* already had used everyone else in the company except me and the wardrobe mistress, and she was too busy, so it fell to me."

For the next decade and even after that, right up to the time she finally retired from Ballet Theatre in 1980, Lucia Chase performing as the Queen Mother had a tremendous impact both on the audience and on the company. Writing nearly twenty years later in the *Washington Post,* Allan Kriegsman described her in the role as "a figure maternal and regal, substantial and diminutive, resolute, magisterial, at once aloof and warm." And also in an obituary written January 11, 1986, Nancy Goldner, the dance critic of the *Philadelphia Inquirer,* observed:

> I doubt that anyone who saw the company's *Swan Lake* could ever forget the dramatic note that Chase invested in the normally regal role of the Queen Mother. Tsk-tsking the waywardness of her son, Prince Siegfried, she took it as a personal offense, as only a mother would, that he preferred some wild swan creature to the perfectly nice debs she had arranged for him to meet at the ball.

Kevin McKenzie, currently the artistic director of American Ballet Theatre and the last dancer appointed by Lucia to be a principal in the company, recalled to me the night when he performed the role of Siegfried in *Swan Lake* for the first time and had to sit onstage beside the Queen Mother while the young girls, competing to win his hand, danced in succession before them:

> Naturally I was nervous, positioned up there next to my boss, trying my best to appear at ease with Lucia right there less than a foot away. At one point she turned toward me as if to confide something. I leaned toward her to listen and heard her say, "Of course, you know, dear, none of them can cook." It was all I could do to nod and keep a straight face.

The Queen Mother was the last of her roles and the one in which she had the least dancing to do, yet it was also the one that allowed Lucia to illustrate qualities that were not only right for the part but also true attributes of herself, the mother and guardian spirit of everyone onstage and indeed of the entire Ballet Theatre organization.

All in all, 1967 was a cornucopia of positives: widespread praise for both the corps de ballet and all the leading dancers, great box office, a new choreographer coming right out of the company, and for Lucia, a new role that appeared made to order.

Yet underneath the euphoria, the same major problems remained: the company still had no home of its own, no place where it could come back to and rest, rejuvenate itself, rehearse, and create on a regular unpressured basis. After twenty-seven years, during which it had made over twenty tours reaching all fifty states and over four hundred cities, plus twelve international trips to some thirty countries in Europe, Russia, Asia, and South America, it was still essentially a nomad, forced to remain on the move simply to stay in existence.

Like food and water, a home is one of the essentials of life. Every creature needs some place of its own, whether a cave, treetop, reef, hole in the ground, hut, or mansion. The same is true for all institutions. John Martin of the *New York Times* expressed it best:

> Not even a company of artists gallant enough to defy snow and rain and heat and gloom can ultimately survive the erosion of endless travel. A ballet company, if it is anything, is an artistic entity and needs to live as such. It cannot exist forever without a home, a center for nourishment and growth, for affection and inspiration. It requires the companionship and support of its relatives and friends across the footlights, who will certainly scold it from time to time but will also hold up its hands in times of uneasiness, forgive it its lapses, and bask in the reflected glow of its accomplishment.
>
> A traveling showcase can do no more than present samples to prospective customers along the road; it cannot manufacture anything, create anything, deliver anything. It can only become increasingly bedraggled. . . .
> Please, Miss Chase, stay home!

Meanwhile, very much at home in New York was "the other company," as Lucia was apt to refer to it: the New York City Ballet, eight years younger than ABT but with certain enormous advantages working in its favor.

Unquestionably, its greatest advantage was its artistic director, George Balanchine. Back in the 1930s and 1940s, when Fokine was the reigning deity, Balanchine not only had fulfilled his promise early on but then continued working to an advanced age, with a long career generally conceded to be the most productive and distinguished of any creator of dances of any time or place.

Between 1955 and 1967, when it might be said that ABT's only successful creative efforts were Robbins's staggeringly difficult *Les Noces* and Eliot Feld's *Harbinger* and *At Midnight,* Balanchine created thirty-two original ballets, including such masterworks as *Pas de Dix* (1956), *Square Dance* (1957), *Agon* (1957), *Stars and Stripes* (1958), *Seven Deadly Sins* (1958), *Episodes* (1959), *La Sonnambula* (1960), *Liebeslieder Waltzer* (1960), *A Midsummer Night's Dream* (1962), *Bugaku* (1963), *Don Quixote* (1965), and *Jewels* (1967). Never has there been such a high level of productivity in the history of dance.

Another great advantage of the New York City Ballet was its general director, Lincoln Kirstein. The son and heir of Louis Kirstein, a partner in the Filene Department Store in Boston, this young Harvard-educated aesthete teamed up with Balanchine in the mid-1930s to found the School of American Ballet, then went on to establish the American Ballet, Ballet Caravan, Ballet Society, and, in 1948, the New York City Ballet, on whose behalf he worked for the rest of his life. It was due to Kirstein as much as Balanchine that New York City Ballet attained certain fundamental benefits that American Ballet Theatre had long sought and still in 1967 sorely lacked, starting with a home.

Way back in the 1940s, Morton Baum was the guiding spirit of the former Masonic Temple on West 55th Street, which had been converted to serve as the low-priced municipal theater known as the New York City Center of Music and Drama. Baum offered City Center to Lucia as a home for Ballet Theatre. However, because the City Center stage was cramped, with very little space in the wings, and also because the house lacked the glamour and prestige that Lucia felt America's premier ballet company deserved, she turned it down. Baum then turned to Lincoln Kirstein, and together they formed a lifelong working partnership, with the New York City Ballet serving as the resident dance company and leading constituent in a complex of opera, drama, and musical entities that Baum banded together under the single protective roof of City Center. In the course of the next fifteen years, the New York City Ballet managed to build a spectacular, predominantly Balanchine repertory, a superb company of dancers, and an immense home audience of ticket buyers, subscribers, and generous supporters.

In the 1960s, the company's most-favored position in New York was further enhanced when it was accorded a new, much more desirable home, thanks again largely to Kirstein's influence and insider contacts. One of his longtime close friends was Nelson Rockefeller, at that point the governor of New York, whose brother, John D. Rockefeller III, was heading the drive to build Lincoln Center. Now, thanks to Governor Rockefeller, Kirstein, and Morton Baum, the New York City Ballet and the New York City Opera, the two leading constituents of the City Center of Music and Drama, were invited to share a brand-new New York State Theater, designed by Philip Johnson, one of the country's leading architects and also a friend of Kirstein.

Lincoln Kirstein had another close friend, McNeil Lowry, who proved to be the crucial powerbroker on a different but equally important front. It was Lowry, a senior vice president of the Ford Foundation, who conceived and proceeded to administer a new program of massive financial support by the Ford Foundation for dance or, more specifically, for ballet in America.

Unlike the prototypical foundation executive who tends to be more of an overseer than innovator, Lowry was an imaginative, dogged, combative champion who had a great impact on education and the arts during the 1960s and 1970s. Physically, he was not particularly impressive. He was medium-sized, slow-moving, tending to give an impression of being somewhat tired and discouraged about the overall state of things. Yet, underneath his passive appearance, Lowry was a bulldog who would push his way into the center of an arena and take charge of all the action from then on until it was done the way he wished.

Besides being a friend of Kirstein's, Lowry was a great admirer of Balanchine. After many months of exhaustive study, travel, and consultation with practitioners of dance across the entire United States, Lowry came to the conclusion that the best way to help the art was not to create a widespread program of support but instead to give a ton of money to ballet's presiding genius and a judicious handful of Balanchine disciples. Consequently, the entire dance world was astounded in 1963 when the Ford Foundation announced it was giving $7,765,750 to a small, highly selective list of ballet companies and one ballet school. Over half of the entire amount, or $3,925,000, was designated for Kirstein and Balanchine's School of American Ballet. Two million dollars was specified for the New York City Ballet, and the remainder was portioned out to four smaller satellite companies in Boston, Pennsylvania, Utah, and San Francisco, all of which were directed either by NYCB alumni or longtime Balanchine associates. It was the largest single contribution in American history ever made to dance, stunning for its overall size but also for the extremely narrow focus of its outreach. There was nothing for Martha Graham, nothing for any modern dance company, and nothing for American Ballet Theatre.

"We are naturally astounded that the Ford Foundation should refuse aid to America's oldest company," was all Lucia could say at the time. It was not just a question of the money that Ballet Theatre failed to receive. It was also a personal affront, a slap in the face to Lucia Chase herself as the company's artistic director and principal leader for so many years, although she would never voice her complaints in personal terms but always as an inexcusable injustice done to the company.

Yet Lowry, for his part, had looked long and hard at Ballet Theatre, and he did not particularly like what he saw there: a weak and undistinguished board, a near-total lack of any organized fund-raising, and a congenital absence of long-range planning. Ballet Theatre appeared to him to be essentially an organization that operated in fits and starts, constantly fighting to overcome chronic deficits and precarious in the extreme. It was not the sort of organization he felt he could safely entrust with Ford Foundation funds. Although his final actions were preceded by a very careful analysis that he personally conducted, exhaustively evaluating the great many ways in which the Ford money could be allocated, ultimately the program he designed and implemented revealed a near-total bias toward Balanchine, his institutional creations, and his aesthetic.

It was also quite clearly a vote of no confidence in Lucia Chase. Lowry knew it. Lucia knew it. In time everyone knew it.

Lucia had one more sorely trying test to deal with. Unhappily for both of us, this one had to do with me, the single most important person left in her world following my brother Tommy's death.

After marrying and leaving Ballet Theatre in 1958, I had spent the next two or three years living with my wife, Carol, on the east side of Manhattan and working on a novel in a miniscule rented room two blocks away. It was Erik Bruhn, then starring in ABT's spring 1960 season at the Met, who suggested that I might look into assisting Robert Joffrey's little ballet company down in the Village.

I had known Joffrey from my Ballet Theatre days when he was a very popular teacher at ABT's ballet school on West 57th Street. Like all struggling dance companies, the Joffrey Ballet needed help, which I was happy to give, for it meant an opportunity for me to feel involved and productive after a day spent alone, writing. It wasn't long before I was doing most of the Joffrey Ballet's business, and about a year later, early in 1962, when the Rebecca Harkness Foundation offered to sponsor the company in a very substantial way, I was hired on as full-time business manager.

After that, things happened quickly. The next two summers became long rehearsal periods, paid for by the Harkness Foundation, which the Joffrey Ballet spent creating new ballets, while in between, the company performed on a 1962–63 State Department–sponsored tour of the Far East. In the fall of 1963, following a performance at the White House for President Kennedy to honor Haile Selassie, the Joffrey Ballet, by this time expanded to twenty-six dancers and a unique repertory largely created by Gerald Arpino, embarked on its sensationally successful tour of the Soviet Union.

But then came a disastrous reversal. The Rebekah Harkness Foundation, which had signed the Joffrey dancers' yearlong contracts with AGMA to cover the Russian tour and the U.S. tour immediately following, decided it wanted to take control of the company, including changing its name from the Joffrey to the Harkness Ballet. When Joffrey, Arpino, and I all objected, the Harkness Foundation, at the end of the U.S. tour, simply ordered all the costumes and scenery to be delivered to its own warehouse. It also appropriated for its own newly instituted Harkness Ballet all the dancers who were still bound by their AGMA contracts (except for two who refused to be taken over and broke their contracts), leaving Joffrey, Arpino, and me proudly defiant but with nothing left of the company we had been running together for the past three years.

We decided to start it up again. Joffrey, the master teacher, began selecting and training a new company; Arpino, who as a choreographer was a very fast worker, turned to creating several new ballets; and I focused on establishing a nonprofit tax-exempt support structure, contacting friends who were starting to make it in the business world but hadn't yet committed themselves to helping other nonprofit enterprises. Within a year, we had put together the makings of a vibrant new Joffrey Ballet company and a Foundation for American Dance to support it. Then two critically important events occurred.

The first was when Morton Baum called from City Center: now that the New York City Ballet had gone over to Lincoln Center, would the three of us be interested in establishing a home base at City Center?

Practically simultaneous with Baum's invitation, McNeil Lowry at the Ford Foundation, who in 1964 had already made a small $35,000 grant to help us get started, offered a second grant of $120,000.

After being left destitute less than two years earlier, we were now off and running. The company was henceforth to be permanently based in City Center, with the venerable theater available to us for fall and spring seasons of increasing length each year, while upstairs, the entire fifth floor was given over to the Joffrey Ballet, its Foundation, and a rapidly growing "Joffrey Circle" of friends organized under the leadership of a dynamic volunteer, Lee Edwards. It wasn't long before a burgeoning schedule built around fall and spring seasons at City Center also included weeklong stays in major cities and a summer residency in the Pacific Northwest centered around Tacoma and Seattle, Joffrey's original home. In April 1968, *Time* magazine devoted its cover to Robert Joffrey's rock-ballet sensation, *Astarte*, which had just been premiered at City Center, and declared in the inside cover article, "This company is leading the way."

The cumulative effect of all these advances by a company that only six years ago had been a small, struggling troupe, based in Greenwich Village and performing one-night stands in the hinterlands, must have been disconcerting, even dismaying, to Lucia. Just as a few years earlier she had had to deal with the original multimillion dollar Ford Foundation grant that completely bypassed Ballet Theatre, now here was the Joffrey Ballet, a much younger company which had none of ABT's resplendent history, time-honored repertory, or long record of national and international service, but which nevertheless had acquired a home base, regular seasons at City Center, two grants from the Ford Foundation, and an annual work schedule already far better than what American Ballet Theatre had been able to piece together after twenty-five years. What made this most difficult for Lucia to stomach was that her son had gone back into ballet, become general director of the Joffrey Ballet, and now was actively competing with her and Ballet Theatre.

This kind of internecine rivalry wasn't supposed to happen inside the family, where Lucia had always considered ballet to be her special domain. She didn't like the fact that I was with the Joffrey Ballet, never congratulated me or even talked to me about the company, and supposedly never broached the subject of the former Greenwich Village troupe's meteoric success in any of her outside conversations, public or private. Instead, the Joffrey Ballet's success had the effect, whenever we were together, of causing my mother to talk more and more, almost incessantly, about all the wonderful things that American Ballet Theatre was doing.

Despite the considerable tension between us professionally, life within our immediate family went on pretty much the same as usual, which meant that on a regular basis, perhaps once a week, my mother, my wife, and I would sit down together for dinner at the apartment. Sometimes there might be others joining us, a guest who was staying upstairs, perhaps a cousin or two, occasionally someone from Ballet Theatre, like Dimitri Romanoff or Enrique Martinez or Charlie Payne or Oliver Smith. Those larger occasions were less stressful than the other times when there were just the three of us, each uncomfortably conscious of the underlying, unspoken competition and working hard to remain cheerful and interested, however forced the conversation might become.

It was difficult. Carol tended to be quiet, always polite, generally nonassertive, and deferential to her mother-in-law. There was not much I could talk about that didn't eventually revolve around what was happening at City Center or the ballet world in general, neither of which were particularly welcome topics for Lucia to hear discoursed upon by her renegade son. As a result, I too tended not to say very much. And so the burden fell on my mother who, rising to the challenge as she always did, ended up doing most of the talking.

Invariably in the course of the evening, the talking became less of a conversation and more and more a nervous, one-sided recital of all the new people coming in and the marvelous things happening at ABT when actually nothing much had changed. It was still the same old story, being repeated over and over.

Finally, the time would come when we could decently stand up to go. I would walk out, feeling tired, somewhat overwhelmed, especially sad, because after all the hype and bravado and incessant talk, I knew that Ballet Theatre was mired in a deadly routine. What made matters worse, at least emotionally, was my awareness that the predicament throttling the company was primarily due to my mother's being either unaware, or too stubborn, or simply unable to accomplish what desperately needed to be done. And so, each time, I would leave with an ache in my heart and a dull despair, that the venerable, brilliant, illustrious American Ballet Theatre could have dug itself into such a deep-trodden rut that it wasn't clear what or who could possible save it.

21. Lucia Chase as Artistic Director

I could strangle her, but I love her.
I have looked up to her for fifteen
years. She's been a mother to me.
She knows me better than anyone.
—Ted Kivett, ABT principal dancer

DESPITE THE tremendously successful season just completed, Clive Barnes on June 11, 1967, wrote in the *New York Times* that even so, Ballet Theatre "would still lack something vital to a really great ballet company—it would lack the imprint of a single recognizable artistic personality."

True enough. And yet there remains another kind of leadership which has less to do with making major administrative or artistic decisions and more with simply functioning out in the field, coping on a day-to-day basis with the myriad problems that confront any large organization. Judging strictly by this arena, there are few if any ballet company directors who were as understanding, effective, or trusted as Lucia Chase.

In a miniature essay, "Directing a Ballet Company," which Lucia wrote for Charles Payne's treatise, *American Ballet Theatre*, she began by saying, "When I am asked what it is I do with Ballet Theatre, I usually reply that I am in charge of the company." Not the board of trustees, not the management, not the Foundation or office staff or lawyers or accountants or stage or production personnel but the performing unit: it was the company dancers she cared most about. They were the people she lived and struggled and performed with, most of them half her age or less, whose personal welfare she considered her primary responsibility.

Amazingly, even after thirty years as director, Lucia still had the mindset of a dancer. As one critic, Deborah Jowitt, expressed in the *New York Times,* "However modest she may be about playing the Queen Mother in *Swan Lake* these days, you suspect that she loves shedding the quietly expensive duds of an executive and grubbing around backstage with the rest of the company." Dancing was her touchstone with Ballet Theatre. As she related to Sally Moore in *On Stage,* "Being in something gives me a dressing room. And it keeps me closer to my dancers. It reminds them I'm one of them." *My dancers*—the two words sum up her feelings about Ballet Theatre.

The rapport went both ways. Ask any ABT dancers what it was like to work with Lucia and immediately there is a very personal, often quite emotional response. Sono Osato, one of the original members, remembers the time in 1942 she was going to a Tudor *Romeo and Juliet* rehearsal. Next to the studio was Lucia's office, which that day was all cluttered with the coats and bags of dancers who were inside working: "I said to her, 'Lucia, wouldn't you like a nice quiet office?' Her answer was quick and firm: 'Oh no, I have to be close to the dancers.' And I thought, 'How marvelous.' I think she felt she had a big family."

We members of her dynastic family on the home front—her two sons and her sisters and cousins and nieces—agreed, having long known and accepted the fact that, along with her blood ties, she had a clan loyalty to this other family called Ballet Theatre.

Cynthia Gregory was quite emphatic about it:

She was like my mother, she really was. I was amazed at what she put up with. We were all her children. I loved that, being part of a family atmosphere. That's what's missing now, that warmth, that family thing. Most companies are being run by men now, more as a corporate thing.

Probably has to be that way, has to be more businesslike, but Lucia put so much of herself into it, that wonderful thing, a woman's touch—we all felt nurtured in a way.

There are so many aspects involved in running a dance company, the word *director* inevitably conjures up images of legendary bygone directors. Like George Balanchine or Martha Graham, who managed single-handedly to create an entire repertory; like Serge Diaghilev, who had the knowledge, taste, and imagination to bring painters, composers, writers, and choreographers together to collaborate on one eye-opening new production after another; like Ninette de Valois, who never relaxed the iron-fisted control she exerted over all aspects of the Royal Ballet. There's no disputing the achievements of these titans, all drastically different yet who by their example helped define what is generally meant in the dance world by the term *director.* It is a useful image as far as it goes but one that fails to convey the distinctive qualities of Lucia Chase.

"If the company had been run by someone else, you might have had better administration," admitted Lupe Serrano, one of the greatest dancers ever to grace the company's roster, "but you would not have had ABT."

> The ship was sinking so many times, it was Lucia's determination that kept it afloat. In fact if she had been more businesslike, probably it would have closed down. She never lost her courage, never lost her nerve. She was a real captain. She certainly knew how to weather storms.

According to Isabel Brown, whose husband and three children also danced in Ballet Theatre, contract time was an ordeal:

> I love Lucia, and I admire and respect all that she has done for ballet, but I dreaded to talk salary with her. By the time she had finished telling me, with tears in her eyes, what I owed to Art, I had not only signed on again without a raise but had agreed to wash the stage down twice a week.

Sallie Wilson agreed that signing a contract was always traumatic:

> Lucia was a genius for making you feel grateful for taking a cut. Or she'd give you a tiny raise, and you'd be so happy. But then she had to be strict, she didn't have enough money.

Cynthia Gregory, on the other hand, felt that times of getting a new contract were always exciting:

> I loved to go sit in that little library in her apartment and have her tell me what we were going to do for the next season, all the different things that were going to happen. She would talk about everybody else but you for a

while—everything else—but I liked that. I got the whole idea she had behind her thinking, what she thought about the season, and I sort of relaxed, and then after a while she'd get around to me.

Bruce Marks, recalling his first week with Ballet Theatre as the company's newest soloist when he was dancing six to eight hours a day, learning several major roles in four totally unfamiliar ballets, so tired in the mornings he could barely get out of bed, recounted how one day Lucia came up to him during a break outside the studio and told him she was tearing up his contract. He felt terribly upset—he thought he had been doing quite well—until she explained that she wasn't firing him but was making him a principal and offering him a new contract.

I said something foolish like it wasn't necessary: "I'm a modern dancer. I've never been in a ballet company before." In reply she simply said those memorable words, "Trust me." From then on, she never wavered in her support, even though there were times when I got some abysmal reviews. As an essentially modern dancer, I didn't have the classic line, but I did have the loyalty of Miss Chase, and for that I was always grateful.

One of the more "difficult" members of the company for Lucia was Eliot Feld, from the beginning right up to the day when he decided he had had enough and suddenly left Ballet Theatre. Yet two decades later, speaking from the stage at ABT's fiftieth anniversary, Feld paid a fond tribute to his former boss:

For me, though I know I'm living in the past, Lucia Chase and Ballet Theatre are one. She was always there. She was at my audition. She handed me my contract. She was at rehearsal. She was always in the wings to put squarely on my head that ugly, dinky little peasant hat from *Giselle* (made of straw with a ton of grapes on top) which I had carefully cocked to the side in order to look debonair. She was on every tour of one-night stands. And she was always on the bus, in the first seat opposite the driver, at 5 minutes to 8:00 each morning, and I mean at 5 minutes to 8. You were not late if you expected to catch the bus. I know, because on my first tour she left me in Chattanooga. And since I had lost my itinerary, I had to call Florence Pettan at the office in New York to tell her that I was in Chattanooga—where the hell was the company?

Like contract stories, there are also reams of bus stories:

Once when we were out in California, we left San Francisco in the middle of the night. The roads were icy, and the bus at one point went off the road into a ditch. All the men got out to push. Slowly we got the bus out and started it up the hill, passing a sign on our right as we continued to push which read, "Welcome to Oregon." Meanwhile behind us the girls had all gotten off the bus and stood wrapped in blankets, huddled around Lucia . . . mother hen and her chicks. When we finally pushed the bus over the hill and it disappeared out of sight, Lucia straightened up and said, "Well, we've lost the bus, so now we'll just continue the tour on foot."

It's startling to hear so many former ABT dancers speak about Lucia in very endearing terms, particularly considering that all the time she was mixing with them, she was also very much their senior and director of the company. Melissa Hayden, forty years after she left the company to go dance with New York City Ballet, recalled Lucia with particular fondness: "She had a wonderful graciousness about her. She never treated us like she was a boss. She was a very upfront person, a very polite lady. I always liked your mother."

Terry Orr claimed Lucia always gave dancers a feeling that they were in a family: "I really felt it was my second home in a way. Leaving California and literally not having any friends or relatives in New York except the few people that I had danced with, I think the idea of joining ABT had a lot to do with the way Lucia made you feel this was a nurturing kind of family to be with."

Nora Kaye wrote about how one year on tour she roomed with Lucia: "She's an early riser and I'm not. Every morning she'd tiptoe around for an hour or so, for fear she'd wake me. Our problems were her problems. She acted like a mother hen for 'her girls.' She'd watch over them and see that they didn't stay out too late."

One comical story has the sound of a folktale but must have been true since it was told to me by several dancers:

The company was in Orlando. A group of us was in the hotel, sitting by a big window, looking out at a pond. At one point Lucia spoke up: "Oh, look at the pond, all those swans—it's like *Swan Lake.*" A moment later, Dimitri Romanoff said, "Take a look now, Lucia." The swans were coming out of the water onto the land—you know the way swans walk, they were waddling. And Lucia said, "Quick, close the curtains. Don't let the company see." The swans were ungraceful, and she wanted things for us to be beautiful.

Lucia just didn't like ugly. Lucia wanted the company to be beautiful, both on and offstage. When it came to selecting new dancers for the company, there might be three or four others sitting in the studio with her—Dimitri Romanoff, the regisseur, or Enrique Martinez or Fernand Nault, assistant ballet masters, perhaps a longtime associate like Tudor or Nora Kaye—but Lucia reserved the right to make the final decisions and would ask herself, "Is the dancer attractive? Does she have charm? Is she alert? Does she project an interesting personality? Is she friendly, amiable, and good-natured?"

These were nonballetic considerations, yet after years of traveling with the company on the bus, staying with them in the same hotels, taking them after performances to glamorous private parties and embassy receptions, she put a high value on having a company who not only got along together when they were by themselves but who also caused people on the outside to enjoy seeing them, being with them, getting to know them. "Lucia had a good eye for picking dancers," according to Lupe Serrano. "One thing she was always very particular about was that the women had to have good feet."

"Blonde, blue-eyed, pretty feet" was the way Eleanor D'Antuono joked about Lucia's preferences. "Pretty feet, pretty face," Terry Orr said, "and the look onstage of being real men and real women."

She took care to provide a good example herself: "She was always beautifully, socially dressed herself in one of her lovely tweed suits and her little shoes," Rhoda Jorgensen said. "And I had the impression she expected that of the kids, too. We didn't get on the bus in our sweat clothes: I always felt I was expected to look nice."

Along with setting an example by her personal appearance, there were a great many little routine things Lucia did which long afterwards were singled out for special mention. Jeannot Cerrone, former company manager, was always impressed by how as a performer Lucia acted and expected to be treated just like everybody else in the company. "She stands in line at the window to pick up her money. And when the company goes on the road, she collects her own baggage when it's unloaded."

That "baggage" was a little red suitcase my brother and I used to see year after year when our mother took it out of the closet and started packing to go off on tour. It was modest and cloth-bound, about as small as a suitcase gets. She kept it for years. It was part of her personality, one of a number of commonplace items—her leopard coat, her gloves, her neat shoes, her trim suits, the smooth leather case with her initials L.C. she always carried with her—which the dancers grew accustomed to seeing, fixed points they hung other memories and feelings on. Rhoda Jorgensen recalled,

> Your Mom was like a Mom to all the kids in the company. I don't mean if you had a heartbreak, that she would take care of that—Moms don't do that anyway. But it was very personal. Lucia always knew what we were about. She was very supportive of male-female relationships, excited when one of the girls had a nice boyfriend, always thrilled when something nice happened to us.

Sallie Wilson, who had a long and illustrious career with Ballet Theatre, said there were no words to tell how she felt about Lucia:

> There isn't anyone like her now. She was always there, rode the bus, sat in the audience every night and applauded. She presented the company, whether she was mad at them, or they were mad at her, she presented them as a jewel in her hand. She was such a real person. Now everyone is a paper doll compared to her. She had a big integrity. She'd do anything to make the show go on, anything not to have to change the program. We had no money, but we always had an orchestra. These things are so easy to throw away. To her, it was very important.

Warren Conover made a special point of her tenacity:

> She could absolutely get the performance on. No matter what happened—a strike, a storm, no matter what—the performance always got on.

There were some very close calls. Cynthia Gregory remembered a time when the company was doing the full-length *Don Quixote* in Washington. She was in the third or fourth cast, which meant she wasn't scheduled to dance in it the first week, so she stayed behind in New York.

> On Sunday morning, Easter morning, Lucia called: "We've had a couple of injuries. Would you mind coming down in case we need you for *Don Q*?" *Don Quixote* was a brand-new three-act production, I hadn't had a dress rehearsal yet or anything, my partner wasn't due in until the following week, but Lucia said, "Please, just get on the shuttle and come down." So I said okay. I barely arrived in my hotel room when the phone rang. It was Lucia.
> "Can you come over to the theatre? We're having a rehearsal." So I went to the theatre, where she greeted me by saying, "I lied. It's not for later. It's this afternoon. We really need you to do it." I was flabbergasted: "You're kid-

ding," I protested, but she wasn't. "Try it. Just try it," she urged. "Otherwise we'll have to cancel. Now what can I get for you?" I told her I hadn't even had breakfast yet. "I'll get you some," she said, and she got me milk. She got me a tuna salad sandwich. Then she got my costume. She put the costume on me. She helped me with my hair, my makeup—she was going to make sure I was going to get on. She believed all the time, was sure I could do it. She wouldn't let me say no. There was no way I could say no. There were times out onstage I didn't know where I was going, but she was right there, standing in the wings, willing the whole thing right up to the end. She could get anybody to do anything.

Another common theme many dancers still talk about was Lucia as a performer. Cynthia Gregory was struck by the way she was so focused. "She did exactly the same thing every time, except she'd make it fresh. It was amazing the way she did it." Rhoda Jorgensen recalled, "Onstage, she would never miss a beat. She was always a performer. Always. Lucia was very much the queen. She was so scary in *Fall River Legend.* It was absolutely awesome what she did with that part." Sallie Wilson said, "She had a theatrical sense that was incredible. She gave me a correction after a performance once that helped me for years. She did *Fall River* until I don't know how old she was, and it was always powerful."

Performing was always the part of her job Lucia loved best. "Being onstage is important to me," Lucia confided in an interview, "because there is a kinship with the dancers which comes from having a theater case, a dressing room, and meeting the same rigors of performance that they do. If conditions in a theater are cramped, or the stage isn't very good, they know that I share that with them. And [referring to her role in *Fall River Legend*] there must be a very useful cathartic effect when they watch me being axed to death."

According to Warren Conover, sometimes her ability as a performer had an influence on the company apart from what she did onstage:

Every once in a while, I would see these little things, like Bonnie Mathis doing your mother's role in *Pillar:* she'd go up to Bonnie in rehearsal, would take her hand, say "do this" or "do that," and it was beautiful. She was passing on this little detail to the dancer coming after her, very, very quietly.

Finally, there were unofficial actions outside the studio and theater that Lucia did privately, without any professional or ulterior motive. Isabel

Brown spoke to me about the time when her husband, Kelly Brown, who had also been a dancer in the company, died:

> The family was scattered at the time. There was a memorial service in Phoenix, but the children couldn't all make it. They felt upset and badly about it afterwards. Lucia heard about it, and she scheduled a separate memorial service in New York. No one asked her to do it. It was all her doing. It was held at St. James Church on Madison Avenue and 71st Street, around the corner from her apartment. She spoke to the minister, she arranged the service. The kids came, the whole company came. Afterwards everyone gathered at Lucia's apartment where she had a beautiful buffet. It meant my children felt they finally had reached closure about their father's death.

Maybe Lucia Chase was not everything one might wish for as an administrator, business manager, or artistic director. But as a human being, either for the dancers in Ballet Theatre or a mother in her own immediate family, she always did everything that could possibly be asked for, and then often a great more.

Original cast of Antony Tudor's dramatic ballet *Pillar of Fire,* which premiered April 8, 1942, at the Metropolitan Opera House. Pictured (left to right) are Hugh Laing (Young Man), Nora Kaye (Hagar), Lucia (Eldest Sister), Annabelle Lyon (Youngest Sister), and Tudor (The Friend). Foto-Semo, Mexico.

Lucia as the Eldest Sister in Antony Tudor's *Pillar of Fire*. A member of the original cast, she continued to perform the role for over two decades. Photo by Hermann Heinrich.

Lucia as the Fourth Song in Antony Tudor's *Dark Elegies*, first performed by Ballet Theatre during its inaugural 1940 season at the Center Theatre. Lucia was a member of the original cast but is pictured here twenty years later in 1960 at the age of sixty-three! Photo by Walter Owen.

Lucia as the implacable matriarch in Kenneth MacMillan's *Las Hermanas,* based on Federico Garcia Lorca's *The House of Bernardo Alba* and first performed by Ballet Theatre in November 1967 at the City Center. In his review of the performance, Walter Terry called Lucia "one of the great dance mimes of our day." Photo by Martha Swope.

For Lucia
affectionately
Agnes

Agnes de Mille, pictured in costume of her ballet *Rodeo*, originally choreographed in 1942 for Ballet Russe de Monte Carlo. Ballet Theatre's production of *Rodeo* premiered in January 1951 with Allyn Ann McLerie in de Mille's role as the Cowgirl, John Kriza as the Champion Roper, and James Mitchell as the Head Wrangler. Photo by Maurice Seymour, courtesy of Ronald Seymour.

Oliver Smith and Lucia, directors of American Ballet Theatre for thirty-five years, 1945–80. Photo by Kenn Duncan.

Lucia in 1953 at the Place Trocadero in Paris with Marc Chagall, designer of sets and costumes for *Firebird.* In reviewing the production, Edwin Denby called Chagall's décor "as wonderful a gift to the season as a big Christmas present to a child. . . . One sits before it in childlike enchantment." Photo by Charles Payne.

Oliver Smith, Lucia, and Justin Colin, president of the Ballet Theatre Foundation,
cutting the cake at the thirty-fifth anniversary party of American Ballet Theatre

My children, Sandy, Eric, and Caroline Ewing, in April 1969, just before their mother's sudden death in July. Photo by Jim Howell.

Lucia in 1982, two years after her retirement, outside High Tide in Narragansett with her poodle, Gendarme, who would accompany her each afternoon as she went to pick flowers for the house.

22. Sherwin Goldman

At ABT, things often happen as
much by chance as by design. Long-
range planning is a luxury Miss
Chase has never felt the company
could afford when there are so many
pressing problems which need day-
to-day solutions.
—Peter J. Rosenwald, *New York*
magazine

J ANUARY 1969: the two-week December season just com-
pleted at the Brooklyn Academy, although distinguished by the superb pairing of Erik Bruhn and Carla Fracci and the addition of *Coppelia* as another
full-length classic to the repertory, did not fare well at the box office, and
the company faced a cash deficit of some $600,000.

Employment for the current year was another problem. There were
some awkward gaps in the upcoming tour, but more alarming, one of its
main elements—a full week in Atlanta—was suddenly blasted when a
plane filled with many of the principal figures of the Atlanta arts commu-
nity crashed. With the cultural leadership of the city decimated, the Atlanta
engagement was cut from an entire week to a single performance, which
meant that the company would be left idle for the remainder of the week.
Furthermore, after the tour, the only firm commitments were three weeks

during the summer in outdoor theaters and another two-week engagement at the Brooklyn Academy in December. Otherwise, there was no foreign tour and, most depressing, no opportunity for the company to perform in Manhattan during all of 1969.

An emergency meeting was called by a small group of Ballet Theatre principals consisting of Lucia and Oliver Smith, Priscilla Stevens and Nancy Zeckendorf (both trustees and two of Lucia's most loyal and conscientious friends), Charlie Payne (who was serving as a de facto administrator of the company), and John Wharton (general counsel for the foundation as well as Lucia's lawyer). During the course of the meeting, there was general agreement that a formal plan should be drawn up and adopted to deal with the company's ongoing operation. The question was, who was the person best equipped to take on this assignment?

Two years earlier, after Harold Taylor had resigned as president and vacated the scene, a concerted effort led by Zeckendorf and Stevens to reconstitute the board had resulted in the election of a young lawyer, Sherwin Goldman, as a new Ballet Theatre trustee. Goldman was a graduate of Yale College (Class of 1961) and Yale Law School who had worked briefly for John Lindsay's 1965 mayoral campaign before joining Debevoise, Plimpton, Lyons & Gates, the same giant New York law firm where my brother had worked until his sailing-accident death in 1962.

Now, in the course of the emergency meeting, Charlie Payne said that he believed that Goldman, although relatively new to the board, had worked out some sort of long-range business proposal for governing the company. In Payne's opinion, it was impossible for a ballet company to operate according to any formally prescribed blueprint—at least Payne confessed it was beyond his powers to conceive of such a plan, and he felt obliged to dismiss himself from the discussion—but before leaving the meeting, he offered to contact Goldman and ask if he might be interested in implementing his idea. A few days later, Payne reported back that Goldman had replied in the affirmative, whereupon the full board of trustees met and agreed to hire him, not simply as the next president to succeed Harold Taylor but in the much more demanding capacity of chief executive officer of Ballet Theatre.

This was quite a radical departure from anything that had been attempted before. All the previous Ballet Theatre presidents were prominent citizens who were not paid employees but who had volunteered their time. Their one prescribed duty was to preside at board meetings over the group of friends, relatives, patrons, and well-wishers who were called trustees but who actually assumed very little responsibility for the workings of the company. While the most recent presidents—Blevins Davis, Byam Stevens, and Harold Taylor—had provided significant personal prestige and business contacts (and, in the case of Davis and Stevens, substantial financial support), they were never officially charged with the responsibility for putting Ballet Theatre's affairs on a sound operating basis but were focused simply on keeping the company going in the same way it always had.

Sherwin Goldman had no such binding attachment to Ballet Theatre's past. He also had a clear–cut image of the organization's endemic ailments and a comprehensive long-range corrective plan that he was anxious to enact. If this blunt-speaking, rather arrogant, often rude Napoleonic figure was not exactly the proverbial winsome knight in shining armor, he came onto the scene precisely when sweeping drastic action was absolutely imperative.

On January 23, 1969, Goldman left Debevoise for his first day of work at Ballet Theatre and was disconcerted to find that no one had set aside a room as a separate office for the foundation's new chief executive officer. But that was only a momentary glitch. It wasn't long after he had settled in that he made the same discovery I had back in 1956 when—considerably younger and less experienced than Goldman—I plunged into Ballet Theatre and found that, in addition to a crisis or two immediately at hand, there was no idea at all on anyone's part of what the company would be doing the following year.

Twelve tumultuous years and scores of highly significant events had taken place since then, but from an operations point of view, little had changed. There were still no long-range plans for the company, "at least not the way we think of plans" was the way Goldman years later described it; no comprehensive budget for the coming year or beyond; and only enough cash on hand for the next couple of weeks, with no visible sources of income after that.

There was one bright spot on the horizon: the American Ballet Theatre was formally selected in 1969 to be the official company for the new Kennedy Center in Washington, D.C. However, until the glittering new theater, still in the planning stages, was built, there was not even a moderately suitable place for ABT to perform in the nation's capital. The situation in New York was equally unsatisfactory. Although there were currently two splendid new theaters at Lincoln Center, neither one was generally available:

the Met Opera House had leased any open time to Hurok, who planned to use it for the big foreign companies he was bringing to the States; and the New York State Theater, controlled by Morton Baum, was dedicated to City Center's two former resident companies, the New York City Ballet and New York City Opera. The only other large New York theaters that could be booked on any sort of a regular basis were the Brooklyn Academy of Music, which was located outside the mainstream of theater activity, or the City Center of Music and Drama on 55th Street, with its cramped stage space and extremely limited number of choice seats despite the house's overall capacity.

With a deficit at hand, very little money coming in, and insufficient future employment, including no appropriate place to perform in its own home city, Ballet Theatre faced a very real possibility that the company might be obliged to close down before the new president had completed his first year in office.

The first imperative was to tackle the crisis caused by the cancellation of the weeklong booking in Atlanta, and here fortune favored Sherwin Goldman. The mother of one of his college classmates happened to be a major figure in Chicago. At Goldman's urging, she organized several of her friends, who were among the city's most influential citizens, into a committee which then met with Bea Spachner, the enterprising woman who had undertaken to renovate and operate Chicago's Auditorium Theatre, the landmark building originally designed by Frank Lloyd Wright and Louis Sullivan. Encouraged by the extreme likelihood that Ballet Theatre would be backed by a powerful resident chapter in Chicago, Bea Spachner agreed to book the company into the Auditorium for the entire time that had been vacated by Atlanta, and in one move the impending crisis was averted. Round One to Goldman.

The second imperative was to secure a theater for an ABT season in New York to coincide with the company's thirtieth anniversary year. The key here was the familiar, all-powerful impresario Sol Hurok. Lucia had already approached him several times, but her efforts had not met with any success, and she had come to think the possibility of getting into the Met was virtually hopeless. Sherwin was not convinced and reopened the issue with Hurok.

A major roadblock turned out to be that Hurok had already contracted to bring England's Royal Ballet in the coming summer to the Met. However, Hurok was also most interested in the possibility of regaining booking rights to American Ballet Theatre. Believing he could postpone the Royal Ballet's opening by a few weeks, Hurok made a verbal agreement with Goldman to present ABT at the Met ahead of the English company.

Getting a signed contract was more difficult. Hurok was constitutionally averse to committing himself in writing, and it took constant pressing before finally Goldman prevailed and got a contract for the Met, much to Lucia's astonishment and delight. Their new working partnership appeared to have started off beautifully.

Unfortunately, Hurok's promise of the Met turned out to be short-lived when Ninette de Valois, the iron-fisted director of the Royal Ballet, refused to grant any leeway on the timetable she had negotiated and insisted on coming to New York in July, according to the original schedule. Hurok was obliged to comply, but in order to safeguard his new relationship with Ballet Theatre, he offered the alternative of an engagement in London at Covent Garden (which the Royal Ballet would now have left vacant), followed by a short tour to Greece, Spain, and Italy. The new schedule effectively solved the greater part of the company's employment problem for the coming year, although for Lucia, the changes were somewhat of a letdown and nowhere near as fulfilling as a gala thirtieth anniversary season at the Met.

As Goldman analyzed the situation he had inherited, the fundamental problem was that Ballet Theatre had always considered itself primarily as an artistic enterprise and had failed to incorporate standard practices that characterize the operations of practically any well-run business. His ultimate aim was to establish a clear definition of what the company was about, where it was going, and how it proposed to get there, yet before tackling that long-range goal, he had to familiarize himself with the multiplicity of crises at hand and decide which problems to tackle first.

Certainly one of the most critical was money. Over the entire span of the previous year, the Foundation had attracted only twenty-four donors in the top category of Patrons (individuals who had contributed $1,000 or more), along with an additional 123 Founder Members who gave $100 or more. Overall, contributions raised from outside individuals were in the vicinity of $50,000, only a tiny fraction of the total amount needed to cover the company's annual operating costs.

One essential part of any prospective fund-raising campaign was to enlist the support of the several national foundations that were committed to supporting the performing arts. Up to this point, with the single exception of the National Endowment for the Arts (NEA), no major foundation had ever given substantial money to help the company—not the Ford or the Rockefeller Foundation, the Rockefeller Brothers Fund, the Mellon Foundation, or several others. In most cases, no applications had been submitted from Ballet Theatre requesting financial assistance. Building a rapport with foundations was a long-term proposition that needed to be started immediately in order even to have any hope of ultimate success.

Another principal problem area Goldman singled out as requiring immediate attention was the inefficient and very costly way the company was currently touring. One-night stands in city after city were impossible for Ballet Theatre to promote from its New York office. Even in the few instances during each tour where an engagement in a single city was longer than one or two days and there was a chance to make a concerted promotional effort, the company lacked the local knowledge, machinery, or staff to handle publicity or ticket sales and was totally dependent on the local manager, who often was either incompetent or placed his own interests first, frequently both. For years Ballet Theatre had been victimized by this setup, and with deficits generated out on the road constantly increasing, unless something was done to alter the system, the cost of touring would soon be prohibitive.

While Goldman was wrestling with these formidable far-flung challenges, Lucia's overriding concern was quite straightforward: to celebrate the thirtieth anniversary of Ballet Theatre.

Prospects for mounting a particularly memorable season were bright. The company, as constituted in 1969, had an incredible roster of principal dancers, including Toni Lander, Royes Fernandez, Bruce Marks, Sallie Wilson, Eleanor D'Antuono, Gayle Young, Cynthia Gregory, Ted Kivett, Mimi Paul, Michael Smuin, and Ivan Nagy. In addition, Lucia set aside her aversion to bringing in guest artists from the outside and was in the process of hiring Lupe Serrano, Erik Bruhn, and Carla Fracci for the thirtieth anniversary, investing them with the innovative title of "Permanent Guest Artists of ABT." As for repertory, new productions being planned for the anniversary season included two all-time classics, Léonide Massine's rollicking *Gaîté Parisienne* and Fokine's *Petrouchka,* which he had restaged on the company back in 1942 with the bewitching Irina Baronova as the doll-like Ballerina; also *The River* by Alvin Ailey, and two works by José Limón, *The Moor's Pavane* and *The Traitor.*

However, there was one problem, by now a sadly familiar one: no theater. With Hurok's original promise of the Met ruled out by Ninette de Valois in favor of the Royal Ballet, the only other location at all suitable was the New York State Theater, but that was tied up by the New York City Ballet, New York City Opera, and other City Center constituents. For Lucia, finding a theater for a thirtieth anniversary season was the number one problem facing the company, more immediate and incontrovertible than any of the sweeping long-range projects Sherwin was talking about.

In June, Lucia was honored at the commencement ceremony of the University of Wisconsin, where she received an honorary degree of Doctor of Humane Letters, "in recognition of her achievements and contributions to the art of ballet both as a dancer and a director." The following month, she planned to rejoin the company, which was scheduled to be in Washington, performing the first of three weeklong summer outdoor engagements. At least that's how she had worked things out in her mind.

Consequently, late in July, she was in Washington at the Carter Barron Theatre when I called her from California, where my wife, Carol, and I, along with our two young sons, Sandy and Eric, were on a family Sierra Club trip with our cousins, the John Chases, high up in the Sierra Mountains. One day in the middle of the trip, after a short hike, Carol fainted, momentarily regained consciousness, but then relapsed and died despite all our efforts to revive her.

Dropping everything, Lucia bid a hasty good-bye to the company, packed, and two hours later was on her way by shuttle to New York City and then on to Millbrook, New York, to devote the rest of the summer to helping me and her three grandchildren cope with our shattering loss.

23. Troubles between Sherwin and Lucia

Last week the company ended its
anniversary season with a four-week
engagement at Manhattan's New
York State Theater that broke all
box-office records in U.S. ballet
history. But even as the final curtain
rang down, accompanied by the now
familiar sound of bravos, ABT faced
a most uncertain future."
—Alan Rich, *New York Times,*
     July 20, 1970

B Y THE FALL OF 1969, Sherwin Goldman had been
working at Ballet Theatre since the beginning of the year, and already,
thanks to his initiatives, a great deal had changed.

As a first step toward building up the foundation's board, there were now
three new trustees: Robert Rubin (later to become U.S. secretary of the
treasury), Lawrence Groo from the investment world, and Stella Saltonstall
(whose husband, David Saltonstall, coincidentally happened to be head
of the giant Mellon Foundation). In addition to joining the board, Stella
Saltonstall had also agreed to serve as chairman of a finance committee, but

only on the condition that Ballet Theatre hire a director of development to plan and run a new department entirely dedicated to fund-raising, a major innovation that was now already in place and beginning to function.

Goldman had also made considerable progress in two other areas he had singled out as his top priorities. Intent on establishing a rapport with some major foundations, he had met several times with both McNeil Lowry at the Ford Foundation and Norman Lloyd of the Rockefeller Foundation, and had even succeeded in obtaining a small grant from the Rockefeller Foundation to assist new choreographers and to expand the company's artistic staff. He had also begun talking with June Arey at the National Endowment for the Arts about the NEA's assisting American Ballet Theatre and other touring dance companies by giving direct subsidies for their out-of-town engagements, and also helping them negotiate more favorable contracts with local theater managers.

Meanwhile, after staying for my wife Carol's funeral service and burial in Millbrook, my mother was instrumental in moving us all to Narragansett where she took charge, particularly of my three children, for most of the month of August. But then after we had all gone home to Millbrook, my children back to their rooms and their friends and the Dutchess School, myself at least for the time being to the Joffrey Ballet, Lucia returned to work in September with one imperative foremost in mind: the thirtieth anniversary of American Ballet Theatre, now only a few months away.

There was still no suitable theater available, either in the spring or at any point during the entire course of 1970, yet she continued to insist that a thirtieth anniversary season should and would take place. If there were problems, there were always problems. No excuses, just get to work.

When the Richard Rodgers Musical Theatre, which was scheduled to perform at the State Theater for four weeks in July, suddenly decided to cancel its season, Goldman sprang into action. Working with Norman Singer, director of the City Center, together they managed practically overnight to switch the State Theater's newly vacated time over to American Ballet Theatre. The State Theater might not be the Met, which was always Lucia's first choice, but it was very good. And immediately afterwards, also thanks to Goldman's earlier negotiations with Hurok, there was now some very substantial employment: the engagement at Covent Garden, followed by a short European tour of Greece, Spain, and Italy, then back to New York for a December season in City Center.

Although Lucia was most grateful for the way Sherwin Goldman had come up with a theater for her anniversary season, she found it quite difficult suddenly to be sharing center stage with him. Goldman seemed to have very far-out ideas and a totally different way of working from hers. Goldman, for his part, felt increasingly beset by complications evolving from Lucia's characteristic modus operandi.

"Lucia saw things as separate units," he observed to me many years later. "A New York season for her, particularly if it was at the Met, was like a great party. After it was over, she'd go to Narragansett and take a deep breath before starting something else . . . like another party."

In contrast to his unswerving battle plan, there seemed to be no continuity in the way the ballet company under Lucia's direction operated. It was like a car that went forward in fits and starts, a giant burst or two and then a lapse, lots of action followed by nothing, with little inkling of what would happen next or assurance that ABT would even keep going at all.

On another front, he encountered a fresh problem from the miniscule success he had securing for ABT a small grant from Norman Lloyd at the Rockefeller Foundation to help pay for creating several new works in the next few years. Lucia, of course, welcomed the idea of getting money from outside foundations. However, the Rockefeller grant had come with certain conditions which made it clear that the funds were not an outright gift but were tied to a specific project that was expected to take several years to complete.

Throughout the three decades Lucia had been with Ballet Theatre, since she was never sure what she and the company could afford to do next, much less several years farther on, she had generally resisted making long-term future commitments. She also didn't like any money given to Ballet Theatre to be restricted in any way: once it was in hand, she wanted it to be available for whatever at the next moment became the company's most urgent need. It seemed Norman Lloyd must have been aware of this, for at the time he made the grant, he had stipulated that the money was only to be used for the grant's expressed purpose of creating new ballets and nothing else. "If this causes you any complications, please let me know," he specifically told Goldman.

It did, and sooner than he or Goldman ever anticipated. In preparing for the anniversary season, Lucia felt it was critical to replace some of the *Swan Lake* costumes, which were beginning to look tawdry, and since the only ready cash around was the new money from Rockefeller, she planned to use that. Goldman, mindful of Norman Lloyd's warning, protested and said she could not. Asking foundations to give money for a particular purpose and then spending it any way you wished was, in his opinion, a sure way to discourage that foundation, and probably others, from ever giving to you again. And yet, for Lucia, whatever was most immediately important for Ballet Theatre was the only thing that mattered, and a bedraggled *Swan Lake* could ruin the entire anniversary season.

The opposing viewpoints quickly turned into a battle about who in Ballet Theatre controlled the money: was it the president and CEO of the Ballet Theatre Foundation, or the director and still the principal supporter of the ballet company? Eventually Lucia agreed not to draw on the Rockefeller money and worked with Sherwin to find ways of paying for the *Swan Lake* costumes and all the other costs involved in the anniversary season. Yet the Rockefeller grant, small and noncontroversial as it was, had the damaging effect of pitting Goldman and Lucia against each other and previewed how their relationship would in time become increasingly combative, even downright hostile.

Meanwhile, the first page of the souvenir program for the thirtieth anniversary season at the State Theater was devoted not, as was the custom, to the ABT company but to the Ballet Theatre Foundation. There was a photo of Goldman in the upper left-hand corner, underneath that a list of the officers and board of governing trustees, and to the right, a pagelong essay—over the signature, Sherwin M. Goldman—that reads less like a report than a manifesto:

> Artistically, the first 30 years of American Ballet Theatre constitute a catalogue of creative productivity unparalleled in the history of American theater. No other organization in our time has generated, nurtured, and given opportunity to so much talent—dancers, choreographers, musicians, composers, conductors, designers.
>
> Institutionally, the same 30 years of American Ballet Theatre have proved less successful. The Foundation still has no broad base of substantial financial support. The Company still has no "home," not even theaters in which regularly to perform, no annual ticket subscribers, no rehearsal facilities, no richly endowed school. If this great Company is to survive the next 30 years, or even the next five, all of this must change and must change rapidly.

This was pretty strong language, particularly for the company's souvenir program, which for years had served as the house organ and official voice of Ballet Theatre. The opening statement in all previous issues had always been enthusiastic accounts of the company's accomplishments. For example, the souvenir program printed five years earlier for the twenty-fifth anniversary season started off with a full-page statement, signed by Lucia Chase and Oliver Smith, naming and extolling each of the Ballet Theatre faithful who had been involved with the company back at its beginning and were still with it in 1965. Another article ended on the same high note: "With high-caliber choreographers and dancers available, and with an international reputation well-established, the next 25 years look bright indeed for American Ballet Theatre." There was no signature, but the message and tone were framed in the same bright, positive way Lucia always talked about the company. It was an article of faith for her to keep any bad news or shadows on the horizon strictly to herself. No matter how bleak conditions might appear, she was invariably quick to assert that the future "looked bright indeed."

But now here was the foundation's new president leading off the thirtieth anniversary issue with a stark assessment of exactly what steps needed to be taken in order to ensure there would even be a future for the company. The essential challenge, Goldman asserted, was to develop "a practical and stable organization in which the creative tumult of a great ballet company can be contained." Never one to mince words, Goldman proceeded to spell out exactly what "containing the creative tumult of the company" meant in practical terms. Beginning with touring: "American Ballet Theatre must get off the road. One-night stands are no longer artistically or economically feasible." Instead, the tradition of bringing ballet to the hinterlands, long the mainstay of the company's existence and one of its proudest accomplishments, henceforth was to be handed over to a small troupe—American Ballet Theatre Players—which the Foundation was in the process of creating.

Meanwhile, the main company should confine its appearances to a handful of "home residencies," major urban centers around the country, beginning with Washington (once the Kennedy Center was completed), Los Angeles, San Francisco, Chicago, and the University of Illinois at Champaign-Urbana, all places that could sustain an engagement of at least a week at a time.

The second imperative, "indispensable to our scheme for the next decade," was to acquire a home theater in Manhattan. Nothing new about this, but the point was accompanied by an admission that there was still no such performing base in sight.

After these two, several other objectives were enumerated: guaranteed annual employment for the company's artistic personnel; new improved facilities at Ballet Theatre's school, both for teaching and for the company's rehearsal and new production needs; the establishment of an endowment to provide scholarships and apprenticeships for promising students aspiring to join the company.

Finally, instead of closing with some sunny assurance that the future looked bright indeed, Goldman wound up with sobering words of warning:

> All of this is going to require, amongst other resources, an enormous amount of money. Without it, all of our glorious plans will come to naught.

None of this frank talk could have been very pleasant for Lucia. She didn't like having the grim realities aired in public. They had always been there, but to her way of thinking, talking about them would only discourage the public and undermine company morale.

Her discomfort went far beyond the new president's statement in the souvenir program. Having been in charge at Ballet Theatre now for almost a full quarter-century, Lucia had grown accustomed to having the last word on everything. Yet now here was a new chief spokesman for Ballet Theatre putting his own personal slant on the company's current state of affairs, enunciating his own comprehensive plan of action, and proposing quite drastic changes and innovations. Understandably, it was not easy for Lucia Chase to sit back and simply accept the master plan that Sherwin Goldman was proposing for American Ballet Theatre.

For instance, there was his National Registry Program, the idea of booking the company only in cities where it could stay at least several days, preferably a week or more. There were only a few cities throughout the country that were big enough to support a week or more of performances. In order to book these extended engagements, it was necessary to make a firm commitment at least twelve months in advance and to guarantee that the company would thereafter return to the same city at roughly the same time for several years. The effect of this objective was that, in order to book these major cities, Lucia was being asked to commit to dates two and three years away while still being ultimately responsible financially for everything else between now and then.

She also had a problem with Goldman's proposal of forming a second company. The idea of another group of dancers, with its own director who would choose its members, set its rehearsal schedules, determine its repertory, in effect do everything that Lucia did for the parent company, was unsettling at the very least.

And there were other changes and innovations—new people starting new activities at the office, restrictions imposed from outside sources on how newfound money was to be used, the switch of the company's preferred performing base in New York from the Met to the New York State Theater, the growing number of unfamiliar faces on the board: all these were starting to make Lucia increasingly nervous. As long as she continued to be the last resort when it came to underwriting the company, she couldn't afford to let others do whatever they wanted.

But her concern wasn't simply about money. At least as Goldman, years later, interpreted her state of mind around this time, Lucia's greatest worry was not that she was always being held captive by the precarious state of the company but just the opposite, that judging by the way things were moving, there might soon come a time when it was decided that she could be dispensed with. The more Goldman worked with her, the more he came to admire her internal fortitude, the way that no matter what happened, she never lost her nerve but always kept going and at the same time kept the company going. "People might quit, conspire against her, say horrible things to her, but she was indomitable: she was not going to be defeated by anything they did or said. In fact, the only fear I ever saw in her was from the idea that at some point she wouldn't be needed and would be turned out." There was no question of that happening, at least not at this point on the eve of the company's thirtieth anniversary.

⁓

Even before it was over, the season at the State Theater qualified as a great success.

Once again, the next-door competition from the Royal Ballet at the Met did not hurt Ballet Theatre's ticket sales but actually increased attendance so that, combined with the lower operating costs at the State Theater compared with the Met, the New York season (assisted by a "generous contribution" from Trans World Airlines) actually made money. Equally significant, both in terms of cash and also of precedent for the future, four of the new productions prepared as highlights for the anniversary had their costs underwritten: *Petrouchka* by Lawrence Groo and the NEA, *Gaîté Parisienne* by Eleanor Clay Ford and the NEA, *The River* by Justin Colin and the NEA, and *The Traitor* by Mr. and Mrs. Frank Lowther.

As for the dancing, principals Lupe Serrano and Cynthia Gregory were described in *Time* magazine as "a good match for the great names of yesteryear." Others also came in for their share of praise: "[Carla] Fracci in *Giselle* ranks among the great dramatic portrayals on any stage"; "Toni Lander and Bruce Marks in *Moor's Pavane* (along with Erik Bruhn and Fracci) demonstrated the company's ability to offer not one but two of the great ballet partnerships of the age"; and (according to Alan Rich in *Time*) "the corps has both an esprit and a discipline that is sadly lacking today in the rival New York City Ballet."

Soon after closing at the State Theater in mid-July, the company left for its Covent Garden engagement and the short tour following that to Greece, Spain, and Italy.

In contrast to the wildly successful and exhilarating visit Ballet Theatre had enjoyed in London in 1946 right after the war when popular acclaim caused it to add an additional two weeks of performances, the reception it received in England this time was markedly reserved. The Royal Ballet had moved out, and the management of Covent Garden was inclined to let the American company taking its place fend for itself. Similarly, the English dance critics, always severe, were noticeably reserved with their praise. It was almost a relief when the time came to leave for the sunshine and enthusiasm of Greece.

Yet Covent Garden turned out to be enormously important to the future of ABT for a completely unanticipated reason: the Kirov Ballet from Leningrad happened to be performing at the same time across the river in Festival Hall, and on off-nights, some of the Russians came to see ABT perform. Included in the group was Natalia Makarova, who had become a top star of the Kirov and one of Russia's most admired ballerinas.

Lucia met Makarova, along with several other Kirov dancers, during an ABT intermission, but at the time, her encounter with Makarova was what might have been described as a nonevent. What no one knew was that, at this critical point in her career, Makarova was feeling emotionally and artistically disenchanted with her current situation at the Kirov and was looking for a chance to perform a wider repertory than was available to her in Russia. She was dazzled by the variety of styles she saw embodied in the American Ballet Theatre, particularly the works of Antony Tudor, and mentioned something along this line to the English critic Clive Barnes at a party following ABT's final Covent Garden performance.

The following week, ABT was in Greece, and Lucia had gone back to the United States and on to vacation in Narragansett. Makarova, on the other hand, did not go back to her native Russia but, at the end of the Kirov's London engagement, left the company and sought asylum in England, at which point things started to happen very quickly.

Barnes, sensing that Makarova's interest in ABT's repertory was more than casual, telephoned Sherwin Goldman, who was then with the company in Greece, to ask if Ballet Theatre was at all interested in having Makarova join the company. Goldman, after conferring transatlantic by phone with Lucia, told Barnes that they were indeed interested and that he was willing to fly immediately back to England. Meanwhile, Lucia sent Makarova a warm letter, asking her to consider joining ABT and even included a specific offer along with a contract.

Returning to London, Goldman met with Makarova and began discussing the possibility of her becoming a regular member of Ballet Theatre. One of the most difficult points was salary: the figure she specified was considerably more than anyone, either in the current company or in the past, had ever been paid. Goldman flew to New York to confer with two particularly dedicated and affluent trustees whom he had persuaded to join the foundation board and who now agreed personally to cover the amount Makarova had requested, whereupon he straightway returned to London and succeeded in getting Makarova to sign a contract to join American Ballet Theatre. Their association was set to begin when the company returned to New York and started rehearsing for ABT's December season at City Center.

Lucia was thrilled. Ever since her first days with Mordkin, she had felt a particular affinity with Russians, loved their language, their food, their emotional natures, everything about them. Now here was a great Russian artist wanting to be part of Ballet Theatre. The joint effort to enlist Makarova marked one of the few occasions when she and Goldman united in spirit and objective, and Goldman's fast, effective action brought a momentary truce to their strained relationship. As Lucia always gratefully acknowledged when talking, not always happily, about Sherwin Goldman, "But one thing I have to say; he got us Natasha."

In the fall of 1970, another momentous event occurred, at least one that was all-important to me and my little family.

After Carol died, I chose to continue living in Millbrook, thereby keeping my children in their familiar rooms at home and in school with their established circle of friends, while I continued commuting to New York and the Joffrey Ballet, where I was still general director.

On top of that rather hectic routine, I had fallen in love again, with Sheila Cobb, who was widowed like myself, with a young daughter of her own. Late in the summer, we decided to get married before the end of the year.

Our wedding took place on the last day of October in Sheila's hometown of Mount Kisco, New York, with my three children and Sheila's daughter, Cecilia, very much in attendance. If it had been dusk instead of high noon, they would probably have appeared in full Halloween costume. (Eric, in fact, did show up by the altar with a hideous set of monster teeth which happily he kept in his pocket.)

Lucia's enthusiastic presence helped persuade my children that life as they knew it was not coming to an end. Caroline at age four, the youngest and smallest, still wasn't altogether sure, particularly when it came time to watch her father go off on his honeymoon and leave her behind.

At the critical parting moment, Lucia took her hand. "Don't you dare let your father see you cry," she said and, squeezing very tight in a no-nonsense grip, stood with her by the door, the Queen Mother and her little grand-daughter whose face I could see as I left all twisted up in a desperate effort to smile.

24. Makarova and Baryshnikov

I always had enormous respect for
her. I just felt her ideas were not
doable. But it was her company
and not mine, so it was becoming
increasingly clear that I might as
well opt out.
—Sherwin Goldman

AKAROVA'S FIRST PERFORMANCE with American
Ballet Theatre—opening night of the company's December 1970 season at
City Center—was originally programmed for her to dance *Giselle* with Erik
Bruhn. However, Bruhn suffered a last-minute injury, and his place was
taken by Ivan Nagy.

Makarova—thousands of miles from her own country, barely able to
speak English, a brand-new member of a totally American company—had
for the past few weeks been thrown into countless rehearsals and been constantly besieged by reporters and dance notables who clamored to speak
to her. Now, without warning, she was being paired with an emergency
replacement she had never danced with.

Yet Makarova was a consummate artist. Seeing her perform earlier that
year up in Canada, Arlene Croce wrote in the *New Yorker* that Makarova
had discovered "that special repose in which dancing is not an act but a

state of being. You could not see the beginning or end of a step—that it seemed to grow from nowhere and vanish."

Fortunately, Nagy turned out to be a strong and gallant partner, and Makarova's debut with ABT was a memorable success. It also marked the beginning of a strong, deep relationship between Makarova and Lucia. The combination of Makarova's being fervently Russian yet choosing to make Ballet Theatre her new home immediately endeared her to Lucia, and soon she would come to be included—along with Irina Baronova, Alicia Alonso, and Nora Kaye—in that chosen company of fabulous ABT dancers who were also Lucia's most cherished personal friends. Makarova was destined to illuminate Lucia's last decade at Ballet Theatre, to the extent that if there was anyone Lucia might have chosen and most comfortably accepted to succeed her when that dreaded time came, it most probably would have been her new Russian comrade-in-arms.

In connection with this question of succession, a small, private dinner party took place in the early 1970s that attracted no outside attention and might been totally forgotten except that Sherwin Goldman, the only attendee now still alive more than three decades later, recalled it as "that wonderful, wonderful dinner at 720, just about the most memorable evening I ever spent."

The dining room at Lucia's apartment, with its sparkling crystal chandelier, dignified Chippendale chairs, and twin sets of glass doors leading out to the balcony terrace, was a formal but warmly gracious setting for the full-course dinners served practically every night whenever Lucia and American Ballet Theatre were in town.

The ostensible purpose of this particular dinner was to discuss the question of who would take over when the time came for Lucia to step down as head of ABT. Lucia had occasionally talked about how she was going to find a successor, but there had never been any formal attempt or even any process set in place to do that. But now this intimate little gathering had been arranged for the specific purpose of considering the succession question on a totally informal basis and, if possible, to come to some kind of unofficial but material understanding.

Those who were invited to attend constituted the ultimate inner circle of Ballet Theatre: Lucia and Oliver Smith, Agnes de Mille, Jerry Robbins, Nora Kaye, Antony Tudor, and Erik Bruhn. These were the tried-and-true old-timers, the Palace Guard. The one "newcomer" was Sherwin, who as president and CEO of the Ballet Theatre Foundation could not very well be excluded from this high-level symposium, so shrouded in secrecy that neither I nor anyone else I have talked to, either in ABT or in our immediate family, ever heard about it.

Ever since the Dick Pleasant days, Lucia had been the commanding voice at Ballet Theatre and still was, but certainly there would come a time. . . and then who would take her place? It only made good sense to discuss the delicate issue now and at least try to have the issue all decided when "that time" did come.

The question couldn't have been an easy topic to introduce while Lucia was sitting at the head of the table in her own dining room, with the others all her invited guests. However, apparently everyone was very relaxed, and the conversation quickly became quite boisterous as they began recounting various adventures and funny times they had spent together. There was never a silent moment, not with Agnes making her crisply enunciated pronouncements, Tudor demonstrating his rapier wit, Robbins at middle age still playing the enfant terrible, and Nora Kaye's commentaries sounding straight from the Bronx, interspersed from time to time by Erik Bruhn's droll Danish humor, while Oliver played pater familias at the other end of the table.

Lucia might well have left most of the talking to others, but there was nothing she enjoyed more than a party, and these were her nearest and dearest pals. Listening to them carry on would certainly have made her radiant, with her hazel eyes sparkling, laughing to the point of tears. On the other hand, Goldman must have felt somewhat of an outsider in the midst of this irrepressible camaraderie. (It's tempting to wonder whether there wasn't the slightest malicious intention on Lucia's part for inviting him to sit in with all her closest compatriots and be made more conscious of just what constituted the time-tested, true Ballet Theatre.)

As for the principal topic that supposedly had brought them all together, the ticklish question of succession never came up. Not even a hint of it. Instead, the conversation around the table was just one rollicking story after another, including many that had been painful or stormy at the time but that now were great fun to laugh about. It all made for a grand night, a delicious meal, as always at Lucia's table, then the formal serving of coffee and liqueurs in the living room, followed by more drinks, continuing on late into the night, no one conscious of time or anxious to go.

And through it all, the great question remained unanswered. It never became a problem; it was just a topic no one wanted to bring up. It would have been too rude, even outlandish, with the Queen Mother happily presiding over the party.

⟨❦⟩

During the summer of 1974, ABT was booked for a six-week season at the New York State Theatre. Makarova by this time had attracted a considerable following in New York, but for this engagement, her greatest contribution came not from her dancing but from the transformation she wrought on the company by directing a new production of the act 4 Kingdom of the Shades portion of Petipa's full-length Russian ballet *La Bayadere*.

Back in 1961, the Kirov Ballet (formerly the Maryinsky) from St. Petersburg caused a sensation when it introduced this act in the company's epochal first appearance in the United States. The Metropolitan Opera audience that night was mesmerized as one female dancer after another appeared in glowing white tutu at the top of a long ramp, swooped into a long languorous arabesque, gradually straightened back, and then slowly began descending the ramp as another dancer appeared out of the wings behind her and repeated the same action. On and on they came, each arabesque exactly like the one before it, all of them perfect, a seemingly endless procession of quiet exquisite bodies. Unhurried, subdued, every movement as though wrapped in velvet, it was the greatest display of discipline and ballet technique that New York had ever seen.

For any ballet company to attempt to match the Kirov in this particular endeavor was begging for an unfavorable comparison. For ABT to make the attempt was particularly risky, due to the widely diverse and individualistic quality of its dancers that had always distinguished Ballet Theatre from other ballet companies. The Royal Danish Ballet, England's Royal Ballet, even the New York City Ballet under Balanchine were all much more uniform in terms of their training and repertories than American Ballet Theatre, with its total mix of choreographers—Fokine, Tudor, Robbins, de Mille, and dozens of others—all exercising a different effect and producing a different look. Yet Makarova's unrelenting, uncompromising, at times ferocious insistence that every girl in Ballet Theatre's corps get the *Bayadere* look exactly right wrought an absolutely transforming effect on the company.

"Makarova's Miracle" was how Arlene Croce described the performance:

She's not only reproduced a masterpiece of choreography, she's taken Ballet Theatre's corps—hardly the most sensitive choreographic instrument in the world—and recharged it from top to bottom. In place of the lifeless gray ensemble that has skated through *Giselle* and *Swan Lake* all these many years, there is now in *La Bayadere* an alert, disciplined, and expressive corps de ballet, trembling with self-discovery.

Thanks to Makarova and *Bayadere,* American Ballet Theatre now exhibited a new classic style and had an international flavor that would attract star dancers from other companies in other countries to join ABT in the years to come.

Significant as *La Bayadere* was to the development of the company, it was not the highlight of the 1974 State Theater engagement. The surprise feature that struck the New York theater-going public like a huge bolt of lightning originated several weeks earlier with a furtive phone call made to Makarova when she was still in London about to leave for the States to supervise final rehearsals of *Bayadere* before the start of the July season.

The call came on June 30, 1974, at 5 a.m. On the line was the Russian superstar Mikhail Baryshnikov, phoning from Toronto where he was on tour with the Kirov. As Makarova described that memorable moment:

> In a trembling voice, stammering and upset, he told me he had taken a firm decision to remain in the West and had already asked for political asylum in Canada. Of course I tried to reassure him in every way and promised to do all that I could for him at ABT—I was flying to New York the next day. . . .

As soon as I arrived in New York, I phoned Lucia Chase (she had heard about Mischa but had never seen him) and described his situation to her. I said I wanted to dance a few performances with him—there would be no other chance for him to dance in New York that summer. Although I was scheduled to dance *Giselle* with Ivan Nagy, I hoped he would understand that this was a true emergency. Soon everything was arranged, and Mischa arrived in New York in the second half of July.

Baryshnikov was already a sensation before he made his first appearance on the North American continent in the early summer of 1974. Still only twenty-six years old and just entering his prime as a dancer, reports of his phenomenal technique and artistry had filtered into the Western world and were soon corroborated by connoisseurs who saw his first performances in Canada. Now that he had defected, Baryshnikov was free to dance anywhere in the world, and Lucia was thrilled that, like Makarova, he had chosen American Ballet Theatre.

The news that Baryshnikov was coming to Lincoln Center caused a furor in the New York dance world. Two weeks before his debut with ABT, the moment tickets for his first performance went on sale at 10 a.m., a line had already formed in front of the box office, and it kept growing until the performance was completely sold out in only a few hours.

Giselle was to be his debut. Although the leading man's role of Albrecht in *Giselle* might not seem to be especially conducive to showing off Baryshnikov's extraordinary talent, his first appearance had an explosive effect on critics and audience alike. At the end of the performance, there were fifteen minutes of standing cheers, dozens of bouquets, rhythmic clapping, and shouts of "Misha, Misha, Misha!"

Following this initial performance or season at Lincoln Center, the impact Baryshnikov was to have on people of all types and walks of life was phenomenal. His effect on young people, particularly girls, was reminiscent of the early Frank Sinatra's hold on bobby-soxers. Poster pictures of him appeared in college dorms and children's bedrooms. Everywhere he went, he was mobbed.

Writing in the *New Yorker* at the end of the season, Arlene Croce observed:

> To watch Baryshnikov dance for the first time is to see a door open on the future. . . . He's unlike anyone else, and he does things I've never seen any other dancer do.

Liza Minnelli in *After Dark* voiced the universal excitement people of all ages felt when she first saw Baryshnikov dance: "Jesus Jesse! How-did-that-happen? how did-he-do-that? what-was-that-again? I-can't-believe-a-human-body-just-did-that!"

Eliot Feld recalled visiting Baryshnikov in a dressing room after one of his performances. "He was dressed in a bathrobe, his feet bare, the muscles and veins in his feet bulging. It was like an anatomy lesson, the power of this foot. I thought, this is like Michelangelo."

Later on, Feld had three chances to choreograph for Baryshnikov that he characterized as "an amazing experience": "I had never driven a Ferrari before. He had gears no other dancer had—a 5th gear, a 6th gear. It was the difference between a little meteor and a comet: he was a comet with a fiery tail, sailing across the sky."

Baryshnikov brought a new excitement to Lucia's lifelong association with Ballet Theatre. What a time this was—first Makarova, now Baryshnikov!

She couldn't stop talking about him and wanted everyone—young and old, aficionado and neophyte—to come see Misha. Ordinarily, ballet company directors don't go out on a limb to rave on and on about a particular member of their company, but in this case, Lucia could not restrain herself. He was, in her mind, the most exciting dancer, and the greatest single addition, ever to join her company.

Meanwhile, throughout his second and third year at Ballet Theatre, Sherwin Goldman had been working hard and effectively. Yet he was not particularly pleased with the way that old habits and procedures persisted throughout the organization. Ballet Theatre, in his opinion, was still not being run right, and at one point he sought guidance from John Wharton, trustee and legal counsel of Ballet Theatre.

"You're asking me to run this business efficiently and control costs, but I can't even get a budget recognized and approved," Goldman said, handing Wharton a comprehensive detailed financial report he had drawn up. Wharton gave it a cursory glance before putting it away in a drawer of his desk.

John Wharton was a profoundly wise legal advocate with an exquisitely subtle understanding of people and what made things work. As a veteran theatrical lawyer, one of the best in the business, to him Ballet Theatre was a bottomless pit financially. However, he was also Lucia's lawyer and confidant, and over the years he had witnessed firsthand how Lucia continued to cling to her preposterous dream. As long as she persisted with this, Wharton believed there was no use trying to force her to think differently. Yet he remained willing to represent and protect her insofar as was legally and humanly possible.

"You're a man of the theater," he said sympathetically to Goldman. "You know what a gavotte is? Well, that's what we have to do. We have to dance a gavotte."

This cryptic response was not the kind of advice or executive support that Goldman had hoped to receive. It was only considerably later that he came to appreciate what this elderly counselor was asking him to accept: that Lucia did not want gruesome details spelled out in advance, as Goldman had done for this latest financial reckoning, just as she had never wanted to know the full extent of any of ABT's previous crises. If she had ever been willing or even forced to face up to what it would ultimately mean in dollar terms for her to press on, the resulting figure in practically every instance would have been more than she was prepared to deal with. Yet at the last minute, she had always chosen to stand fast and pay up, and because she had done so, now—after over thirty years of financial crises—American Ballet Theatre was still in existence, an achievement and personal legacy which John Wharton deeply admired. Which was why on this occasion he put the budget projection away in his desk and told the young man seated across from him that he just had to carry on as best he could.

After this maddeningly abstruse conversation with Wharton, Goldman continued to press for his long-range plan to make Ballet Theatre into a viable operation. However, it was becoming increasingly clear to him that the opposition he was encountering was not simply a question of resolving a series of differences on how to deal with one problem after another but was essentially a personal contest for control. The longer he continued working at Ballet Theatre, the more he found himself working at cross purposes or even in direct conflict with Lucia. Relations between them continued to deteriorate to the extent that, in an interview that appeared the following year in *New York Magazine,* Goldman admitted that for the last two and a half years of his time at Ballet Theatre, he and Lucia hardly spoke:

> She fought me on my determination to have annual guaranteed employ-ment for dancers, a permanent artistic staff, a building for the school, and most important, the development of long-term commitments with major arts centers around the country to assure ABT performances year after year. It was always my intention to build an organization which didn't need me or any other individual. Lucia wanted a road show which couldn't operate without her.

At one point, early in 1973, it appeared to Goldman that he was about to land a massive grant from the Ford Foundation. The windfall, which he had been working on for some time, involved Ford's setting aside $1 mil-lion as a reserve fund which the Ballet Theatre Foundation could draw on in times of crisis, always providing that any money drawn out of the fund would be replaced by the end of the year, leaving the million intact for the next twelve-month cycle. The intent of the proposed underwriting was to even out the drastic cash shortfalls that tended to occur each year between the company's regular seasons in New York, which were now producing considerable amounts of income.

The grant promised to come at least very close to putting Ballet Theatre's year-to-year financial operation on a sound footing and represented a tre-mendous breakthrough, a culmination of so much that Goldman had been trying to accomplish since taking over control of Ballet Theatre Foundation. The only catch was that, instead of his being able to use this munificent prize as a grand way to retire gracefully from the scene, Goldman was told by McNeil Lowry at the Ford Foundation that he had to remain at Ballet Theatre at least another year in order to ensure that the Ford money was properly administered. Otherwise no grant.

In February 1974, Lawrence Groo, who had been recruited as a trustee by Goldman and was currently serving as chairman of the finance committee, sent Lucia the following letter:

> I am writing at this time of turmoil in Ballet Theatre's financial history to bring into focus two important changes. . . .
>
> (1) Board members will be raising more money among themselves and from outside: the commitment will be made by the board meeting next Friday. While it won't raise anything near $713,000, it will be larger than ever before. . . .
>
> (2) This year could prove to be the last difficult year for private financing until fiscal 1978. ABT wouldn't need financial assistance from you during these years.

This would have been welcome news to Lucia if the letter had just ended there. Instead, Groo went on to explain the reasoning behind his hugely optimistic conclusion. Actually, if the Foundation tried to repeat everything it had done this past year, there would be a deficit of $400,000. However, this deficit could be avoided if, for the current year, the company undertook to perform just one, instead of two, New York appearances. After that, the next two years' deficits (1975–76 and 1976–77) would be covered by the million from the Ford Foundation, and it would again be possible to have both a winter and a summer season in New York.

"It seems clear," Groo concluded, "that your tremendous burden of financial contribution could be ended after this year. However, to get to next year, we have to get through this."

Lucia was experiencing some extreme financial pressures of her own. Three decades of constant substantial contributions to Ballet Theatre had brought her personal finances to a point where she could no longer come up with large amounts of readily available cash. The trust arrangement established by Tom Ewing in his will ensured that his wife would in any event still have money to pay for her private life, but beyond that, it had become increasingly difficult for Lucia to continue acting as the company's principal individual sponsor.

She must have notified the Ballet Theatre Foundation board of this exigency, because the following month, the trustees held another meeting, after which Groo wrote her a second letter reporting how "the Board had not adjusted to the urgent realities of the new situation":

> It is naturally sympathetic to conditions which forced the withdrawal of over $600,000 in budgeted support from Miss Chase. The only possible action to remove that large a sum from expenditures—(which) was canceling the NY season—was decided against. No actions of any kind were taken to control or cut costs this year, or to assure chances of ABT's survival when current year is over.

As a conscientious trustee and sound businessman, Groo was sincerely distressed by this irresponsibility on the part of the board, and he went on to lay out for Lucia his own recommendations of what should be done:

> No new productions or expenditures for foreign dancers except those approved at meeting. Board should direct and monitor strict adherence to the budget. Rehearsal overruns should be avoided. Ford F. money must be kept segregated and secure because it is ABT's link to financial aid in future. Board should pass budget for fiscal 74–75 no later than 4/30/74. Advise canceling NY season. Feel the $500,000 cannot be raised. Better to lose a NY season than ABT's life.

From a strictly business point of view, this all made very good sense. However, it completely failed to take into account the indomitable will that had prevailed at Ballet Theatre for the past thirty-three years and was still planted in the driver's seat. After having announced her intention to withhold any further immediate support, she penciled in a series of little calculations at the bottom of Groo's letter: "Colin $50M . . . Groo $25M . . . LC $75M . . . Rubin $10M; duP $5M."

The names referred to current board members: Justin Colin (BTF treasurer), Larry Groo (chairman of finance committee), herself down for $75,000, Robert Rubin, and Mrs. S. Hallock du Pont. Altogether these estimates of possible contributions, as construed by Lucia, only amounted to $165,000, a long way from the $500,000 goal, but still it was a good start. Enough to avoid postponing the season, which was unthinkable.

A few weeks later on, still in the spring of 1974, Sherwin Goldman addressed a group of arts administrators and foundations and at one point in his talk stated that in his opinion, the object of grantsmanship—obtaining grants from foundations—was to manipulate figures in order to qualify for the most outside assistance possible.

The underlying situation which prompted his remark was that, despite the congratulatory statements about the company's vastly improved status printed in ABT's 1974–75 souvenir program, the company was still hovering close to insolvency, if not actual bankruptcy. Rather than make a completely open disclosure of all the stark realities confronting the company, Goldman had for some time attempted to put the best possible face on ABT's finances in his applications to the several major foundations that, acting in concert, had it within their power to put the company on a sound financial basis.

The problem was that each of these foundations tended to have a different objective. The Ford Foundation was not interested at all in covering ABT's regular annual deficit: quite the opposite, its $1 million grant was offered strictly as a reserve fund and would only be finally available if the running deficit was covered for the upcoming three years without resorting to any of the Ford money. The effect of this condition was that Goldman had to produce for Ford financial statements showing that the company was in a position each year to cover its operating costs.

In contrast to this very positive set of figures, in order to gain the support of both the New York State Council on the Arts and the NEA in Washington, it was necessary to emphasize how there was invariably a drastic shortfall between the company's earned income and its operating expenses while touring either New York State or the United States, and consequently— without a substantial subsidy from both sources—an operating deficit was unavoidable and potentially disastrous.

In order to deal successfully with these two opposite viewpoints on funding, Goldman was obliged to produce different sets of figures, one of which showed the company finances in good order, the other pointing up a fiscal emergency.

While this was a tricky maneuver, if not downright deceptive, it was not the first time that ABT and its Foundation had not been totally honest about its financial figures, particularly when it came to detailing the contributions made over the years by Lucia Chase, often a principal portion of ABT's annual income. Instead, there had been a sort of tacit agreement on the part of the Foundation's board to accept and report whatever Lucia was willing to reveal of her personal support of the company, and because (until very recently) there was no development office submitting formal grant applications and exchanging financial figures back and forth with outside funding parties, there were few occasions and very little pressure to produce comprehensive and totally accurate financial statements.

When Goldman changed this pattern and instituted an aggressive campaign to solicit corporate and foundation support, he faced the dilemma of either disclosing all facts and figures, a course that was not particularly apt to inspire immediate and massive outside support, or submitting separate and often opposite versions of ABT's finances, depending on which set of figures was most likely to gain the most positive response. Clearly, at this time, ABT's survival was on the line, and whatever facts and figures Goldman promulgated were solely fashioned to save the company from extinction. Also, the figures were generally accurate insofar as they went: if they did not present the entire truth, they at least gave a clear picture of the particular problem being addressed.

His random remark about manipulating figures went unnoticed at the time, but it was picked up later by someone at the New York State Council on the Arts, which reacted by delaying approval of a new 1974–75 grant for ABT until Goldman clarified exactly what his words meant. Two months later, his original statement and the Council's reaction to it became big news when they were reported by Anna Kisselgoff on the front page of the *New York Times* and caused something of an uproar. The following day, also in the *Times*, Arthur Levitt, the New York State controller, announced that he intended to make a special audit of all the financial figures of American Ballet Theatre and Ballet Theatre Foundation for the past two years; and in the same *Times* article, Goldman was quoted as admitting that the Ballet Theatre Foundation at one point had fashioned a big artificial deficit in order to qualify for an installment of the four-part cash reserve grant from the Ford Foundation.

After that, in an effort to come clean and also to clear up the massive confusion, Goldman submitted a comprehensive list of corrections and adjustments that also covered Ballet Theatre Foundation's applications to the National Endowment for the Arts. This was critical because, during the years 1969–73, the NEA had given Ballet Theatre $1,124,250 and was now questioning some of the company's expenditures as well as the reliability of the receipts reported to be matching the NEA grants. When told his accounting system did not meet NEA's grant requirements, Goldman was alleged to have said that ABT had too many important things to do to keep its books any other way, a rash statement that caused Lewis Lloyd (the New York Arts Council's program director for the performing arts) to comment publicly that either Goldman was a remarkably poor manager or something bad was going on at ABT.

In short, Goldman's frank admission, reprinted in the *New York Times*, that yes, he was a manipulator of figures, profoundly shocked much of the philanthropic world. The idea that the official financial statements of a nationally renowned arts organization were not to be trusted struck at the heart of the way in which all foundation and government support of the arts was based. The only acceptable recourse, in the opinion of almost everyone within and outside Ballet Theatre, was that this man must go. Otherwise Ballet Theatre's future relations with important sponsors—especially the NEA and the New York State Council on the Arts—would be gravely endangered.

For the next few months Goldman remained on the scene, cooperating fully with the state controller's investigation, and in time he was cleared of any wrongdoing. However, the damage had been done, and for the good of the entire ABT organization, he voluntarily retired at the end of the year.

Sherwin Goldman had served as CEO and president of the Ballet Theatre Foundation from 1969 until 1974. This was not a particularly lengthy tenure, yet the innovations he had introduced and the results achieved during his five-year stint were astounding.

Back in 1969, when he came into office, the financial support (aside from Lucia Chase) being given to ABT and its Foundation was so extremely limited as to be practically insignificant: only one foundation and two individuals gave more than $1,000, and there were only 321 contributors overall. Five years later, in 1974, after the completion of Goldman's first five-year plan, there were sixteen "Benefactors" who had given $10,000 or more to the Ballet Theatre Foundation; fifty-two "Patrons" who gave $1,000 or more; and twenty-four "Donors" contributing $500 each. Overall, in 1974, there were fifteen times as many contributors who, together, gave ten times as much money as in 1969.

The company's earned income recorded similar huge increases, the total for 1974 amounting to 500 percent more than five years earlier. During the same period, the salaries of principal dancers tripled, and the average of artists' salaries nearly doubled.

A comparison of the company's tours over the same five-year period shows a similar drastic change: in 1969, ABT spent eighteen weeks on the road, reaching forty-six cities; in 1974, the company was out performing twenty-five weeks or over 30 percent longer, yet was required to travel to only twelve cities.

As for the Ballet Theatre School: by 1974, a long-range plan to build seven studios had been completed, a professional training division had been established, and an apprentice program was firmly in place.

Finally, under Goldman's prodding, a monumental transformation had occurred in ABT's office where a development department now was conducting an ongoing fund-raising effort. Also, for the first time in ABT history, in 1974 a comprehensive budget was drawn up, considered, and adopted by the board of trustees.

Despite the disruptive controversy during the final year over his reputed manipulation of figures, by the time he resigned, Goldman was formally cleared of all wrongdoing. Furthermore, in just five years, he had succeeded in establishing a business operation for the Ballet Theatre Foundation that earned the approval and ongoing support of the Ford and Rockefeller Foundations, the New York State Arts Council, and the National Endowment.

"Sherwin Goldman was the first person who had some idea of how Ballet Theatre really should be run," Nancy Zeckendorf said in assessing his role within the organization. "He was a real executive director, and as long as he kept his distance, it was okay. But Sherwin was Sherwin," was the way she wryly put it, acknowledging that at the same time that he was putting things on a business footing, he caused Lucia to feel she was losing control, and that being the case, there was no way the two of them were going to work things out between them.

Years later, when asked what he felt best about all that he had managed to accomplish, Goldman's response was low-key and nowhere near what he might have claimed for himself.

The answer he gave referred to *La Bayadere* and the transformation Makarova was able to impose on ABT: in order for her to pull that off, the company had to be put on a much sounder footing.

"There had to be a proper ramp built for all those dancers to come down," Sherwin Goldman explained. "I guess I helped build that ramp."

25. Twyla Tharp's *Push Comes to Shove*

[Lucia Chase's] name appears
only passingly in ballet reference
books, and she modestly shares her
directorship of ABT with designer
Oliver Smith and choreographer
Antony Tudor. But were it not for
her quiet drive, her quintessential
optimism, and the firm fist beneath
her demure white gloves, ABT
would never have survived, let alone
reached its present heights.
—Peter J. Rosenwald, *New York
Times*, November 10, 1975

THE MID-1970s began as an especially golden moment for Lucia, a period of grace, like a late summer afternoon, when many of her goals and dreams for the company came to fruition.

Besides Baryshnikov and Makarova, Rudolf Nureyev came to direct and to dance in his production of *Raymonda*, and Erik Bruhn was back, along with Ivan Nagy and Fernando Bujones, to lead the company's men, while the women's contingent included Cynthia Gregory, Carla Fracci, Gelsey Kirkland, Sallie Wilson, Martine van Hamel, and Eleanor D'Antuono . . . an eye-catching array of talent.

The Foundation, thanks largely to Sherwin Goldman, had an active board of trustees headed by a new president, Justin Colin, who took a very close interest in the company and, in addition, proved to be exceedingly generous. As described by BTF trustee Nancy Zeckendorf,

> He was a business person, but he really understood that you had to take chances in show business. When people on the board would say things like "We should cut out Makarova, we should eliminate this and that," he would say, "You can't do that." Sherwin would have done the same. Justin was not only a business person, he understood about theater.

Another great improvement in the company's overall picture was that the Kennedy Center in Washington, D.C., was finally completed, and American Ballet Theatre was granted special status within it as its premier dance company. At last ABT could count on a beautiful, welcoming home base in the nation's capital where it could perform a number of weeks at the same time year after year.

Soon there would be a similar breakthrough in an even more critical locale. Early in 1976, Tony Bliss, the patrician lawyer who had just agreed to take on the top job of running the Metropolitan Opera, hired Jane Hermann, a well-known figure in Manhattan theater circles, to explore the possibility of the Met's instituting its own Metropolitan Opera Ballet Company.

A few months later, Hermann—at a lunch meeting with Bliss—alerted him to the fact that Hurok Associates, which still held the option on any free time at the Met, was rumored to be, in her own words, "on the verge of going belly-up." What this portended was that Bliss, in his new capacity as the Met's chief administrator, might soon face the devastating prospect of six or more weeks when the house would be completely empty, with no rent money coming in.

Bliss was understandably alarmed and asked Hermann what she thought he should do. Her response was a rather radical proposal which, as Hermann commented to me in her usual unequivocal way, "saved American Ballet Theatre." The idea of starting a new ballet company at the Met, she told Bliss, just didn't make sense: it would saddle the Met with the huge cost of hiring close to 100 more people; there was not enough studio space at the Met to accommodate a permanent on-site ballet company; and finally, if such a company were established in-house, then it would of necessity take over most of the available lease-time at the Met and in the process might well put the American Ballet Theatre right out of business. Instead, why not let her book ABT as a regular lessee into the Met for a guaranteed eight-week season every year?

Bliss approved the idea, and straightway a contract was drawn up between the Met and Ballet Theatre Foundation. As Hermann delights in recounting, there were no lawyers involved, just herself, Tony Bliss, and Justin Colin. It was a simple, straightforward deal: the Met would provide the house crew and pay the advance costs and all front-of-house expenses; Ballet Theatre would provide the company and repertory. The box office receipts would be split down the middle, with 50 percent going to each party. It took only a couple of days to get the final agreement drawn up and signed. The grand result—which was particularly welcomed by Lucia, who had often said, "We exist in order to perform at the Met"—was that for the next several years, American Ballet Theatre was able to schedule extended seasons at the Met where it would attract huge audiences amounting to over 90 percent of the great opera house's capacity.

While all this was pending, the company in 1975–76 managed several notable successes, beginning with a gala thirty-fifth anniversary performance at City Center on January 11, 1975.

The program opened with *Les Sylphides,* the same ballet which had introduced Ballet Theatre to the world thirty-five years earlier at the old Center Theatre, now no longer in existence. Two of the original cast members of *Sylphides* back in 1940—Lucia Chase and Karen Conrad—were in the audience at City Center on the night of the gala opening, along with many of the most distinguished alumni who had ever danced with the company, including Irina Baronova, Agnes de Mille, Anton Dolin, André Eglevsky, Royes Fernandez, Maria Karnilova, Nora Kaye, John Kriza, Hugh Laing, Antony Tudor, and Igor Youskevitch. Also prominent in the audience were former first lady Jacqueline Kennedy Onassis and her daughter, Caroline Kennedy. According to society columnist Suzy Knickerbocker,

> It was one of those truly glittering evenings in the theater, with a star-studded gang on stage and an audience that wasn't half bad either . . . with everyone applauding madly and shouting "bravo" and "brava" when they weren't awe-struck and gasping at the inspired dancing.

Before the performance, the word backstage that night among the dancers was "Don't go near Agnes—she's loaded for bear." Apparently she and Lucia had gone together to try on their costumes for *Judgment of Paris,* and Lucia fitted into her costume, Agnes did not. Fortunately her ill-humor had worn off by intermission time, and she gave one of her patented de Mille "knock-em-dead" speeches to the audience. Then Lucia and Oliver Smith were called up on stage by Angier Biddle Duke, the city's commissioner of civic affairs and cultural events, and presented with the Handel Medallion, NYC's highest cultural award, for their distinguished service in the cause of the arts.

The gala offered a full program of divertissements, one crowd-pleaser after another: Erik Bruhn and Cynthia Gregory together in *Miss Julie;* Baryshnikov and Gelsey Kirkland performing a pas de deux from *Le Corsaire;* the Rose Adagio from *The Sleeping Beauty,* with Gregory accepting individual roses from Eglevsky, Dolin, and Youskevitch; and finally, a spectacular finish when (according to Sally Moore in *On Stage*) everyone returned for a final bow, "at center of attention the petite, erect figure of Lucia Chase, the heart, soul, and main support of the U.S.'s leading ballet company."

"It was like having my whole family back," Lucia exclaimed backstage afterwards. "It dropped years away. I caught up with so many people. It was one of the great joys of my life."

When asked how long she planned to continue, she smiled reassuringly: "I couldn't possibly think of retiring. Things might go wrong, and I'd have to be there to make them right. But I promise you right here and now a fortieth anniversary." At that point, there didn't appear to be an end in sight or any reason to call it quits.

One year later, practically to the day, with the Met not yet available because of the opera company's winter schedule, American Ballet Theatre booked itself into the medium-sized Uris Theater. The public interest in so many great dancers—particularly its craze for Baryshnikov—was intense, and a number of the performances were quickly sold out.

Excitement reached a peak early on when a new work, *Push Comes to Shove* by Twyla Tharp, was premiered on January 9, with Baryshnikov in a leading role. Tharp, who was generally known as a modern dance choreographer, startled all of Baryshnikov's rabid fans by presenting their idol in rehearsal clothes—T-shirt, trousers, and leg warmers (designed by Santo Loquasto)—and sporting a derby hat and campy outfit. At first people didn't know how to react: the august art of ballet was being presented as a fun show, and the revered Baryshnikov was exhibiting outrageously unfamiliar talents as a comic. But then, as the whole audience caught on and started to enjoy the transformation, the Uris began to rock. By the time the curtain came down, the new work—and particularly Mischa—had caused a sensation.

Only one year earlier, practically to the day, Arlene Croce had delivered in the *New Yorker* a withering report, calling ABT "a company which since 1950 had not commissioned one ballet of lasting merit." According to her, watching its new works then was "like listening to cracked 78 rpm records being played on the finest stereo equipment." Now, thanks to Tharp's *Push*, Croce reversed positions and was totally positive:

> After two performances, I believe it is a real work of art and an entrancing good time in the theatre. . . . Fortunately for us all, it is a great big hit, and it will be around for a while. [Twyla Tharp] has given Ballet Theatre a flash act, and left us yelling for more.

Lucia's reaction was even more exuberant. In an article she wrote two years later for Charles Payne's *American Ballet Theatre*, she cited the premiere of an outstanding new ballet as the ultimate exhilaration for her in her position as company director:

> The satisfaction I experienced on the opening nights of, for example, *Pillar of Fire, Fancy Free,* and *Theme and Variations,* was doubled following the premiere of *Push Comes to Shove.* That evening alone would have convinced me that my thirty years as co-director of Ballet Theatre, with all the headaches, had been well worthwhile.

During the past couple of years, ever since Baryshnikov made his daring leap from the Kirov straight into the American Ballet Theatre, he had been working around the clock, learning an astounding number of new roles which all seemed magnified by his phenomenal technique and enthralling personality. In his first six months with the company, he had danced seven ballets, five of them new to him. The following year, he took on twelve more, nine of which were new. In 1976, he danced nine more, eight of which were new. As he said at the time, "Every encounter with a new choreographer is like a celebration for me."

In April 1978, the company returned to the Met, and once again the great theater was regularly packed to near-capacity. Everything augured well when, early on in the course of the ten-week season, the shocking news broke. Warren Conover described to me what happened:

> We were in dressing-rooms getting ready, about to do a performance, when everyone was called on stage. Your mother was on stage, holding

Baryshnikov's hand. She told us how Mischa had always wanted to dance for Balanchine, and so four weeks from now, he was going to be leaving the company. She wanted us all to hear it firsthand before reading about it in the papers. That was very hard for her, but she did it.

Then Lucia stood by, still holding his hand, as Baryshnikov addressed the company:

The last four years at American Ballet Theatre have been a wonderful time for me. When you are thirty and have a few more years to dance, it's now or never.

That was it. Just two sentences. After a moment's stunned silence, everyone turned and went back to their dressing rooms to prepare for the evening performance.

In a public statement shortly afterwards, Baryshnikov amplified on what he had said to the company:

In Russia, Balanchine is an incredible symbol of uncompromised creative genius. . . . I would love to be an instrument in his wonderful hands. So many opportunities to try myself out. . . . Slowly I realized that I would never forgive myself if I did not try.

Nancy Zeckendorf remembers the whole Baryshnikov rupture very clearly, particularly the day that Mischa actually left to go to the City Ballet:

We were all devastated in the office, and Lucia came in. She adored him like a son, doted on him, and we all expected she'd be falling apart, but she was incredible: she just said, "Now we have to understand that Mischa has to grow, that he wants to go, and we have to appreciate that and let him go. He'll come back." She was so philosophical about it. We all just hated him for what he did. But she was like a queen. Her behavior—I'll never forget it—she didn't bad-mouth him, be angry about it. . . . She was very, very generous.

Still, it was a bitter blow to her.

⸻

Soon there was worse to follow.

After three years with Justin Colin as president of the Foundation, the general situation was vastly improved compared with the start of the decade. Sherwin Goldman had accomplished an enormous amount, but there was still a great deal to be done, especially with regard to the company's operating deficit, which kept rising despite constantly increased income from both donations and box office revenue.

One thing that Goldman did accomplish before he left was to reestablish good relations with the National Endowment in Washington. Feelings had temporarily chilled over the issue of his admitted manipulations of financial figures, but this was corrected when further investigation cleared him of any wrongdoing, with the result that, in January 1977, the NEA awarded Ballet Theatre Foundation $1 million in the form of a 3:1 challenge grant. Essentially, what this meant was that, including a $1.7 million shortfall that still had to be cleared up, a grand total of $6.33 million had to be raised in the next three years.

Obviously this new fund-raising challenge was way beyond anything that Lucia could cope with. Financially, at least, this huge new fiscal imperative effectively relegated her to the sidelines. The challenge was also manifestly more than the current board of trustees felt they could manage by themselves. The only recourse they could agree upon was to enlarge their ranks and power, particularly to enlist a new chairman of great magnitude, someone who, besides having a sizable personal fortune, also had wide-ranging contacts with the industrial, business, and financial world.

One of the most dedicated and dynamic of the current trustees was Charles McWhorter, an AT&T executive with very close ties to the White House and the Republican Party. Due largely to his efforts, the chairman and CEO of Pepsi-Cola, Donald Kendall, was invited to join the board and, early in 1978, was elected president of Ballet Theatre Foundation.

It was a bold, if somewhat incongruous, arrangement for both parties. Kendall certainly was a powerful figure in the business world, but he was not particularly well versed in the arts. As one trustee (who declined to be named) recalled:

> First thing Kendall said when he came onto the board was, "I want you to know, I just saw the best ballet in the world. I saw the Russian Ballet." He didn't know ballet from a hole in the wall, but he loved Baryshnikov—loved to smoke cigars with Baryshnikov. That's the way it started.

Along with Kendall came a new executive director, Herman Krawitz, who had been a teacher of arts management at Yale under Robert Brustein, and before that had spent twenty years at the Metropolitan Opera under Rudolf Bing. According to the same trustee,

When Kendall got on board and brought Krawitz in, it really got to be a whole other thing. Kendall didn't want anyone around he couldn't tell what to do. I guess you'd say that he was intent on getting Mischa back and putting him in Lucia's place. Also, there were people on the board who felt it was time for Lucia to go. I don't know why, because she was doing what she was always doing, but the difference was that now, suddenly, she was no longer in charge.

The transition was engineered quietly and with a minimum of fuss. In fact, no one afterwards was quite sure how the actual transfer of power had been arranged. It didn't appear to have been a principal item of business that was formally proposed to the board, openly discussed, and finally determined by any kind of a vote. It was just decided, somehow, somewhere, totally outside any limelight, and after that, there was just a formality to be settled in private between Don Kendall and Lucia.

They met in the library of her apartment, the same little study so many dancers had referred to regarding their contract talks. Now there was one more contract to be discussed in the familiar paneled room.

Not much about it had changed in the nearly half century since Lucia and Tom had originally moved into the apartment. It had been their favorite sitting room. The walls were still lined with the handsome leather-bound books Tom had inherited from Uncle Alex. The portrait of Lord Howe, painted by Sir Joshua Reynolds, still hung over the fireplace. An oversized blue leather chair for reading was in the far corner, across from the small red sofa where Lucia always sat. On this particular afternoon, Kendall came to talk to her about her own director's contract, which had only been recently instituted for the first time in her long history at Ballet Theatre.

It would remain intact, he assured her, until it was due to expire, which wouldn't be for almost two more years. However, at that point in time, he regretted to tell her, it would not be renewed. And with that, a few minutes later, Kendall stood up, left the room, and went down in the elevator.

Lucia continued sitting on the little sofa, staring at nothing particular, thinking private thoughts for a long while before finally stirring, taking a deep breath, then slowly walking back upstairs and into her bedroom to get ready for dinner.

26. Baryshnikov Replaces Lucia

Lucia was an institution. Yes, I loved and hated her at the same time. But now she's leaving, and I'm working for a bunch of rich board members and society people. Well, I don't care about them.

—Statement by ABT dancer during 1979 strike negotiations

THE *New York Times* broke the news on January 7, 1979: "Lucia Chase to Quit Ballet Theatre Post as of Sept. 1, 1980."

The announcement came in the form of a statement by Donald Kendall, chairman of the Ballet Theatre Foundation, who said that Miss Chase's decision "is accepted with deep regret. Her devotion and dedication to the Ballet Theatre have created an institution of the highest caliber." According to Kendall, Miss Chase would remain "in full charge" until her departure, would be involved in selecting her successor, and would also remain as a director on the board.

Lucia was reported to be not available for comment, but Oliver Smith, speaking for her, stated that she was in total agreement with this decision: "The change was planned in the interest of the longevity of Ballet Theatre, and since we have been co-directors for close to thirty-five years, it is only natural that we concern ourselves with this artistic responsibility." He said that he planned to resign at the same time.

Herman Krawitz, executive director of Ballet Theatre Foundation, was quoted in the same article as saying that the news should be viewed as "the commencement of a process of an orderly transition to a change in artistic administration":

> When I was engaged, the company owed $850,000 for services and had difficulty meeting its payroll. The debt is now $300,000. The financial mess will be virtually cleared up by spring.

The news of the big change at Ballet Theatre was carried in a number of other papers, both as news articles and editorials. For the moment, as long as Lucia refrained from making any comment and no mention was made of who her successor might be, there was little additional to add. About the only offbeat aspect of the nationwide coverage was that every single one of the reports underestimated her age (which at the time was actually eighty-one): the *New York Times* said she was "reportedly" in her seventies, the *Herald American* in Boston cited seventy-three, and her hometown *Waterbury Republican* referred to her seventy-one years. The across-the-board inaccuracy was not surprising, since Lucia had been adamant all her life about never revealing her age.

This reticence was generally true of all five of the Irving Chase daughters, but it became particularly pronounced in Lucia when she seriously took up dancing in the mid-1930s, when she was already thirty-eight years old, an age so late in life for a dancer that confirming it would have practically obliterated her chances for a performing career. From then on, practically everyone underestimated her age by at least ten years, and she took care never to correct them. Now, four decades later, when she looked about fifty or sixty at the most, she was almost eighty-two, with still another year and a half to go before the date appointed for her to step down.

Just as she had always refused to discuss either her age or the money she'd contributed to Ballet Theatre over the years, now her impending retirement became another forbidden topic. Whenever the subject was broached, she limited her response to saying that when the time came, "she would neither resign or retire but would simply relinquish her post."

In January 1979, the company toured the west coast, spending more than half of the time in California. Now that so much surrounding ABT's future was unsettled and overshadowed by various reports of financial and administrative turmoil, the west coast media picked up the scent and zeroed in with a vengeance. "The ABT has some problems," the local critic wrote following the company's weeklong appearance in San Francisco:

> To begin where it hurts most tellingly, the artistic policy of the ABT directors Lucia Chase and Oliver Smith, disaster-bound for years, is bankrupt. Based on the superstar system, the company is dancing on thin ice: with Nureyev, Baryshnikov, and Nagy gone, only two top males (Bujones and Dowell) carry the premier danseur banner. The repertory is withered; the latest extravaganza—Baryshnikov's *Don Quixote*—was a vulgar, expensive attempt at multiple burlesque which crashed and burned, fast and loud; the corps, male and female, was only occasionally excellent.

After a good deal of negative comment on the recent past and present, the article returned to the question of the company's management, claiming that it seemed unlikely that Miss Chase would "cut herself free from the company she founded 38 years ago, into which she has poured a reported $30 million, most of her fortune." The article concluded by saying there were surely troubles ahead, and in order to sort these out, "the leadership of ABT's powerful board chairman Don Kendall is crucial."

Practically everyone, within and outside Ballet Theatre, had swung around to share this same belief in the importance of Kendall to the company's future. Even Lucia, who must have bristled at the way she was effectively being shouldered out of the picture, recognized that the immediate goal of ensuring the company's survival was now beyond her financial means and rested squarely in Kendall's hands.

A letter she dashed off to one of her nieces is particularly revealing. Written on Rose Hill stationery and dated April 30, 1979, it begins:

> I'm at the hairdresser, so at last a minute to write to thank you for the wonderful check for the Ballet which I handed immediately to the Comptroller. We cheer at every one that comes in to help Kendall get the $3 million for our Nat'l Endowment challenge grant.

The letter goes on to talk about the current company season at the Met:

> Tonight we have our Gala for the same purpose [to raise money to help match the NEA grant]. I just came from the orchestra rehearsal, and it should be a wow. You should see Anthony Dowell and John Curry, the skater in his 1st ballet performance—they're in long tails and high silk hats, and

they are terrific. I do hope you're planning R.I. [Rhode Island] in the summer. I'll go soon to open the houses and expect to move up June 29th for a real vacation—can hardly wait.

Everything about Lucia's letter sounds the same as ever. Even the handwriting is just as it was half a century earlier. No matter how far beyond her control the current activity around Ballet Theatre threatened to become, Lucia remained the Queen Mother—calm, even-handed, standing erect and unfazed as she surveyed the turbulent party scene.

She had always been able to pick herself up. Always, that is, until now when—four days before the end of the Met season—an article appeared in the *New York Times* stating that Ballet Theatre was seriously considering Baryshnikov to be its new artistic director to succeed Lucia Chase.

According to all reports, Lucia never knew about this leaning toward Baryshnikov until she opened the newspaper that morning. She didn't believe it at first, until she picked up the phone and made a call that confirmed it might indeed be true.

Two weeks later, the decision of Ballet Theatre's trustees was officially announced: Mikhail Baryshnikov, currently still dancing with the New York City Ballet, was scheduled to rejoin ABT in the dual capacity as artistic director and principal dancer on September 1, 1980. Until then, according to Ballet Theatre Foundation chairman Don Kendall, Miss Chase would continue in full charge.

For Lucia to have her retirement, a dreaded prospect she refused to talk about or even acknowledge, publicly proclaimed in the press was distasteful and very hard to carry off in a dignified manner. But that was only the start of the problem: what made it particularly difficult for her was that her successor was to be Baryshnikov, the same Misha she had welcomed and for whom she had provided a safe haven when he was on the run, the dancer she adored and praised to the skies, the public icon whom she had come to regard practically like a son and had encouraged to do whatever he wished, even when, two years ago, it meant his leaving American Ballet Theatre. Now for him to come back and take over her position, it was almost as though it were he, and not Don Kendall or the company's financial crisis, that was responsible for forcing her out.

What made the whole situation much worse was that her replacement was such a dazzling personality—the most compelling and heroic figure in the entire dance world—that the natural reaction of everyone inside and out of ABT was to rejoice that the company now would have none other than the glorious Baryshnikov as its new head. It seemed no one was impervious to the excitement generated by the news. Even Lucia's longtime secretary, the enchanting and deeply loyal Florence Pettan, who for some thirty years had stood constantly by her, now looked on the arrival of Misha as a veritable epiphany or divine-coming about to descend into the world of ABT.

For Lucia, after nearly four decades of performing, touring, underwriting practically every deficit, working day and night for Ballet Theatre, never complaining but always encouraging and exhorting, now—with the finish line plainly in sight—to have all heads turning expectantly to greet the new figure about to walk in and take over center stage was almost too much to bear.

On the same devastating plane, though much less personal, a new cataclysmic change was brewing through the upper and lower ranks of ABT.

The first signals of trouble came midway through the May 1979 Met season when the company's dancers, acting in concert, issued a statement detailing a number of drastic changes in pay scales and working conditions which they wished to see incorporated in the basic union contract, which was due to expire on August 31.

Submitting such a formal proposal several months in advance was quite unprecedented and constituted a clear notice from the dancers that the old way of doing business—agreeing to practically whatever terms of employment they were offered—was no longer acceptable. Even more unusual was the decision reached by the dancers that they would no longer entrust their case to the union but had hired an independent outside lawyer to handle their side of the negotiations.

There was no immediate response from the management of Ballet Theatre to the initial notice, and since the existing contract was not due to expire until the last day of August, the spring season at the Met continued on unaffected to its closing date on June 9, with little indication of the monumental disruption that lay ahead.

In August, another celebrated Russian dancer, Aleksandr Godunov, emigrated and soon afterwards signed a contract to join ABT. The event was particularly noteworthy because the salary he was reported to have been offered was $150,000, an extraordinarily high fee for a dancer, possibly the highest ever recorded in the dance world. What gave his contract even greater notoriety was that negotiations finally were just starting between the dancers and Ballet Theatre over the new AGMA basic contract: for Godunov to have been offered $150,000 constituted a startling largesse on the part of Ballet Theatre when its management, at the same time, was claiming it could afford only a small fraction of the increases the dancers were seeking for themselves.

On August 23, one week before the actual deadline date, both sides agreed to extend the current AGMA contract until one party gave the other formal written notice, two weeks in advance, of either a strike or a lockout. This concession was critical, considering that ABT's two-week fall season at the Met was due to commence immediately following Labor Day. As a result, the Met engagement took place without an AGMA contract, and the truce continued another three weeks until October 5, at which point Allan Jaffe, legal counsel for the Ballet Theatre Foundation, gave notice to Leonard Leibowitz, the dancers' lawyer, that as of October 19, ABT was canceling all work until a new basic union agreement had been worked out. With that signal of an impending lockout, the battle was on.

It would prove to be quite a confrontation. For practically the first time in history, an entire company of dancers had marshaled together a cohesive, rigorously organized, and united front. As explained by ABT principal dancer Gelsey Kirkland,

> In the past, dancers haven't taken total responsibility for saying what they need. This is the beginning of a thinking process among dancers about their needs for more money. They've taken a tremendous leap in educating themselves in that area.

A feature article by Ken Sandler in the *Washington Post* described the new situation:

> Traditionally, life for most American ballet dancers has consisted of hard work, low wages, and sacrifice. And traditionally they have accepted it, killing the present pain with dreams of future stardom and the money it might bring. At ABT, however, dreams are no longer acceptable in lieu of what the dancers consider a decent wage—not just enough for subsistence but a little luxury as well.

The dollar gap between the two sides was dismayingly large. The dancers were calling for an overall package increase of around 60 percent over what they were currently being paid, whereas Ballet Theatre was offering less than a third of the dancers' demands. As explained by Joyce Moffat, ABT's general manager,

> We agree there are ills that go back historically with American dancers, but I don't think Ballet Theater can be expected to solve them all in one contract. Particularly not the same year when the budget was reported to be $8.4 million, of which $2.7 million still has to be raised and when Ballet Theatre up to now has never raised more than $1.7 million in a single year.

This didn't exactly jibe with the news that, at the same time Ballet Theatre was pleading poverty, it had offered Godunov such a spectacularly large salary. However, this inconsistency in itself never became an issue: the dancers uniformly maintained throughout the negotiation talks that they did not object to an acknowledged superstar receiving a monumental reward for his exceptional talents. What particularly aggravated them was the way that both the stagehands and the musicians hired to work ABT's performances were always paid substantially more than the dancers. After all, the public was paying to see the dancing, not to admire the stagecraft or hear the music.

According to the *Washington Post* article, there were also two psychological issues influencing the negotiations:

> The first is a maturing process in which the dancers have realized that most of them will never achieve stardom and the big money. They are resigned to the long-term prospect of lives at corps de ballet and soloist salaries. These salaries currently do not allow for many luxuries and are generally inadequate to support families. The second is the collapse of ABT's matriarchal society and "family" feeling—largely because the company's co-founder and de facto ruler, Lucia Chase, has been pressured to resign, effective next September. Much of her power has already been assumed by others.

The article went on to quote Dr. Harvey Kaplan, a well-known New York psychoanalyst:

> The matriarchal structure of the company served to repress the dancers' economic assertiveness—as long as Lucia Chase was there, she kept this assertiveness depressed. With Chase retiring, the dancers feel even more exploited because they identify with her as being abused.

A principal dancer of ABT expressed much the same sentiment:

At the end of each year, Lucia used to call each of the dancers into her office and ask what you'd like to do next year. You'd say this role, and that role, and a promotion, and usually you wouldn't get most of what you wanted. She would go into her act that "Oh, there's no money," or "We're taking this ballet out of repertoire, so you can't do it," or something like that. But at least you thought Lucia cared. This year, Lucia says one thing, and they [ABT officials] say something else. You don't know who is running the company.

However disconcerting the transition to a new management was to the company, for Lucia it was much more severe. The impending changeover, combined with the lockout, had the doubly devastating effect of undermining her authority and also of distancing her from the dancers. No longer was she the sole person who had all the answers, who could give the final okay, who determined exactly what was being offered and withheld in a dancer's contract. Suddenly it seemed that she was neither a dancer like one of them, nor was she the person they could come and talk to about their future. Instead, she had been virtually consigned to the sidelines while the negotiations—between the company dancers, represented by a militant strike committee, and the Ballet Theatre management team of Donald Kendall, Herman Krawitz, and Joyce Moffat—were being thrashed out by the dispute's opposing lawyers, Jaffe and Leibowitz. Whereas up to now there had always been one compact entity that was ABT, now there were two conflicting and rapidly solidifying separate camps, and Lucia was not particularly welcomed, nor did she feel she properly belonged, in either one.

The lockout continued with growing intensity throughout the fall. On October 29, the dancers—dressed in costumes, wearing ballet shoes, and carrying signs like "I'd rather dance than walk but have no choice—Locked Out"—staged a public demonstration on the sidewalk outside the ABT office. Two weeks later, there was another demonstration, this one held in front of Lincoln Center, in which other prominent outside figures—the celebrated actress Helen Hayes, dance star Carmen de Lavallade, along with several members of the New York City Ballet—marched in support of ABT's dancers.

The following week, Ballet Theatre made what it called its final offer. It was rejected, 72–0, by the dancers. Suddenly it seemed not only possible but quite likely that the company's December engagement at the Kennedy Center in Washington would have to be cancelled.

On November 29, Kendall wrote a lengthy letter to the dancers in which he pleaded for both sides to reach a reasonable understanding. It was not right, in his view, for the dancers to reject the idea of putting the whole issue up for arbitration when Ballet Theatre was prepared to accept whatever final settlement an independent arbiter laid out. It was equally hard for him to understand why the dancers would not even sit down and talk face-to-face with some of the governing trustees: surely there was no harm in that. He described the Foundation as willing to offer more in the coming year, but there was a limit to how much money it could raise in the immediate future, probably not more than $1 million, so there had to be some concessions from what the dancers were demanding. The dancers' committee refused to back down, saying this was their one and only chance to gain a decent living wage. As a result, early in December, the Kennedy Center season was cancelled.

There were far greater dangers looming in the new year. The next date to be threatened was the fortieth anniversary of American Ballet Theatre, which was scheduled to take place early in 1980. Back at the time of the thirty-fifth anniversary in 1975, Lucia had said she couldn't make any promises far into the future, but at least she would guarantee that there would be a gala celebration of the company's fortieth anniversary. Now that commitment was not at all certain.

Looking ahead, immediately following the fortieth anniversary season was the company's tour to California, which was all booked and would soon be in jeopardy. Then early in December, Anthony Bliss, head of the Metropolitan Opera, issued a warning that if no settlement was reached soon, the Met would have to reconsider the ten-week season ABT was scheduled to perform beginning next May. The Met just would not be comfortable, Bliss said, without having its standard five months of advance time for marketing and promotion efforts. "If ABT loses part or all of that season, the loss could jeopardize future Met seasons and in fact the company's existence."

Dancers around the globe were all watching. It was said that, whatever happened, the entire dance world might never be the same again.

The same was certainly true for Lucia. At the very twilight of her career, it was far beyond her ability to cope—financially, professionally, personally—with this strike by the dancers. No longer could she present herself as a dancer and ally herself with the rest of the company who were out walking on the picket lines, any more than she could join in with the management team which only a few months ago had banded together to ease her out of the picture. Practically overnight, she was irrelevant. There was nothing she could do but stand by on the sidelines while lawyers for the two combating sides worked to find a way for the company to continue.

Neither side knew what to do with her or how to react to her presence. They were both almost embarrassed just to see her, waiting around on the outskirts, desperately hoping that somehow the terrible issue could be resolved before time ran out. Yet if the California bookings at the start of the year, and the Met season immediately following, ended up being canceled, the dancers might not be able to stay around, and with the company dispersed, there was no assurance it could be brought back together again. It was this desperate urgency, the realization on both sides that perhaps this time it really was "now or nevermore," that at the very end of the year, on December 20, 1979, a new basic agreement between Ballet Theatre and AGMA, the dancers' union, was ratified that would be in effect through August 31, 1982.

Under the forthcoming contract, a new dancer in the corps who had been paid $235 a week would now receive $300, $325 the following year, and up to $400 by the end of the third year. The overall cost to Ballet Theatre of the new agreement was estimated to be several million dollars. As so often with a strike, neither side was particularly happy with the settlement, yet the ultimate disaster had been averted.

That same week, on December 15, 1979, a letter written by Irina Baronova arrived from Switzerland. "My darlingest Lucia!" it began:

> Just a note to tell you how upset I am at reading of the troubles ABT is going through! Not knowing "both sides of the coin," I cannot have an opinion. All I want to say is: You, Lucia Chase, are a great lady! You have done for the art of ballet more and for longer than anyone in the history of ballet. Dancers of almost 3 generations have had a "home" you started and lovingly kept to develop their talent and achieve themselves! Choreographers, many started their first efforts in your company. You made it possible. The public, thanks to your love and devotion for our art, had 40 years of pleasure! Whatever happens now, do not get upset. You shall be always honored, admired, and never forgotten by those who like you are genuinely serving their art and loving it like you do, and you will be, and are already, "the great lady of the ballet art." To you, my darling, I make a deep curtsey, and I say thank you, and I am proud I am one of your "children." I fervently hope all the troubles

will resolve themselves and your great work will go on forever. "Long life to American Ballet Theatre!!" May 1980 be a happy one, for you, all your ABT, and all those that work with it. I love you tenderly.

Irina

–♾–

Lucia had promised that there would be a fortieth anniversary for Ballet Theatre, and good to her word, it took place at the Met in the spring of 1980.

The season opened in true ABT style with a gala performance that practically all the renowned alumni of the company attended from all over the country, even the world. The single opening performance grossed more than $415,000, close to the entire cost of any one of the early years of Ballet Theatre, with tickets selling at 50 to 100 times what it cost to attend the company's opening night forty years earlier when the top price was $3.30 ($2.20 for the following nights). In return, the anniversary audience was treated to a historic celebration of four decades of American dance.

At the end of the program, the realization of what the whole evening meant swept over the Met Opera House as, one by one, the legendary figures appeared out of the wings and stepped out onto the stage: Anton Dolin, the leading male dancer of the company's opening years; Antony Tudor, its premier choreographer; Agnes de Mille and Jerry Robbins, the two other members of the company's creative triumvirate; Nora Kaye, generally considered the leading dramatic ballerina of her time; the fabulous partnerships of Igor Youskevitch/Alicia Alonso and Erik Bruhn/Carla Fracci; also Maria Karnilova, Muriel Bentley, Sono Osato, Ruth Ann Koesun, Miriam Golden, Annabelle Lyon, Toni Lander, Melissa Hayden, Violette Verdy, Donald Saddler, and many others; then finally, Lucia Chase and Oliver Smith, codirectors for the past thirty-five years of American Ballet Theatre.

De Mille stepped forward to speak. Of all the central figures in Ballet Theatre's inner circle since the beginning, she and Lucia had interacted like two cats occupying the same house, both jealously protecting their own special turf, circling around each other, occasionally coming together to spat or openly fight, but then making up soon afterwards and moving on, an indomitable pair of sparring sisters and the truest of all believers in Ballet Theatre. De Mille may not have had the choreographic genius of Tudor or

Robbins, the dancing skills of Baronova and Alonso, or the elegant figure of an ABT dancer, but when it came to selecting just the right words and delivering them with arch, acid precision, no one was better.

She started off by reading a telegram from President Jimmy Carter, in which he and Rosalynn sent their "warmest wishes." She then continued in her own words, carefully enunciating each one as she projected her voice directly to every person seated in the house. She wanted to make sure that they understood what she believed was gospel truth, that it was Lucia Chase's drive and tenacity that had kept Ballet Theatre alive all these years, longer than Diaghilev's Ballets Russes, longer than almost any dance company in the Western world, how Lucia was pure New England, nine-tenths granite, made of the same material as the yeoman farmers who fought behind stone walls to beat the British. It was an outpouring of vintage Agnes de Mille, as captivating as any show onstage.

Then Antony Tudor, the spare, wizardlike dean of Ballet Theatre, came out with a puckish smile to deliver a huge bouquet of red roses into Lucia's arms. The dancers performed a surprise "You Are There" reenactment of Lucia's own dancing roles within the company. Then everyone stepped back and left her out there, alone before the entire Met audience, by now on its feet cheering, while from the flies high above, a shower of rose petals cascaded down on her head and about her feet and covered the stage.

This adulation continued for another six weeks. Congratulatory messages came in from all across the country: Los Angeles County sent "best wishes and health" to Lucia Chase. The Minnesota Dance Theatre offered a testimonial: "For Lucia, the gratitude and the love from those of us who have been nourished and enlightened, who have been inspired by all that she has given to us in the world of dance." Anton Dolin, now back in England, sent a personal message: "My very dear Lucia, thank you for wonderful evenings of great ballet, 'Great Lady of the American Dance.'" The state of Connecticut presented Lucia Chase with the state's medal for her service to the arts. But it was two other awards that came to her in the course of her remaining days as company director that probably meant more to Lucia than any other honor she had ever received in her life.

The first was an honorary doctorate from Yale, delivered at the university's annual graduation ceremony on May 25. After a lifetime of being a fervent Yalie, cheering for the college in downtown New Haven through whose doors had passed several generations of her family, including her father, husband, and both her sons, Lucia Chase proudly stood on the graduation platform and received from President Bart Giamatti her own honorary degree from the university. Connecticut's foremost intellectual institution was officially recognizing one of the state's most outstanding daughters.

As close as the Yale degree was to Lucia's heart, it was topped by an award given by another president the following month. On the South Lawn of the White House, President Carter presented Lucia and twelve other recipients with the U.S. Medal of Freedom, the nation's highest civilian award. Receiving the award—"for their passionate commitment to their convictions"—were the photographer Ansel Adams, the late scientist and author Rachel Carson, Archbishop Iakovos of the Greek Orthodox Church, the late President Lyndon Johnson, the retired director of Washington's NAACP, Clarence Mitchell, ornithologist Roger Tory Peterson, Admiral Hyman Rickover, singer Beverly Sills, poet Robert Penn Warren, actor John Wayne, author Eudora Welty, playwright Tennessee Williams, and along with this most distinguished company, the mother of American Ballet Theatre, Lucia Chase.

The Met Opera House, Yale University, and the White House, all in the course of six weeks: surely it was time to step down. But Lucia still didn't feel ready to let go.

As she reported to the *New York Times* early in May, "I shall stay on the board. I'll have to get to the trustees and teach them something about a ballet company. I don't think they know much about ballet."

As she liked to say, *resign* and *retire* were two words that were not in her vocabulary. Nevertheless, like it or not, her time was officially up, and on September 1, 1980, Mikhail Baryshnikov took over as artistic director of American Ballet Theatre.

27. Last Years

When American Ballet Theatre
dances, they dance for Lucia.
—Mikhail Baryshnikov

IN SEPTEMBER 1980, when she was displaced as ABT's artistic director, Lucia was eighty-three years old. She never admitted her age (in fact, she went to considerable lengths to conceal it), but claimed she acted this way for professional reasons: if everyone knew her true age, they might begin to question whether she was still capable of directing a major ballet company.

Yet there was probably a more fundamental explanation: like a great many people, Lucia was afraid of growing old. "Old" and "Lucia" were a contradiction in terms. They didn't belong together. She had always been first in line everywhere, the fastest walker, the quickest to get dressed, the most tireless worker, the most enthusiastic party girl. It was more than a point of pride. It was her way of signaling to the world, and also of reassuring herself, that however many changes might be taking place elsewhere, everything in her particular world, beginning with herself, was still the same as it had always been.

Once she no longer had an active role in Ballet Theatre, she tried carrying on much the same as usual, making regular appearances at the office, sitting in on the board of trustees meetings, attending most performances when the company was dancing in New York, even making several trips to join up with it when it was off on tour. But of course it wasn't the same. People no longer came to her with all their problems and often did not know how to react when she suddenly appeared in their midst. It was particularly awkward for the dancers, who felt hesitant about paying a great deal of attention to Lucia now that they were working for Misha. Many of them felt she had been badly treated, even that, indirectly, it had been their fault for not having stood up and protected her, so that now they felt almost guilty and tended to avoid her.

There were, of course, exceptions. Like Terry Orr:

Sometimes she would call up ahead of time and ask me to sit with her during a particular performance, and of course I was always glad to do it. She had been such a large part of my life and my career. Besides, I was very fond of her and enjoyed being with her. She wanted me to tell her all about any new members in the company and was curious to hear how everyone else was getting along. I felt sorry for her. She seemed wistful and a little sad, although never admitting as much.

Sallie Wilson was more direct:

It broke her heart. She went on tour the next year, and they treated her like a nonperson. The stagehands looked out for her, would get a chair for her, but no one else did. She said, "I don't care if they don't want me. It's my company." But she did care . . . desperately.

"Suddenly she was an old woman," Agnes de Mille wrote years later, "but she maintained her Connecticut steadfastness." She still dyed her hair auburn, wore trim suits and dresses, still walked with incredible rapidity in her smart little shoes, and held her spine straight as a soldier's. She religiously continued to go to performances and sat in the seats that were permanently reserved for her. She also went backstage as often as she liked. But she no longer sat in rehearsal rewriting her casting lists, no longer devoted days of discussion to the contract arrangements. And she said little: "I have an open mind," she remarked, "an open mind but a closed mouth."

When asked how she felt about being cut off from the company, her answer was brief and straight to the point: "As long as there are full houses and good reviews, I shall smile and keep quiet. When the houses and reviews are not so good, I'll stop smiling and speak up."

Cynthia Gregory recalled once when Lucia came to see the company in San Francisco:

The president was there, so they had to drop us off four blocks away. Lucia said, "No, don't worry. I'll be fine," and she went tripping down the steep hill. I always think of her doing that. I thought, wow, she's amazing.

Priscilla Stevens, who made several trips with Lucia, had seen this same independent streak time and again:

Lucia was always Lucia. She didn't demand special attention, didn't assume that particular favors should be done for her. After her retirement, she deliberately adopted another much lesser role. It was not, for instance, the role of the director emeritus, which would have been the way of Dame Ninette [de Valois, longtime director of England's Royal Ballet], who kept her mystique and remained an unbelievable power right up to the time of her death. With Lucia, somehow her operative element disappeared with her retirement. As far as she was concerned, she was no longer a part of it, so it was gone. That sounds worse than what I mean to say. It was just, "If I'm not running it, I'm not a part of it." This feeling of being an onlooker rather than a participant came from her own unqualified personal modesty. With Lucia, there was never any suggestion of anything like "You know, guys, if it weren't for me, you wouldn't be seeing any of this." Not with her, ever.

At home, those of us who were closest to her were especially concerned. Ballet Theatre had been so much a part of her life. Now with it gone, there was a great void with nothing substantial to fill it.

Even though she was a longtime and prominent New Yorker, it was remarkable how totally removed she was from the day-to-day activities that engaged most other women of her rank in the city. She belonged to no clubs. She didn't meet friends for lunch or spend afternoons at the movies or shopping or pampering herself. She had none of the customary pastimes: she didn't play bridge, attend lectures or concerts, visit museums, read books, or have any hobbies or private pursuits to absorb her time. Although she did maintain a busy household, with guests and family moving in and out much of the time, this had been going on for years, and thanks to the stalwart household staff at the apartment, life on the home front generally ran smoothly whether she was there or not.

The next three years were in ways the most difficult time she had ever faced since Tom had died nearly half a century earlier. Once again, the dominant element in her life had been snatched away, and suddenly there was nothing: no place she had to go, no imperative she had to face, no urgency or crisis or even mundane daily task to claim her attention. It didn't feel natural, nor did it seem right, according to her code of personal conduct, to be suddenly, totally at leisure. Her only recourse was to keep acting as though not all that much had changed and that she still had such a busy schedule there just weren't enough hours in the day to get everything done.

Lucia was fortunate during this period to have Lisa Alberg in the apartment. Lisa had come to work as a maid sometime in the late 1960s, but gradually, without any fuss, she had become much more than that. She was not just the de facto manager of the household but a true friend for Lucia all hours of the day, as well as one of the most loyal and understanding helpers who had ever worked for our family. Now, during this very difficult postretirement period, Lisa was a quiet, sympathetic presence, ready to attend or listen or slip away, a totally safe and uncritical audience who hugely helped fill in the empty spaces.

Another great presence during this time was my teenage daughter, Caroline. For two years, she had boarded in New York with close friends of ours while attending the Brearley School in Manhattan. In the fall of 1981, Caroline moved over to spend her junior and senior years with "Lolo" at the apartment. So now there was a bright and loving member of the family who was always there, at least one person for Lucia to have dinner with, whether or not anyone else was staying at the apartment. Whenever there were guests, she and Caroline would eat in grand style in the dining room. Otherwise, they ate on trays in the library, granddaughter and grandmother, one seventeen and the other eighty-five, together night after night, which was very good for each of them.

Besides Lisa and Caroline, there were two others who were invaluable to Lucia in these later years. The first was a small, quiet man we only knew as Andy, who had taken on the assignment, usually at night, of chauffeuring Lucia wherever she wanted to go. For a long while, we thought Andy was like any other limousine driver for hire in New York, except that he was unusually good at the job, very smooth and knowing, always there when you looked for him, with a little smile and a helping hand, making sure that Miss Chase and whoever was with her got to the Met on time, leaving them not way out in front with the whole Lincoln Center plaza to cross but at the private entrance underneath the opera building. Afterwards, at the end of the performance, Andy would be back there waiting, always first in line, poised to deliver Lucia safely home again.

He rarely talked and never confided any information about himself. It was only gradually, by putting together little bits and pieces gleaned in the course of time and many trips, that we learned that he had his own company, a firm of private investigators, that he was an accredited black-belt expert in jujitsu, that he carried a gun at all times with him in the car, and most remarkable, that he never drove for anyone else, only for Miss Chase, whom he apparently had decided to take on as his personal responsibility.

The other mainstay in Lucia's life outside the apartment was Frances, the cheerful, undemonstrative housekeeper who lived in and took care of Rose Hill, the family homestead in Waterbury, which Lucia had taken over when her father had died. Frances was another example of what Agnes de Mille would have called pure, undiluted New England. She didn't mind being left alone in the big house on the hill. Her only company was Lucia's giant poodle, Gendarme, who lived either in the kitchen or in the yard just outside the kitchen window. Frances and Gendarme were two familiar, friendly presences ready to greet Lucia as she began regularly taking the train from New York to Waterbury to spend each and every weekend at Rose Hill.

All the bedrooms at Rose Hill were now empty, but Lucia still slept way up on the third floor, in the same room she had had as a small girl. "Wouldn't dream of changing," she would always say whenever it was suggested. That was the whole point of her keeping Rose Hill. It was there to be used as it had always been, the place to go for Thanksgiving and Christmas, as well as for the traditional Chase family party the day after Christmas, which "Cousin Lucia" hosted every year for nearly 100 Chases from all over Connecticut and surrounding states. Now Rose Hill had the further function of providing my mother with a destination and focal point for the end of each week, when she would see Gendarme and talk to Frances and get her car out of Rose Hill's garage to drive to her sister Dee's house in nearby Middlebury for Sunday lunch, a routine to cling to, a reminder that not everything had passed by.

Summers were better, when she left New York and went to Narragansett, opening up the houses in June. Narragansett was another routine that never changed, except there was no longer any reason for hours of phone calls to New York or Washington or California each morning. Otherwise, the days unfolded exactly the same way, mornings to the Dunes Club for a swim, then lunch, afternoons spent on errands and perhaps a trip out to Sunset Farm for milk and vegetables, back home in time to take Gendarme for a short walk, stopping along the way by the little garden next to Moonraker (the house built in memory of my brother, Tommy) to pick flowers to bring back to High Tide. She was a small woman in her eighties, straight as a soldier, taking a huge poodle on a leash walk alone. Then cocktails on the porch, followed by a full table for dinner practically every night.

For these summer months, Lucia slipped back quite effortlessly into her nonballet world. It didn't really matter that the company was off somewhere else: it often had been when she was in Narragansett. As usual, there was the high point when E.I. came over from England and moved into Tommy's room right next door to our mother's bedroom. For the next two or three weeks, the two sisters spent every day together, with Dee just a mile up Ocean Road—all three totally devoted to each other.

Sometime in August, Sheila and I would arrive with our four children. The first night, there would be a family gathering with Lolo on the porch, each grandchild bringing a little present which Lucia would open with great excitement and joyful surprise, as though we were all onstage celebrating a birthday party with Lolo presiding. For the next two weeks, or as long as we were there, she would take charge of their lives, swimming and lunching at the beach, talking and laughing together, her little miniature company, afterwards with Lolo always in the driver's seat of her white Lincoln four-door convertible, ready and happy to go to the next stop wherever it happened to be.

But then changes began to occur. Edward Carmody, Dee's husband, who for years had served as Lucia's wise mentor and head male of the family, died in his family home in nearby Middlebury, Connecticut. A young cousin my mother particularly loved, who used to rent one of the family houses in Narragansett every summer, died of cancer. The following summer, Gendarme became ill, and Lucia took to going every afternoon to the veterinary clinic ten miles away in a desperate all-out effort to save him, but to no avail.

Lucia was starting to have health troubles herself, fleeting spells that occurred usually at night when, for a moment, she would lose track of the conversation before suddenly coming back, pretending nothing had happened, and hoping no one had noticed.

There had been other scary incidents in the past. Ten years earlier, Antony Tudor and I chanced to meet at a National Endowment meeting in Washington, and he made a particular point of asking me how Lucia was. When I seemed surprised at his concern, he made an excuse and rushed off. I straightway called the apartment. Lisa answered, and I asked to speak to my mother: "She isn't here, Mister Alex." "Where is she?" Lisa, clearly ill at ease, said she couldn't say. I said she had to. Well, apparently she was at the hospital, but no one was supposed to know. I found out she had fainted on a Madison Avenue bus and, after seeing a doctor, was directed by him to check into the hospital to be fitted with a pacemaker.

Another more recent time, in the Chicago airport, already retired but on her way to meet up with the company, she became disoriented, sat down for a long while, and never did make the company rehearsal where she had been expected. Everyone was worried, but she never gave any explanation.

Then, back in New York, in the fall of 1983, she had a massive stroke. Lisa came into the library and found her slumped on the sofa. An ambulance took her to the hospital.

At one point along the way, an attendant in the ambulance, anxious to find out how badly off she was, asked a few basic questions: What was her name? What day of the week was it? Lucia mumbled some answers that were barely intelligible until he asked her age.

Quick as a flash, Lucia spoke up: "Who wants to know?"

"The doctor."

"Well, then the doctor can ask me," she snapped, and shut her eyes.

⸻

She never really recovered. After a few days, it was possible to take her out of the hospital and back to the apartment where she was essentially immobilized, either confined to her bed or in a wheelchair, sometimes quite lucid, more often in a world of her own.

An around-the-clock system was set up to take care of her, with a nurse upstairs in the bedroom with her. Lois Mander, a wonderfully understanding and efficient friend, took on the job of coming in every day to handle the household affairs, take care of the phone calls and all correspondence, and make whatever special arrangements were needed. Meanwhile Lisa's presence nearby seemed to have a beneficent calming effect on Lucia.

For about a year, there was only a very gradual worsening of her condition. At first, she was still able with help to be moved about the apartment. On one very special occasion, Nancy Zeckendorf gave a small dinner party staged especially for Lucia, with Tudor and Hugh Laing as guests. She sent a car with chauffeur to bring Lucia and take her home afterwards, and planned everything so that she would feel comfortable and at ease. It was like an old-time Ballet Theatre get-together, the kind that Lucia would most enjoy and that only a particularly kind and generous friend could carry off with style and grace.

That was her last excursion. Otherwise, the only people to see Lucia were those who came to the apartment. I was living and working in Millbrook, two hours north of the city, but tried to drive in two or three times a week to see her. Besides me and a few other members of the family, she had occasional visitors, particularly Oliver Smith and Antony Tudor, the latter somewhat surprising, since he wasn't generally considered to have a particularly warm and caring nature. Tudor came quite often and would sit by her bedside and talk to her as though everything was perfectly normal.

On one of his last visits, Lucia took to tapping a balloon which had been attached to her bedstead into Tudor's face. Tap into his face, tap, tap, tap again into the face. Rather than pull away, he kept his forehead there where the balloon could hit it. This from Tudor, who was famous for subjecting dancers to such cruel treatment in rehearsal that he would reduce them to tears.

After more than a year confined to her bedroom, there was little reason to hope for any recovery. Lucia's doctor said as much, but just to check with the best possible authority, a call was made to Dr. Fred Plum, eminent attending neurologist at New York Presbyterian Hospital, who kindly consented to come by to examine her himself.

In a recent letter, Dr. Plum reaffirmed what he had told me back in 1985:

> I clearly recall visiting your mother at 720 Park Avenue in New York. She had suffered a severe stroke in the left cerebrum which caused both a right-sided hemiplegia as well as a severe loss of her language. She barely uttered any words and could not understand verbal language. She turned her head inconsistently and weakly to the right, but showed little knowledge of language. Her nursing care had been excellent, and she apparently smiled when someone spoke her name. I am not sure how much she identified other persons, but she reacted intentionally with her left-sided arm, weakly. She didn't appear to suffer at any time.

There seemed to be nothing to do after that but just carry on. The expense of around-the-clock nursing was considerable, and at one point Lucia's accountant issued us a warning that there was only sufficient money left in her trust to pay for a few more months of care. Amazing, that her fortune which had originally been in the millions had been diminished down to the point where now it was about to run out.

I remember one morning downstairs in the library discussing the problem with Lois Mander and how it now appeared necessary to give notice to James, the butler. There was certainly no longer any need for a butler, and letting him go would mean a considerable saving.

Just then, we could hear James upstairs in my mother's bedroom. He had a penetrating voice anyway, and now that Lucia was not responsive, he had developed the habit of almost shouting in order to get through to her:

"I'LL NEVER LEAVE YOU, MRS. EWING. YOU CAN COUNT ON ME!"

Lois and I looked ruefully at each other: what to do in the face of that?

And then, hard to believe but absolutely true, about a week later, a call came from the bank that handled what was left of Lucia's trust. Apparently Ganna Walska, the opera singer whom Alex Cochran (Tom's uncle and my namesake) had married aboard ship on the Atlantic in a momentary infatuation some sixty years earlier and then quickly divorced, had died in California. According to the terms of the trust fund that had been established as part of the legal settlement ending the marriage (which lasted barely a month), the fund had been designated on her death to revert to Alex Cochran, then, if he was deceased, to Thomas Ewing Jr. or his beneficiaries, which meant Lucia. So now there was money left to carry on for at least another year.

As it turned out, this money was barely needed. A few months later, on January 8, 1986, my mother died in her bed.

—◦—

Lucia Chase's picture was on the front page of the *New York Times* the following day. In the four-column obituary written by Jack Anderson, Mikhail Baryshnikov was quoted in a tribute to his predecessor at Ballet Theatre:

> She was a realist, but she lived like an idealist, and in the darkest time she could force the sun to shine. She stood by us all with love and a will of iron and a heart like a lion.

The *Washington Post* printed a testimonial entitled "Appreciation," which ran across the entire page:

> The image of Lucia Chase most familiar to Washingtonians was her portrayal of the Queen Mother in the American Ballet Theatre's production of *Swan*

Lake—a figure maternal and regal, substantial and diminutive, resolute, magisterial, at once aloof and warm. That's how we'll remember her. Those qualities were not only right for the part, but real attributes of the person. What's more, the same characteristics define Chase's historic role—she was, if you will, the sovereign mother of American ballet.

And Anna Kisselgoff, chief dance critic for the *New York Times,* wrote a farewell article ten days later in the *Times* Sunday edition that concluded with the following encomium about Ballet Theatre and its longtime leader:

It had been a company with a family feeling, deeply personalized behind an institutional façade. It will always be remembered as Lucia Chase's company.

28. Memorial Service

She was not creative in any usual
sense. She will leave no ballets
behind, no books, not even memoirs.
But she will leave many, many
memories.
—Clive Barnes, *New York Post,*
January 1986

FUNERAL SERVICES for Lucia were held on the following Monday, January 13, 1986, at St. James Church just around the corner from her apartment. She was buried in the Ewing family plot at Oakland Cemetery in Yonkers next to her husband, Tom, and her son Tommy.

The extreme austerity of the St. James service, which allowed for no eulogies or remembrances, had a dispiriting effect on our family. Thankfully her friends in the ballet world decided to hold a memorial in her honor three months later in the Bruno Walter Auditorium at Lincoln Center. The event was organized by Donald Saddler, an original member of Ballet Theatre, with assistance from Lois Mander, who had taken care of Lucia's affairs for the past two years, and Genevieve Oswald, curator of the Dance Division of the New York Public Library for the Performing Arts. The auditorium was thronged with friends and admirers from all the different places and periods of Lucia's life. There was a wonderful bustle and warm feeling in the air, like the anticipatory spirit in a theater before the curtain rises.

Oliver Smith, appropriately the opening speaker, began in his calm, un-hurried tone of voice:

> Today we honor a great American, Lucia Chase. All of us are here to express our love and gratitude for her enthusiasm and enormous effect which she had on each of our lives.

It was a relationship that he and Lucia shared for thirty-five wonderful years, he went on to say, throughout which she had steadfastly employed and cared for dancers all over the world, provided an artistic home for Antony Tudor and dozens of other celebrated or emerging choreographers, and produced an imposing succession of the full-length classics.

> Those of us who knew Lucia remember her trim figure, her erect carriage, her New England sense of values. She spoke in a low, well-modulated voice, often quickly and breathlessly, too, as if there was never enough time for all she had to say. . . . Lucia enjoyed festivity and dressed elegantly to celebrate it: how often we would hear the rustle of her gown as she entered her box just before the curtain rose.
>
> Lucia could have enjoyed a social existence and entirely indulged herself with its sybaritic pleasures. Instead, she spent her fortune and her entire en-ergy in helping create and sustain one of the world's great dance companies. Her main concern was artistic excellence, professional behavior, and sur-vival. She saw the company through wars, fires, financial instability, and in-ternal turbulence, always with faith in its future existence. . . . What greater or more generous gift could one leave for us to admire and cherish?
>
> Thank you, dear Lucia.

His dignified, measured words set the stage for all the other speakers who followed.

Sono Osato, another original member of Ballet Theatre, spoke next and recalled those early days on tour:

> I complained a lot. I got soot in my eyes. I got a stiff neck. I got a terrible backache, and my legs and feet got very swollen from sitting in the bus all night. Lucia never complained, and she danced a lot in those days.

Donald Saddler and Maria Karnilova stood together to read messages from several who were unable to come—Irina Baronova from Switzerland; Robert Joffrey, Gerald Arpino, and the Joffrey company, which was in

Chicago; Alicia Alonso from her home in Havana, Cuba. They were followed by Nancy Zeckendorf, Morton Gould, Anna Kisselgoff, Jerome Robbins, Mikhail Baryshnikov, and Cynthia Gregory. Alicia Markova, a governor of the Royal Ballet, vice president of the Royal Academy of Dancing, and president of the London Ballet Circle, said she was "here today to bring our tribute from England to honor dear Lucia: We're very fortunate that she didn't choose to own a string of race horses, that she chose artists, dancers, instead."

Then Antony Tudor:

Lucia knew how to battle. She could fight. At her apartment, the way she would lie in bed and move the right hand, just give you a slight pressure on the hand, and you knew she would come through in a second, but you wondered what she was going to come through with. Was she going to win this battle or not? She couldn't win every battle, but she sure tried.

And after Tudor, Agnes de Mille offered a farewell tribute to her old comrade-in-arms:

I loved what Lucia stood for and loved what she fought for. She would listen to others, then she would judge very quietly by herself. And act. At bottom, Lucia knew what was right, what was wrong, what was good, what was sound, what linked with the earth roots. . . .

When I think of Lucia, I think of a quality of loyalty. If she liked you, and she didn't always, but if she did, and she gave her trust and her faith, it was for life. And she maintained her friendship and her associations sometimes long past when it was advisable, for business reasons, to do so. But oh my God, what a marvelous quality to find in the theater as we know it, which is cut-throat! But she wasn't. She was steadfast.

Agnes concluded her remarks with the following:

In April 1944, *Tally-Ho*, my ballet, was having its New York premiere at the Met. I was nervous as hell, and Lucia, who was in *Tally-Ho*, let me use her dressing room. We had adjoining tables and were both very busy. When I sat down at my table—now remember the date, 1944—I noticed a small flower box, and it contained a large bunch of violets. Very beautiful, old-fashioned ones, with a handwritten card—from my husband who was overseas fighting the war. All I had for over a year were V-mail letters that the army sent through. But nothing else. I never had anything that he had touched. I said,

"Lucia! This is from my husband." She looked at me with great wide eyes. "How wonderful!" she said, and the tears poured down her cheeks. Then we went on with our makeup.

And with that, Agnes turned the podium over to me to wind up everything.

I had to take a very deep breath. Standing there that afternoon, before so many of Lucia's fellow dancers and friends and relatives, I wanted to tell the whole story, all about Lucia, my mother. Of course it was an impossible task. Just as now, there is still so much more to be said. Perhaps best to end with a little story from long ago that I told that afternoon.

When my brother and I were quite small boys, maybe eight and ten, we started a tradition of taking our mother out on her birthday. Just the three of us, mother and two sons, out on the town.

We took full charge of the corsage, the restaurant, and afterwards a show: I remember we saw *The Hasty Heart* and *Finian's Rainbow* and *South Pacific.* With a little practice and age, we got better at it, but the first time was a near disaster because we weren't very well prepared—financially— and long before the evening was over, it was pretty clear we were going to run out of money.

I didn't register a thing about the last act of the show because I was panicked about how we were going to cope afterwards. I mean you couldn't just say, "Hey, Mom, let's walk home"—to 70th Street and Park from 46th Street west of Broadway, at 11 o'clock at night, on your mother's birthday. Yet we only had about 50 cents left between the two of us. We decided to go down first class, waved for a taxi and started off, with the meter already beyond our combined resources.

Something must have given us away because suddenly our mother said we'd been doing so much, she wanted to get in on the fun, and with that, she flipped a five dollar bill on the floor of the cab. My brother and I almost knocked ourselves out diving for it.

Mom laughed, said she'd never had such a good time, and then sat back, happy to have been able to help us carry on with our show.

Index

Illustrations have been grouped together, into two sections. Section 1 follows page 108 and Section 2 follows page 258. The photographs in these sections are referred to accordingly; for example, 1.9 indicates section 1 of photos, page 9 of the insert.

ABT. *See* American Ballet Theatre
Adams, Ansel, 310
Adams, Diana, 133, 148
Adams, George, 206
Advanced Arts Ballets Inc., 40–42, 60, 160
Advanced Productions Inc., 37
African American dancers, for *Black Ritual (Obeah)*, 58, 79
AGMA. *See* American Guild of Musical Artists
Ailey, Alvin, 143
Alaska, 223
Alberg, Lisa, 314, 317
Aleko, 98, 99
Alex Smith & Sons Carpet Company, 11, 16–17; Ewing, Tom, inherits, 18, 19. *See also* Zuckert, Harry
Allied Arts Ballets Inc., 32–33
Alonso, Alicia: at 40th ABT anniversary, 308; with Eglevsky in *Giselle*, 134; glory days of, 236; Kaye *v.*, for top billing, 151; as Lizzie in *Fall River Legend*, 150–51; in Lucia's inner circle, 277; piloting transport plane, 167; returning to

Cuba, 163–64; Youskevitch partnered with, 134, 136, 142, 148, 150–51
Alonso, Fernando, 163–64
American Ballet Theatre (ABT), 244; 3rd New York season, 90–91; 10th anniversary, 165–66; 15th anniversary, 170; 25th anniversary, 214–21; 30th anniversary, 273; 35th anniversary, 292; 40th anniversary, 308–10; 1940s and 1950s ballet popularity due to, 169; in all fifty states, 223; "American" added to "Ballet Theatre" (1956), 186; artistic staff, 183, 234, 267; attempted take-over of, 235–36; Barnes' reviews of, 220, 228, 238, 240, 241, 250; Baronova joins, 88–90; Baryshnikov joins, 280–82; Cannes fire disaster, 192–96; Chicago Civic Opera performance, 77–78; at Claridge Hotel, Buenos Aires, 173–75; closed for finances (1948), 151–52; Covent Garden performances, 125, 128–33, 267, 273; dancer's strike, 302–7; debut of, at Center Theatre (1940), 60–61, 65–69, 82; de Mille's departure, 187–88; Dolin joins, 54–55; Ewing, A., with, 180–81, 184–85, 186–91; Fokine joins, 53–55; fundraising instruments, 70–71, 78–79, 160–61; Godunov's contract with, 302–3; Howard joins, 54–55; invited to Washington D. C., 211–13; Laing joins, 54–55; Lucia's

directing of, *2.6*, 123–24, 131–33, 137–40, 151–52, 193–94, 234–38, 260, 277–78, 290, 293; Majestic Theatre performances, *1.9*, 78–83; Makarova joins, 273–74; "Makarova's Miracle" with, 279–80; Martin's critiques of, 67, 68, 81, 91, 113–14, 119, 139, 150, 170, 187, 195, 198–99, 201–2, 242; Massine joins, 98; at the Met, 27, 87–88, 92–98, 109, 112–14, 116–20, 125–28, 133, 140, 147–51, 164–65, 170, 188, 195, 197–99, 291–92, 300–301, 303–6, 308–10; Mikhail Mordkin Ballet company renamed "Ballet Theatre," 52; in need of home, 144–45, 185–87, 196, 197, 211–13, 242, 247, 270, 291; Palacio de Bellas Artes performances, *1.10*, 90–91, 98–101; Palais de Chaillot performances, 167; Pleasant's master plan for, 48–53, 58–61, 69, 95; Policy and Planning Committee, 234–36; Rockefeller Foundation's support, 289; start-up money for, 49–50; *Swan Lake* ushering new era for, 236–37; Terry's reviews of, *2.4*, 28, 67, 68, 91, 96, 134, 198, 241; tour in Mexico, *1.10*, 90–91, 98–101, 171; tour in South America, 172–75; tour in Soviet Union, 200–201; tours in Europe, 187–88, 192–94, 274; transcontinental tours, 102–8, 116, 136–39, 165, 169–70, 201; Tudor joins, 54; WWII impacting, 53–55, 102–3

American Ballet Theatre (Payne), 235, 250–51

American Guild of Musical Artists (AGMA), 59, 302–6

American National Theatre and Academy (ANTA), 166, 172–73, 176

Anderson, Jack, 319

Andrews, John William, 11, 15

ANTA. *See* American National Theatre and Academy

Arey, June, 267

Argentina, 172–75

Arpino, Gerald, 246–47

Arrick, Larry, 190–91

Artistic committee, 133, 234–36

Artistic staff, 234, 267; in 1956, 183

Ashton, Frederick, 54, 129; *Les Patineurs*, 134; Pleasant's invitation to, 51

Astarte, 248

Atlanta, 259

At Midnight, 244

Balanchine, George: choreography to Tchaikovsky's Suite no. 3, 144; *Complete Stories of the Great Ballets*, 37; *Concerto Barocco*, 123; distinguished career of, 243–44; esteem for Petipa's *Sleeping Beauty*, 33; Ford Foundation favoring, 245–46; *Jewels*, 244; Pleasant reaches out to, 51, 54; Tallchief married to, 164; *Theme and Variations*, 142–44, 194; works produced between 1955 and 1967, 244; as world's preeminent choreographer, 33

Ballet Associates, 122–23

Ballet Caravan company, 66, 244

Ballet Presentations Inc., 78–79

Ballet Rambert, 54, 80; response to Cannes fire disaster, 193

Ballet Russe, *1.7*, *2.5*; De Basil's, 37, 39, 87, 88; Hurok representing, 86, 133; Massine as choreographer for, 93; Mordkin, Mikhail, joins, 27; performance of *Petrouchka* in Paris (1911), 101; *Sleeping Beauty* brought to West by, 33. *See also* Diaghilev, Sergei

Ballet Russe de Monte Carlo, 86; 1940s and 50s popularity of ballet due to, 169; Denham's, 44, 87; Hurok presenting, 37

Ballet Society, 244

Ballet Theatre. *See* American Ballet Theatre

Ballet Theatre Foundation Inc. (BTF): bids for home in Lincoln Center, 185–87; Colin as president of, 291–92; Davis as president of, 183; Ewing, A., as executive secretary, 180–81, 184–85, 186–91; Goldman's leadership in, 262, 263–67, 270–72, 282–84, 287; Groo's recommendations to, 284–85; Stevens, B., as chairman of Board of Trustees, 222–23; tax-exempt status, 137, 160–61; Washington, D.C., 212–13

Ballet Theatre Inc., 70–71, 78–79, 160

Ballet Theatre School, 271, 289

Ballet Theatre Workshop, 188–90

Barnes, Clive: on ABT's lack of artistic leadership, 250; on ABT's luck turning, 241; on Feld (1967), 240; on *Les Noces*, 220, 228; linking Goldman and Makarova, 273–74; on *Swan Lake* (1967), 238

Baronova, Irina, *1.7, 1.10*, 292; 1979 letter to Lucia, 307–8; in *Bluebeard*, 100; hospitalized, 107–8; joins ABT, 88–90; in Lucia's inner circle, 277; Pleasant's invitation to, 51; Toumanova, Riabouchinska and, 37, 88; *Voices of Spring*, 55–56, 66, 67, 93

Baryshnikov, Mikhail (Mischa): departs ABT, 294–95; joins ABT/debuts in *Giselle*, 280–82; Kirkland with, in *Le Corsaire*, 293; in *Push Comes to Shove*, 293–94; as successor to Lucia, 301–2, 310; tribute from, 311, 319

Bator, Victor, 186

Baum, Morton: Kirstein, Lincoln, partnership with, 244; offers Center Theatre to ABT, 145, 247

Bennett, Isadora, 69

Bentley, Muriel: in ABT's 15th anniversary, 170; at ABT's 40th anniversary, 308; in *Fall River Legend*, 150–51; in *Fancy Free*, 117; stalwart of ABT, 133; on working with Tudor, 92–93

Berlin, Germany, 167–68

Bernstein, Leonard, 117–20

Bessy, Claude, response of to Cannes fire disaster, 193

Biddle, Livingston, 226–27

Billy the Kid, 66, 232

Bing, Rudolf, 296

Black Ritual (Obeah), 58, 79

Bliss, Anthony (Tony), 291, 292, 306

Bluebeard, 101; Baronova and Markova in, 100; at London's Royal Opera House, 130; Lucia as Queen Clementine, *1.10*, 56, 75, 99, 113; as smash hit, 95

Blumenthal mansion, West 54th Street, 77

Bogota, Colombia, curfew in, 171–72

Bolm, Adolph: *Firebird*, *2.7*, 126–28; *Mechanical Ballet*, 58; *Peter and the Wolf*, 58, 75, 105; Pleasant's invitation to, 51; Romanoff's tutelage under, 34; with San Francisco Opera Ballet, 34

Bolshoi Ballet, 27, 200, 230

Bournonville, August, 214

Bowman, Patricia: in ABT's 15th anniversary, 170; joins Mikhail Mordkin company, 40

Broadway Theatre, 133–36, 201

Brooklyn Academy of Music, 31; 1968 ABT at, 259; 1969 ABT at, 260

Brooks, Randy, 174

Brown, Isabel, 252, 258

Brown, Kelly, 258

Brownsville Labor Lyceum, Brooklyn, 85

Bruhn, Erik: at 40th ABT anniversary, 308; ABT's 30th anniversary, 273; in Danish Royal Ballet, 160; Fracci partnered with, 239; in *Giselle*, 170; Martin's praise for, 201; *Miss Julie*, 194, 195, 293; as "Permanent Guest Artist of ABT," 264; Phoenix Theatre workshop with, 189; in *Raymonda*, 290; replaced by Nagy in *Giselle*, 276; *Time's* praise for, 273; world-renowned, 238–39, 259

Bruno Walter Auditorium, Lincoln Center, 321

Bryn Mawr College, *1.3*, 8–9

BTF Inc. *See* Ballet Theatre Foundation Inc.

Bujones, Fernando, *Raymonda*, 290

Butler, John, 189

Cannes, France, fire disaster in, 192–96

Capezio, 193

Caprichos, 166; for ABT's 25th anniversary, 214

Carmody, Basil, 146

Carmody, Deirdre, 146, 206–7

Carmody, Edward, 29, 76, 146, 316

Carnaval, 68, 100; rehearsals (1939), 58

Carnegie Hall Studio, 10, 38–44, 58

Carter, Jimmy, 309, 310

Carter Barron Theatre, Washington, D.C., 265

Carver, Alex, 11

Cassidy, Claudia, 212

Center Theatre. *See* Radio City Music Hall, Center Theatre

Central American touring, 214

Cerrone, Jeannot, 192, 255

Chagall, Marc, *2.7*, 98, 126

Chase, Dorothy (Dee) (Lucia's sister, Mrs. Edward Carmody), *1.2*, 7, 22, 76, 124, 146

Chase, Elizabeth Irving (E.I) (Lucia's sister, Mrs. John Griffith-Davies), *1.2*, 7, 22; at Greystone Farm, 124–25; response to Martin, 199

Chase, Elizabeth Kellogg (Lucia's mother), *1.1*, 6

Chase, Irving (Popsie) (Lucia's father), *1.1*, *1.2*, 6, 14–15, 29, 50

Chase, Lucia, *1.2*, *1.3*, *1.8*, *2.7*, *2.10*; Baronova's 1979 letter to, 307–8; Baryshnikov as successor to, 301–2, 310; Baryshnikov's tributes to, 311, 319; championing *Swan Lake*, 234–37; closing ABT (1948), 151–52; debut in Mordkin Ballet's *The Sleeping Beauty*, 34–37, 44; de Mille and, 9–10, 72, 80–81, 162, 233–36, 308–9; diphtheria of, 8; "Directing a Ballet Company" by, 250; directing ABT, *2.6*, 123–24, 131–33, 137–40, 151–52, 193–94, 234–38, 260, 277–78, 290, 293; director contract expires, 297–302; Dolin's tribute to, 113; early roles, 56–57; as Eldest Sister (*Pillar of Fire*), *2.1*, *2.2*, 56, 195; elected to RAD, 131; Fokine/Tudor as favorite choreographers, 29, 100; as Fourth Song in *Dark Elegies*, *2.3*, 57, 80; as fundraising instrument, 196–97; in *Giselle* (Mordkin Ballet), 37, 44; Goldman *v.*, 269–72, 277–78; as Greedy One (*Three Virgins and a Devil*), *1.9*; Gregory on, 251, 252–53, 256–57, 312–13; Handel Medallion presented to, 293; Hayden on, 254; home life, *1.4*, 5, 6–7, 21, 23, 26–27, 73–77, 99, 114–15, 146–47, 314–15; humor of, 75–76; Hurok on, 155; Hurok/Talbot and, 120–23; illness/death of, 316–20; inner circle of friends, 277; Kaye on, 254, 277; launching *Swan Lake*, 225–26, 228; Martin's appraisal of, 139, 195, 198–99; Mordkin, Mikhail, relationship to, 27, 28–32, 56–57; "one of the great dance mimes of our time," *2.4*; at Palacio de Bellas Artes, *1.10*, 90–91, 98–101; in *Petrouchka*, *1.7*, 99, 107–8; *Pillar of Fire* championed by, 92–97; as Queen Clementine (*Bluebeard*), *1.10*, 56, 75, 99, 113; as Queen Mother (*Swan Lake*), 56, 241–42, 251, 275, 319–20; at Rose Hill, *1.4*, 5, 6–7, 76, 146–47, 315;

Smith, O., with, *2.6*, *2.8*, 29, 117–20, 123–24, 126, 129, 131–33, 187, 214, 230, 260, 277–78, 308, 318; start-up money for ABT, 49–50; as Stepmother (*Fall River Legend*), 56, 150–51, 195; Stevens, P., on, 313; succession of, in ABT, 277–79, 298–302; Talbot's dispute with, 120–23; tax court, 112–13, 156–58, 177, 178–80; Terry on, in *Las Hermanas*, *2.4*; Tom (husband) and, *1.4*, 10–14, 15–17, 19–24, 25–26, 29; U.S. Medal of Freedom awarded to, 310; University of Wisconsin honorary doctorate, 265; voice of, 75; Yale honorary doctorate, 309–10

Chase, Marjorie (Lucia's sister), *1.2*, 99

Chicago Civic Opera, ABT at, 77–78

Chujoy, Anatole, 68, 87

Claridge Hotel, Buenos Aires, 173–75

Clarke, Cecilia (Lucia's daughter), 275

Clarke, Mary, 212

Clifford, Henry, on ABT's artistic committee, 133

Cobb, Sheila, 275

Cochran, Alex Smith, 11, 16–19, 319

Cochran/Ewing extended family, 11, 14, 17–18, 179

Coleman, Emily, 217

Colin, Justin, *2.8*, 272, 285; as BTF president, 291–92

Colombia, ABT's tour in, 171–72

Columbia Concerts Corporation, 40

Comden, Betty, 118

Connecticut, service to the arts medal from, 309

Conover, Warren, 256, 257, 294–95

Conrad, Karen, 38, 67, 79, 292

Constantia, 198

Contract, dancer's: dispute over, 302–7; prior to 1948 closing of ABT, 151–52

Copland, Aaron, on artistic committee, 133

Coppelia, 259; ABT's full-length, at New York State Theater, 236; at Met (1911), 27

Costa Rica, 171

Covent Garden: ABT at, 125, 128–33, 267, 273; response to Cannes fire disaster, 193; Royal Ballet at, 239

Croce, Arlene: critical of ABT, 240; on

Makarova, 276; reversing appraisal of
ABT, 294
Cruikshank, Frank, 32–33
Cuba, 163–64
Cullberg, Birgit, 194, 198
Cunningham, Merce, 143
Curry, John, 300

Dance Magazine, 170
Dance News, 68, 87, 166, 170, 194
Danilova, Alexandra, Pleasant's invitation
to, 51
Danish Royal Ballet, 160
D'Antuono, Eleanor: in 1969, 264;
Raymonda, 290
Dark Elegies, 214; critically acclaimed,
93; Kaye on, 94; Lucia as Fourth Song
in, 2.3, 57, 80; at the Met (1948), 148;
rehearsals (1939), 58; revival of, 134;
Tudor's critical acclaim from, 148
Das Lied von der Erde, 148
D'Autuono, Eleanor, 239, 255
Davies, Robertson, 106–7
Davis, Blevins, 159–61, 163, 166–68, 173,
183
Death and the Maiden (Howard's), 51, 58
De Basil, Col. Wassily, 37, 39, 87; Hurok's
relationship with, 88
Debevoise, Plimpton, Lyons & Gates
(law firm), 1.6, 204–6; Goldman with,
260
De Lavallade, Carmen, 305
De Mille, Agnes, 1.9; 1965 works by, 214;
ABT's 15th anniversary, 170; ABT's 25th
anniversary, 214; ABT's 35th anniver-
sary, 292; on artistic committee, 133,
234–36; Black Ritual (Obeah), 58, 79; in
Cowgirl costume (Rodeo), 2.5; deserting ABT, 187–88; Fall River Legend,
56, 75, 77, 79, 148–51, 195, 214–15, 236;
The Four Marys, 214; Harvest Reel,
135; on Kaye's performance as Lizzie
(1948), 150; Lucia and, 9–10, 72, 80–81,
162, 233–36, 308–9; Majestic Theatre
premiere, 79–80; New York Herald
Tribune article by, 224–25, 227; Phoenix
Theatre workshop with, 189; Pleasant's
invitation to, 51; on Robbins at Fancy
Free debut, 119; Rodeo, 2.5, 79, 232;
Sebastian, 189; Swingin' the Dream,

58, 60; Tally-Ho, 79, 111–12, 116, 118, 139,
214; tribute at Lucia's memorial, 323–24
Denby, Edwin, 2.7, 128, 136
Denham, Serge, 44, 87. See also Ballet
Russe de Monte Carlo
Designs with Strings, 166
De Valois, Ninette, 129, 143, 265, 313
D'Harnoncourt, René, 228
Diaghilev, Sergei, 1.7, 98, 101; Mordkin,
Mikhail, joins Ballet Russe, 27;
Nijinska's relationship to, 55; Sleeping
Beauty brought to West by, 33, 34;
valuable attribute of, 143. See also
Ballet Russe
Dialogues (Serenade for 7), 198
"Directing a Ballet Company," 250
Distant Dances (Osato, autobiography),
104
Dolin, Anton, 1.10, 89, 103–4, 309; in
ABT's 15th anniversary, 170; at ABT's
35th anniversary, 292; at ABT's 40th
anniversary, 308; in Bluebeard, 100;
in Fair at Sorochinsk, 1.8; Giselle, 58;
joins ABT, 54–55; Pleasant's invitation
to, 51; Princess Aurora, 91, 95; Quintet,
58; in Rose Adagio (from The Sleeping
Beauty), 293; Sevastianov's listing of,
93; tribute to Lucia, 113; version of
Swan Lake, 68
Dollar, William, Constantia, 198
Don Domingo de Don Blas, 98, 99
Don Quixote, 200, 244, 256
Doris Duke Foundation, 188
Douglas, Scott, 195
Dowell, Anthony, 300
Dowling, Robert, 173, 176
Drozdoff, Vladimir, 32, 33
Duke, Angier Biddle, 293
Duncan, Don, 69
Duncan, Isadora, 87
Du Pont, S. Hallock, 161, 285

Eckl, Shirley, 117
Ecuador, 172
Edinburgh Festival, 166
Edwards, Lee, 248
Eglevsky, André, 134; at ABT's 35th an-
niversary, 292; with Alicia Alonso in
Giselle, 134; in Rose Adagio (from The
Sleeping Beauty), 293

Eisenhower, Dwight D., 169
Eldest Sister, Lucia as (*Pillar of Fire*), *2.1, 2.2*, 56, 195
Embree Concert Service, 52–53
Essen, Viola, *32, 34, 37, 38*; in ABT's 15th anniversary, 170
Etudes, 228; for ABT's 25th anniversary, 214
European tours: in 1960, 187; Cannes fire (1958), 192–96; government-sponsored (1950), 166–68; government-sponsored (1956), 188; Greece, Spain, Italy, 267, 273
Ewing, Alex C. (Sandy) (Lucia's son), *1.6*; at American Ballet Theatre, 180–81, 184–85, 186–91; birth of, 19; early home life, 26–27, 73–77, 114–15; at Joffrey Ballet, 246–49; marriage to first wife, Carol Sonne, 191, 206–7, 246, 249, 267; marriage to Sheila Cobb, 275; Pleasant's outing with, 83; tribute at Lucia's memorial, 324
Ewing, Bill (Lucia's brother-in-law), 22, 23
Ewing, Caroline (Lucia's grandchild), *2.9*, 275, 314
Ewing, Carol Sonne (Lucia's daughter-in-law), 191, 206–7, 246, 249, 265, 267
Ewing, Eric (Lucia's grandchild), *2.9*, 265
Ewing, "Mater" (Lucia's mother-in-law), 25–26
Ewing, Sandy (Lucia's grandchild), *2.9*, 265
Ewing, Sheila Cobb (Lucia's daughter-in-law), 275
Ewing, Thomas (Tommy) (Lucia's son), *1.6*, 16–17, 99, 180–81, 213–14; early home life, 21, 23, 25–27, 99; sailing accident, 204–7, 211
Ewing, Tom (Lucia's husband), *1.4*, 15–17, 29; birth of sons to, 16–17, 19; business pressures on, 18–20; illness/death of, 20–24, 25–26; Lucia courted by, 10–14

Facsimile, 134–35, 142–43
Fair at Sorochinsk, The, 126; Dolin and Lucia in, *1.8*
Fall River Legend, 75, 77, 79, 215; for ABT's 25th anniversary, 214; Alicia Alonso in, 150–51; de Mille's challenges working on, 148–50; early glory days

of, 236; Lucia as Stepmother in, 56, 150–51, 195
Fancy Free, 99, 116–20, 130, 232; early glory days of, 236
Feld, Eliot, 253; *Harbinger*, 239–41, 244; *At Midnight*, 244
Fernandez, Jose, 58; *Goyescas*, 58
Fernandez, Royes, 226, 239; in 1969, 264; at ABT's 35th anniversary, 292
Filene's Department Store, Boston, 244
Finch, Clyde, *1.3*
Firebird, *2.7*, 126–28
Fisher, Tom, 137–38
Fokine, Michel, 31; ABT joined by, 53–55; *Bluebeard*, *1.10*, 56, 75, 95, 99, 100–101, 113, 130; *Carnaval*, 58, 68, 100; as greatest living ballet choreographer, 51; *Helen of Troy*, 98, 99, 100; last days of, 99–100; *Les Sylphides*, 57, 58, 66, 67, 100, 130, 139, 194, 236, 292; as Lucia's favorite choreographer, 29, 100; *Petrouchka*, *1.7*, 75, 98–101, 107–8, 139, 264, 272; rehearsals (1939), 58; *Scheherazade*, 126; Sevastianov's listing of, 93
Fonteyn, Margot, 51, 129; response to Cannes fire disaster, 193; unable to join ABT, 54
Ford, Eleanor Clay, 272
Ford, George, 213
Ford Foundation: ABT's ongoing support from, 289; Balanchine favored by, 245–46; Goldman's progress with, 267; Joffrey Ballet's grant from, 247–48
Foundation for American Dance, 247
Four Marys, The, 214
Fourth Song, Lucia as, *2.3*, 57, 80
Fracci, Carla: ABT's 30th anniversary, 264, 273; ABT's 40th anniversary, 308; *Giselle*, 239; partnered with Bruhn, 239, 259; as "Permanent Guest Artist of ABT," 264; *Raymonda*, 290; *Time's* praise for, 273
Fram Corporation, 206
Freebooters, The, 10–11
Froman, Mae, 95
Fundraising instruments: absence of tax-exempt status, 137; ABT Inc., 70–71, 78–79, 160–61; authorized nonprofit tax-exempt status, 160–61; Ballet

Associates, 122–23; Lucia's, 196–97; Pleasant *v*. Zuckert, 40–42

Gaîté Parisienne, 93, 264, 272
Gala Performance, 79, 93, 194; bringing recognition to Tudor, 148
Garland, Robert, 135
Gaudenzi, Mme. (singing instructor), 15
Gendarme (poodle), *2.10*, 316
George Blumenthal mansion, West 54th Street, 77
Gest, Morris, 27
Giselle: Alicia Alonso and Eglevsky in, 134; Bruhn's and Markova's performance in, 170; Fracci and Bruhn in, 239; full-length at New York State Theater, 236, 273; Lucia in Mordkin, Mikhail, production of, 37, 44; Makarova and Baryshnikov in, 280–81; Makarova and Nagy in, 276–77; Markova and Baranova displayed in, 95; Mordkin, Mikhail, production taken over by Dolin, 55; rehearsals (1939), 58; *Time's* praise for, 273; Youskevitch in, 134, 164–65
Giamatti, Bart, 310
Goberman, Max, 144
Godunov, Aleksandr, 302–3
Golden, Miriam, at ABT's 40th anniversary, 308
Goldfish, 55
Goldman, Sherwin: achievements, 288–89, 291, 295–96; admission statement in *New York Times*, 288; business approach of, 263–67, 271–72, 282–83; grants secured by, 268, 283–84, 289; Lucia v., 269–72, 277–78; Makarova's ABT contract via, 274; National Registry Program concept of, 271; as new CEO, 260–62, 288–89; on opting out, 276
Goldner, Nancy, 242
Gollner, Nana, 51, 79, 120, 148; Pleasant's invitation to, 51
Goodyear, A. Conger, 161
Gould, Morton, 117, 149
Goyescas, 58
Graham, Martha, 143, 246
Great American Goof, The, 57, 66, 68; rehearsals (1939), 58

Great Depression, 18, 19, 38
Greedy Virgin, Lucia as (*Three Virgins and a Devil*), *1.9*
Green, Adolph, 118
Greenwich Village Follies, 27
Gregory, Cynthia: in 1969, 264; on Lucia, 312–13; on Lucia's directorship, 251, 252–53; on Lucia's directorship re *Don Quixote*, 256–57; *Miss Julie*, 194, 195, 293; overnight stardom of, 239; in *Raymonda*, 290; in Rose Adagio (from *The Sleeping Beauty*), 293; *Time's* praise for, 273
Greystone Farm, Gloucestershire, 124–25
Groo, Lawrence: financial plan for ABT, 284–85; trustee for ABT Foundation, 266; underwrites *Petrouchka*, 272

Hamlet, 160
Handel Medallion, 293
Hanes, De Witt, 8
Harbinger, 239–41, 244
Harkness, Rebecca, 246–47
Harkness Ballet, 246–47
Harvard Law School, *1.6*
Haskell, Arnold, 131
Hawaii, 223
Hayden, Melissa: at 40th ABT anniversary, 308; on Lucia, 254; stalwart of ABT, 133
Hayes, Helen, 305
Hecksher, August, 226
Helen of Troy, 98, 99, 100
Hepburn, Katharine, 28
Hering, Doris, 170
Hermann, Jane, 291–92
High Time Promotions, 160
Hill, James, 159
Hillbright Enterprises Inc., 160
Holland, H. Brian, 177
Home, ABT's need for, 144–45, 185–87, 196, 197, 211–13, 242, 247, 270, 291
Honorary doctorate degrees: University of Wisconsin, 265; Yale, 309–10
Hosmer, Stephen Titus, 8
House of Bernardo Alba, The (Lorca), *2.4*
Howard, Andrée: *Death and the Maiden*, 51, 58; joins ABT, 54–55; Lady into Fox, 51, 58; Pleasant's invitation to, 51; rehearsals (1939), 58

Hudson Theatre, 41
Humor: Baryshnikov's talents, 293–94;
    Bluebeard, 1.10, 56, 75, 95, 99, 100–101,
    113, 130; *Judgment of Paris,* 56, 58, 75,
    139, 148, 292; Lucia's, 75–76; *Three
    Virgins and a Devil, 1.9,* 56, 75, 79,
    80–81, 120
Humphrey, Hubert, 228, 229
Hurok, Sol, 82, 84–86; ABT's break from,
    125–28, 178–79; association with ABT,
    87–92, 101–2, 120–21; Ballet's Theatre's
    obligation, 122–23; De Basil's relation-
    ship with, 88; on Lucia's control, 155;
    Lucia *v.* Talbot and, 120–23; presenting
    Ballet Russe de Monte Carlo, 37; rep-
    resenting Ballet Russe, 86; unappre-
    ciative of Tudor's work, 92–95; Zuckert
    and, 89–90
Hurok Associates, 178; "on verge of going
    belly-up," 291
Hurok Attractions Inc., 87, 95

I Dedicate. See Pillar of Fire
Imperial Russian Ballet, 9
Internal Revenue Service: 1948 U.S. Tax
    Court hearings, 112–13, 156–58; 1953
    U.S. Tax Court trial and verdict, 177;
    1954 U.S. Tax Court appeal, 178; 1956
    U.S. Tax Court final decision, 178–80;
    tax-exempt status, 137, 160–61
International Exchange Program, 171,
    230–31
Interplay, 134

Jacob's Pillow, Mass., 89
Jaffe, Allan, 303, 305
Jardin aux Lilas: for ABT's 25th anni-
    versary, 214; bringing recognition to
    Tudor, 93, 148; rehearsals (1939), 58
Javits, Jacob, 228, 229
Joffrey, Robert: Ballet Theatre Workshop
    with, 188; Alex Ewing working for,
    246–47; Joffrey Ballet company, 246–
    49; as notable director, 143; Phoenix
    Theatre workshop with, 189
Johnson, Lyndon B., 226–27, 310
Johnson, Philip, 185
Jorgensen, Rhoda, 255, 256, 257
Journal (Thomas Ewing III), 214
Journey, 189

Jowitt, Deborah, 241, 251
Judgment of Paris, 75, 139, 148, 292;
    Lucia's Minerva in, 56; rehearsals
    (1939), 58
Julliard School, 185

Kahn, Otto, 27
Kaplan, Harvey, 304
Karnilova, Maria: in ABT's 15th anniver-
    sary, 170; at ABT's 35th anniversary,
    292; at ABT's 40th anniversary, 308;
    unable to return to ABT, 164, 308; on
    working with Tudor, 94
Kaye, Nora, 79, 134–35, 167, 174; at 40th
    ABT anniversary, 308; at ABT's 35th
    anniversary, 292; Alicia Alonso versus,
    for top billing, 151; as artistic direc-
    tor, 234; in *Fall River Legend,* 150;
    glory days of, 236; hospitalized, 149; in
    Lucia's inner circle, 277; on Lucia's ma-
    ternal approach, 254; Martin's praise
    for, 170, 195; in *Pillar of Fire, 2.1,* 92, 94,
    95, 96; stalwart of ABT, 133; in *Swan
    Lake,* 170; on Tudor's influence/tech-
    nique, 94, 95
Kelly, Gene, 54; Pleasant's invitation to, 51
Kendall, Donald, 296–97, 298–300, 305,
    306
Kennedy, Caroline, 292
Kennedy, John F., 247
Kennedy Center, Washington, D. C., 291
Khivira, Lucia as *(Fair at Sorochinsk), 1.8*
Khrushchev, Nikita, 200–201
Kidd, Michael: Pleasant's invitation to, 51;
    on railways in 1940s, 103
Kimball, Arthur, 20
Kinross homestead, Yonkers, 25, 114
Kirkland, Gelsey, 303; Baryshnikov with,
    in *Le Corsaire,* 293; in *Raymonda,* 290
Kirov Ballet, 273–74, 279
Kirstein, Lincoln, 185, 244–45
Kivett, Ted, 239, 250; in 1969, 264
Knickerbocker, Suzy, 292
Koesun, Ruth Ann, 148, 173, 239; at ABT's
    40th anniversary, 308
Korean War, 167–68
Krawitz, Herman, 296–97, 305
Kria, 205–7
Kriegsman, Allan, 242
Kriza, John, 117, 135, 148; at ABT's 35th an-

niversary, 292; as Champion Roper in *Rodeo*, *2.5*; glory days of, 236; stalwart of ABT, 133

Krupska, Dania, 150

La Bayadere: full-length at New York State Theater, 236; Makarova's direction in, 279–80

Lady from the Sea, 198

Lady into Fox, 51; rehearsals (1939), 58

La Fille Mal Gardée, 37, 44; ABT's reception in Buenos Aires, 174; Nijinska's restaging of, 55, 57, 58, 68, 174; rehearsals (1939), 58

Laguardia, Fiorello, 100

Laing, Hugh, 148; at ABT's 35th anniversary, 292; glory days of, 236; joins ABT, 54–55; in *Pillar of Fire*, *2.1*, 92, 94; Pleasant's invitation to, 51; stalwart of ABT, 133; on Tudor's technique for dancers, 94

Lander, Harald, mounting *La Sylphide* (1965), 214

Lander, Toni, 239; in 1969, 264; at ABT's 40th anniversary, 308; *Time's* praise for, 273

Lang, Harold, 117, 119

Larssen, Harry, 73

La Scala, Milan, 239

Las Hermanas, Lucia in, *2.4*

La Sylphide, 236; at ABT's 25th anniversary, 214

Le Beau Danube, 93

Le Corsaire, 293

Leibowitz, Leonard, 303, 305

Lenin Sports Palace, 201

Les Noces, 215–17, 220, 228, 240, 244

Les Patineurs, 134

Les Sylphides, Fokine's, 66, 67, 130, 139, 194; ABT's 35th anniversary, 292; full-length at New York State Theater, 236; Lucia coached for, 57, 100; rehearsals (1939), 58

Lewisohn Stadium, 77

Lichine, David, *1.8*, 100; in ABT's 15th anniversary, 170

Lied von der Erde (Mahler), 148–49

Límon, José (*The Moor's Pavane*), 264; *Time's* praise for, 273

Lincoln Center for the Performing Arts, 185–87; for ABT's 25th anniversary, 214; Baryshnikov in *Giselle* at, 280; Bruno Walter Auditorium, 321

Lindsay, John, 228, 229, 260

Lion and the Mouse, The (Bryn Mawr play), *1.3*

Litz, Katharine, 188

Lloyd, Norman, 267, 268

Lorca, Frederico Garcia, *2.4*

Loring, Eugene, *1.9*; *Billy the Kid*, 66, 232; *Great American Goof* choreographed by, 57, 58, 66, 68; Pleasant's invitation to, 51; rehearsals (1939), 58

Los Angeles, Calif., 105, 106, 309

Lowry, McNeil, 245–46, 247, 267

Lowther, Mr. & Mrs. Frank, 272

Lucia. *See* Chase, Lucia

Lyon, Annabelle, *1.9*; in ABT's 15th anniversary, 170; at ABT's 40th anniversary, 308; in *Pillar of Fire*, *2.1*, 92

MacMillan, Kenneth, *2.4*; *Journey*, 189; *Winter's Eve*, 188

Mahler, Gustav, 148–49

Majestic Theatre, *1.9*, 78–83

Makarova, Natasha: on Baryshnikov's defection, 280; *Giselle*, 276–77, 280–81; joins ABT, 273–74; *La Bayadere*, 279–80

"Makarova's Miracle," 279–80

Mamoulian, Reuben, 13

Manchester, P. W., 170

Mander, Lois, 317, 319, 321

Maracci, Carmelita, 50

Markova, Alicia, 113; in ABT's 15th anniversary, 170; in *Bluebeard*, *1.10*, 100; *Giselle*, 170; Pleasant's invitation to, 51

Marks, Bruce, 239, 253; in 1969, 264; *Time's* praise for, 273

Martin, John, 67, 68, 81, 150; ABT lauded by (1943), 113–14; ABT reviewed by (1947), 139; on ABT's endless travel, 242; on ABT's third New York season, 91; bombshell from (1960), 198–99; Bruhn lauded by, 201; on creating new works, 187; on eighteenth season at Met, 195; on *Fancy Free*, 119; Kaye lauded by, 170, 195; Lucia critiqued by, 139, 195, 198–99; Serrano praised by, 201–2; Youskevitch praised by, 170

Massine, Léonide: *Gaîté Parisienne*, 93, 264, 272; joins ABT, 98

Mathis, Bonnie, 257

MCA. *See* Music Corporation of America

McKenzie, Kevin, 242

McLerie, Allyn Ann, 2.5

McWhorter, Charles, 296

Mechanical Ballet (Adoph Bolm's), 58

Melziner, Jo, 148

Mendelssohn, Gordon, 50

Met. *See* Metropolitan Opera House

Metropolitan Opera House (the Met), 37, 125–28, 140, 185; ABT (1942), 92–98; ABT (1943), 109, 112, 113–14; ABT (1944), 116–20; ABT (1948), 147–51; ABT (1949), 164–65; ABT (1956), 188; ABT (1979), 300–301; ABT Foundation contract with, 291–92; ABT's 40th anniversary, 308–10; Ballet Russe at, 133; *Coppelia* (1911), 27; dancers' strike impacting, 303–6; Hurok's lease of, 87–88; Martin on ABT's eighteenth season, 195; as rehearsal home for ABT, 197

Mexico: Palacio de Bellas Artes opera house, *1.10*, 90–91, 98–101; as part of South American tour, 171

Miami, 239–40

Midsummer Night's Dream, A, 244; Reinhart in, 33

Mikhail Mordkin Ballet: Lucia in, 34–37, 44; Pleasant as de facto manager, 41; renamed "Ballet Theatre," 52

Mikhail Mordkin Studio of the Dance Arts: Bowman joins, 40; founding of, 28; Pleasant as office manager, 38–40

Minerva, Lucia as (*Judgment of Paris*), 56

Minnesota Dance Theatre, 309

Miramar residence, 6, 10, 13

Miss Julie (Birgit Culberg's), 194, 195, 293

Mitchell, James, 2.5

Modern dance, Ford Foundation ignores, 246

Moffat, Joyce, 303, 305

Moonraker house, 213–14, 316

Moore, Sally, 251

Moor's Pavane, The. See Límon, José,

Mordkin, Michael, Jr., 37, 42, 47

Mordkin, Mikhail: disinherited, 55–58; *Giselle* produced by, 37, 44; *Goldfish*,

55; joins Ballet Russe, 27; Lucia's relationship with, 27, 28–32, 56–57; Mikhail Mordkin Studio of the Dance Arts, 28, 38–40; Pleasant usurps, 41, 44–48; Sevastianov's listing of, 93; *Sleeping Beauty* produced by, 32–37

Moscow, USSR, 200–201, 230–31

Moylan, Mary Ellen, in ABT's 15th anniversary, 170

Music Corporation of America (MCA), 136

Nagy, Ivan: in 1969, 264; *Giselle*, 276–77; *Raymonda*, 290

Narragansett, Rhode Island, 6, 32, 73, 76; family at, after Carol Ewing's death, 267; family at, after Tom Ewing's death, 26; Mordkin, Mikhail, invited to, 30; retirement years at, 315–16; summer days at home in, 114–15; Tom's marriage proposal to Lucia at, 12–13

National Endowment for the Arts (NEA), 226–28, 267, 272; ABT's ongoing support from, 289, 296; Goldman's grant application to, 287–88

National Registry Program, 271

Nault, Fernand, 255

NEA. *See* National Endowment for the Arts

Nemchinova, Vera, 27

New York City Ballet, 185–86; advantages of, 243–45; Ford Foundation's grant to, 245–46; L. Kirstein's establishment of (1948), 244; as "the other company," 243

New York City Center of Music and Drama, 185, 186, 241, 244, 267

New York City Center theatre, *2.4*, 139–41, 145, 267, 292–93

New York Hippodrome, 87

New York Master Institute of United Arts, 32

New York Public Library for the Performing Arts, 185, 321

New York State Council on the Arts, 287; ABT's ongoing support from, 289

New York State Theater, 185; ABT's 1960 performance, 272–73; ABT's 1967 spring season at, 234–37, 238–41; ABT's 1974 performance, 279–80; ABT's twenty-fifth anniversary celebration at, 214–21

New York Times, 288, 298, 310; announcing Baryshnikov's directorship of ABT, 301

Nijinska, Bronislava: with Diaghilev's ballet, 55; *La Fille Mal Gardée* reconstructed by, 55, 57, 58, 68, 174; Pleasant's invitation to, 51

Nijinsky, Vaslav, *1.7*, 55, 101; Sevastianov's listing of, 93

Nimbus, 166

Nonprofit tax-exempt status, 137, 160–61

Nureyev, Rudolph. *See Raymonda*

Nutcracker, The, full-length production at New York State Theater, 236

Oakland Cemetery, Yonkers, 25, 207, 321

Oceanographic Laboratory, Woods Hole, Mass., 206

Ode to Glory, Yurek Shabelevski's production of, 50, 58

Office staff, in 1956, 182–83

Oklahoma!, 132, 149

Onassis, Jacqueline Kennedy, 292

On Stage, 103

On the Town, 131, 135

Onysko, John, 162, 183

Orlin, Terry, 183

Orr, Terry, 255, 312

Orthwine, Rudolf "Rudy," 32–33, 37–39, 45, 47, 52

Osato, Sono, 104, 251; in ABT's 15th anniversary, 170; at ABT's 40th anniversary, 308; tribute at Lucia's memorial, 322

Oswald, Genevieve, 321

Page, Ruth, 50, 137

Page-Stone Ballet Company, 50

Palacio de Bellas Artes opera house, *1.10*, 90–91, 98–101

Palais de Chaillot, 167

Paris Opera House: Ballet Russe's *Petrouchka* (1911), 101; Mikail, Mordkin, with Pavlova at, 27

Pas de Quatre, 139

Paul, Mimi, in 1969, 264

Paul, Randolph, 177

Paul, Weiss, Wharton, Rifkind, & Garrison law firm, 235

Pavlova, Anna, 28, 87; at Paris Opera House, 27

Payne, Charles, 95, 109, 136–37, 167, 260; *American Ballet Theatre*, 235, 250–51

Pay scale, dancer's complaint over, 302–7

Peck, Gregory, 228

Pendleton, Dick, 206

Persichetti, Vincent, 117

Peru, 172

Peter and the Wolf, 75, 105; rehearsals (1939), 58

Petipa, Marius: *La Bayadere*, 279–80; *La Sylphide*, 214, 236; as world's preeminent choreographer, 33

Petrouchka: Ballet Russe performance in Paris (1911), 101; Fokine's revival of, *1.7*, 75, 98–101, 107–8, 139, 264, 272; Lucia as Ballerina in, *1.7*, 99, 107–8

Pettan, Florence, 162, 183, 221, 302

Phoenix Theatre, 188, 189

Pillar of Fire, 75, 120, 148, 194, 214–15; early glory days of, 236; Lucia as Eldest Sister in, *2.1*, *2.2*, 56, 195; Russian ballet *v.*, 92–97

Pinocchio, 60

Pleasant, Richard (Dick), 220, 221; as Ballet Theatre manager, 77–78; on creating new works, 187; fundraising, 40–42; master plan of, 48–53, 58–61, 69, 95; Mordkin, Mikhail, usurped by, 41, 44–48; as Mordkin Ballet de facto manager, 41; as Mordkin Studio office manager, 38–40; obliged to step down, 82–83; offer to Balanchine, 51, 54; as secretary of Advanced Arts Ballets, 40–41; Zuckert and, 41–43

Plum, Fred, 318

Point Judith Country Club, 10

Poland, invasion of, 53

Policy and Planning Committee, 234

Portrait of a Young American (Andrews), 11

Pravda, 201

Princess Aurora, 91, 95

Princeton University, 9, 38

Push Comes to Shove, 293–94

Queen Clementine, Lucia as (*Bluebeard*), *1.10*, 56, 75, 99, 113

Queen Mary, 129

Queen Mother, Lucia as (*Swan Lake*), 56, 241–42, 251, 275, 319–20
Quintet, Dolin's, 58

RAD. *See* Royal Academy of Dance
Radio City Music Hall, Center Theatre, 40, 58; ABT's 10th anniversary (1950), 165–66; ABT's debut season (1940) at, 60–61, 65–69, 82; Baum offers, as home for ABT, 145, 247
Railway touring, in 1940s, 103–4
Rambert, Marie, 54, 80, 143
Raymonda, Nureyev's production of, 290
Rebecca Harkness Foundation, 246–47
Reed, Janet, 117
Reinhart, Max, 33–34
Remisoff, Nicholas, 126
Riabouchinska, Tatiana, Toumanova, Baronova and, 37, 88
Rich, Alan, 273
Richard Rogers Musical Theatre, 267
River, The, 264, 272
River Club, East 52nd Street, 197
Robbins, Jerome, *1.9*, 277; at ABT's 40th anniversary, 308; on artistic committee, 133, 234–36; de Mille on (*Fancy Free*), 119; deserting ABT, 187–88; *Facsimile*, 134–35, 142–43; *Fancy Free*, 99, 116–20, 130, 232, 236; *Interplay*, 134; *Les Noces*, 215–17, 228, 240, 244; *On the Town*, 131, 135; undercutting Lucia, 233–36
Rockefeller, John D., III, 185, 245
Rockefeller, Laurence, 50
Rockefeller, Nelson, 185, 245
Rockefeller Foundation, 267; ABT's ongoing support from, 289; grant with strings attached from, 268–69
Rodeo, 79, 232; de Mille in Cowgirl costume for, *2.5*
Rodgers, Richard, 228
Rodriguez, Alfred, 189
Romanoff, Dimitri, 33, 38, 148, 254, 255; Bolm's tutelage of, 34; Christmas with Chase family, 146; Martin's recognition of, 165
Romeo and Juliet, 148
Rose Adagio, from *The Sleeping Beauty*, 293
Rose Hill homestead, *1.4*, 5, 6–7, 76, 315;

Christmas and Thanksgiving at, 146–47
Rosenwald, Peter J., 259, 290
Roslavleva, Natalia, 201
Ross, Herbert: ABT's 25th anniversary, 214; *Caprichos*, 166, 214; *Dialogues (Serenade for 7)*, 198; Phoenix Theatre workshop with, 188, 189
Royal Academy of Dance (RAD), 129–30, 131
Royal Ballet, Covent Garden, 239; response to Cannes fire disaster, 193
Royal Danish Ballet, 193
Royal Theater, Copenhagen, 214
Rubin, Robert, 285; trustee for ABT Foundation, 266
Russian ballet, 87; Ballet Russe, *1.7*, *2.5*, 27, 33, 86, 93, 101, 133; Ballet Russe de Monte Carlo, 37, 87; Bolshoi Ballet, 27, 200, 230; Kirov Ballet, 273–74, 279; Petipa's *Sleeping Beauty*, 33; Petipa's works, 33, 236, 279–80, 314; *Pillar of Fire v.*, 92–97
Russian Imperial Ballet company, 33

Saddler, Donald, 321; in ABT's 15th anniversary, 170; at ABT's 40th anniversary, 308; Phoenix Theatre workshop with, 189
Sadler's Wells Ballet, London, 54, 129
Saltonstall, David, 266
Saltonstall, Stella, trustee for ABT Foundation, 266
Sanders, Job, 189
Sandler, Ken, 303
San Francisco Opera Ballet, 38; Bolm in, 34; Reinhart in, 33–34
Sargasso, for ABT's 25th anniversary, 214
Saroyan, William (*Hearts in the Highlands*), 66
Saunderstown, Rhode Island, 115; Spindrift house in, 99
Scarborough Beach Club, 11–12
Scheherazade, 126
School of American Ballet, 244
Scott, Raymond, rehearsals (1939), 58
Scotti, Antonio, 20
Sebastian, 189

Selassie, Haile, 247

Serova, Sonia, 9

Serrano, Lupe, 170, 195, 226, 252, 255;
ABT's 30th anniversary, 273; critically
acclaimed, 238; Martin's praise for,
201–2; as "Permanent Guest Artist of
ABT," 264; *Time's* praise for, 273

Sevastianov, Gerald (Gerry), 88–90, 111;
unappreciative of Tudor's work, 92–96

Shabelevski, Yurek, 50, 58

Shadow of the Wind, 148

Sheldon, Irving, 206

Sills, Beverly, 310

Singer, Norman, 267

Sleeping Beauty, The, 236; Balanchine's
esteem for Petipa's, 33; Dolin's
Princess Aurora adapted from, 91,
95; full-length at New York State
Theater, 236; Lucia's debut in, 34–37,
44; Mordkin, Mikhail, excerpts from,
32–37; Rose Adagio of, 293

Smalley, Dave, 206

Smith, Eric, 207

Smith, Oliver: as ABT codirector, *2.6, 2.8*,
29, 117–20, 123–24, 126, 129, 131–33, 187,
214, 230, 308, 318; on artistic committee, 133; *Fall River Legend* set by, 149;
Les Noces set by, 217; tribute at Lucia's
memorial, 322

Smuin, Michael, in 1969, 264

Sokolow, Anna, 189

Sonne, Carol, 191, 206–7, 246, 249, 267

Sorell, Walter, 212

Sorrento, Maine, 14

South American touring: Argentina,
172–75; government sponsored, 171–75,
214. *See also* Mexico

Souvenir program, ABT's 30th anniversary, 269–71

Soviet Union tour, 200–201

Spanish dancers, for *Goyescas*, 58

Spessivtzeva, Olga, 34

SS Washington, 55

St. James Church, memorial for Brown,
Kelly, 258

St. John's Episcopal Church, Waterbury,
Conn., *1.4*

St. Margaret's School, Waterbury, Conn.,
5, 162

St. Paul's School, N.H., 163

St. Petersburg, Russia, 33

Stanislavsky Theater, 200–201

Stepmother, Lucia as (*Fall River
Legend*), 56, 150–51, 195

Stevens, Byam: ABT Foundation
Chairman of the Board, 222–23; retirement from Foundation, 233

Stevens, Priscilla, 260; on Lucia, 313

Stevens, Roger, 226–27

Stock market crash of 1929, 18

Strand Theatre, Waterbury, Conn., 10

Stravinsky, Igor, 126; *Les Noces* music by,
215–17

Studebaker Theatre, Chicago, 38

Sunset Farm, Narragansett, R.I., 6, 10;
marriage proposal at, 12–13, 15

Swan Lake, 58, 68, 75, 95, 134, 170, 193;
Barnes on 1967 production of, 238;
costumes for, 268–69; Dolin takes over
directing of, 55; Lucia's championing of, 234–37; Lucia's launching of,
225–26, 228; Queen Mother role in,
56, 241–42, 251, 275, 319–20; rehearsals
(1939), 58; ushering new era for ABT,
236–37; Youskevitch in, 134, 164–65

Swenson, Ellen, 74

Swingin' the Dream, 58, 60

Sylvester, Jerry, 74

Tack, Augustus Vincent, 67

Takeover, Wharton thwarting attempted,
235–36

Talbot, Alden, 116, 222; Lucia's dispute
with, 120–23

Tallchief, Maria, 164

Tally-Ho, 79, 111–12, 116, 118, 139; for ABT's
25th anniversary, 214

Taras, John: *Designs with Strings*, 166; on
railway touring in 1940s, 103–4

Tax Court, 112–13, 156–58; appeal (1954),
178; final verdict (1956), 178–80; trial
and verdict (1953), 177

Tax-exempt status, 137, 160–61

Taylor, Harold, 228, 260; involvement in
undercutting Lucia, 234–35; "new image" for ABT by, 233–34

Taylor, Paul, 143

Teatro de Colon, Buenos Aires, 174–75

Tempelhof Airport, Germany, 167

Terry, Walter, 28, 67, 68, 134, 198, 241; commenting on third New York season, 91; on Lucia in *Las Hermanas*, 2.4; on *Pillar of Fire*, 96

Tetley, Glen, 214; ABT's 25th anniversary, 214

Tharp, Twyla, *Push Comes to Shove* by, 293–94

Theatre Guild, 14, 15

Theme and Variations, 142–44; Cannes fire impacting, 192–96

The Three-Cornered Hat, 93

Three Virgins and a Devil, 56, 75, 79, 80–81, 120; Lucia as Greedy One in, *1.9*

Times Square, in 1942, 117

Titania Palast, 167–68

Toronto, 105, 106, 280

Toumanova, Tamara (with Irina Barakova and Tatiana Riabouchinska). 37, 88

Train travel, 102–3

Traitor, The, 264, 272

Transcontinental tours: 1942–1943, 102–8; 1943–1944, 116; 1946–1947, 136–39; 1949–1950, 165; 1950s, 169–70; 1960, 201; Goldman's practical approach to, 270

Truman, Harry S., 159

Tudor, Antony, 309, 316, 318; 1948 at the Met, 148; ABT's 15th anniversary, 170; ABT's 25th anniversary, 214; ABT's 35th anniversary, 292; ABT's 40th anniversary, 308; on artistic committee, 133; *Bluebeard*, *1.10*; *Dark Elegies*, *2.3*, 57, 58, 80, 93, 94, 134, 148, 214; deserting ABT, 187–88; *Gala Performance*, 79, 93, 148, 194; Hurok unappreciative of, 92–95; *Jardin aux Lilas*, 58, 93, 148, 214; joins ABT, 54–55; *Judgment of Paris*, 56, 58, 75, 139, 148, 292; Karnilova on, 94; Kaye on influence/technique of, 94, 95; as Lucia's favorite choreographer, 29, 100; Massine v., 93; *Nimbus*, 166; *Pillar of Fire*, *2.1*, *2.2*, 56, 75, 92–97, 120, 148, 194, 195, 214–15, 236; Pleasant's invitation to, 51; *Romeo and Juliet*, 148; Russian ballet v., 92–96; Sevastianov's listing of, 93; *Shadow of the Wind*, 148; slow

worker, 143; tribute at Lucia's memorial, 323; *Undertow*, 121–22, 125–26, 143, 148

U.S. Coast Guard, 206

U.S. Congress, 176

U.S. Medal of Freedom, 310

U.S. Secretary of State, 168

U.S. State Department, 171, 194, 231; ABT's Soviet Union tour sponsored by, 197, 200–201

U.S. Tax Court: 1948 hearings, 112–13, 156–58; 1953 trial and verdict, 177; 1954 Court of Appeals, 178; 1956 final decision, 178–80

Undertow, 121–22, 125–26, 143, 148

Union, dancer's contract, 302–7

"University of the world," 159

University of Wisconsin, 265

Uris Theater, 293

Van Hamel, Martine, in *Raymonda*, 290

Verchinina, Nina, 51

Verdy, Violette, 194, 195; at ABT's 40th anniversary, 308

Vestoff-Serova School, 9

Vladimiroff, Pierre, 27

Voices of Spring, 55–56, 66, 67; to show off Baronova, 93

Walska, Ganna, 319

Washington Post, 303, 304, 319

Waterbury, Conn.: Lucia's childhood home in, *1.4*, 5–7, 6–7, 76, 146–47, 315; Mordkin, Mikhail, *Sleeping Beauty* at, 32–37; St. John's Episcopal Church at, *1.4*; Strand Theatre, 10

Waterbury Clock Company, *1.1*

Webster, David, 128

West 58th Street apartment, 15–19, 277–79; home life at, 73–77, 314–15

Westover School, Conn., 202

Wharton, John, 29, 78, 136, 260; thwarting attempted takeover, 235–36

White, Stanford, 6

Wilson, Sallie, 194, 239, 252, 256, 257, 312; in 1969, 264; *Raymonda*, 290

Wiman, Anna Deere, 78

Wiman, Dwight Deere, 50, 78, 161

Wind in the Mountains, The, 214

Windsor, Elizabeth (princess), 130
Windsor, Margaret (princess), 130
Winter Garden Theatre, 165
Winter's Eve, 188
World War I, 8–9
World War II, 74, 124, 129; ABT influenced by, 53–55, 102–3, 105

Yale Law School, 260
Yale University, 9, 163, 181, 296, 309–10
Yankee Clipper, 66
Young, Gayle, 239; in 1969, 264
Youskevitch, Igor: at ABT's 35th anniversary, 292; at ABT's 40th anniversary, 308; Alicia Alonso partnered with, 134, 136, 142, 148, 150–51; glory days of, 236; Martin on, 170; in Rose Adagio (from *The Sleeping Beauty*), 293; in *Swan Lake* and *Giselle*, 134, 164–65; in *Theme and Variations*, 142, 144

Zeckendorf, Nancy, 317–18; as BTF trustee, 260; on Colin as BTF president, 291; on Goldman's contributions to BTF, 289
Zorina, Vera, 50
Zuckert, Harry, 39, 136; Baronova's report to, 107; fundraising, 40–42; Hurok and, 89–90; Lucia's relationship to, 29; Pleasant and, 41–43; as treasurer of Advanced Arts Ballets, 60; Wharton takes over for, 235

Chancellor emeritus of the University of North Carolina School of the Arts (chancellor 1990–2000), Alex Ewing was formerly general director of the Joffrey Ballet in New York (1965–70), chairman of the Foundation for American Dance, board member of the New York City Ballet's School of American Ballet, a member of the dance panel of the National Endowment for the Arts, and chairman of the Dance Collection of the New York Public Library. He is also an honorary trustee of American Ballet Theatre's Ballet Theatre Foundation Inc. in New York.